PAN-AFRICAN ISSUES IN CRIME AND JUSTICE

Interdisciplinary Research Series in Ethnic, Gender and Class Relations

Series Editor: Biko Agozino, Cheyney University of Pennsylvania, USA

This series brings together research from a range of disciplines including criminology, cultural studies and applied social studies, focusing on experiences of ethnic, gender and class relations. In particular, the series examines the treatment of marginalized groups within the social systems for criminal justice, education, health, employment and welfare.

Also in the series

Main Issues in Mental Health and Race
David Ndegwa and Dele Olajide
ISBN 1 84014 812 8

A Critical Analysis of the Contributions of Notable Black Economists
Kojo A. Quartey
ISBN 1 84014 147 6

Dehumanizing Discourse, Anti-Drug Law, and Policy in America
A 'Crack Mother's' Nightmare
Assata Zerai and Rae Banks
ISBN 0 7546 1545 6

The National Question in Nigeria
Comparative Perspectives
Edited by Abubakar Momoh and Said Adejumobi
ISBN 0 7546 1234 1

Maintaining our Differences
Minority Families in Multicultural Societies
Edited by Carol D.H. Harvey
ISBN 0 7546 1246 5

Constructing Lived Experiences
Claudia Bernard
ISBN 1 84014 938 8

Pan-African Issues in Crime and Justice

Edited by

ANITA KALUNTA-CRUMPTON
University of Surrey, Roehampton, UK

BIKO AGOZINO
Cheyney University of Pennsylvania, USA

Routledge
Taylor & Francis Group
LONDON AND NEW YORK

First published 2004 by Ashgate Publishing

Published 2017 by Routledge
2 Park Square, Milton Park, Abingdon, Oxfordshire OX14 4RN
711 Third Avenue, New York, NY 10017, USA

First issued in paperback 2017

Routledge is an imprint of the Taylor & Francis Group, an informa business

British Library Cataloguing in Publication Data
Pan-African issues in crime and justice. -
(Interdisciplinary research series in ethnic, gender and
class relations)
1. Crime - Africa 2. Criminal justice, Administration of -
Africa
I. Kalunta-Crumpton, Anita, 1962- II. Agozino, Biko
364.9'6

Library of Congress Cataloging-in-Publication Data
Pan-African issues in crime and justice / edited by Anita Kalunta-Crumpton and Biko Agozino.
p. cm. -- (Interdisciplinary research series in ethnic, gender, and class relations)
Includes bibliographical references and index.
ISBN 0-7546-1882-X
1. Criminal justice, Administration of--Africa. 2. Crime--Africa. I. Kalunta-Crumpton, Anita, 1962- II. Agozino, Biko. III. Series.

HV8267.A2.P36 2003
364.96--dc22 2003058290

ISBN 13: 978-1-138-20527-7 (pbk)
ISBN 13: 978-0-7546-1882-9 (hbk)

Contents

List of Contributors

Biko Agozino (Ph.D.) is an Associate Professor in the Department of Social and Behavioral Sciences at Cheyney University of Pennsylvania. Previously he was a Senior Lecturer in Criminal Justice, Liverpool John Moores University. He studied at Edinburgh University, Scotland; Cambridge University, England; and the University of Calabar, Nigeria. His publications include *Black Women and the Criminal Justice System: Towards the Decolonisation of Victimisation* in 1997, which launched the Ashgate Interdisciplinary Research Series in Ethnic, Gender and Class Relations of which he is editor. He is also the co-author (with Unyierie Idem) of *Nigeria: Democratising A Militarised Civil Society* which was published by the Centre for Democracy and Development in 2001, and the author of *Counter-Colonial Criminology: A Critique of Imperialist Reason* which was published by Pluto Press in 2003.

Jon Alexander (Ph.D.) is a Political Scientist and teaches at Carleton University in Ottawa, Canada. A former Fellow at the Center for the Study of Democratic Institutions, he has taught at UCLA, Emory University and Columbia University in the United States, and has lectured in nine other countries. His research interests include philosophy of science and technology, S&T policy, democratic theory, political communications, social engineering, and comparative law and public policy. He has published five books and numerous articles in English and French (with translations into Spanish and Swedish) in for example, the American Political Science Review, the Canadian Political Science Review, Public Administration Review, Canadian Review of American Studies, Reseaux, Mondes en développement, and Nouvelles de la science et des technologies. His main hobby is fundraising.

Robert Kwame Ameh (Ph.D.) is an Assistant Professor at the Department of Sociology, University of New Brunswick, Canada. He received his doctorate in criminology from Simon Fraser University, Canada. His teaching and research interests include the application of international human rights norms in other cultures; youth justice; restorative justice; and the sociology of law. He is currently researching Truth and Reconciliation Commissions with focus on the ongoing national reconciliation exercise in Ghana, West Africa.

Ogbonnaya Oko Elechi (Ph.D.) is an Assistant Professor of Criminal Justice at the University of Wisconsin, Parkside. He received his Ph.D. from Simon Fraser

University, Canada. He also holds two degrees from the University of Oslo – Norway, where he worked closely with Professor Nils Christie. Dr Elechi's teaching and research interests are diverse – including African Indigenous Justice Systems; Restorative and Transformative Justice Systems; Community Policing; and State, Human Rights and White Collar Crime. His recent articles on Restorative Justice have been published in the International Journal of Comparative and Applied Criminal Justice and the International Review of Victimology.

Alice Itani (Ph.D.) is Professor of Sociology at the Instituto de Biociências of Universidade Estadual Paulista (University of State São Paulo) in Rio Claro. She is also a researcher in work and health programs funded by Conselho Nacional de Desenvolvimento Cientifico e Tecnologico CNPq (Scientific and Technological National Institute) and Fundação de Amparo à Pesquisa do Estado de São Paulo Fapesp (Scientific Research Foundation). She received a Ph.D. in Sociology from École des Hautes Études en Sciences Sociales, Paris. She is the author of *Metroviarios et travail automatisé, Labour and health in aviation*, and *Violence in the educational agents imagery*. At present, she is dedicated to questions around childhood in Brazil. She lives in São Paulo.

Marlyn J. Jones (Ph.D.) is an Assistant Professor in the Division of Criminal Justice, California State University, Sacramento. Her interests include issues of race, class and gender; human rights; social justice; drugs and immigration policy analysis; and Caribbean crime and criminal justice issues. She teaches in areas such as women and criminal justice, and minority groups and criminal justice

Anita Kalunta-Crumpton (Ph.D.) teaches criminology at the School of Business and Social Sciences, University of Surrey, Roehampton, United Kingdom. She has published extensively and internationally on issues of race, crime and criminal justice. Her research interests include race and drugs, and comparative criminal justice.

Annelie Odendaal is a senior lecturer in sociology at the University of Namibia. She was born in 1956 in Usakos, Namibia where she completed most of her schooling before she matriculated in 1974 at Gymnasium High School, Potchefsroom, South Africa. After obtaining a Master's degree in sociology in 1984 from the University of Stellenbosch, South Africa, she returned to Namibia and established the country's first Sociology department at the Academy for Tertiary Education (now the University of Namibia). She is currently registered for a Ph.D. at the University of Utrecht, The Netherlands. Her essay 'Crime, Social Change and Social Control in Namibia: An Exploratory Study of the Namibian Prisons' is based on some of her Ph.D. research findings on criminal violence and convicted violent offenders in Namibia, Southern Africa.

Ihekwoaba D. Onwudiwe (Ph.D.) received his Ph.D. from the School of Criminology at Florida State University. He is currently an Associate Professor of Criminology at the University of Maryland Eastern Shore where he serves as the director of the graduate program in criminal justice. His book, *The Globalization of Terrorism* was published by Ashgate in 2002.

Emmanuel C. Onyeozili (Ph.D.) is an Assistant Professor of Criminology and Criminal Justice in the Department of Criminal Justice, University of Maryland Eastern Shore. He obtained his Bachelor's degree in History from the University of Ibadan, Nigeria; a Master's degree in Criminal Justice Administration from Clark Atlanta University, United States; and his Doctoral degree from Florida State University, United States. His writing and research interests are in the areas of African criminology, policing and social control, and gender studies.

Udo C. Osisiogu (B.Sc., Benin; M.Sc., Lagos; M.Phil., Cambridge; Ph.D., Hull) holds a Bachelor's degree in Sociology and Anthropology and a Master's degree in Sociology from universities in Nigeria. He also holds graduate degrees in Criminology from universities in the United Kingdom. His academic interests include economic and property crimes, youth crime, theory, policing, and crime prevention. At present, he works for a non-profit organisation in Toronto, Canada.

Camy Pector, a widely travelled Arab political scientist, studied at l'Universite de Paris-Sorbonne (Paris IV), and at Arizona State University. She worked for several years in Germany, writing in Arabic, English, French and German. Her interests include the politics of health, comparative political cultures, and the sociology of law. She is currently studying the politics of the internet, and the ensemble of technologies relating to Digital Video Disks.

Wagner Volpe is one of the experts in Statistics in Brazil. He obtained an M.Phil. in Experimental Statistics from Universidade de São Paulo. He was a professor at Universidade Estadual Paulista (University of the State São Paulo) in Rio Claro between 1987-1998. At present, he is a professor in Faculdade Santa Marcelina and other universities teaching Statistics and Bio-Statistics. He teaches Physics in Colégio Nossa Senhora do Rosario (High School N.S. Rosario). He is the author of *Urbanisation and Violence in Rio Claro 1980-1991*. He lives in São Paulo.

Miranda Young-Jahangeer is a lecturer in the Drama and Performance Studies Department at the University of Natal in Durban South Africa. She was previously working in the Graduate Programme for Cultural and Media Studies at the same university. She is currently pursuing her Ph.D. in the area of Prison Theatre in KwaZuluNatal with specific focus on how gender and power relations are articulated through popular participatory performance.

Introduction

ANITA KALUNTA-CRUMPTON and BIKO AGOZINO

Pan-Africanism is a political and scholarly movement, which focuses on primary contradictions that confront people of African descent wherever they may be in the world (Abdul-Raheem, 1996). The idea was borrowed for the focus of this book because the criminological crisis facing people of African descent in many parts of the world today amounts to a primary contradiction. Poor people of African descent share a common experience of under-representation in privileged institutions but over-representation in prisons. At the same time, criminology has been monopolised by European and North American universities while remaining conspicuously absent in African universities with the exception of South Africa (Agozino, 2003). What is more, even in Europe and North America, criminologists of African descent are relatively excluded from the discipline. This book is designed to identify the potential advances in knowledge that criminology could make by being less provincial and by learning from the experiences and ideas of people of African descent.

For many years, individual nations in the West have contextualised and conceptualised criminology to suit their differing territories and concerns. However, recent years have seen a growing interest in comparative criminology, which now means that countries compare notes thereby broadening the parameters of criminological knowledge. This exercise has been particularly evident within Europe and between Europe and North America. In this ongoing criminological quest for comparative research across countries and continents, Africa remains a relatively neglected territory and relatedly, pan-African concerns are marginalised. Thus, although criminology assumes the position of an established discipline, its influence is in fact limited by its primary focus on the West for both theoretical and empirical substance.

This book aims to contribute to the growth of criminology on a global level. Drawing upon materials on pan-African issues in crime and justice across the globe, the collection offers a convergence of criminological endeavours from both western and African standpoints. Western criminology is acknowledged as a significant angle from which to comprehend crime and justice as they are conceptualised in a non-western scenario. While this consensus is explored, differences and specifics in a non-western crime context are simultaneously revealed in the various criminological contributions on crime and justice in black societies around the world. The overall pattern of approach centralises the place of relativity and diversity in analyses of crime; it sees a society's crime scenario as being congruent with its own structural make-up. This is to say that the historical, political, cultural, social and economic structures of a society individually and collectively define and shape the creation and sustenance of crime. Likewise, such structural influences pattern responses to crime and criminality, in the form of law making, law enforcement and social control.

In Chapter 1, Anita Kalunta-Crumpton provides an overview of criminology's treatment of crime and justice issues relating to people of African descent. The author highlights a central point – such treatment is hegemonic in its approach and as such has the tendency to subordinate perspectives aired from an African experience. Drawing upon data from the United Kingdom (UK) in particular, the dominant-subordinate relationship between criminology and pan-Africanism is further illustrated in debates surrounding the experiences of black people in the UK criminal justice system.

Chapter 2 is the first of a range of illustrations interpreting crime and justice issues from an African perspective. The chapter looks at the gender discrimination embedded in the 'trokosi' system practised in parts of West Africa. According to the author, the system involves the selection of a female child by her family to 'serve in a shrine in reparation for crimes committed by other members of the family'. In analysing the effects of the 'trokosi' practice on women, Robert Kwame Ameh unveils some of the complexities and contradictions surrounding traditional practices and human rights issues.

Jon Alexander and Camy Pector present an overview of the workings of the justice system in Egypt in Chapter 3. In doing so, they argue that social control in Egypt is hampered by a detrimental configuration of politics, religion and law. The effect is that there are no set guidelines as to what constitutes a deviant behaviour. Similarly, issues of gender, race and class are suppressed. According to the authors, western control theories fail to provide sufficient answers to crime and justice questions in Egypt.

Chapter 4 takes a critical look at imprisonment as a form of punishment for violent offenders in Namibia. Here, Annelie Odendaal places this crime control strategy within the context of Namibia's historical, political and socio-economic structures. Ultimately, the critical endeavour argues for crime prevention measures, which are holistic and encompass *inter alia* efforts to alleviate socio-economic deprivation.

In Chapter 5, Udo Osisiogu provides a detailed criminological analysis of fraud, particularly advance fee fraud, from a western perspective. The chapter derives its substance from the author's Ph.D research study of a sample of fraud cases that occurred across the globe, and in particular the United Kingdom, between 1994 and 2001. Through a case study of Nigeria, a country popularly associated with advance fee fraud, the author constructs an analytical framework, which recognises the political economy of developing countries in criminological explanations for the perpetration of fraud.

In Chapter 6 Ihekwoaba Onwudiwe analyses the emergence of advance fee fraud otherwise known as 419 offences after the relevant Nigerian Criminal Code section. His study of the problem reveals weaknesses in western criminology theory and suggests the need to develop new theoretical insights for tackling such a huge criminological problem. At the same time, he warns against racial profiling of Nigerians as the only ones who engaged in fraud as some campaigners against the phenomenon tend to do. This chapter complements the theoretical review of the same problem by Udo Osisiogu in Chapter 5.

Chapter 7 introduces readers to the dire conditions under which women of African descent live in Brazil. Itani and Volpe document that the conditions of women as victims of violence are very poor in Brazil but that the conditions of black Brazilian women are even worse. To make matters worse, documentation of black women who were victims of violence is not adequately kept by the officials giving the impression that such serious crimes are grossly under-reported. The emphasis in the official statistics is on women who committed violent acts against abusive partners but even in such statistics, black women are under-represented. The significance of this chapter is the broad definition of violence against women to include violent working conditions outside the homes instead of focusing on domestic violence the way many western criminologists do. This should serve as a lesson to all criminologists that violence at places of work for black women is more significant outside their homes especially in a society with significant leisure classes such as Brazil where black women are more likely to find work as domestic servants who routinely endure hostile working conditions.

In Chapter 8, Young-Jahangeer continues the focus on violence against women of African descent by studying South African women who were in prison for killing their abusive spouses. She presents an analysis of prison dramas staged by the women and the result of interviews with the women to demonstrate that the women remain defiant towards a patriarchal society that would repress any woman who dares to challenge hegemonic masculinity. This chapter complements the focus of Chapter 7 by again highlighting that the most violent conditions for black women is not always the domestic setting but sometimes even within the criminal justice system with the support of the patriarchal media that chastise the women in prison and try to distort their assertions in order to demonize them.

Chapter 9 continues the focus of women of African descent by analyzing the role of Nigerian women in the traditional restorative justice systems that contrast sharply with the punitive obsession of western societies. Even though African women remain under the domination of patriarchy, they are accorded more significant roles in the resolution of disputes in traditional African societies than their counterparts in Europe and North America. Ogbonnaya Oko Elechi suggests that western criminologists could learn more by taking seriously the innovative ways that African cultures attempt to resolve disputes in restorative fashions.

In Chapter 10, Marlyn Jones completes the special focus on women of African descent by analyzing the repression of Jamaican women under the pretext of the war against drugs. The chapter considers alternatives to the war on drugs including the alternative of legalization, which a government commission of enquiry recently recommended to the country. The implication here is that many of the women who are incarcerated could have been free to carry on legitimate businesses. Instead, many more women are being locked up in Jamaica, Europe and North America for drugs offenses.

In Chapter 11, Emmanuel Onyeozili reminds us that the crimes that have affected people of African descent most adversely are not the crimes committed by individual offenders but crimes that are inflicted in the guise of punishment. He uses the term 'gunboat criminology' to theorize the fact that centuries-old injustice within the relationships between Europe and Africa constitutes a suitable subject matter for pan-African criminology.

Chapter 12 concludes the book by highlighting the lessons that people of African descent could learn from criminology in their struggle for reparations and what criminologists could learn from the movement for reparations. A review of existing criminological theory shows that most of them are not relevant to the monumental struggles for reparations and suggests that by studying the reparations movement, criminologists stand a chance of advancing their discipline.

Taken together, the chapters in this book could serve as a timely resource for people of African descent as we try to develop an Africa centered theory of justice. By developing original conceptual tools with which to interpret the African historical experience of relevance to deviance and social control, these chapters will help to start filling the gap that still exists in African studies and in criminology. African and African American Studies, Black Studies and Pan-African Studies tend to focus on the discovery of great deeds of Africans and so writing on deviance and social control could lead into the pitfall of denigrating Africans. On the other hand, criminology carries on without adequate awareness of the fact that people of African descent are over-represented in the criminal justice system, suggesting that criminologists should take required courses in Black Studies.

References

Abdul-Raheem, T. (ed.) (1996), *Pan-Africanism: Politics, Economy and Social Change in the Twenty-First Century*, Pluto Press, London.

Agozino, B. (2003) *Counter-Colonial Criminology: A Critique of Imperialist Reason*, Pluto Press, London.

1 Criminology and Orientalism

ANITA KALUNTA-CRUMPTON

Introduction

Mainstream criminological knowledge as we know it is reflective of a western view of the social world. It represents a hegemonic position of western conceptualisation of crime, criminality and criminal justice. What the dominant criminological enterprise is slow to represent is a process of doing criminology from the standpoint of 'others' outside the West. For one, the voice of Africa and Africans is a long way short of being embraced into the centre of the defining process of western criminology, which fundamentally assumes a divide between the definer and the defined. These two categories mirror firstly, the dominant position of those who define as represented in the western perspective and secondly, the subordinate position of those (that is, non-westerners) who are recipients of definitions popularly pursued in criminological inquiry. It is an arrangement that builds on concepts of race and which transcends domestic boundaries to reach global parameters. Within the domestic context, this divide cannot manifest itself any better than in the ways in which race has been dissected within academic analyses of crime. In North America and Western Europe for example, 'race', a term inundated with negative meanings, is commonly utilised to apply to non-whites. More revealing of this racial demarcation is the position of people of African descent as often the subject of inquiry in debates about crime. For instance, to study race and crime is to fundamentally explore such issues as the patterns and causes of black peoples' engagement in criminal acts; to study race in law enforcement is to primarily parade black people's encounters with agencies of the criminal justice system. Regardless of any differences in objectives embraced in such debates, whether it purports to establish a conservative or a radical or a liberal stance, the race-specific approach normally features the existence of a problem worth examining and defining. Addressing race therefore is particularly about analysing, defining and understanding the 'problematic' of blackness.

As already noted, the influential place of hegemony in criminological approach to studying black people is not confined to scenarios in western societies but can also be transposed onto situations outside the West, that is in 'black' societies across the globe (Cain, 2000). This of course is not to claim that criminology holds much positive interest in pan-African issues outside the West. Western criminological interest in 'black' societies in Africa and the Caribbean, for instance, is very limited perhaps due to a belief that these societies have nothing worthwhile to contribute to international comparative criminological research. Such belief could naturally stem from a historical backdrop of white hegemony through which western criminology has itself tended to adopt an absolutist position in defining pan-African issues against western perspectives and standards. As such, any conceptions that black societies have nothing useful to offer criminology can seem to coincide with centuries of ethnocentric viewpoints, which have defined and still define various facets of 'blackness' as inferior to the superior whiteness of the West. It is from this standpoint that we can relate to criminological neglect of, and/or 'interest', in people of African descent around the world.

This chapter firstly presents a review, by no means exhaustive account, of criminology's relationship with issues relating to people of African descent. It draws attention to the place of race in the criminological journey from the classical period to contemporary times, and in doing so, demonstrates the intersection of theory and practice. And as a case study, it reviews the workings of the UK (United Kingdom) criminal justice system to exemplify the practical significance of criminology *vis-à-vis* race. Secondly, the chapter searches for a criminology, which exists outside the dominant western framework, and concludes by calling for a criminological recognition of pan-African concerns, particularly from the point of view of people of African descent around the globe.

Understanding Crime and Justice

Criminology developed principally out of western culture and therefore it is reflective of western perspectives. From classical to postclassical criminologies, the place of people of African descent in the range of criminological endeavours has varied in significance. Classical perspectives and their core notions of social contract, utility and rationality held principles that displayed no direct application to race. Explicit questions of race started to arise in the 19th century with the development of positivist criminology and its scientific approach to the study of criminal behaviour. Under this criminological stance, popularly associated with the Italian school founded by Cesare Lombroso, it was claimed that criminal behaviour was biologically determined (Lombroso, 1876; Ferri, 1895). By linking crime to certain physical characteristics, Lombroso concluded that criminals were genetic throwbacks to more primitive forms of human species, which he referred to as *atavistic*. This conclusion drew upon his study of criminals in which he observed that criminals shared many anatomical similarities with savages and non-whites. Examples of those physical similarities were voluminous ears, receding forehead, fleshy lips, darker skin colour, small skull, and thicker and curly hair. Lombroso's ideas were widely received and influential. As Garland (1985) observed, positivist criminology 'developed from the idiosyncratic concerns of a few individuals into a programme of investigation and social action which attracted support throughout Europe and North America' (cited in Roshier, 1989, p.20).

The positivist theories that differentiated the 'criminal type' from the 'noncriminal type' were premised on assumptions of superior and inferior races representing white and non-white races respectively. For one, the principles of biological positivism were centrally beneficial to Europe's move towards the colonisation of the supposed inferior non-white territories following the end of the slave trade in the 19th century. Slavery itself had thrived on notions of white racial superiority articulated by European philosophers of 'The Age of Reason' (Eze, 1997). The belief that intelligence, reason and civilisation can only be found among the white race justified the subjection of Africans to hostile and savage slave labour since as was perceived, their stupidity, lack of intelligence and indolence meant that they were not suited for anything requiring the application of reason (Walvin, 1971, 1973; Fryer, 1984). Biological positivism was greatly influenced by biological evolutionary theories upheld by theorists such as Charles Darwin. Darwin's (1859) *On the Origin of Species* and his concepts of *natural selection* and *the survival of the fittest* not only implied a natural divide between superior and inferior races. It also denounced contact between the two for fear of contamination of the former by the latter. For the 'superior' race to therefore maintain its purity and superiority, it must resist any forms of threat of racial degeneration. Those assumptions were utilised to justify the need for colonialism and the subordination of the 'lower' races in Africa, the Caribbean and elsewhere; they were linked to the idea of trusteeship, which also underlined the philosophies of colonial domination by the 'superior' race.

Within western nations in North America, Europe and elsewhere, the establishment of the eugenics movement founded by Francis Galton towards the latter part of the 19th century (Galton, 1869; Goring, 1913) was to pave the way for the practical implications of Darwin's theory of natural selection. The fundamental mission of the eugenics movement to purify the genetic stock of the white race had from the late 19th century entailed formulating ways of causing the extinction of social categories, defined as socially unfit, undesirable and of low intelligence, through selective breeding. Essentially this involved preventing those 'inferior' categories from reproducing as exemplified in the programme of involuntary sterilisation practised in southern states of the United States (US). Among those included in the eugenicists' list were black people (Miller, 1997). Incidentally, the eugenics movement gained a great deal of its strength from the growing interest in the relationship between crime and intelligence amongst North American and European psychologists. Works on intelligence testing popularly claimed that intelligence was not only biological and fixed but was also related to criminality whether directly or indirectly (Goddard, 1912, 1914; Jensen, 1969; Eysenck, 1971; Hirschi and Hindelang, 1977; Wilson and Herrnstein, 1985).

The implications of these observations for race have been more obvious than not. Psychologists have used IQ scores to uphold the view that white Americans have by far more superior intelligence than their African-American counterparts. And this difference in intelligence is largely attributed to genetic differences between the two groups. Relatedly, differences in crime rates between African-Americans and European-Americans have attracted explanations within this intelligence-biology framework, with the overall argument linking the perceived low IQ among African-Americans to the recorded higher crime rate for this racial group (Gordon, 1976; Hirschi and Hindelang, 1977). Despite the fact that the IQ-race-crime studies stood to invite an array of controversial debates and criticisms (Kamin, 1977), including evidence of methodological shortcomings such as the lack of clarity and consensus as to what IQ scoring measures, and the influence of cultural bias on IQ tests, it is a line of thought that has resurfaced in recent years. Herrnstein and Murray's (1994) book, *The Bell Curve* is a recent reminder of the IQ controversy. The authors reiterated that intelligence is largely a biological factor; that differences in IQ scores coincide with differences in class and racial origins; and that crime and delinquency are conversant with low IQ.

Both Lombrosian biological positivism and its offshoot, psychological positivism, locate the causes of crime in the individual. Notwithstanding the sensitive nature of these theories, their philosophies of individualising crime continue to surface. Explicitly and implicitly, race continues to be a part of this process of understanding criminal behaviour. Such racial influence is further illustrated in the conservative theory of the *underclass*, another major individualistic approach to crime (Murray, 1984, 1990). Here, the underclass are identified by their 'culture of poverty' caused because they possess certain 'unconventional' cultural features (that of poverty), which are passed on from one generation to another, and which prevent them from taking advantage of available opportunities to escape poverty. Such cultural features, which include above all illegitimacy and single-parenthood, unemployment and welfare-dependency, and crime, are commonly found amongst the lower-class sections of society. In the United States, these are known to be largely composed of African-Americans and Hispanics; in Britain, the 'emerging underclass' can include black communities (Murray, 1996).

Alongside psychological explanations of crime, Lombroso's legacy of positivism also evolved into various social theoretical strands that have overtly or covertly manifested the race ingredient in our understanding of crime and criminality. The Chicago School's influential social disorganisation theory demonstrates a strong relationship between crime and poorer areas of society. Referred to as the *zones in transition*, those 'crimogenic areas', often occupied by immigrant populations including high numbers of African-Americans, were characterised by low levels of social integration, high levels of socio-economic deprivation and relatedly high rates of crime (Shaw, 1929; Shaw and McKay, 1942). Merton's (1938) anomie and strain theory, also influential, focused on the crime-producing effects of social structural factors. His central argument sees crime as a product of problems of *strain* that arise out of a disjunction between culturally defined goals and the legitimate means of achieving those goals. Herein, the lower class is clearly predicted to be more likely to resort to crime as a response to situations of anomie and strain caused by the contradiction between the two elements. This prediction is even more apparent for black and other visible minority ethnic communities given their higher levels of socio-economic deprivation across nations in North America and Europe, for example (Sampson and Wilson, 1995; Massey and Denton; 1993; Commission on Systemic Racism in the Ontario Criminal Justice System, 2000; Brown, 1984; Penal Affairs Consortium, 1996).

Notwithstanding the notable shift of positivist accounts of criminal behaviour from the 19th century individualistic theories to the 20th sociological perspectives, race has remained a significant feature, particularly in its implicit connection to the class basis for understanding criminality. Within the series of attack on sociological positivism that emerged in the middle of the 20th century and other subsequent criminological advances that were to follow, the impact of race has been felt. Like the practical illustration of the individualistic approaches instanced in the eugenics movement, the sociological pursuits and their offshoots have also had practical implications for race.

Sociological Theory and Implications for Race, Crime and Criminal Justice with Particular Reference to the United Kingdom

By the 1950s, the sociological aspect of criminology developed in the United States had started gathering influence in the United Kingdom (Tierney, 1996). The US impact showed itself more clearly in the popularity that the North American subculturalist tradition had gained in the UK sociological studies of crime during the 1950s and 1960s. The specific area of interest to UK subcultural theorists was the delinquency of lower-class youth (Mays, 1954; Morris, 1957; Downes, 1966), and in this endeavour, the primary focus of UK subcultural theories was white working-class males. Not only was the cultural context of black youth's actions relatively marginalised in the literature but also what existed, as Hobbs (1997, p.811) observed, tended 'to be presented in terms of its relationship to the police, as a social problem, rather than as an entity in its own right; a courtesy afforded to white youth, whose every stylistic nuance was pored over by academics'. Implicit in Hobbs' observation is that while UK criminological interest in black youth was relatively insignificant at the time, the black presence was generally felt in other more powerful discursive sites such as the political, media and criminal justice arenas. For example, societal reactions to the urban disorders of the post-1945 period symbolised race within the various images that brought together issues of black immigration, inner-city deprivation, and law and order in political and popular discourses (Solomos, 1988, 1993). At those influential discursive levels, the descriptions of black people as a 'problem' also harboured potential and actual practical implications for this racial group, especially in terms of policing and other criminal justice responses to crime (Hunte, 1966; Humphrey and John, 1971; Humphrey, 1972).

The relatively minimal recognition assigned to issues relating to black people and crime in sociological criminology started to change towards the late 1970s when academic concerns about police-black community relations and black over-representation in crime figures started to grow and attract importance (Hall et al.,

1978; Demuth, 1978). Until the 1990s when the compilation of arrest statistics assumed a national status following the introduction of section 95 of the 1991 Criminal Justice Act, information on arrest figures had since the late 1970s been gleaned from London-based arrest data put together by the Metropolitan Police. Findings from those series of arrest data show arrest rates for black people to be disproportionate in comparison to the London population and also to be higher than that for other racial groups in every category of offence. For example, under the now defunct 'sus'[1] law, arrest figures for 1975 showed that black people comprised 40.4% of all 'suspected persons' arrests in the London Metropolitan District; in 1977 and 1978, the 'sus' arrest figures for blacks were 44% and 43% respectively (Roberts, 1982; Demuth, 1978). Moving into the 1980s, the problem of black disproportionate presence in crime figures had become a crucial debatable subject in sociological questions about crime and criminal justice. The 'race and crime' debate as it is commonly termed welcomed the dominant influence of sociological criminology, which by the 1960s was supposed to have severely marginalised the influence of biological positivism. It was an inquiry principally pursued by the disparate approaches taken by critical criminology/sociology and left realism. The former highlights the impact of race and criminalisation on the black crime rate, and in doing so prioritises the role of micro- and macro-level processes of racialisation of crime through which racial imageries associating black people with crime are constructed (Gilroy, 1987a, 1987b; Centre for Contemporary Cultural Studies, 1982). Conversely, the latter underplays the place of race by centralising the role of class in attempts to understand black crime figures (Lea and Young, 1984).

This latter approach seemed to have received more recognition at least within 'administrative' or 'governmental' criminology due to its tendency to lean towards the cause-and-effect positivist paradigm of mainstream criminology. By advancing the argument that the marginalised and disadvantaged socio-economic position of black people is consistent with high black offending and invariably reflective of the high black crime rate, left realism adopts the stance of sociological positivism. Doubtless, the black community suffers an adverse and complex form of socio-economic marginalisation not experienced by other racial groups (Oppenheim, 1993; Penal Affairs Consortium, 1996). Given theoretical justifications, stemming from the strain theories put forward by Merton (1938), Cohen (1955), and Cloward and Ohlin (1960) for locating crime prevalence amongst those at the lower-end of the social strata, left realism sees black people as making the crime choice in response to their deprived socio-economic circumstances (Lea and Young, 1984, 1993). To denounce allegations of racism levelled against it by critical theorists, left realism referred to the high crime victimisation rates experienced by the black community, arguing that the majority of crime is both intra-racial and intra-class. Even though this perspective acknowledges the wider influence of structural factors such as the role of the political economy and racial discrimination on the black community's socio-economic situation, it nonetheless conceptualises and promotes elements of individual pathology by somewhat shifting blame of racial discrimination away from influential criminal justice apparatuses.

These left realist conceptions imply that crime figures are accurate indicators of offending rates. In effect, discretionary powers of stop and search accorded the police bear no racially based impact on the high black arrest rate or on other policing decisions around cautioning, charging and bail. This is despite the preponderance of evidence pointing to the determining role of race at various stages of policing – from stop and search (Willis, 1983; Jones, 1986 et al.; Skogan, 1994) to charging decisions (Landau, 1981; Landau and Nathan, 1983; Commission for Racial Equality, 1992; Home Office, 1998). At other stages of criminal justice, the race effect is undermined by invoking the class framework not simply in its causal link to criminality but also in how it constitutes a strong determining ingredient in criminal justice practices relating to bail and sentencing decisions, for instance. Within this context, legally-provided decision-making criteria such as employment and status of residence are claimed to disadvantage black people in light of their overall marginalised socio-economic position (Crow and Simon, 1987; National Association for the Care and Resettlement of Offenders (NACRO), 1993).

The class context of understanding black people's encounters with the criminal justice system and its seemingly primary objective to wholly or partly dismantle the race factor that often grounds accusations of discrimination is evident across western nations. This approach is not confined to academic circles but can also be found amongst other powerful discourses and practices. In Canada where black people are also over-represented in arrest and prison figures (Commission on Systemic Racism in the Ontario Criminal Justice System, 2000), the class explanation, whether as a precursor to crime or as an integral part of criminal justice decision-making, is known to find significant favour among criminal justice officials. The US crime figures also present the disproportionate presence of people of African descent, particularly for drug offences (Lusane, 2000). Popular attempts to dissect this problem have also drawn on intersections of race, class and crime. For example, Steffensmeier and Demuth (2001, p.152), having summarised some of the negative and criminal stereotypes of African-Americans, point out that amidst the stereotypical images, 'black offenders are socio-economically disadvantaged and are presumed to lack the resources they need to thwart the imposition of legal sanctions...' They add:

> For these reasons, the lack of resources, coupled with attributions that associate black offenders with a stable, enduring predisposition to future criminal activity or dangerousness, is thought to increase sentence severity for black defendants.

Clearly, theorising the black deprivation-crime connection in the UK context has placed some explanations on the wider structural political, social and economic forces, which produce socio-economic inequality, and which in turn leads to crime (Pitts, 1986; Scarman, 1981). Some others have explicitly individualised the link by adopting the 'blaming the victim' approach. The latter, popular within administrative criminology, exhibits notions of conservative theory outlined above. According to Ryan (1976), such an individualistic approach is often used to hide the injustices suffered by the marginalised sections of society. For people of African descent, one notable instance of the 'blaming the victim' strategy is shown in alleged handicaps in black families. In the UK, explanations for black youth involvement in unlawful acts have made strong references to the supposed failure of the black family to adequately socialise their young ones due principally to the high numbers of single-parent families within this racial group. Black families have been known to make up the highest percentage of one-parent households (see Hall, 1989) headed by a black woman (Chigwada, 1991). The perceived failure of the black family to instill fatherly responsibilities in black males is viewed as a pathological characteristic and an expression of family breakdown – features which are seen to sit comfortably with criminality and subsequent involvement with the criminal justice system. Furthermore, as single parents, black women are believed to violate the traditional English family structure and values.

To a significant extent, such notions about black women are evidenced to influence their encounters with the criminal justice system (Chigwada, 1991; Chigwada-Bailey, 1997; Agozino, 1997) where they, like their male counterparts, are over-represented in relation to crime figures (Home Office, 1993, 1998). The disparity that unfavourably confronts black men in the criminal justice process is also witnessed, albeit doubly, by black women who are disadvantaged by their gender position as women and their racial background as black. Black women face greater likelihood of being subjected to police suspicion, stopped and searched, denied a police caution and arrested than their white counterparts (Chigwada-Bailey, 1997; Agozino, 1997). At other stages in the criminal justice process, black women's experiences of differential and discriminatory treatment is evident. They face a higher possibility of being refused bail but instead remanded in custody; their chance of receiving a custodial and a lengthier prison sentence is higher than that of their white counterparts in similar circumstances (ibid.). This picture of black females' (and other minority females') relationship with the criminal justice system is by no means unique to the UK as Sudbury (2002, pp.59-60) highlights:

> Aggregate rates of increase in prison populations under-represent the impact of the prison boom on black women, women of colour and indigenous women. In all the countries mentioned above (which are Britain, Australia and Canada, *my emphasis*), oppressed racialized groups are disproportionately represented. For example, in New South Wales, while all women's imprisonment increased by 40% in five years, aboriginal women's incarceration increased by 70% in ony two years. In Canada, aboriginal people comprise 3% of the general population and 12% of federal prisoners... African Canadians are also disproportion-ately policed, prosecuted and incarcerated... In the U.S., Latinas and African-American women make up 60% of the female prison population. And despite their small numbers in the population, Native Americans are ten times more likely than whites to be imprisoned... Finally 12% of women

> prisoners in England and Wales are African-Caribbean British passport holders compared to 1% of the general population...

Very important to note is that foreign nationals charged or sentenced for drug importation largely influence the disproportionate presence of black women in prisons in western societies such as the UK and the US. In June 1997, black foreign nationals made up 80% of the U.K female foreign nationals serving a prison sentence for a drug offence (Home Office, 1998). In the US, the war waged on drugs has had a disproportionate impact on black women from around the globe, who serve longer sentences in US prisons than their white counterparts. As Sudbury (2002, p.60) states: 'The crisis of women's prisons can...be read as a crisis for black women and women of colour worldwide'.

Clearly, the US-led war on drugs, which emerged in the 1980s is one of the most glaring contemporary endeavours by the West to extend and impose a western-initiated crime and justice agenda on non-western societies. Assigning blame on the drug trafficking role of non-western nations for the drug problem of the West has been a popular and highly favoured political rhetoric in the drug war demonstrated in North America and Britain in particular (Green, 1998). The Jamaican 'yardie', the Colombian 'cartel' and the Nigerian drug baron/courier instance popularised images of drug trafficking as an imported phenomenon. These images are translated into practical implementations of repressive punitive measures, especially aimed at drug traffickers from the Caribbean, West Africa, South America, Asia and those of visible minority ethnic groups resident in western societies, despite the fact that a vast number of them are located at the bottom-end of the drugs trade (Green, 1998; Lusane, 2000).

Outside the domestic scene, the West's influence is instanced in the use of US-led foreign policies to coerce drug producer and transit countries into complying with the West's drug policy. Green (ibid.) refers to how the West's economic assistance to such countries has tended to balance against their performance in fighting the West's drug war. Responsibilities assigned to drug producer countries have included eradicating and replacing drug crops with alternative 'licit' crops; for transit countries such as Nigeria, their duty is concerned with strengthening their domestic drugs law enforcement policy and practice in order to control international drug trafficking. Nowhere in the drug war agenda is significance given to the drug victimisation experiences of non-western societies. The link between the drug trade and the devastating effects of the strained political economy of the developing world on its people has not been of concern to the West (ibid.). Similarly, the drug-related health plight of people of African descent is insignificant in the West's drug policy agenda. According to Lusane (2000), there is a high number of drug-related HIV/AIDS cases in Caribbean societies, similar to the situation in the US where great numbers of African-Americans are affected by the spread of HIV and AIDS caused by intravenous drug use. A similar scenario is also seen to affect blacks in other societies such as sub-Saharan Africa. Meanwhile, the situation of people of

African descent as victims of the drug problem is a fact that is sidetracked in the ongoing global drug war that makes them a convenient scapegoat.

Overall, the recognition accorded the position of black people as victims of crime is one that is far outweighed by the relevance given to their perceived position as perpetrators of crime in western societies. This is demonstrated in other forms. Take for example the issue of racial violence and harassment in the UK. The sequence of political responses to white perpetration of racial violence and harassment towards minority ethnic groups is one of the glaring illustrations of how black peoples' experiences of victimisation tend to be relegated to the bottom of political priorities. Despite the fact that incidents of racial attacks on black and other visible minority ethnic groups had become obvious as far back as the early 20th century (Gordon, 1983; Hiro, 1992), and had shown a dramatic increase by the 1990s (Hesse et al., 1992; Virdee, 1995), political intervention was insignificant. According to Solomos (1993, p.192), the 'nature of the response to racial attacks both by the government and the police for most of the past decade' remained 'low key'. This, he adds:

> ...contrasts sharply with the oft-expressed views of the police and government on the criminal activities of young blacks, and the amplification of images of black crime in the popular media on an almost daily basis. By contrast, the policy response to racial attacks and related phenomenon has been muted and at worst non-existent.

Although the legislative intervention in the form of the 1998 Crime and Disorder Act has given significant recognition to this problem, it was a legislative transition that owed a great deal to the widely publicised 1993 racist murder of the black youth, Stephen Lawrence. This incident was sustained at the centre of official and political controversy due principally to the perseverance of the Lawrence family. Across the Atlantic, the relative neglect of black victimisation is evident. For example, in the US this can be illustrated in the way cases of rape victims are interpreted within the context of race and gender. Rapes by black men on white women are more likely to be reported, to be dealt with seriously in the legal process, and to attract extensive publicity (Cuklanz, 1996; Chancer, 1998). Such black-on-white rapes 'are most likely to result in severe prison sentences...' (Ferraro, 1989, p.156). Conversely, the victimisation of black women receives no such recognition (Chancer, 1998).

Criminology Beyond the West?

Criminology originated, survives and prospers on a western platform. Relatedly, understandings of crime and justice have found favour from that angle. Amidst this scenario is a pan-African viewpoint, which is yet to gain significant recognition within mainstream frameworks of western criminology. This is despite the advent of postmodernism and its denunciation of universalism. While the pan-African voice in a western domestic context can be said to be struggling to be significantly heard, that which is based outside the West seems to be almost excluded from the criminological pursuit. Under these circumstances, pan-African issues are popularised from a non-African perspective, which itself is primarily western, absolutist and hegemonic in its interpretations.

Cain's (2000) paper on *Orientalism, Occidentalism and the Sociology of Crime* offers some illuminating illustrations of the above scenario. In a critique of western criminology and its 'hegemonic tendencies', she analyses the orientalist and occidentalist orientations adopted in western criminology towards crime and justice interpretation at a global level. Whilst orientalism negativises and/or idealises the practices and cultures of non-western nations, occidentalism 'presumes the 'sameness' of key cultural categories, practices and institutions' (p.239) and denies the existence of a difference. The policy, economic and scholarly implications of information based on these approaches for both the informers and the recipients are unveiled by Cain who on the basis of research-based data drawn from the Caribbean preaches the importance of giving recognition to diversity in its own right. Thus, included in Cain's (2000, p.258) advice to criminologists are:

- avoid orientalism in both its negative and its romantic guises…
- avoid occidentalism, both in its denial of difference and in its self regarding interpretation of all difference as resistance…
- encourage the capacity to see the Other as her own subject; use other people's writings about their situation to feed into improved abstractions…

Of particular interest to this essay is Cain's detailed illustration and analysis of the issue of occidentalism, which I see as the most apparent and a major driving force behind the hegemonic ideals of criminology. By way of example, Cain refers to issues of 'age', 'victimization and poverty', and 'community safety and neighbourhood watch' to show the theoretical and practical representations of occidentalist criminology in the Caribbean context. In doing so, she observes that these concepts are not cultural universal entities. The points of difference between the Caribbean and the West include: (1) the relationship between age and crime is different, and show that unlike the West, the crime rate in the Caribbean is lower among young people; (2) unlike western societies where crime victimisation (including personal and household crimes) is shown to be prevalent amongst the socio-economically deprived, the Caribbean situation shows crime victimisation to be more evident amongst the higher income groups; and (3) the Caribbean agenda for neighbourhood watch is informal in practice with no links to a state agency unlike the more official neighbourhood watch scheme practised in the West.

The reasons for the differences lie principally with the differences in the societal contexts within which those entities occur. However, as Cain importantly points out, these are differences that have been ignored in western occidentalist models upon which Caribbean discourse and practice towards crime and justice have *themselves* rested. For example, the Caribbean response to crime victimisation is that which thrives on 'the export of a model of community policing based on an inappropriate presumption of the generalizability of western victimization patterns' (ibid., p.245). Those 'western victimization patterns' allege the greater vulnerability of the deprived and this theory consequently amounts to the over-policing of the deprived in the Caribbean crime scene.

What Cain describes as 'hegemonic tendencies' of occidentalist (and orientalist) criminological discourses are rooted in a historical backdrop of ethnocentric conceptions of white superiority and non-white inferiority. As partly shown in earlier sections above, those images were useful to the slave trade and colonialism. To most people, slavery and colonialism have been and gone. But in reality their practical embodiments are still lingering, albeit indirectly, in the form of neocolonialism. And criminology is no exception to exposure to this new form of colonialism. Neocolonial criminology not only sidetracks diversity at both domestic and global levels but it also has the tendency to impose its mainstream definitions upon those whom it aims to define. This has, for instance, meant that within the domestic settings of western nations, critical approaches to the treatment and experiences of black people in the criminal justice system have often been met with those popular responses which overtly or covertly construct black people as *the problem*. Broadly speaking, either that the label on black people as 'the problem' is justified in biological and psychological terms as an inherent quality, or it is interpreted in sociological terms, which tend to patronise or pathologise their circumstances. The latter stance invokes, for example, the class status and single-parent arguments as justifications while the IQ account can exemplify the former. Herein, no significant interest seems to be assigned to black people of middle-class background, those in stable coupled relationships or those with 'high' IQ levels, who in any case are also susceptible to the theoretical and practical ramifications of these negative lines of thinking (Kalunta-Crumpton, 2000).

In her essay entitled *The Color of Crime: External and Internal Images*, Russell (2000) provides some description of the absence of a divide and rule strategy in analyses of black criminality. With reference to the US, she narrates how the amount of media focus on crime committed by a minority of black people far outweighs the recognition given to the law-abiding black majority. As she argued, statistical inferences often claim that 'one in three young black men is under the jurisdiction of the criminal justice system', and in so doing 'what …goes unacknowledged is that if 33.3% are in the justice system, then 66.7% are not' (p.19). But what do we know about the '66.7%'? Russell appropriately states that the black 'noncriminal majority is an untapped resource' (p.25); this category is 'frequently overlooked as a resource for analyzing crime and justice issues' (p.19). Instead, familiar images of black people, which have surfaced uppermost in race-crime debates, regardless of western geographical boundaries, are reflected in portrayals such as 'inherently criminal', 'aggressive', 'anti-authoritarian', 'violent', 'threathening' and 'dangerous'. Such labels, which sometimes accompany anti-racism campaigns by black people, serve to promote what Cain (2000) describes as occidentalist 'interpretation of all difference as resistance'. Through ongoing reproductions of such representations in both theoretical and practical criminological concerns, this common trend in understanding the position of black people has tended to abnormalise and subordinate their differing standpoint.

Examples abound to unveil hegemony in criminology's attitude towards pan-African issues in the western scene. The global context of hegemonic criminology is an extension of the situation in the West, and is seemingly more damaging principally because its occidentalist approach sustains and thrives on the relative absence of western awareness, or even western denial of alternative non-western theorising. In fact, from the outset of contact between Europeans and Africans on the coasts of Africa, cultural relativity was denied by scholars, travellers and traders alike amidst their ignorant assumptions of a cultural universal premised on western ideals. Thus, while Africans were besotted with their physical features and cultural make-up, Europeans in contrast described and treated those characteristics with contempt (Husband, 1982). Alleged sexual abnormality ascribed to polygamous relationships in Africa and the Caribbean, and the interpretation of African traditional religion as heathenism instance negative representations that dominated European ideological constructions of Africans (Walvin, 1973; Barker, 1978) and subordinated any relevance of cultural difference and diversity. Although more subtly, contemporary times have carried on this traditional line of reasoning about African issues including attempts to ignore them. Within the discipline of criminology, the relative absence of non-western African experience is a further sign of western apathy towards difference. This is not to say that the African experience has nothing productive to offer mainstream western criminology.

Interestingly, while it seems that ethnocentrism about difference is a western creation and a right specific to the West, the fact remains that it is not. Non-western societies hold racially-based ideologies differentiating them from others. Fenton (1999, p.85) cites Dikotter (1992, p.5) as stating that 'every civilisation has an ethnocentric world image in which outsiders are reduced to manageable spatial units'. Referring to the Chinese, Dikotter narrates how as far back as the 8th century, the Chinese viewed non-Chinese as barbarians; white Europeans were defined as 'deathly white' with sub-human physical qualities (Fenton, 1999). Such ethnocentric views are also found in Africa as revealed in the following two observations:

> As early as 1621 one writer told of the 'jetty coloured' negroes, 'who in their native beauty most delight, /And in contempt doe paint the Divell white' (cited in Husband, 1982, p.45).

> Unlike the Afro-Caribbean, the West African did not undergo a traumatic uprooting nor did he suffer the indignity of slavery. Hence he had not developed the feeling of 'intimate enmity' towards the British the Afro-Caribbean had. He did not suffer from the anxiety and neurosis about his colour that was part of the Afro-Caribbean subconscious. He did not wish

> to be white, nor was he a product of a 'white-based' society. Indeed, in his culture white was the colour of death. He did not suffer from self-contempt, nor did he wish to run away from his past. Quite the contrary. West Africans were rooted in their past and their own socio-cultural tradition (Hiro, 1992, p.65).

These instances demonstrate the crucial significance of cultural relativity and the existence of a strong African cultural base from which alternative theorising can emerge, and influence western criminology and related disciplines. It is now a question of whether criminology is willing to tap into that culture as a resource in its own right.

Conclusion

Relegating pan-African experience to the margins of criminology crucially deprives the mainstream the opportunity to benefit and learn from the culture of Africans, and especially its origins in Africa. The African continent presents a very fertile ground with rich and interesting information that criminologists around the globe can utilise with a view to broadening and enhancing their theoretical and empirical knowledge. To achieve this would mean dismantling the hierarchical structuring of differences in order of their normality and abnormality; refraining from undermining the importance of difference in its own right; and refraining from simply studying and presenting 'other' subjects as passive recipients of definitions. Instead criminology needs to aim at encompassing *all* as active expressions in criminological definitions.

In short, Cain's (2000) suggestion for 'interactive globalization, rather than hegemony' for the purpose of 'mutual and reciprocal learning' captures an important way forward for criminology.

Note

1. Refers to the arrest of a person under s.4 and s.6 of the 1824 Vagrancy Act for loitering in a public place with intent to commit a crime.

References

Agozino, B. (1997), *Black Women and the Criminal Justice System*, Ashgate, Aldershot.

Barker, A. (1978), *The African Link*, Frank Cass, Britain.

Brown, C. (1984), *Black and White Britain*, Heinmann, London.

Cain, M. (2000), 'Orientalism, Occidentalism and the Sociology of Crime', *British Journal of Criminology*, vol. 40, pp.239-260.

Centre for Contemporary Cultural Studies (1982), *The Empire Strikes Back*, Hutchinson, London.

Chancer, L. (1998), 'Gender, Class and Race in Three High-Profile Crimes', in Miller, S. (ed.), *Crime Control and Women*, Sage, London.

Chigwada, R. (1991), 'The Policing of Black Women', in Cashmore, E. and McLaughlin, E. (eds), *Out of Order*, Routledge, London.

Chigwada-Bailey, R. (1997), *Black Women's Experiences of Criminal Justice*, Waterside Press, Winchester.

Cloward, R. and Ohlin, L. (1960), *Delinquency and Opportunity*, Free Press, New York.

Cohen, A. (1955), *Delinquent Boys*, Free Press, New York.

Commission for Racial Equality (1992), *Cautions v. Prosecutions: Ethnic Monitoring of Juveniles by Seven Police Forces*, Commission for Racial Equality, London.

Commission on Systemic Racism in the Ontario Criminal Justice System (2000), 'Racism in Justice: Perceptions', in Neugebauer, R. (ed.), *Criminal Injustice*, Canadian Scholars' Press, Toronto.

Crow, I. and Simon, F. (1987), *Unemployment and Magistrates' Courts*, NACRO, London.

Culkanz, L. (1996), *Rape on Trial*, University of Pennsylvania Press, Philadelphia.

Darwin, C. (1859), *On the Origin of Species, The Works of Charles Darwin*, vol. 15, John Murray, London.

Demuth, C. (1978), *'Sus': A Report on the Vagrancy Act 1824*, Runnymede Trust, London.

Dikotter, F. (1992), *The Discourse of Race in Modern China*, Hurst and Co., London.

Downes, P. (1966), *The Delinquent Solution*, Routledge and Kegan Paul, London.

Eysenck, H. (1971), *Race, Intelligence and Education*, Temple Smith, London.

Eze, E. (1997), *Race and the Enlightenment*, Blackwell, Oxford.

Fenton, S. (1999), *Ethnicity*, Macmillan, London.

Ferraro, K. (1989), 'The Legal Response to Woman Battering in the United States', in Hamner, J., Radford, J. and Stanko, B. (eds), *Women, Policing and Male Violence*, Routledge and Kegan Paul, London.

Ferri, E. (1895), *Criminal Sociology*, Fisher Unwin, London.

Fryer, P. (1984), *Staying Power*, Pluto, London.

Galton, F. (1869), *Hereditary Genius*, Macmillan, London.

Garland, D. (1985), 'The Criminal and his Science', *British Journal of Criminology*, April.

Gilroy, P. (1987a), *There Ain't No Black in the Union Jack*, Hutchinson, London.

______ (1987b), 'The Myth of Black Criminality', in Scraton, P. (ed.), *Law, Order and the Authoritarian State*, Open University Press, Milton Keynes.

Goddard, H. (1912), *The Kallikak Family: A Study in the Heredity of Feeble-Mindedness*, Macmillan, New York.

_____ (1914), *Feeblemindedness*, Macmillan, New York.
Gordon, P. (1983), *White Law*, Pluto, London.
Gordon, R. (1976), 'Prevalence: The Rare Datum in Delinquency Measurement and its Implications for the Theory of Delinquency', in Klein, M. (ed.), *The Juvenile Justice System*, Sage, Beverly Hills, California.
Goring, C. (1913), *The English Convict*, Home Office, London.
Green, P. (1998), *Drugs, Trafficking and Criminal Policy*, Waterside Press, Winchester.
Hall, S., Critcher, C., Clarke, J., Jefferson, T. and Roberts, B. (1978), *Policing the Crisis*, Macmillan, London.
Hall, T. (1989), 'Black People, Crime and Justice', in Russell, E. (ed.), *Black People and the Criminal Justice System*, The Howard League for Penal Reform, London.
Herrnstein, R. and Murray, C. (1994), *The Bell Curve*, Free Press, London.
Hesse, B., Rai, D., Bennet, C. and McGilhrist, P. (1992), *Beneath the Surface: Racial Harassment*, Avebury, Aldershot.
Hiro, D. (1992), *Black British White British*, Paladin, London.
Hirschi, T. and Hindelang, M. (1977), 'Intelligence and Delinquency: A Revisionist Review', *American Sociological Review*, vol. 42, pp.572-587.
Hobbs, D. (1997), 'Criminal Collaboration: Youth Gangs, Subcultures, Professional Criminals, and Organised Crime', in Maguire, R., Morgan, R. and Reiner, R. (eds), *The Oxford Handbook of Criminology*, Clarendon Press, Oxford.
Home Office (1993), 'The Prison Population in 1992', *Home Office Statistical Bulletin*, 7/92, Home Office, London.
_____ (1998), *Statistics on Race and the Criminal Justice System*, Home Office, London.
Humphrey, D. (1972), *Police Power and Black People*, Panther, London.
Humphrey, D. and John, G. (1971), *Because They're Black*, Penguin, Handsworth.
Hunte, J. (1966), *Nigger Hunting in England?* West Indian Standing Conference, London.
Husband, (ed.) (1982), *Race in Britain*, Hutchinson and Co Publishers, London.
Jensen, A. (1969), 'How Much Can We Boost IQ and Scholastic Achievement?', *Harvard Educational Review*, vol. 39, pp.1-123.
Jones, T., MacLean, B. and Young, J. (1986), *The Islington Crime Survey*, Gower, Aldershot.
Kalunta-Crumpton, A. (2000), 'Black People and Discrimination in the Criminal Justice System: The Messages from Research', in Marlow, A. and Loveday, B. (eds), *After MacPherson*, Russell House Publishing, Dorset.
Kamin, L. (1977), *The Science and Politics of IQ*, Penguin, Harmondsworth.
Landau, S. (1981), 'Juveniles and the Police', *British Journal of Criminology*, vol. 21, no.1.
Landau, S. and Nathan, G. (1983), 'Selecting Delinquents for Questioning in the London Metropolitan Area', *British Journal of Criminology*, vol. 28, pp.128-149.
Lea, J. and Young, J. (1984), *What Is to Be Done About Law and Order?* Penguin, Harmondsworth.

______ (1993), *What Is to Be Done About Law and Order?* (2nd edn), Pluto, London.

Lombroso, C. (1876), *L'Uomo Delinquente*, Fratelli Bocca, Turin.

Lusane, C. (2000), 'We Are the World: Race and the International War on Drugs', in Henry, C. (ed.), *Foreign Policy and the Black (Inter)National Interest*, State University of New York Press, Albany.

Massey, D. and Denton, N. (1993), *American Apartheid*, Harvard University Press, Cambridge, Mass.

Mays, J. (1954), *Growing Up in the City*, Liverpool University Press, Liverpool.

Merton, R. (1938), 'Social Structure and Anomie', *American Sociological Review*, vol. 3.

Miller, J. (1997), *Search and Destroy*, Cambridge University Press, Cambridge.

Morris, T. (1957), *The Criminal Area*, Routledge and Kegan Paul, London.

Murray, C. (1984), *Losing Ground*, Basic Books, New York.

______ (1990), *The Emerging British Underclass*, Institute for Economic Affairs, London.

______ (1996), 'The Underclass', in Muncie, J., McLaughlin, E. and Langan, M. (eds), *Criminological Perspectives*, Sage, London.

NACRO (1993), *Evidence of the Links Between Homelessness, Crime and the Criminal Justice System*, Occasional Paper, NACRO, London.

Oppenheim, C. (1993), *Poverty: The Facts*, Child Poverty Action Group, London.

Penal Affairs Consortium (1996), *Race and Criminal Justice*, Penal Affairs Consortium, London.

Pitts, J. (1986), 'Black Young People and Juvenile Crime: Some Unanswered Questions', in Matthews, R. and Young, J. (eds), *Confronting Crime*, Sage, London.

Roberts, B. (1982), 'The Debate on 'Sus'', in Cashmore, E. (ed.), *Black Youth in Crisis*, George Allen and Unwin, London.

Roshier, B. (1989), *Controlling Crime*, Open University Press, Milton Keynes.

Russell, K. (2000), 'The Color of Crime: External and Internal Images', in Neugebauer, R. (ed.), *Criminal Injustice*, Canadian Scholars' Press, Toronto.

Ryan, W. (1976), *Blaming the Victim*, Vintage, New York.

Sampson, R. and Wilson, W. (1995), 'Toward a Theory of Race, Crime and Urban Inequality', in Hagan, J. and Paterson, R. (eds), *Crime and Inequality*, Stanford University Press, Stanford, California.

Scarman, Lord (1981), *The Brixton Disorders 10-12 April 1981: Report of an Inquiry by the Rt Hon. the Lord Scarman*, HMSO, London.

Shaw, C. (1929), *Delinquency Areas*, University of Chicago Press, Chicago.

Shaw, C. and McKay, H. (1942), *Juvenile Delinquency and Urban Areas*, University of Chicago Press, Chicago.

Skogan, W. (1994), *The Police and Public in England and Wales: A British Crime Survey Report*, HMSO, London.

Solomos, J. (1988), *Black Youth, Racism and the State*, Cambridge University Press, Cambridge.

______ (1993), *Race and Racism in Britain*, Macmillan, London.

Steffensmeier, D. and Demuth, S. (2001), 'Ethnicity and Judges' Sentencing Decisions: Hispanis-Black-White Comparisons', *Criminology*, vol. 39, pp.145-178.

Sudbury, J. (2002), 'Celling Black Bodies: Black Women in Global Prison Industrial Complex', *Feminist Review*, vol.70, pp.57-74.

Tierney, J. (1996), *Criminology*, Prentice Hall/Harvester Wheatsheaf, London.

Virdee, S. (1995), *Racial Violence and Harassment*, Policy Studies Institute, London.

Walvin, N. (1971), *The Black Presence*, Orbach and Chambers, London.

______ (1973), *Black and White*, Penguin, London.

Willis, C. (1983), *The Use, Effectiveness and Impact of Police Stop and Search Powers*, Home Office, London.

Wilson, D. and Herrnstein, R. (1985), *Crime and Human Nature*, Simon and Schuster, New York.

2 Human Rights, Gender and Traditional Practices: The Trokosi System in West Africa

ROBERT KWAME AMEH

Introduction

Membership of the global village and the community of nations has meant the subjection of developing countries to scores of international laws, treaties, conventions and understandings. Inevitably, the vigorous processes of globalization and localization engender some dilemmas and tensions, and nowhere are these more manifested than with regard to issues of law and social control in traditional societies. Across Africa, evidence of these dilemmas and tensions have expressed themselves in raging controversies surrounding hitherto accepted traditional and cultural practices such as female circumcision, witch villages, marital practices, funeral and widowhood rites, and inheritance practices. This chapter highlights some of the human rights and gender issues raised by the traditional and religious system of *trokosi* found among some ethnic groups in West Africa. The *trokosi* system among the Southern Ewe of Ghana will be presented to illustrate these issues.

What is Trokosi?

Trokosi is an aspect of the traditional religious and crime control practices of the Dangme, Ewe, and Fon ethnic groups in Ghana, Togo, and Benin along the West African coast. Generally, it is a practice whereby a child, usually a virgin, is selected by her family to serve in a shrine in reparation for crimes committed by other members of the family. Such a child becomes known as a *trokosi*, an Ewe word, which could be variously translated as 'wife of a god', 'a person consecrated to a god' or 'slave of a god'. Whereas children of both sexes could be called upon to serve as *trokosis*, the tendency has been for more girls and women, than boys and men, to do so. The tales of horror and exploitation told by *trokosis* from interviews with them, were summed up by Ameh (2001, pp.271-272) as follows:

a. Abandoned at the shrines by their parents or other relatives at a tender age, in some cases as young as seven years old;
b. Some did not know why they were so abandoned. For those who knew, the reason has often been a crime of commission or omission by a parent or other relative;
c. The crimes ranged from stealing, adultery, having sex with a *trokosi*, and failure to redeem a pledge made to a deity;
d. Waking up as early as 5:00am, doing the domestic chores, working long hours on the farm, having unwanted sex with the priests and bearing children, no access to medical care, and lack of education constitute their normal daily living;
e. In addition, their movements are restricted to the confines of the shrine, unless with the permission of the priests. Their clothing is largely limited to the famous blue-black piece of cloth and the identification raffia necklace; and
f. *Trokosi*s describe the practice as unfair, inhuman, degrading, and a practice no human being should undergo. In fact, they all describe the practice as slavery.

Other scholars (Dovlo and Adzoyi, 1995; Nukunya and Kwafo, 1998), human rights practitioners (Ababio, 1995; Bilyeu, 1999; International Needs Ghana, 2001; Short, 2001) and several local and international reporters (Amoah, 1998; Azumah, 1998; French, 1997) have confirmed the experiences of *trokosis* as outlined in the summary above.

The duration of the stay of a *trokosi* in a shrine is supposed to last from between six months to three years, depending on the gravity of the crime and the shrine at which one is serving. But in practice, once the girls are assigned to the shrines, their families are not enthusiastic about procuring their release as *trokosis* become objects of fear in the practising communities due to the stigma attached to them. Once they are sent to the shrines, families maintain only minimal, or in some cases sever all, contacts with them. Consequently, the practice of *trokosi* could be defined as bondage for life as most girls serve at the shrines for the rest of their useful lives.

It is now commonly accepted among researchers and practitioners that there is considerable variety in the practice of *trokosi* as one moves from one shrine and practicing community, to another. At the recent West Africa Sub-Regional Workshop on *Trokosi*, it became clear that there are differences in *trokosi* practice and also between the three sub-regional countries of Ghana, Togo and Benin. In Benin for example, fewer girls/women live in the shrines, and human rights organizations are more focused on other human rights abuses such as child trafficking, which they consider as more urgent than the *trokosi* issue. Thus, the Benin delegates, and to some extent the Togolese, could not fully share in Ghana's preoccupation with the anti-*trokosi* campaign.

In Ghana, *trokosis* could be grouped into three main categories. There are *trokosis* who, like Samuel in the Bible, were offered by their parents to serve in the shrines in appreciation of the help of the gods in their conception and birth. These are the *dorfleviwo*, also known as *baviwo* among the Tongu-Ewes (Dovlo and Adzoyi, 1995: 7). *Fiasidis*, a second category of *trokosis*, are initiates of the Nyigbla and Yewe religious orders, and may be given by their families, inducted by the deities, or voluntarily choose to serve in the shrines. These particular *trokosis* are perceived as the "wives of the gods" and consequently, are treated with respect by all in the community including the priests and their husbands. They own property and are not considered poor by community standards (Greene, 1996; Ameh, 1998). This is the more humane version of *trokosi* practice, which is found among the Anlo Ewes. A third category of *trokosis*, which has become the subject of Ghana's *trokosi* debate and anti-*trokosi* campaign, is the focus of this chapter. These *trokosis* serve in shrines in atonement for crimes committed by other members of their family. They offer free domestic and agricultural labor and sexual services to the priests and other shrine functionaries. Consequently, their rights to determine their own marriage and sexual partners are violated. Ideally, their families are responsible for their upkeep in the shrines. Yet, no sooner had these families sent these girls and women to the shrines than they forget about them. With the priests unable to provide their basic survival needs, these girls risk a life of extreme deprivations, which sometimes compromise their health. These *trokosis* are mainly found among the Tongu-Ewes and the Dangmes.

The *trokosi* system as described above raises several issues and opens up several lines of inquiry of interest to social scientists such as criminologists, legal scholars, human rights practitioners, and anthropologists. The lines of inquiry could be grouped into two broad categories. First is the purely academic analysis of the issue of *trokosi*. For example, criminologists and legal scholars may be interested in the violations of several national and international laws and conventions, wrongful convictions, and the issue of serving time for a crime committed by another person as embedded in *trokosi* practice. Other social scientists such as historians engaged in the study of *slavery* and slavery-like practices such as bondage may also find the issue of *trokosi* fascinating as *trokosi* is definable as bondage or slavery since *trokosi* women and girls are virtually owned by the shrine priests and elders. As explained earlier, the *trokosi* experience could become a lifelong bondage to the shrine priests who control their movement and appropriate their labor and sexual services, for most of their useful lives. *Trokosis* who die or become sexually unattractive must be replaced. Social anthropologists may be interested in the traditional norms, values, religious, and social control values that underpin the practice. For why would someone in his right mind send one of his own offspring into a life of bondage?

The second major line of inquiry would be to address the policy issues emanating from the *trokosi* problem. This may be of interest to policy scientists, policy makers, and human rights practitioners. How do we deal with the *trokosi* problem to ensure effective and positive change? Or even more generally, how do we confront controversial traditional practices? Ameh's (2001) attempt to grapple with these questions has revealed that Non-Governmental Organizations (NGOs) and individuals have played a more pro-active role in Ghana's '*trokosi* problem', both at the local and national levels, than the government. Consequently, an analysis of social movements, interest groups, and policy theory and practice must also be part of any complete understanding of the *trokosi* problem. The two lines of inquiry are, however, closely interrelated. For example, one cannot fully explain and develop an effective policy to combat the practice if one does not also grapple with a key question raised in the first line of inquiry such as, "What accounts for the origin, development and sustenance of the institution of *trokosi*?" This would require following the social anthropologist's lead in placing the practice within the context of the traditional religious and crime control institutions of *trokosi* practicing communities. The multiple perspectives from which *trokosi* could be analysed illustrate the complexity of the issue, and demands that researchers and practitioners eschew any simplistic approach to the problem. But while all these approaches and issues are important for a complete understanding of the institution and practice of *trokosi* it is beyond the scope of this chapter to address them all. Consequently, the rest of this chapter will be devoted to addressing only two issues: the human rights and gender issues that emerge from the *trokosi* system.

A Human Rights Approach to Trokosi

The anti-*trokosi* campaign in Ghana has mainly been defined as an international human rights issue. The human rights violations of the institution and practice of *trokosi* have been well articulated by Ababio (1995), Bilyeu (1999) and Short (1995, 1997, 1998a, 1998b). Among them, they discuss a long list of Ghanaian laws and international human rights instruments that the practice of *trokosi* violates. These include the violation of relevant sections of the constitution of the Republic of Ghana, the African Charter of Human and People's Rights, the United Nations (UN) Convention on the Rights of the Child, and the UN Convention on the Elimination of All forms of Discrimination Against Women (CEDAW). But granted that the *trokosi* system is a gross violation of international human rights norms, two practical but related questions need to be addressed: (i) how do we get people of other cultures such as *trokosi* practitioners to implement international human rights norms? (ii) how do we make change meaningful and acceptable to practitioners of controversial cultural practices in general?

A review of the international human rights literature reveals the universalism-versus-relativism debate as one of the major dilemmas and tensions surrounding the application of international human rights norms in other cultures. Two central issues of contention emerge in this debate. First, is whether non-western societies have conceptions of human rights. A related question is whether, if so, those conceptions are valid and should be recognized by the UN. Western scholars such as Howard and Donnelly (Donnelly, 1982a, 1982b; Howard, 1986, 1992, 1993,

1995; Howard and Donnelly, 1986) observe that human rights can only flourish in liberal regimes and are therefore peculiar to western societies. Consequently, they argue that non-western societies have no notion of human rights. Howard and Donnelly define human rights narrowly in terms of the western liberal ideals of personal autonomy, equality, and free market. Several African scholars disagree with Howard and Donnelly. Motala (1989), Busia (1994) and wa Mutua (1995) argue that all societies of the world have standards of human dignity and the worth of human beings in both its collective and individual personalities. To them, these standards form the basis of human rights the world over and, hence, these societies could not be described as not having conceptions of human rights. Based on the anthropological literature, these scholars provide evidence from the political and social systems of pre-colonial African societies to make a strong case for human rights in these societies. They see communitarian principles and their system of duties and obligations as unique aspects of the African human rights system. Labelled differently by various Africans as 'African humanism', 'African personality', 'African cultural fingerprint', among others, these writers argue that these are equally valid as any other conceptions of human rights.

The second major issue of contention in the universality/relativity debate in human rights is whether the existing UN human rights instruments have universal applicability. Howard (1986, 1992, 1993) and Donnelly (1985) have championed the view that the current regime of international human rights norms is universally applicable. On the other hand, the relativists, mainly scholars from the non-western world, such as Motala, Busia, and wa Mutua contend that since western conceptions of human rights do not adequately capture the wide range of notions of human rights which obtain in other societies, current international human rights laws are not universally applicable. Consequently, the latter support the idea of multiple standards for measuring conformity to international human rights norms.

The position of the African human rights scholars seems more plausible than that of the western universalists in addressing controversial traditional practices because it reckons with the reality of the African situation as it considers the history, indigenous values and practices, and the current socio-economic experiences of the people. The reality of the situation of the vast majority of Africans today is that they are economically deprived and live in inaccessible regions. Consequently, they find pre-colonial African socio-cultural institutions and practices (that is, the only ones most are familiar with) more relevant and reliable than the modern, western-imported ones. This reality cannot be ignored in any attempt to implement international human rights norms in Africa. Besides, there are elements of universalism in the position of African academics. Their argument that all societies have conceptions of human rights and that some commonalties could be found across all societies of the world contains the seeds of a different type of justification for the universality of human rights than the one offered by western universalists. Renteln (1990) pursued the idea of cultural commonalties and human rights through her 'cross-cultural universals' approach, which demands that universality in human rights should be based on universals across cultures. An-Na'im (1992) further developed Renteln's 'cross-cultural universals' approach by adding to it the elements of internal cultural discourse, cross-cultural dialogue, and local activism. This approach bridges the gap between the relativists and their opponents because while recognizing the universal applicability of international human rights norms, it argues strongly for sensitivity to local cultural norms and values in its implementation. The approach essentially gives ownership of the process of change and primary responsibility to local people involved in a particular issue. The emphasis is on dialogue, education, and cultural sensitivity. This contrasts sharply with the condemnation, a demeaning and contemptuous attitude towards other cultures, and a top-down approach that is characteristic of current efforts to eradicate controversial traditional practices in non-western cultures.

The 'cross-cultural universals' approach could easily be supplemented with Nagan's (1993) 'comprehensive orientation' to human rights, an orientation which demands that human rights practice be pursued within the socio-cultural context of the practising community. It requires that the views of all stakeholders (including those of people in practising communities), and not only those of scholars, powerful political interests, and international human rights agencies, must be reckoned with in human rights practice. Nagan calls this the 'contextual policy oriented approach' to human rights.

African human rights scholars, however, acknowledge that like any other human rights system of the world, the African pre-colonial system had both its merits and demerits. In this vein, Gyekye (1996) came to the conclusion that even though African societies cherish communal values, they also recognize individual values. Gyekye, however, acknowledges that some Africans may have a problem striking a balance between communal and individualistic values. In practice, the negative impact of the problem of imbalance between communal and individual values weighs more heavily on women and children than on men, as would be discussed in the next section. Hence, African scholars argue that contemporary African countries should fashion their human rights systems on positive aspects of their pre-colonial cultural and social values and discard the negative aspects such as discrimination and oppression of women and children.

Gender Issues in the Trokosi System

Until the recent emergence of feminism as a dynamic academic discourse, the experiences and knowledge of women were subjugated in academia just as in traditional society. Common to all feminisms is the issue of giving recognition to the experiences, knowledge, identity, and voice of women in the construction of the realities of society. In this way, feminism, at the very minimum, adds gender to all issues in society (Einstadter and Henry, 1995; Lilly et al., 2001; Phillips, 1996). While sex deals with biological differences, gender connotes 'socially constructed and historically variable relationships, cultural meanings, and identities through which biological sex differences become socially significant' (Laslett and Brenner, 1989 cited in Phillips, 1996, p.242).

In Africa, gender differences find their strongest expression in cultural and traditional religious institutions and practices. Communal values, a key component of African culture that is expressed through the principle of collective responsibility, are often given precedence over individual values (Gyekye, 1996; Nukunya, 1969, 1997). Unfortunately, in almost all such cases it is the individual rights of women and girls or children that are sacrificed for the benefit of the whole society. Almost every imaginable controversial customary African practice – circumcision; witch villages; funeral and widowhood rites; *rites de passage*; inheritance practices; marriage practices such as polygamy, levirate, sororate, child marriage, spousal veto, and brideprice; and *trokosi* – either apply only to females or impact on the individuality of females more negatively than males. In fact, there is a mountain of evidence from African scholars (Adjetey, 1995; Armstrong et al., 1993; Ncube, 1991; Savell, 1996) that this is not a problem of African societies' disdain for individual values but rather that of an inability to strike a balance between communal and individualistic values to a disproportionate disadvantage to women.

In this context, a key question that has constantly been asked at *trokosi* fora ever since the issue became identified as a national social problem in Ghana in the early 1990s has been, 'why is it always girls and women?' (International Needs, 1995, 1998, 2001). It could be argued that the principle of patrilineal descent among *trokosi*-practising ethnic groups, whereby family is defined through the male line, and which makes males more important than females, accounts for this. Yet, the plight of women in matrilineal societies in Africa does not look any different from that of their counterparts in patrilineal societies. The discrimination against wives and their children and the violation of their rights with regards to inheritance rights on the death of a husband among the matrilineal Akan ethnic groups in Ghana, such as the Asante, testifies to this plight. Upon the death of a husband in traditional Asante society, it is his extended family, and not his wife or children, that inherit his property regardless of the contribution of the wife and children in the acquisition of the property. This practice prompted the enactment of the Intestate Succession Law (Provincial National Defence Council (PNDC) Law 111) with the aim of rectifying the situation. According to the Federation of International Women Lawyers in Ghana (Ghana Review International Newsreel (2001a, 2001b), this law has, however, been largely ignored by the people. To this extent, the patrilineal descent argument may not fully account for the sacrifice of the individuality of the African woman on the altar of communal values.

There is, however, evidence that the individuality and dignity of the African woman may be more respected in matrilineal societies than in patrilineal societies. In this respect, Adjetey (1995) has argued that the African woman has an individualized personality, dignity and freedom, which must be recognized, respected and exercised. With examples from traditional (matrilineal) Asante society, she shows how some Ghanaian women in the past exercised rights even in the political and other spheres and how this changed with the imposition of colonization. In this vein, she contends that what constitutes African customary law today is a product of evolution resulting from African customs, imported colonial common and civil law notions, and religious concepts from Christianity, Islam, and traditional African religions. This product, she contends, constitutes a male view of custom as it represents the views of influential and powerful male traditional rulers and colonial (usually male) appointed leaders. It is then credible to posit that the predicament of the African woman is only partially due to the value placed on the principle of patrilineal descent in African societies. Patriarchy seems a more cogent explanation of the African woman's situation. It refers to the system of male domination over women, whereby 'that which is considered masculine is typically more highly valued than that which is feminine' (Curran and Renzetti, 1994, p.272). Patriarchy cuts across all social systems the world over, whether patrilineal or matrilineal, developed or underdeveloped.

From a policy perspective, a key issue that needs to be addressed, however, is that of change. Like others, Adjetey (1995) contends that customs and traditional norms can adapt to the changing needs of society and argues persuasively for change. To this end, she rightly advocates for a strong infusion of not only feminist values but also of the core Western value of respect for the individuality of a person. In this regard, several scholars (Armstrong et al., 1993; Bilyeu, 1999; Ncube, 1991) including Adjetey suggest that African women stand to benefit greatly from the implementation of certain provisions of the conventions and treaties of the international human rights regime such as the Convention on the Elimination of all Forms of Discrimination Against Women (CEDAW), Convention on the Rights of the Child, the Slavery Covenant, the Forced Labour Convention, the International Bill of Rights, the International Covenant on Civil and Political Rights, and the International Covenant on Economic, Social and Cultural Rights. These scholars have also called for the implementation of national laws and regional conventions such as the African Charter on Human and People's Rights. This is a legal approach to the problems faced by African women, which I find problematic, especially within the African context, as discussed below.

The author has maintained elsewhere that an approach based on dialogue and education is more effective in producing change than any other means in dealing with a belief system (Ameh, 1998, 2001). This position does not negate the utility of law in attempts to procure change. Law could strengthen the hands of the party in whose favor it works, but it, especially criminal law, does not by itself possess the capacity to persuade proponents of a belief system to adopt change. Several cultural institutions and practices in Africa have religious components, which qualify them as elements of the belief system of the people. Like human rights, religious systems lay claim to a higher morality or order. In this sense, human rights and religious systems are both hegemonic and compete against each other for the loyalty of citizens (An-Na'im et al., 1995). Consequently, law, *per se*, has limited efficacy in effecting change in attitude and behaviour with respect to controversial traditional practices. Legal practitioners in Ghana such as Anita Ababio (1995) (then Executive Director of the Ghana Law Reform Commission and member of the Federation of International Women Lawyers (FIDA)) and Emile Short (1995, 1998b, 2001) (Commissioner of the Ghana's Commission on Human Rights and Administrative Justice (CHRAJ)) were quick to acknowledge the limitations of law in dealing with the *trokosi* problem. It was based on this realisation and acknowledgment that the anti-*trokosi* campaign in Ghana adopted a strategy of education and dialogue, which has proved very effective in dealing with the *trokosi* problem (Ameh, 2001, 1998).

Another reason why a legal approach may not be effective in dealing with the problem of women and controversial traditional practices is that Ghanaian women, like other African women, do not have a culture of using the courts to fight for their rights. In fact, this is a pattern, which equally applies to Ghanaian men, even though it is worse in the case of women. A study done by the Ghana Law Reform Commission (1995) on the impact of constitutional provisions on female ritual practices in Ghana aptly captures the issues involved. According to the report of the study, women's rights issues are usually not brought before the courts despite the enactment of numerous relevant legal instruments. The report (ibid., p.22) stated:

> First, many women cannot afford the legal costs involved in litigation. Second, the high illiteracy among women makes them unaware of such provisions. Third, there are still too few active women's organizations which would be willing to undertake class or representative actions on behalf of women victims.

There are few instances in which the courts have been used to fight the violation of rights regarding controversial traditional practices in Ghana. However, the report indicates that even in those few instances the courts in Ghana have been through a dilemma dealing with the cases. This is due to the fact that although African Traditional Religion is legal by the laws of Ghana, findings from traditional religious practices are not legally acceptable evidence in the law courts. Consequently, a legal approach may not be the best for dealing with women's rights issues in African societies.

Further, in the attempt to infuse feminists values into the African socio-cultural environment, policy makers should do well to take note of the findings of several studies on women in Africa. Greene (1996, p.43) sums up these findings in her study of women in Anlo-Ewe, a sub-group within the Southern-Ewe:

> Females as a group did not constitute a homogenous body within their societies. Distinctions existed among women based on their status as free or slave, as individuals associated with royal or non-royal families, and as persons who were advantaged or disadvantaged based on their marital status, age, or specialized roles. These same studies also emphasize that those women who were in stronger economic, political, or religious

> positions often sustained their status by actively subordinating, for their own benefit, the interests of other women who were under their authority.

While these findings are from studies of African women in pre-colonial times, the situation of African women today is no different, just as it was even during the colonial era. There are different categories of women in Africa: some exercise enormous power while others do not, and those who exercise power often end up subjugating their fellow women for their own benefit.

The works of Robertson (1983) and Jones (1995) have shown how influential Ghanaian women during the colonial era sold, bought, and kept female slaves. The slaves were not only of economic value in terms of their role in providing labor in the economic activities (mainly petty commerce) of the mistresses and caring for the young and old, but they also served to boost the mistresses' status in society. Today, while influential Ghanaian women no longer sell or buy slaves, concerns have been raised about the practice of keeping "house-maids" also known as 'house-servants', 'house-helps' or 'maid-servants' by affluent women and families. Almost every household that considers itself wealthy, especially among the urban middle and upper class, keeps a minimum of one 'house-maid'. Except for their titles, the functions of 'maidservants' are not drastically different from that of female slaves of colonial Ghana discussed by Robertson (1983) and Jones (1995). Also, the maidservants of contemporary Ghana are not purchased in the strict sense of the word. Whereas boys or even men are also kept as servants, the predominant number of house-servants in Ghana are girls or women. Clearly, the 'maidservant problem' is not only a female issue as maidservants serve all members of a household, including men. In a typical Ghanaian home, however, it is generally the women, and especially the wife, who have primary responsibility for doing the house chores. Since doing these chores has become the main function of maidservants, and the wives play a deciding role in acquiring and firing them, the 'maidservant problem' is often presented as that of the western educated, middle/upper class Ghanaian woman, who is addressed as 'Madam'. It is the Madams who have the resources to retain the services of maidservants. But the author sees the problem as a middle- and upper class, affluent Ghanaian men and women problem. This position, however, does not weaken the author's argument that powerful Ghanaian, and therefore, African women participate in the exploitation and abuse of their less fortunate female counterparts.

While it is only fair to say that some servants are treated with decency by their mistresses, the exploitation and abuse of maidservants is an open secret in Ghana and yet a largely ignored subject by Ghanaian scholars. Maidservants sometimes even suffer sexual abuse at the hands of their masters and the older male children in the household, work long hours, and some are often starved. The situation of servants has raised concerns in recent times not only among the public, as portrayed in the vicious maidservant stories often carried by Ghanaian media, but has also been raised in Parliament. On 2 August 1996, after Parliament was informed of the first ever mass liberation of *trokosi* women and girls from a shrine, Mr. J. A. Cobbinah, MP for Evalue Gwira, made the following statement:

> Mr. Speaker, the release of girls and women from the *trokosi* shrine is indeed a step forward in our attempt to empower women. But as I always say on the floor of this House, there is one other area where women are in bondage; and that area is that if we look at the very women who are spear-heading the crusade for the empowerment of women, we see that most of them have maid-servants in their houses who do not receive the education which their own children do have. This is another area that we must highlight. Mr. Speaker, I want to appeal to such women to consider the need to liberate these young girls, if the *trokosi* shrine has taken this gigantic step in releasing the girls who used to be in bondage… (Republic of Ghana Parliamentary Debates, 1996, column 1376).

Two years later, the maidservant problem was again raised in the Ghanaian Parliament during the debates that followed the introduction of The Children's Bill in 1998. In his contribution to the debate, Mr. Kosi Kedem, MP for Hohoe South, stated:

> Mr. Speaker, clause 13 talks about the protection of the child from torture and degrading treatment, and straightaway some people's minds may go to customary practices like *trokosi* and things like that. But, Mr. Speaker, I can assure you that some of our children suffer lots of cruelty even in normal homes where they are employed as housemaids or house-helps. Some of them work into the night; some of them are employed at very tender ages of 5, 6, 7, 10 years; and they are denied education. They are misused in the houses. And the people who employ these people as housemaids or house-helps and deny these children their rights are the people who are also advocating for the rights of children – some of them… My message is, that, as much as possible we should try to rescue the child from those people, from the well-to-do in society who employ our children at tender ages to serve them in their houses and deny them their right to education… I would like to appeal to gender and women liberation movements and organizations to do something seriously to rectify the situation… (Republic of Ghana Parliamentary Debates, 1998, columns 612-615).

It is not surprising that on both occasions that the maidservant issue was raised in Parliament, it did not generate many debates. Based on the author's familiarity with the situation in Ghana, it would not be out of place to say that almost every Parliamentarian has at least one maidservant in his or her home. Thus, even though The Children's Act (Act 560) passed in the latter part of 1998 prohibits exploitative child labor (Sections 12 and 87) and child labor at night (Section 88), one is not sure if the lawmakers specifically had maidservants in mind when these sections of the Act were approved. Comparing the plight of maidservants in the homes of the rich to that of *trokosis* in shrines, as discussed earlier, the question that comes to mind is, 'is there a difference between the two categories of girls and women'? For one, *trokosis* are sent to shrines against their will by their families, while only some girls and women become maidservants against their will, having been forced into the situation by their families. Also, maidservants are fed and a significant percentage are paid wages, even if some are underfed and their wages are almost always below the national minimum wage. In contrast, *trokosis* must feed themselves while in the shrines and are not even allowed to partake in the produce of the farms they work. Further, rural girls and women constitute the majority of maidservants in urban Ghana. And for lots of rural people, the status of maidservant represents upward, and therefore positive, mobility on the social scale. *Trokosis*, on the contrary, are stigmatised and become objects of fear in the community, ruining any chances of marriage to men from their own communities.

But do these differences diminish the elements of exploitation of labor, denial of basic rights such as education and health (food), and sexual abuse experienced by both categories of women and girls? It seems as if the two groups only occupy different points in the continuum of exploitation and abuses faced by the African woman at the hands of both powerful men and women, with *trokosis* located at the harsher and more severe end of the gamut. Proponents of the *trokosi* system such as the Afrikania Mission have drawn the attention of the members of the Federation of International Women Lawyers (FIDA), who, together with International Needs Ghana and CHRAJ, are at the forefront of the anti-*trokosi* campaign in Ghana, to the maidservant problem (Ameve, 1999, 2000). The practice of maidservants needs the critical attention of scholars and must definitely be addressed in any attempt to rectify the problem of customary practices that perpetuate gender inequality in Africa. However, the issue, just like the general problem of child labor, must be approached from the context of the culture, traditions and specific realities of not only the African woman, but also that of African societies in general.

Conclusion

The traditional crime control and religious practice of *trokosi* is a complex phenomenon that raises several issues of interest to criminologists and other scholars. This chapter examined only two of the many issues involved – human rights and gender. The human rights concerns revolve around the relativism-universalism debate in the literature on human rights in Africa with the central question being how best to approach the implementation of international human rights norms in other cultures such as Africa. A key argument raised in this chapter is that in order for any policy approach to the *trokosi* problem to be effective, it must take cognisance of the unique socio-cultural belief systems that produced and maintain the practice and the contemporary realities of the people in the practicing communities.

The gender discrimination endemic to the *trokosi* system is quite obvious: why is it only women and girls that have to endure such an inhumane practice? To reverse this trend, the temptation has been for scholars to call for a legal approach embracing the implementation of the full range of conventions and norms of the international human rights regime. The author has argued that since African societies do not have a culture of fighting for their rights through the courts, a legal approach would not be an effective means for achieving respect for the individuality of the African woman. In addition, most African women are not even aware of the existence of legal provisions that protect their rights; even if they are, they do not have the resources to pursue a legal challenge in the courts. In this context, it would seem a more reasonable approach to emphasize educational policies rather than criminalize the discrimination and oppression of African women.

Equally important is the recognition that African women do not constitute a homogenous unit. Throughout history, there have been different classes of women in Africa with varying degrees of power and authority. Unfortunately, some powerful women, just like men, subjugate their fellow, less powerful women to their own advantage. The author used the practice of 'maidservant' or 'house-servants' in Ghana to illustrate this situation in the chapter. A commonly acknowledged problem, yet an academically ignored subject, the contemporary issue of 'maidservants' cannot be overlooked in any attempt to rectify the inequality that women suffer in African societies. Hence, it needs to be further researched.

References

Ababio, A. (1995), 'The Legal Basis for Abolishing the Trokosi System', *International Needs Report of the First National Workshop on Trokosi System in Ghana*, Accra, pp.37-43.

Adjetey, F.A. (1995), 'Reclaiming the African Woman's Individuality: the Struggle between Women's Reproductive Autonomy and African Society and Culture', *The American University Law Review*, vol. 44, pp.1351-1381.

Ameh, R. K. (1998), 'Trokosi (Child Slavery) in Ghana: A Policy Approach', *Ghana Studies*, vol. 1, pp.35-62.

______ (2001), *Child Bondage in Ghana: A Contextual Policy Analysis of Trokosi*, Unpublished Ph.D. dissertation, Simon Fraser University, Burnaby, British Columbia, December.

Amoah, A.E. (1998), 'The Transformation of Trokosi', *Daily Graphic*, May 15.

An-Na'im, A.A. (ed.) (1992), *Human Rights in Cross-Cultural Perspectives: A Quest for Consensus*, University of Pennsylvania Press, Philadelphia.

An-Na'im, A.A., Gort, J.D., Jansen, H. and Vroom, H.M. (eds) (1995), 'Preface', in An-Na'im, A.A., Gort, J.D., Jansen, H. and Vroom, H.M (eds), *Human Rights and Religious Values: An Uneasy Relationship?* Grand Rapids, William B. Eerdmans Publishing Company, Michigan.

Armstrong, A., Beyani, C., Himonga, C., Kabeberi-Macharia, J., Molokomme, A., Ncube, W., Nhlapo, T., Rwezaura, B. and Stewrat, J. (1993), 'Uncovering Reality: Excavating Women's Rights in African Family Law', *International Journal of Law and the Family*, vol. 7, pp.314-369.

Azumah, V. (1998), 'What Next After Trokosi?', *Daily Graphic*, June 24.

Bilyeu, A.S (1999), 'Trokosi – The Practice of Sexual Slavery in Ghana: Religious and Cultural Freedom vs. Human Rights', *Indiana International and Comparative Law Review*, vol. 9, pp.457-504.

Busia, K.A. Jr. (1994), 'The Status of Human Rights in Pre-Colonial Africa: Implications for Contemporary Practices', in Arnolds, E., McCarthy-Arnolds, E., Penna, D.R. and Cruz Sobrepenia, D.J. (eds), *Africa, Human Rights and the Global System*, Westport, Greenwood Press, Conn.

Curran, D. and Renzetti, C. (1994), *Theories of Crime*, Allyn and Bacon, Boston.

Donnelly, J. (1982a), 'Human Rights and Human Dignity: An Analytic Critique of Non-Western Human Rights Conceptions', *American Political Science Review*, vol. 76, pp.303-316.

______ (1982b), 'How are Human Rights and Duties Correlative?', *Journal of Value Inquiry*, vol. 16, pp.287-294.

______ (1985), *The Concept of Human Rights,* Croom Helm, London.

Dovlo, E. and Adzoyi, A.K. (1995), *Report on Trokosi Institution*, Report commissioned by International Needs, Department for the Study of Religions, University of Ghana, Legon-Accra.

Einstadter, W. and Henry, S. (1995), *Criminological Theory: An Analysis of its Underlying Assumptions*, Harcourt Brace College Publishers, Forth Worth, TX.

French, H.W. (1997), 'Ritual Slave of the Fetish Priest', *The New York Times*, January 20.

Ghana Law Reform Commission (1995), *The Impact of the Constitutional Provisions on the Customary Disabilities of Women in Ghana: Report on the Abolition of Ritual Slavery, Forced Labor and Other Related Practices*, Accra, Ghana.

Ghana Review International Newsreel (2001a), 'Custom Hampers Intestate Law – FIDA', June 14, Retrieved on June 15, 2001 from http://www.mclglobal .com/History/Jun2001/14f2001/14fln.html.

Ghana Review International Newsreel (2001b), 'Intestate Succession Law Yet to have Impact – FIDA', June 7, Retrieved on June 15 2001 from http://www. Mclglobal.com/History/Jun2001/07f2001/07fln.html.

Greene, S.E. (1996), *Gender, Ethnicity, and Social Change on the Upper Slave Coast: A History of the Anlo-Ewe*, Heinemann, Portsmouth, NH.

Gyekye, K. (1996), *African Cultural Values: An Introduction*. Philadelphia, Sankofa Publishing Company, PA.

Howard, R. (1986), 'Is there an African Concept of Human Rights?', in Vincent, R.J. (ed.), *Foreign Policy and Human Rights: Issues and Responses* Cambridge, Cambridge University Press, New York.

______ (1992), 'Dignity, Community and Human Rights', in An-Na'im, A.A. (ed.), *Human Rights in Cross-Cultural Perspectives: A Quest for Consensus,* University of Pennsylvania Press, Philadelphia.

______ (1993), 'Cultural Absolutism and the Nostalgia for Community', *Human Rights Quarterly*, vol. 15, pp.315-338.

______ (1995), *Human Rights and the Search for Community*, Westview Press, Boulder, Colorado.

Howard, R. and Donnelly, J. (1986), 'Human Dignity, Human Rights, and Political Regimes', *American Political Science Review*, vol. 80, pp.801-817.

International Needs Ghana (1995), *Report of the First National Workshop on Trokosi System in Ghana,* Accra, Ghana, July.

International Needs Ghana (1998), *Report of the Second National Workshop on Trokosi System in Ghana*, Accra, Ghana, April.

International Needs Ghana (2001), *Report of the First West Africa Sub-Regional Workshop on Female Ritual Servitude*, Accra, Ghana, February.

Jones, A. (1995), 'Female Slave-Owners on the Gold Coast: Just a Matter of Money?' in Palmie, S. (ed.), *Slave Cultures and the Cultures of Slavery*, University of Tennessee Press, Knoxville.

Laslett, B. and Brenner, J. (1989), 'Gender and Social Reproduction: Historical Perspectives', *Annual Review of Sociology*, vol. 15, pp.381-404.

Lilly, J.R., Cullen, F.T. and Ball, R.A. (2001), *Criminological Theory: Context and Consequences*, Sage Publications, Thousand Oaks, CA.

Motala, Z. (1989), 'Human Rights in Africa: A Cultural, Ideological, and Legal Examination', *Hastings International and Comparative Law Review*, vol. 12, pp.373-410.

wa Mutua, M. (1995), 'The Banjul Charter and the African Cultural Fingerprint: An Evaluation of the Language of Duties' *Virginia Journal of International Law*, vol. 35, pp.339-380.

Nagan, W.P. (1993), 'The African Human Rights Process: A Contextual Policy-Oriented Approach', in Cohen, R., Hyden, G. and Nagan, W.P. (eds), *Human Rights and Governance in Africa*, University Press of Florida, Gainsville.

Ncube, W. (1991), 'Dealing with Inequities in Customary Law: Action, Reaction, and Social Change in Zimbabwe', *International Journal of Law and the Family*, vol. 5, pp.58-79.

Nukunya, G.K. (1969), *Kinship and Marriage Among the Anlo Ewe*, The Athlone Press, London.

______ (1997), 'The Land and the People', in Agbodeka, F. (ed.), *A Handbook of Eweland Volume I: The Ewes of South-eastern Ghana,* Woeli Publishing Services, Accra, Ghana.

Nukunya, G.K. and Kwafo, S.K. (1998), *Report on De-Criminalising Trokosi: A Research into the Nature and Operations of Ritual Enslavement in South Eastern Ghana*, National Population Council, Accra.

Phillips, S.D. (1996), 'Discourse, Identity, and Voice: Feminist Contributions to Policy Studies', in Dobuzinskis, L., Howlett, M. and Laycock, D. (eds), *Policy Studies in Canada: The State of the Art*, University of Toronto Press, Toronto.

Renteln, A.D. (1990), *International Human Rights: Universalism versus Relativism*, Sage Publications, Newbury Park.

Robertson, C. (1983), 'Post-Proclamation Slavery in Accra: A female Affair?', in Robertson, C. and Klein, M. (eds), *Women and Slavery in Africa*, The University of Wisconsin Press, Madison.

Savell, K.L. (1996), 'Wrestling with Contradictions: Human Rights and Traditional Practices Affecting Women', *McGill Law Journal*, vol. 41, pp.781-817.

Short, E.F. (1995), 'Trokosi—Legal or Illegal?', International Needs Ghana, *Report on the First National Workshop on Trokosi System in Ghana*, pp.22-8, Accra, Ghana.

______ (1997), 'Trokosi Transformation', unpublished speech delivered on 18 July at Trokosi liberation ceremony, Dzangpong Shrine, Tokpo, Ghana.

______ (1998a), 'Keynote Address', International Needs Report of the Second National Workshop on Trokosi System in Ghana, pp.59-62, Accra, Ghana.

______ (1998b), 'Securing the Inalienable Rights of Trokosi Women and Children in Bondage', International Needs Ghana, *Report of the Second National Workshop on Trokosi System in Ghana*, pp.73-76, Accra, Ghana.

______ (2001), 'Harmonising the Laws, Policies, and Programmes to Transform Female Ritual Servitude in the West Africa Sub-Region', paper presented at the First Sub-Regional Workshop on Ritual Servitude in Accra on February 7, Ghana.

3 Crime, Justice and Social Control in Egypt

JON ALEXANDER AND CAMY PECTOR

Introduction

> If democracy is the first pillar of government then there is no democracy without justice and no justice without a law giving everybody his right and defining for everyone of us duties and obligations on the basis of equality among citizens and non-discrimination between one group and another, no matter how strong (President Husni Mubarak, 1986, quoted in Brown, 1997, p.123).

This chapter's thesis is that Egypt's legal system forms part of a state control apparatus that effectively prevents matters pertaining to class, race and gender from becoming public issues. How does law-based social control dissipate potential class, race and gender issues? Let us first examine the background within which this control occurs.

Ancient Egypt created the world's first civilian police force, but colonialism bequeathed a paramilitary police system. For 50 years the government has maintained martial law, partly due to challenges by Islamists seeking to transform Egypt into a theocracy. Two societal paradigms contend. The challengers oppose the ruling class by demanding the establishment of Islamic rule of law. The state elite focuses on retaining privilege while fostering economic development through western-oriented capitalism. Judges serve for life, seldom being dismissed without serious cause. They occasionally curtail arbitrary authority, which paradoxically helps to buttress a status quo that sustains extreme inequalities. Centralized in the Justice Department and administered by the Supreme Council of Judicial Organs, Egypt's quasi-independent judiciary prudently underwrites elite interests and helps to centralize authority. Judicial independence and user-friendly courts help show citizens that Islamist proposals to base society on Islamic law (*shari'a*) are unnecessary because the current system works. Social control entails mechanisms 'brought into play to react to (prevent, reduce, and detect) crime and secure obedience to social norms' (Deflem, 1994, p.355). Egypt's criminal justice system may or may not reduce crime. It does punish wrongdoers, and it helps keep the ruling class in power. Jill Crystal (2001, p. 469) writes:

> In the Middle East, rulers use the criminal justice system, as rulers do everywhere, to achieve two related ends: to maintain order, generally, and to maintain a particular order – to preserve the regime in power and the interests and values of those who support it.

This is especially crucial in Egypt where the opposition's single-minded objective is to change the legal system, but where leaders feel a powerful culture-based inability to give in to pressures (as democracy would require), and where cultural factors help to ensure that forgiving one's enemies will remain virtually impossible.

Egypt's court system uses no juries. Containing remnants of Islamic law, it combines elements of France's Napoleonic Code. Judges are fact-finders – supervising a judicial corps (*niyaba*) that represents state interests while investigating and prosecuting crimes. Egypt's judiciary (*quada*) imposes political and economic elite interests on society, obscuring this behind a mask of legitimacy. Courts serve the status quo partly by shoring it up directly. They also allow small, individualized resistances that encourage system adaptation without producing large changes. Courts serve the rich less through direct judgments than by buttressing the stability that the rich need to retain and expand their wealth (Brown, 1997). While not necessarily reducing crime, the legal system does help reproduce a particular political, economic, racial and gender order (Deflem, 1994). Although genuine, Egyptian judicial independence faces practical limits.

Social Control of the Judicial System

A symbolic rupture that helped politicize the judiciary via the Judges Club occurred at 2:00 a.m. in October 1989. Security forces arrested and tortured a student suspected of Islamist activity. His father was a prominent judge, whose house the forces invaded without judicial warrant. The police soon released the son, but only because judges mounted intense pressures through the Judges Club, which emerged as a civil liberties champion (Brown, 1997). The state then moved to impose direct control over lawyers. The Lawyers Syndicate was once arguably Egypt's most powerful interest group, standing up to government and defending civil liberties and rule of law (*siyadat al-qanum*). During President Anwar Sadat's regime (1970-81), it attacked the Law of Shame, which outlawed criticism disrespectful of presidential authority. Although that law survived, throughout the 1970s the Lawyers Syndicate provided virtually the only legal opposition to state policies.

During the 1980s several members of the Islamist Muslim Brotherhood became Syndicate Board members. They opposed normalizing relations with Israel. In 1981, Parliament passed a law dismissing the Board. The Supreme Court ruled this unconstitutional. In 1986 the Syndicate staged a strike against the continuing emergency laws, and in 1988 campaigned against illegal abuses and illegal detentions (Metz, 1990). Muslim Brothers swept 17 of 24 Board positions in 1992. Two years later police tortured to death a lawyer representing Islamist militants. A thousand Cairo lawyers gathered to march from Syndicate headquarters to demand his autopsy report and the release of 34 other lawyers being held without charges.[1] To prevent the march, Interior Ministry security forces fired tear gas into the Syndicate's building and injured about 100 people (Holder, 1994). In January 1996, the government again disbanded the leadership, appointing a panel to operate Syndicate affairs. Police officers with law degrees infiltrated to keep watch (El-Ghobashy, 2000). By January 1999 the government approved elections for the 24-seat Board, but on seeing that several Muslim Brothers would be running, it soon resumed control by implementing a law that would allow it take over if an election did not achieve a 50% vote. The lawyers called an election, however on voting day security forces and police (equipped with guns, batons, tear-gas and police dogs) deployed around the syndicate's headquarters and occupied it to prevent the vote required to end sequestration (Apiku, 1999).

Although the legal profession's drive to install rule of law is important, this effort operates within strict boundaries because Egypt's legal system serves state social control. As Brown, 1997, p.124) states:

> As suspicious as they may sometimes be of executive influence, Egyptian judges tend not to behave as freestanding actors mediating between that state and the society or between different social actors, but as enforcers of state policy, no matter how impartially and principled.

Suppression by Means of a Never-Ending Emergency

The Egyptian Constitution has now been superceded by martial law for a full half century. The task of consolidating the revolution that overthrew the monarchy was long since accomplished. However, an Islamic religious awakening has since the 1970s divided Egypt and sustained a legal and political combat zone within which the state imposes draconian forms of social control. Western development ideologies, cultural, economic and political influences have deeply rent the unity for which Islamic culture and law both strive. This severe division refuses to heal fully. The *Qur'an* devotes few verses (80 of 6219) to law and is silent on most legal issues (Crystal, 2001). Despite recent experience in Iran and elsewhere, a state based upon Islamic law does not necessarily have to be repressive (Bassiouni, 1982). Powerful interrelated themes of legitimacy and accountability run through Islamic political thought. Unlike Christianity's division of life into a city of God and a city of Man ('render unto Caesar'), for Islam there is but one city – one in which the politically-based control system has long lacked legitimacy in citizens' eyes.

The government undermined legality by introducing a military court system and another emergency tribunal system, both designed to punish political opponents under a guise of law. Once a case enters a military or emergency tribunal, one may expect a conviction with no appeal to civilian courts allowed. Trials *in absentia* or *in camera* (eliminating any effective defense) are common. Judgment is too swift for truly deliberative procedures. Ignoring complaints of torture, these bodies contravene liberal legality. Although regular judges prefer repression to occur in these arenas rather than in the real courts, these two realms do not comfortably coexist. Nonetheless, the government use of extraordinary tribunals has paradoxically helped to preserve the regular courts' independence. One need not wholly squelch the judiciary when one can invoke martial law (*hukm 'urfi*) and use it for political purposes through non-judicial courts. As Brown (1997, p.77) observes, the 'use of exceptional courts helps explain why much of the judiciary was accorded some degree of autonomy for so long – the regime had other ways of insuring favorable results'. Military tribunals first started trying civilians. Once exceptional measures extended well beyond military realms, politicians posited a 'state of emergency' (*halat al-tawari'*). Security trial bodies headed by a Supreme State Security Court formed to hear cases involving political and military security. According to Crystal (2001, p.480):

> These extrajudicial courts range from showy tribunals stripped of due process, offering the form but not substance of a real trial, to shadowy summary tribunals where police, courts, and corrections all merge. Security and military tribunals typically share the outward appearance of court systems: laws are discussed in a place that resembles a court and the process for the most part precedes the corrections phase: there is a process, just not due process.

The government may respect nonpolitical personal rights (it remains illegal to criticize the president or other officials) but it denies public assembly rights by outlawing peaceful protest or distributing critical literature. People charged often get their cases dismissed, especially if they can establish that they were tortured. However, they may have received permanent injuries, and will usually have served long non-terms in prison awaiting trial. Living conditions and health care in prisons are so severely appalling that officials routinely bar Red Cross observers.

For years torture was centralized in the Interior Ministry's Cairo offices, which issue most non-judicial arrest warrants (search warrants are unnecessary), however in the fight against Islamists, torture has spread increasingly to local police stations. Handcuffed, blindfolded suspects are questioned while being punched, kicked and beaten with sticks, batons and whips and suffering electric genital shocks. They are often stripped and hung by the wrists, doused with hot or icy water, and left without heat in cold weather. Except for the threat of rape, female prisoners' torture displays total gender equality (State Department, 2000). Tortured people often die incidentally but sometimes torture culminates in deliberate murder. Investigating judicial officers, the *niyaba*, often suppress evidence of torture and refuse to investigate individual cases. This became so blatant that in protest the Lawyers Syndicate in 1994 called a strike, which evoked violent clashes as state security forces attacked some of Egypt's leading lawyers (Brown, 1997). The Interior Ministry, which relies heavily on torture, ignores disagreeable court decisions. Beyond torture, it practices other forms of illegality not even countenanced by martial law. For example, it may kidnap a political dissident's whole family, holding them hostage to force a suspect to surrender, sometimes killing family members one by one if this fails (Metz, 1990). Mahmoud Muawad died on October 21, 1999 in Damanhour prison. His crime was being the brother of a man a military court had *in absentia* convicted in April 1999 (State Department, 2000).

This approach generates a vicious circle: control efforts thwart challenges but radicalize another generation of young, lower- and lower middle-class males who form new Islamist groups to attack the system anew – with serious crimes that energize new state crimes. Meanwhile, the system helps ensure that most class, race and gender issues will remain effectively unaddressed.

The Structures of Suppression

Police power is centralized under the Interior Ministry, which conducts elections, combats ordinary crime, operates civil defense, maintains prisons, controls borders, conducts political intelligence, prevents subversion and averts sabotage. In each governorate (sing. *muhafazah*, pl. *muhafazat*), the presidentially appointed governor and the police director reports to the Interior Ministry on security matters. Police ranks resemble army ranks, their structure martially hierarchical. At the street level, patrolmen receive few job-related benefits and their pay is meager. This leads patrolmen implicitly to demand bribes (*rashwa*) for ignoring infractions. At higher levels too, corruption is widespread, including complicity in drug smuggling.

Several primary and secondary intelligence services perform police functions. These include the General Intelligence and Security Service (*Mukhabarat el-Aama*) in the Presidential Office, and the Military Intelligence Service (*Mukhabarat el-Khabeya*) in the Ministry of Defense. The State Security Investigations Sector (*Mubahath el-Dawla*) resides in the Interior Ministry. The Ministry of Interior's Deputy Minister for Public Security oversees public safety, travel, emigration, passports, port security, and criminal investigations. The Deputy Minister for Special Police controls prison administration, civil defense, police transport, communications, traffic, tourism, and the State Security Service (*Jihaz Amn al-Dawla*). The *Jihaz Amn al-Dawla's* 300,000 paramilitary troops guard public buildings, hotels, strategic installations, and foreign embassies, direct traffic and control crowds. They attack student disturbances, intimidate industrial strikers and peasant demonstrators, and fight Islamist activities. These poorly paid men are conscripted mainly from rural areas, having failed to meet military standards. In 1986 a rumor spread that the three-year conscription term would rise to four. The force rioted. Security troops set Cairo tourist hotels and nightclubs afire, leaving hundreds dead or wounded and producing enormous property damage. The Interior Ministry dismissed 20,000 conscripts; another 8,000 deserted (Metz, 1990). What it lacks otherwise, this force makes up in sheer pervasiveness. Its presence denies citizens any meaningful ability to change their government, or raise political issues pertaining to class, race or gender.

Maintaining public order includes suppression of what might in the absence of martial law be legitimate political activity. *Mubahath el-Dawla* enforces domestic security, conducts investigations, and questions and tortures detainees to gather information and to intimidate. Its size is secret, but huge, dwarfing America's CIA and FBI together. It represses public meetings or discussions by regime opponents. It quashes local political activities, using informer networks to monitor subversives, opposition politicians, journalists, union leaders, feminists and human rights activists, diplomats and suspicious foreigners. This agency spies on Islamist, feminist and human rights organizations, government departments, public sector companies, labor unions, parties and mass media. It monitors telephone calls and opens letters of political opponents and suspected subversives. It enforces political loyalty much like East European *Nomenklatura* networks that formerly buttressed Communist Party rule. In 1986 Islamist *Al-Jihad* (Holy War) defendants charged forty *Mubahath el-Dawla* officers with torture. The court found that *Mubahath el-Dawla* had indeed tortured *Al-Jihad* members, but also that the complainants lacked sufficient evidence to link particular defendants with specific victims (Metz, 1990).

What is being Suppressed?

Gender

The new prevalence of women's veiling symbolizes this generation's lost gains. The Islamic religious awakening hurt women's status by energizing male dominance. Unescorted, unveiled females are vulnerable to verbal sexual harassment from young males. Officially illegal but seldom charged, this patriarchal social control occurs ubiquitously, but within strict bounds. Increasingly working outside their homes, many women veil to help avoid such encounters. As criminal offenders, women receive harsher treatment than do men in some respects but not all. Laws often discriminate against women. For a woman to marry outside Islam is a crime, as is a married woman leaving Egypt without her husband's permission. However, the all-male judges often favor women by more lenient sentencing. Similarly, if a police officer feels that prosecution could harm a female offender's reputation or family, or that she was a victim of circumstances, she may be let off. Middle- and upper-class males get far better treatment than lower class females but since this culture views women as less capable, it also may treat them as less culpable. Courts enforce society's duty to protect them.

Female genital mutilation (*tahara*), though formally outlawed in hospitals and clinics, is universally performed (97%), almost exclusively by women (Dillon, 2000). Convictions of the mutilators are almost nonexistent. Prostitution is a crime, and an increasing number of middle-class prostitutes (lacking economic necessity) receive harsh treatment if caught. A husband raping his own wife is no crime. Rape is a crime against women and gang rape with abduction is a capital offense. Sexual assault is a lesser unisex crime. Rape is under-reported, often being punished by the family without recourse to law. Women carry the cultural burden of family honor in their own behavior and that of female relatives. Having been raped reduces a woman's and even her sisters' social value. To restore honor, family members might force the victim to marry her rapist, or may even kill her. Murder's most common form is honor killing, which mainly affects women, both as killers and as victims, usually for presumed sexual infidelity. Often a mistaken presumption produces a killing for naught (Digges, 2002).

Infanticide, almost always done by women to female babies, is the most under-reported crime and, like abortion, is rarely prosecuted. Conversely, Egyptian women favor the use of poison to murder adults, a *method* punishable by death. Drug smugglers often constitute the female prison's largest group. If a man finds his wife having intercourse with another man and kills her, he serves up to six months; in a reverse situation, she may be imprisoned for life. She can have only one husband, but the man can marry up to four wives simultaneously. Adultery is essentially a crime against the husband's private rights. Should his wife receive a prison term for adultery, he can free her by agreeing to resume marital relations. The wife can charge the husband with adultery only if it occurs inside the matrimonial home (Mohsen, 1990).

The *shari'a* or Islamic religious law currently has limited applicability. In the Prophet's time no prisons existed, and today the *shari'a* courts' jurisdiction is largely limited to personal status issues, mainly marriage, divorce, child custody and inheritance. In 1985, the government started reviewing statutes (6,000 laws and 10,000 peripheral legal acts), promising to change those conflicting with Islamic law so that the *Shari'a* would become the spirit of the law as the Islamists had long been insisting should occur (Metz, 1990). This largely cosmetic action appeased conservatives, undercutting Islamist arguments for more fundamental reforms. Civil and criminal law, though perhaps increasingly influenced by the *shari'a*, are nonetheless man-made, imported legal codes. Changes have marginally favored women's rights. The fact that the regime's main opponents seek to restore tradition – and that this opposition is the only one in sight – helps to determine how women's rights play out in everyday life. Since the Islamists favor radical reforms of male supremacy, minimizing women's rights helps the state to forestall and minimize chances of Islamist opposition.

A case in point is the fate of the voter education project jointly led by the Ibn Khaldoun Center for Development Studies and the League of Egyptian Women Voters. Both organizations were shut down and their leaders arrested during the 2000 election for activities that were part of a campaign to increase female voting and political participation. In a second trial during 2002, the 63-year-old Khaldoun Center's leader, political sociologist Saad Eddin Ibrahim, was again sentenced to seven years imprisonment with hard labor. One main female collaborator, Nadia Abdel Nour, got two years, while another, Magda Al Bey, got three years with hard labor. Acting under the emergency regulations, a state security court convicted them of receiving funds from the European Union (EU) without state permission, and fraudulently misusing those funds – even though the EU, after having conducted a thorough audit, categorically denied the charge's validity. Another, extremely vague, crime of which they were convicted was 'tarnishing Egypt's image' abroad by issuing critical reports (EU 2002). The day before his arrest, Ibrahim had angered current Egyptian President Mubarak by charging that in grooming his son to succeed him Mubarak was trying to create a hereditary republic (*Washington Post*, July 30, 2002). In 2000, Ibrahim and the feminists were together pursuing female voter registration through means reminiscent of the 1960s U.S. civil rights movement. They were also accurately claiming that the government was using state and police power to perpetrate numerous, widespread, systematic voting irregularities. Their arrest and show trials virtually brought the feminist movement as well as the pro-democracy movement in Egypt to a dead standstill. That repressive effort has since cost the Egyptian nation enormously because it has evoked a tremendous chorus of criticism from around the world, and especially from the US, the European Union and the world's non-governmental human rights movement.[2] Ibrahim faced a third trial in 2003.

Social Class

The state has retained freedom of action, partly because it remains decoupled from society. In Habermas' (1987) terms, a 'system' functions independently from its 'lifeworld' whenever action-coordination mechanisms downplay communication in favor of such steering mechanisms as money in the economic system and power in the political system. Egypt radically reoriented its foreign policy in the 1970s, rejecting its former USSR mentor and allying with America. An open door policy (*infitah*) removed restrictions on foreign investment. This attracted huge capital inflows. They scarcely contributed to economic development, but did have social consequences. The accompanying deregulation stimulated businesses to compete for foreign aid dollars. This helped produce a significant *nouveau riche* class. It also overstimulated a westernized, import-dependent consumer market to the detriment of local goods and services (Ismael and Ismael, 1991). The ensuing hyperinflation wiped out fixed income families. Economic disparities, always large, became much greater. The International Monetary Fund and World Bank induced structural readjustment that forced economic privatization, which in turn produced extensive hardships. These deteriorating conditions might well have produced an enormous crime wave, but this did not happen.

Upper-class beneficiaries share contempt for regular courts, which treats them like anyone else and impedes business with cumbersome delays. The *nouveau riche* class has developed elaborate mediation and arbitration arrangements that help its members bypass the courts. The old-money upper-class and upper middle-class, especially women, also rarely go to courts, which they view as unruly, low class and degrading. Resorting to court would violate old-money families' honor code, and might as well jeopardize family property interests (Antoun, 1990). In contrast, regular courts are user-friendly for lower- and lower middle-classes. Cumbersome and slow, they are overused. Regular court fees are low, and cheap lawyers abound. Judges respond seriously to conflicts that another country's judges might well consider 'garbage cases'. Elsewhere, lower- and lower middle class people may feel uncomfortable in court, unfamiliar with its procedures and awed by its majesty. Egypt's regular courts enter into the lower-class lifeworld, treating virtually any claim or dispute. This makes non-elite Egyptians more willing to litigate than even the famously litigious Americans. People who would never take problems to police parade woes before judges. Socially and politically subordinate groups' ability to use the courts is highly developed, even sophisticated. Far from being last resorts, many lawsuits arise simply to put extra pressure on adversaries.

The courts' willingness to entertain virtually any dispute helps foster a formal equality. Lower-class people are of course far more likely to lose cases than middle- or upper-class litigants but judges deliberately offer tools to weaker parties. Courts are especially user-friendly to tenants facing eviction and to battered wives (battering affects every third wife, but no shelters exist). Common people criticize the judiciary for not reining in arbitrary executive power, but when facing eviction they happily accept judicial relief (Brown, 1997). In this patriarchal society a man may divorce his wife by ritual act not requiring recourse to court; a wife desiring divorce must go to court with either provable grounds or a willingness to give up everything. However, judges are exquisitely attuned to differential social status and resources, and have great leeway in making decisions. Courts treat verbal abuse as a crime, and physical abuse as a grave infraction. Judges have been known to encourage a wife to demand *mahr mu'akhkar* (alimony) as well as the apartment and furniture.

Do lower-class-friendly courts help diffuse conflict that might otherwise be politically aggregated and focused in ways that might challenge the *status quo*? Do they induce people to view their disputes as individual problems rather than larger, perhaps class-based, race-based or gender-based phenomena? We have as yet no social science studies to help shed light on these questions, but the probable answer is yes. The twice-imprisoned Egyptian political sociologist Saad Eddin Ibrahim (1980) has cast light on social class factors in the religious awakening. Studying the extremist movements, he concluded that, aside from the Muslim Brotherhood (professional, middle-class, nonviolent), Islamist groups grew primarily out of lower middle and middle-class sectors, especially among those of recent rural, lower class backgrounds. The typical recruit was a young male student newly experiencing life free from conventional social controls in a large, metropolitan area that was itself under heavy foreign influence. Such students open their eyes to find a society grossly unequal in power and wealth; their unmet expectations seem tied to a continued pattern of foreign dependence and influence. For them, the westernized but authoritarian political elite of unbelievers had secured its position as servants of imperialism by abandoning both Islam and the national interest. Without a lower class-friendly court system, perhaps such angry young men would be far more numerous. Today, a significant proportion of the unemployed consists of well-educated young people just entering the labor market. Due to structural readjustment they are no longer guaranteed state jobs on graduation. The unemployment rate for women is twice that for men. As Nadan Fergany (1998, p.13) reports:

> Unemployment rates are highest for graduates of intermediate education and next highest among graduates of higher education (indicating a negative societal rate of return to education, taking employment as a criterion).

This failure leads both to a brain drain to the rich Gulf states and to the West – and to discontents likely to fuel another generation of Islamist activism.

Race

Ethnically and racially, Egypt's 70 million people are mainly homogeneous. There are some 780,000 Bedouins, 77,000 Beni-Amers, and 30,000 Berbers. The state leaves these Moslem ethnic minorities alone (Joshua Project, 2002). Another 234,000 Gypsies, widely suspected of harboring pickpockets, receive continual police attention. A very long-standing quasi-racial confrontation concerns relations between the Arab majority and the ethnic and religious minority represented by the Copts, who are overwhelmingly Christians.

Islamist groups reject Marxism and westernization, accept private property and profit, but want to limit their anti-egalitarian consequences through a moral/legal code and a welfare state. Some, such as the Muslim Brotherhood, favor nonviolence. Others, such as *Al Jihad* and *Jamaat al Islamiyah* (Islamic Group) believe only violence can overturn the state. Still others stand between these extremes. The government fights back partly by appointing and paying the salaries of religious leaders (*imams*) who officiate in mosques, and by proposing sermon themes for them and then monitoring their sermons (State Department, 2000). In Southern (Upper) Egypt, Islamists and police have together targeted the country's some eight million Copts. By the 1960s, the government had nationalized most private Copt businesses. This and resurgent discrimination led millions to leave permanently. President Sadat encouraged militant Islamic groups to aid his struggle against socialist followers of the previous President Nasser. By the 1980s, militant Islam's resurgence helped produce escalated assaults on both Copts and foreign tourists. Ironically, militant Islamists financed the attack that produced President Sadat's own assassination by using money they had robbed from Coptic retail shops (Kepel, 1993). The Copts suffer from official repression as well as frequent attacks by Islamist militants. For example, in 2002 a farmer from Nag'a al-Keeman village in Upper Egypt some 290 miles South of Cairo was arrested for allegedly turning his home into a church. Local Muslims had complained that they heard praying coming from the home. In this case, police may have acted to forestall a planned attack on the house by Muslim neighbors (Copts Daily Digest, 2002).

One of the crimes of which political sociologist Saad Eddin Ibrahim was convicted in 2002 was that he 'tarnished Egypt's image', in part by writing about ethnic strife between Muslim Arabs and Coptic Christians. His Ibn Khaldoun Center for Development Studies did monitor this strife, and Ibrahim himself once described government bungling of a particular incident. In 1998, Muslim police investigating the murder of several Copts in Upper Egypt's Al-Koseth village tortured many hundreds of Copts as part of the investigation. Ibrahim (1999) wrote):

> The clumsiness and arrogance of the government is to tell the Coptic bishop to say that nothing had happened. Then the EOHR [Egyptian Organization for Human Rights] made a report, and sent it to the government to answer as usual, but they ignored it. Then two months after the incident, the world began to know about it. The cover-up was reality-denial, unnecessary. Then they used the EOHR as a scapegoat, and fabricated a cheque from the British embassy – outright lying, extortion, very cheap... Egyptians are fair-minded and tolerant. But we get a terrible reputation because of mishandling and mismanagement of problems that all societies have.

The primary visible racial minority consists of a million Black Nubians. The Kingdom of Nubia once lay in Southern Egypt, extending into the Sudan. Virtually all Muslims, Nubians spoke a non-Arabic language and enjoyed a reputation for outstanding honesty. Their crime rate was virtually absent, limited to matters of honor and passion. For millennia, the government left the Nubians largely alone to police themselves. During the 1960s the government built the high Aswan Dam. This solved the Nile's age-old problem of annual flooding, increased arable land, and generated enormous amounts of hydroelectric power. It also created the world's largest artificial lake, 300-mile-long Lake Nasser, which permanently flooded the Nubians' valley homeland. Hundreds of Nubian villages with their spacious, ornate and unlocked homes, lush palm groves, ancient temples and ancestral graveyards disappeared, forcing Nubians to relocate (TourEgypt, 2002).

Those displaced received cement block housing laid out in resettlement village grids, and one year's salary. The government indiscriminately forced Nubia's three antagonistic ethnic groups to live together. This housing proved extremely unsatisfactory, even an impetus to crime. The Aswan Dam had great national value, eliminating most flooding of the Nile, but for Nubians it spelled cultural genocide. Ancient customs quickly eroded in the exigencies of settlement life. Having lost their ancestral homes and unsatisfied with their Spartan quarters, most eventually migrated to cities where they had to learn Arabic. They began to forget their native language. As displaced persons whose traditional culture was largely destroyed, the Nubians harbor enduringly hard feelings. One Nubian explained: 'We are also experiencing crime and social problems, maybe similar to other communities but nothing we ever had before, like murders and stealing. In the past everyone knew each other and there were no strangers among us' (Miles, 1994, p.36). In Cairo there is now a Society for the Revival of Nubian Traditions, and a few Nubians have returned to live on the banks of the lake that submerges Old Nubia. Wherever they live, the decultured Nubians now lock their doors.

Modes of Criminal Behavior

Despite enormous social and gender inequality, international statistics show Egypt to be among the safest, most law-abiding societies. Petty theft happens, mainly purse snatching or pickpocketing, but rarely involves violence. Of 2,000,000 drug users, some 250,000 are heroin addicts (Metz, 1990). Addicts often steal to buy drugs that cost them some US$1 billion a year. Small dealers receive sentences up to life with hard labor but major dealers buy immunity with bribes to high officials. In rural areas, crime victims often seek direct retribution but seldom go to authorities, especially in cases involving personal or family honor. Murder is uncommon, occurring mostly within families – matters of passion, honor or vengeance. In cities, white collar crime, tax evasion, smuggling, and currency black marketing are rife. Governmental favoritism and graft, kickbacks and bribes to officials occur everywhere (Metz, 1990).

Abject city slums are almost as safe as other areas. Some forms of begging endearingly approach illegality. We sometimes see in Cairo a woman with children who gets rotten eggs free from a grocery store and, carrying them on a busy street in a head bowl, appears to trip, smashing the eggs to elicit sympathetic gifts. Desperation-born ingenuity takes more ominous, criminal forms. Proliferating on city streets are homeless beggar children whose faces and bodies display horrible mutilations designed to elicit sympathy. However, as the UN's (United Nations) developing country criminal victimization figures show, true crime is rare. Within a five-year period, according to a UN (1995) report, criminal statistics for vehicle theft was only lower in India than Egypt; for attempted burglary only Indonesia; for burglary with entry, and for true sexual crimes no other country was lower than Egypt. One major crime source these statistics omit is government.

An international non-governmental organisation called Freedom House has surveyed press freedoms permitted by the world's governments, using a continuum showing near total press freedom (Iceland=12) vs. totalitarian controls (Taliban Afghanistan=100). For both broadcast media and print, Freedom House rated: (1) laws and regulations that influence media content, (2) political pressures and controls on media content, (3) economic influences over media content, and (4) repressive actions such as direct censorship or violence against journalists. Egypt's composite score of 69 places it far toward the totalitarian end, a worse violator of mass communication rights than such other 'unfree' countries as Cambodia (62) Croatia (63), Djbouti (62), Eritrea (68), Ethiopia (64), Ghana (61) Lebanon (62), Morocco (51), Niger (68), Nigeria (68), etc. (Freedom House, 1999). The government owns all broadcast media and the large daily papers. Officials censor the rest. They closely control magazines and weekly newspapers, partly by requiring that the government itself do their printing. Creating any independent press operation requires governmental approval. In 1999, at least 34 journalists were awaiting trial or under investigation, four were sentenced to prison, and two were released after four months without a charge. Authorities halted publication of more than 30 newspapers (Freedom House, 1999). A few publications put censored articles on websites outside Egypt. Because organized political activity is essentially forbidden and where it occurs anyway is systematically suppressed, citizens perceive political parties mainly as political newspapers.

Conclusion

Criminologists may posit deviance as residing outside dominant social norms. Social control theorist, Hirschi (1969, p.23) 'assumes a common value system within the society or group whose norms are being violated'. This theory applies across racial, gender and class boundaries in Holland, UK, Australia, Canada and Belgium (Junger and Marshall, 1997). Egypt lacks a single unified bond from which deviants rebel due to personal or social inadequacies. Criminologists may also view the state as social control's singular locus. When acknowledging both hidden and obvious injuries of class, gender and race, one might presume impotent, subordinate victims. Foucault (1979), like mainstream American political scientists, more correctly views any major exercise of power as inescapably involving a superior-subordinate relationship. In such a relationship subjects often play active roles.

Hirschian theory applies poorly to states with authoritarian elites whose illegal behavior continually regenerates disloyal opposition, and to the extended families that in Egypt constitute the most effective policing units. Egypt has powerful indigenous, religious-based, culturally-molded social controls, outside the state, acting pervasively through extended family units. This control system is far more effective than the state's. State controls serve to insulate and protect a political elite and an economic *nouveau riche* elite, but traditional mores impose actual overall law and order. Social legality does not derive from the state's defense of elite privileges because in confronting opposition groups, the state itself sometimes uses criminal and terroristic tactics. 'Terrorism', according to the Penal Code, includes merely 'obstructing the work of authorities' (State Department, 2000). Often the victims themselves may create cultural action spaces hidden from the state's panoptical gaze, where effective social interaction proceeds without state regulation. In villages, policing bends to fit local mores, and the village head person (*omda*) acts by common consent as a referee to settle disputes. This is how it has been from time immemorial, which in Egypt goes back a long way.

What will the future bring? Crime prevention mostly comes from a web of institutional settings that promote human development in daily life in families, communities and schools. The legal institutions of policing and criminal justice are far less important; they mainly pick up cases when the informal social institutions fail. Egypt enjoys strong families and communities. Its citizens love to be in the streets, for they are inveterate people watchers. They do not hesitate to get involved, to stop a fight, or even a thief. This tendency shows no sign of abating. It is the real secret of Egypt's extraordinarily low crime rates. In 1985, the government started making birth control supplies readily available. Soon the birth rate had dropped from 39 to fewer than 25 per 1,000 people. Nonetheless, Egypt's population is expected to jump from today's 70 million up to 95.8 million by 2025 (World Reference, 2002). Islamists oppose contraception, so if they become more influential this figure could rise dramatically. Since arable land is limited, this is a crucial issue. Another problem is the education system where weaknesses are extensive. Schools rely too heavily on rote memory and not enough problem solving. They are impractical. But even the best schools could not overcome the broader structural life chance determinants that place recent graduates among the highest number of unemployed.

Egypt can never develop normally until it ends the state of emergency it uses to fight the Islamists and avoid in the process any effective opposition to the state elite arising from civil society. One key question is whether the Islamist challenge has effectively ended. Here we find a vicious circle. People turn to political Islam partly due to being disenchanted by gross and widening economic inequalities. They see enormous class, race and gender inequality being buttressed by an autocratic and corrupt government, but would-be reformers can find no effective political stage on which to fight. They want to overcome corruption and the foreign cultural values brought in via mass media, businesses and tourists. Many are enraged by sex tourism, which is partly why the state recently cracked down on overt homosexual behavior. Even though this activity is not itself a crime, police charge people with debauchery. After a 2001 raid on downtown Cairo's Queen disco boat, a state security court tried 52 men and convicted 26.[3] Thus Islamists do impact upon public policy, as the government continually strives to undercut their potential appeal.

The Islamists' most serious strategic blunder came in 1997 when radicals gunned down scores of tourists in Luxor. The idea was to frighten tourists from coming to Egypt. This certainly happened. However, the killing backfired drastically by producing a national revulsion against fundamentalism. Some radicals retreated south to camps in Islamist Sudan. Others declared a truce. Still others, displacing their anger against the US, went to Afghanistan and other bastions of anti-Americanism. Though virtually declaring victory, the state did not remove martial law. It knows the Islamist movement feeds on poverty, unemployment, corruption and despair – conditions that remain strongly in force. The movement may be quiescent within Egypt; it is far from dead.

Egypt remains in thrall to western capitalism. A US$31 billion debt (Commerce Department, 2002) remains following massive debt relief and other IMF concessions that Egypt won in 1991 as a Gulf War coalition partner. This all helped improve macroeconomic performance, but the business class was the only real beneficiary. By the late 1990s, financial pressures on the economy and the Egyptian pound had returned. Tourism had been a US$2 billion business employing one in every six workers. It stopped cold following the September 11, 2001 US attack by Egyptians and Saudi Arabians. The greatest economic problems are all chronic: low productivity, poor management, excessive population growth and massive urban overcrowding. Although Egypt is potentially rich in human resources, depending on one's criteria, between 50% and 90% of Egyptians are poor. The real living standard in the mid-1990s was lower than in 1958. The economic squeeze required by structural adjustment led to near starvation and widespread malnutrition, which produced serious stunting (low height for age) and wasting (low weight for height), both signs of irreversible physical and mental damage. In 1992, 25% of children were stunted; by 1996, stunting afflicted 30%. These children, weak of body and mind, are unfit to compete in a society of untrammeled capitalism (Fergany, 1998). If they can function at all, some will make up the next generation's wasted Islamist cannon fodder. Unemployable university graduates will lead them, and stunted, army-rejected *Jihaz Amn al-Dawla* conscripts will persecute and torture them.

Otherwise, the state will remain autocratic and commit its crimes with impunity, and the problems of class, race and gender will remain very largely unaddressed. The system seems both willing and able to continue its effective suppression of independent political activity. Rich men will continue to enrich themselves with strong state support and the state elite will continue to prosper. Perhaps rich women will make small further gains. Unable to act politically, such groups as poor women, orphans, gays, lesbians, Gypsies and Nubians are likely to find themselves being driven further into crime. Nonetheless, the overall crime rate in civil society will remain extraordinarily low.

Notes

1. The government was then holding 30,000 political detainees. Some 22,000 would remain following release in 1999 of 6,000 being held without charges (State Department, 2000).
2. President Bush announced that, due to the Ibrahim case, the US would consider no new aid to Egypt beyond the almost US$2billion provided for by the Camp David Accord (State Department, 2002).
3. In Arab novels, gay sexual relations with foreigners are often a metaphor for western domination, so this case resonated strongly (Whitaker, 2001).

References

Antoun, R.T. (1990), 'Litigant Strategies in an Islamic Court in Jordan', in Dwyer, D.H. (ed.), *Law and Islam in the Middle East*, Bergin & Garvey, New York.

Apiku, S. (1999), 'Syndicate Crisis Takes on New Proportion', *Middle East Times*, http://www.metimes.com/issue99-13/eg/syndicate_crisis_takes.htm.

Bassiouni, M.C. (1982), 'Sources of Islamic Law, and the Protection of Human Rights in the Islamic Criminal Justice System', in Bassiouni, C. (ed.), *The Islamic Criminal Justice System*, Oceana Publications, London.

Brown, N.J. (1997), *Rule of Law in the Arab World*, Cambridge University Press, Cambridge.

Commerce Department (2002), 'Middle East Business Development Missions-Egypt-Economy', October 1999, http://osecnt13.osec.doc.gov/obl/me99.nsf/docs/egypt-economy.

Copts Daily Digest (2002), 'Copt arrested for allegedly turning his home into a church', July 1 2002, http://www.amcoptic.com/copt_arrested_for_allegedly_turn.htm.

Crystal, J. (2001), 'Criminal Justice in the Middle East', *Journal of Criminal Justice*, vol. 29, pp.469-82.

Deflem, M. (1994), 'Social Control and the Theory of Communicative Action', *International Journal of the Sociology of Law*, vol. 22, pp.355-73.

Digges, D. (2002), 'Victims of Honor', http://www.cairotimes.com.

Dillon, S.A. (2000), 'Healing the Sacred Yoni in the Land of Isis: Female Genital Mutilation is Banned (again) in Egypt', *Houston Journal of International Law*, vol. 22, pp.289-312.

El-Ghobashy, M. (2000), 'Where have all the Lawyers Gone?', *Cairo Times*, vol. 4, Issue 8, April 27-May 3, http://www.cairotimes.com/news/lawsynd.html.

European Union (2002), 'Commissioner Patten deplores ruling of Egyptian State Security Court against Saad Edin Ibrahim', July 30, free_saadeddin_ibrahim@yahoogroups.com.

Fergany, N. (1998), *The Growth of Poverty in Egypt*, Almishkat, Giza, Egypt.

Foucault, M. (1979), *Discipline and Punish: The Birth of the Prison*, Vintage, New York.

Freedom House (1999), *Press Freedom Survey 1999: Country Ratings - Press Freedom Worldwide*, January 1, http://www.freedomhouse.org/pfs99/reports.Html.

Habermas, J. (1987), *The Theory of Communicative Action: Lifeworld and System: A Critique of Functionalist Reason*, vol. 2, Beacon Press, Boston.

Hirschi, T. (1969), *Causes of Delinquency*, University of California Press, Berkeley.

Holder, R.C. (1994), 'Human Rights', *Washington Report on Middle East Affairs*, American Educational Trust, Washington DC.

Ibrahim, S.E. (1980), 'Anatomy of Egypt's Militant Islamic Groups: Methodological Notes and Preliminary Findings', *Journal of Middle East Studies*, vol. 12, pp.423-53, pp.481-99.

Ibrahim, S.E. (1999). 'Encouraging Signs: The Bungling of the Al Kosheh Crisis Obscures a Few Positive Steps the Government's Taken to Improving the Situation of Copts', *Cairo Times*, vol. 2, Issue 25, February.

Ismael, T.Y. and Ismael, J.S. (1991), *Government and Politics in Islam*, CBS Publishers, New Delhi.

Joshua Project (2002), 'Index of Original Joshua Project Peoples in Egypt', http://www.joshuaproject.net/Assets/Profiles/jpcxegy.htm.

Junger, M. and Marshall, I.H. (1999), 'The Interethnic Generalizability of Social Control Theory: An Empirical Test', *Journal of Research in Crime and Delinquency*, vol. 34, pp.79-113.

Kepel, G. (1993), *Muslim Extremism in Egypt: The Prophet and the Pharaoh*, University of California Press, Berkeley.

Metz, H.C. (ed.) (1990), *Egypt: A Country Study*, Library of Congress, Federal Research Division, Washington DC.

Miles, H. (1994), 'A Lost Ancient Land', *Middle East*, no. 236, pp.35-38.

Mohsen, S.K. (1990), 'Women and Criminal Justice in Egypt', in Dwyer, D.H. (ed.), *Law and Islam in the Middle East*, Bergin & Garvey, New York.

State Department (2000), *1999 Country Reports on Human Rights Practices: Egypt*, Bureau of Democracy, Human Rights, and Labor, Washington, DC.

State Department (2002), 'Regular Briefing with Spokesman Philip Reeker', August 15, free_saadeddin_ibrahim@yahoogroups.com.

TourEgypt (2002), 'Nubia through the Ages', Cairo American College, http://touregypt.net/historicalessays/nubiac1.htm.

United Nations (1995), *Criminal Victimisation in the Developing World*, United Nations Publication no. 55, Rome, UNICRI, New York.

Whitaker, B. (2001), 'Homosexuality on Trial in Egypt', *Guardian*, November 19, http://www.guardian.co.uk.

World Reference (2002), 'Egypt: the People', http://www.travel.dk.com/wdr/EG/mEG_Peop.htm.

4 Crime, Social Change and Social Control in Namibia: An Exploratory Study of Namibian Prisons

ANNELIE ODENDAAL

Introduction

Crime is increasing in most regions of the world, and Southern Africa and Namibia are no exceptions. As crime disrupts social order, punishment, including imprisonment, has been used throughout time to protect society against crime. Crime, especially violent crime, is increasing rapidly in southern Africa, and alarmingly so, in Namibia. This chapter discusses crime, social change and social control within the Namibian context; it gives particular reference to imprisonment as a form of formal and legal punishment in Namibia today. It will also include findings from the author's research with violent offenders in Namibian prisons from 1998 to 2000. To understand the relevance of studying crime and violence in post-independence Namibia, the chapter firstly locates this problem within the contexts of Southern Africa and Namibia's history. A brief overview of Namibian society will therefore introduce this chapter.

Namibia: Country Profile

Situated in the south-western part of Africa, Namibia covers an area of 824,269 square kilometres. It is bounded by two major deserts that cover 22% of the total land area: the Namibia Desert, that runs along the entire coast of Namibia, and the Kalahari along the southern and central-eastern borders of Namibia. Namibia shares its borders with Angola and Zambia to the north, South Africa to the south, Botswana to the east and the Atlantic Ocean to the west. With a population of approximately 1.8 million, Namibia has a population density of 1.7 persons per square kilometre. This is among the lowest in the world. The population is unevenly distributed throughout the country due to environmental conditions and historical factors. Approximately 68% of the population lives in rural areas. (Lombard et al., 1995).

Until independence in March 1990, Namibia was occupied and ruled for more than a century by Germany and subsequently South Africa. With independence a constitutional government was installed which guaranteed democracy and equality for everyone in Namibia. For the majority of Namibians, the history of colonial rule was characterised by dispossession, national oppression and poverty. The policies of Apartheid in particular led to racial and ethnic fragmentation within Namibian society and communities were segregated geographically, economically and socially. The small, but diverse Namibian nation comprises 11 ethnic groups. Eighty-six per cent of the population is black, 6.6% white, and 7.4% racially mixed (Lombard et al., 1995). Approximately 48.7% of the population are male, and 51.3% female, with a sex ratio of 95 males per 100 females. The population growth rate is estimated at 3.1% per annum. Namibia has a classic age-sex pyramid indicative of a developing country with 50% of the population under the age of 15. The age-sex ratio is slightly skewed in that 43% of all males and 41% of all females are under the age of 15. However, by the age of 65, there are 4% males and 5% females. This is because men tend to die more than women in the 20-35 age groups due to accidents and violence. Life expectancy at birth in Namibia is 59.1 years for men and 62.8 years for women (Lombard et al., 1995).

The country's Gross Domestic Product (GDP) was N$16,826 million (US$3,042 million) in 1998 (United Nations Development Programme (UNDP), 1999). Although Namibia has been classified as middle income country prior to its independence and as such has been considered one of the richest countries in sub-Saharan Africa, it displays many characteristics similar to several poor and developing countries in Africa. It still bears the scars of a colonial economy characterised by a high dependency on exports (53% of GDP) and imports (63% of GDP), lack of manufacturing and industrial sectors and unequal distribution of infrastructure, resources and social services. The unemployment rate of people able to be economically active is nearly 40%, and affects primarily the black majority. Only 66% of the labour force was economically active in 1991 (UNDP, 1999). By 1992, 35% of men and 29% of women in the age group 15-19, and 21% of men and 24% of women in the age group 20-29, were unemployed. (Lombard et al., 1995). The effects of unemployment in the rural areas in particular are to some extent tempered by the extended family system, which acts as a network for both social and economic support. Relatives who are wage earners in urban employment, and who maintain links with 'home', remit wages to their families. Children of disadvantaged families are frequently reared by less impoverished families. The major employment sectors are the formal wage sector, commercial agriculture, and the mining and fishing industries, while subsistence agriculture and the informal sector on the peri-urban and urban fringes account for substantial non-formal or hidden employment. The Namibian GDP per capita was N$10,011 (US$1,810) in 1998. (UNDP, 1999). However, there is still a large gap between the GDP of the top 5% of the population (mostly whites) that accounts for 71% of the national GDP, and the poorest stratum of the population (55%) that accounts for only 3% of the national GDP) (Lombard et al., 1995). The gini coefficient for inequality in income distribution was 0.70 in 1993 (UNDP, 1999).

At present more than two-thirds of the population live in absolute poverty in the rural areas, while only a minority in the predominantly white, urban sector has access to incomes, housing and public services. In comparison to other sub-Saharan countries, rates of fertility, infant and maternal mortality, preventable diseases, malnutrition, teenage pregnancies, illiteracy, unemployment, crime and migration to urban areas in Namibia are high. Many people in the rural and urban areas, especially women, have opened *shebeens* (liquor outlets) to combat unemployment and to create an income for themselves and their families. The distribution and sale of alcohol also brings an outcome to Namibia's remote areas and squatter camps in terms of economic activity. Children are enabled to attend school with money from alcohol sales, while families climb out of absolute poverty through successful alcohol trade. *Shebeen* incomes have been estimated to range from N$60 (US$6) to N$300 (US$30) per week for smaller *shebeens*, and to about N$1,000 (US$100) per week for those appearing like small shops. This amounts to N$3,120 (US$312) per year at the lower end and N$52,000 (US$520) at the upper end. In Namibia where the average annual income per capita for 90% of the population is N$800 (US$80), alcohol trade is a rewarding business. Alcohol trade is a major source of jobs and incomes for the poor (UNDP, 1999). However, the excessive and increasing use and abuse of alcohol in Namibia largely contributes to unwanted and teenage pregnancies, the spread of HIV/AIDS, crime and violence.

Rapid social change, which includes a growing increase in poverty and unemployment since independence as well as changes in social norms and values, most likely contributed to the escalation of crime in Namibia. Crime as a national phenomenon is believed to cost Namibia up to 15% of its gross domestic product annually. Social structures have weakened as a result of Namibia's colonial and Apartheid experience and a prolonged war prior to independence. The Contract Labour System in particular, undermined Namibian family structures. This system recruited men from the rural areas to temporarily migrate for contract employment to 'white' areas. Rural poverty generated massive migration to urban centres after independence. Nevertheless, urbanisation under German occupation and South African Apartheid rule already placed enormous pressure on family structures and destroyed support structures of the extended family. The escalating process of urbanisation has a serious impact on traditional family life and value systems. While dislocating traditional systems and making family members more vulnerable in the westernised urban culture where the individual or nuclear family has to be more self-reliant, urbanisation is also recognised as a positive factor in bringing various cultures together and enhancing the process of nation-building.

Demographic tendencies exacerbate the increase of crime in Namibia. Windhoek, the capital city, is the largest and fastest growing city in the country. While there is no sign yet of relieving unemployment, Windhoek is struggling to find ways of dealing with a high influx of people, ever-rising unemployment and escalating organized crime. Windhoek currently has an annual population growth of 5.4%. Fifty per cent of all crime in Namibia is believed to be centered in Windhoek. In the first two years of independence, crime was reported to be on the increase and urbanisation and unemployment were identified as possible causes. This however did not come as a surprise, since studies conducted prior to independence already predicted that, in view of past policies, crime would increase (Bukurura, 2000). During colonial times, political status and economic class were mainly racially determined, and traditional and customary legal structures lost their influence to a great extent. With the country's extreme imbalances in access to resources, criminal activity soon became a legitimate and socially acceptable coping mechanism for the majority of the population that was racially in a disadvantaged position. Street crime flourished among mainly black, lower socio-economic groups in urban areas. It became a major strategy for survival in a situation where culture and tradition lost their supportive and moral strengths. White collar and corporate crimes were hidden and associated with mainly white individuals from middle or higher socio-economic classes.

Currently, in independent Namibia, property crime is driving many Namibians to turn their homes and automobiles into fortresses. In 2000 alone there were 9,600 reported cases of housebreaking and 1,200 reported causes of motor vehicle and motorcycle theft. This amounts to a daily average of 26 burglaries and three cases of motor vehicle and motorcycle theft (Namibian Economic Policy Research Unit (NEPRU), 2002). Furthermore, police statistics indicate that, on average, one murder per day is committed in Namibia while one rape occurs every 30 minutes each day in Namibia. In independent Namibia, Namibians are still confronted daily with violence, and the relatively high levels of crime and violence have a devastating impact on the general quality of life for most people, especially the poor. Even though regarded as relatively peaceful in comparison to its southern African neighbours, South Africa, Zimbabwe and Angola, crime and violence steadily increased in Namibia since the country's independence. Murder, rape, robbery and domestic violence mark the lives of many Namibians today and police statistics confirm that suicides are also on the increase. Conversely, in pre-independence Namibia and the period of Namibia's struggle against Apartheid, social, political and structural violence dominated the Namibian scene while other forms of violence such as family violence, interpersonal violence and small-group violence continued backstage. Since the complex and growing situation of interpersonal violence in contemporary Namibia is reflected in the rest of southern Africa, concerted efforts are needed to address crime and violence in the region as a whole.

According to the Southern African Development Community (SADC) Regional Human Development Report 2000, violent crimes such as murder, rape and assault have topped the list for Southern Africa since 1994, but the most numerous have been crimes against property. Crime distribution data (crime per 100,000 habitants) on a number of selected SADC countries for 1998 show that Namibia takes a strong lead in most crime categories in comparison to the five other selected neighbouring countries: Angola, Mauritius, Tanzania, Zimbabwe and Swaziland (UNDP, 2000). These Southern African countries have populations up to twenty times bigger than that of Namibia, which stands at approximately 1.8 million. The crimes examined include car-jacking, burglary, theft, robbery, corruption and other economic crimes (UNDP, 2000). Although the crime distribution does not include statistics for South Africa, indications are that South Africa might well be the country with the highest violent crime rate in the southern African region. Statistics for 1997 indicated 57 murders per 100,000, and 188 armed robbery victims per 100,000 people in South Africa for 1997 alone (Newham, 1999). According to the crime figures, 45.17 Namibians were murdered for every 100,000 habitants in 1998. This is by far higher than Swaziland with 17.6 per 100,000 people, Angola (10.41 per 100,000), Zimbabwe (9 per 100,000), Tanzania (6.51 per 100 000) and Mauritius (4.36 per 100 000). The Namibian statistics for sex offences, rape, serious assault and theft are alarmingly high. Namibia has the highest rape rate (34.38 per 100,000) after Swaziland (69.22 per 100,000), and ranks third highest (42.1 per 100,000) for sex offences after Swaziland (90.02 per 100,000) and Zimbabwe (54.5 per 100,000), and second (466.8 per 100 000) after Swaziland (474.23 per 100 000) for serious assault. Theft of all kinds was highest in Namibia (1879.78 per 100 000).

According to the SADC Regional Human Development Report 2000, crimes have a negative influence on investment confidence, on production and other aspects of the economy. Crimes also contribute to loss of physical capital and crimes can lead to violence. The report states that most of these crimes have been associated with economic hardships in the SADC region as a whole and in certain countries in particular, and points out that the levels and types of crime are the result of a range of local, national and regional factors. These include political and economic instability, the quality of policing and the availability of guns and other weapons.

Social Perceptions and Popular Approaches to Crime Prevention

Measuring the extent of violence and criminality in society is a difficult task, since crime reported to the police is known to be only a reflection and a limited indicator of what is otherwise a wider social problem. To complicate this task, crime usually evokes strong emotional reactions. Sensational media reporting, anger and fear shape public opinion and often resort into distorted perceptions of crime and unsystematic reasoning in society. In order to understand public perceptions and fears of criminality in Namibia, one only has to look at the number and flourishing businesses of security companies and establishments. It is believed that the number of these businesses has increased from twenty or less before independence to between 40 and 70 at present (Bukurura, 2000).

Often perceptions of crime and corrections are distorted by informal methods of reasoning. The general public, professionals and legislators are influenced by social perceptions of crime when they develop crime control strategies. Punishment is also getting more profitable for technologically advanced countries. Security devices in the form of behaviour modifying equipment for prisons are currently a remarkable resource for American technology. Many countries of the world today are keen to invest in weapons and advanced technology to control prisoners. Politicians everywhere generally profit when crime gets more media exposure. They use public fear of crime to their advantage by promising to fight crime and doing so by building more prisons.

In Namibia today, it is the government's primary objective to protect citizens. Therefore it spends 16% (N$1,368m/US$136.8m) of its expenditure on security services. Individuals pay a further N$343m (US$34.3m) on property insurance, N$433 (US$43.3) on security installations and N$274m (US$27.4m) on private security services every single year. Security related expenditure and criminal activities is estimated to absorb at least N$2,650m (US$265m), a minimum of 11% of the nation's GDP every year (NEPRU, 2002). It is argued that the Namibian Constitution gives a lot of emphasis to the protection of criminals. There is a suggestion that that the Constitution is partly to blame for the inability of criminal justice institutions to handle crime. There appears to be a belief that, if criminal justice institutions and officials had more powers, as existed before independence, it would enable them to successfully deal with crime. In July 1998, the Minister of Fisheries and Marine Resources, Dr Abraham Iyambo stated in Parliament that 'crime is a national problem which requires concerted efforts from all of us to eliminate it from our society'. The Minister of Water and Rural Development, Helmut Angula, called for a consultation with traditional leaders over combating crime, and Parliament was urged to draw on the wisdom of traditional leaders in the quest to reduce crime. Furthermore, to upgrade the Justice Ministry system, opposition party member, Alois Gende suggested that the public participate in neighbourhood watches to help combat crime (Inambao, 1998).

Community involvement in prisons was recently introduced in Namibia and is encouraged by new legislation. In August 1998, the Prison Act of 1998 came into force. The new Act provides for community involvement in Namibian prisons to aid the rehabilitation of prisoners. This approach, however, is still alien in Namibia. Existing fears and suspicion are currently holding back community prison rehabilitation projects. The Namibian society is nevertheless encouraged to deal with crime by means of community involvement. Traditional leaders, men, women and specific youth groups are challenging crime through legal reform, conferences, media campaigns, demonstrations and development projects.

Law Reform in Namibia

The Namibian experience probably provides one of the best examples in history as to how law was used in an attempt to bring about deliberate social change. Law, introduced to Namibian society in the guise of the Namibian Constitution, was to promote a peaceful revolution in social relations by reshaping racial and sexual attitudes and beliefs in a manner far more ambitious than ever before. Whether law will eventually change the rich variety of underlying, deeply rooted mores in Namibian society is an interesting question of time, since the Namibian Constitution was written from outside the culture of the people. The fact that the majority of Namibians now have to live by an alien value system may have tremendous consequences for their Constitution's social legitimacy and maintenance.

At the onset of law reform, however, Namibia's Law Reform and Development Commission showed its commitment to legal reform through a participatory approach by involving the public and private sector as well as civil society in debates on legal reform. The most revolutionary impact of law reform on social change in independent Namibia is most likely to be found in the country's gender relations. Amending and implementing laws to enhance the individual status of women in Namibia introduced a significant change in the relationship of men and women. Certain new Namibian gender laws now criminalise some long established patterns of male behaviour in the country. While certainly improving the legal position of women in Namibia, the 1996 Married Persons Equality Act, for example, is also believed to have contributed to the severe spin-off in widespread violence against women in the country. Implementing the country's Combating of Rape Act in May 2000 is therefore seen as yet another breakthrough in protecting women against men by means of law. This Act, however, is by all means gender neutral and gives legal recognition to the fact that men can fall victim to rape too, just as women can become the perpetrators of rape. A number of women have already been charged with the rape of minor boys, whereas a few cases of men raping other men have been reported. It nevertheless took Parliament ten years to pass and implement this law. This law is expected to have even greater consequences for gender relations in the country since it allows for the prosecution of rape within marriage. Women's groups are now eagerly awaiting the implementation of the country's new Domestic Violence Act of which the bill has already been tabled.

Both the Namibian Combating of Rape Act and the proposed Domestic Violence Bill are regarded revolutionary and progressive in international legal circles. In many African countries a woman is considered a minor who cannot enter into legal contracts without the consent of her father or husband. In the new Namibia, a woman has equal rights and can purchase, dispose of and bequeath property without the supervision of a man. Simultaneously, a woman with matching experience and qualifications is entitled to equal pay for equal work with her male counterparts. However, the Namibian society is traditionally a male dominated society. It is one thing for legislators to make laws that promote gender equality. Yet, it is quite another to implement the meaning of these laws in families and workplaces. Not only is it difficult for men to transcend culturally sanctioned behaviour and practices that harm women, it is also a challenge for women themselves to overcome their own ingrained submissiveness.

Violence against women and children, including rape and child abuse, continues to be a widespread problem in independent Namibia. Women continue to experience serious legal and cultural discrimination. Racial and ethnic discrimination and severe disparities in education, health, employment and working conditions continue. Discrimination against indigenous peoples persists, especially in remote rural areas where people are often unaware of their rights. Forced labour, also of children, still occurs.

The Criminal Justice System

Historically, political structures have determined how different social classes are treated by the criminal justice system. Economics, through the tendency to exploit cheap labour, played a vital role in punishment and corrections, as did religion and technology. Religion has had considerable impact on the belief that offenders ought to be morally reformed whereas many methods for torture and punishment have emerged from technology. After independence, the Namibian government inherited many state institutions from South Africa, and unrealistic expectations that better living conditions would be delivered immediately were destined to be frustrated. The most distrusted institutions before independence were the police, the justice system and correctional services.

In contemporary Namibia, the new Namibian criminal justice system has not yet produced respected social resources of authority, and some members of the general public feel that Namibia's criminal justice system fails to suppress crime successfully. Popular public opinion also blames the new government's attempts to establish human rights awareness in Namibia for the current crime situation. There is a strong belief in Namibia today that crime can be stopped through reforming or transforming the criminal justice system in one or more ways. It was suggested in Parliament that the Ministry of Justice be upgraded to bring about a drop in rising crime statistics. It is believed that crime should be dealt with by introducing tougher sentences, recruiting more police officers, using sophisticated technology and toughening up prison rehabilitation programs. Shortly after independence, for instance, there was public demand to reintroduce the death penalty in Namibia. This approach however, wants to resolve crime problems within the criminal justice system alone and ignores other factors that underpin crime such as historical, social, political and value systems.

Tougher sentences for violent crimes were nevertheless introduced, with no bail allowed for rapists. In addition, the police force was expanded and special police units were introduced to cope with crime. Due to the increase in criminality and sophistication of crimes committed after independence, the Namibian Police decided to establish specialized investigation units within the service, namely the Commercial Crimes Investigations Unit in March 1993 and the Serious Crimes Unit in February 1994 (Bukurura, 2000). Currently imprisonment is used as the main strategy for crime-control and prevention in Namibia. With the country's prevailing crime situation, correctional services have lately come under increasing attention. Attempts to introduce better coordination and cooperation between the Namibian police, courts and correctional services have yet to bear fruit. Lack of co-ordination within the criminal justice system significantly adds to the numerous problems facing effective rehabilitation practices within Namibia's prisons. For example, effective correctional services depend on effective prosecution, which depends on effective police investigation. All of these depend on successfully transforming the responsible state institutions and building up public confidence in them.

Prison overcrowding, institutional violence and public perceptions that correctional services fail to adequately protect society contribute to already existing social problems that are underlying crime. These problems include poverty, structural violence, substance abuse and inadequate education. The Namibian public however, believes that prisoners receive 'five star treatment'. Meanwhile manpower shortages, lack of expertise, violence and corruption within the system hamper effective rehabilitation in Namibia's prisons. Correctional services are the key to dealing with problems of criminal behaviour. It is generally believed that effective rehabilitation of criminals will solve the crime problem by eliminating recidivism. Theoretically, the aim of imprisonment is to protect society from dangerous offenders. Traditionally, imprisonment aims at rehabilitation, deterrence, retribution and incapacitation. Yet, after a decade of ineffective crime-control strategies, Namibia's criminal justice system, which includes correctional services, is perceived to be in crisis.

The reason for the existence of a criminal justice system is social control. The aim of the criminal justice agencies is to control crime, provide criminal justice and the treatment of offenders, and hence, maintain community safety. Imprisonment is contemporary society's form of control and punishment. Punishment is thought to fulfil a number of functions in society. It is imposed for retribution so that the offender suffers as well as the victim ('an eye for an eye'). It is done for the sake of deterrence in the hope to instill fear of punishment in potential offenders. It is done for rehabilitation under the assumption that offenders will not repeat their crimes. Finally, it is done for social protection because imprisonment temporarily handicaps imprisoned offenders to commit further crimes in society. The criminal justice process, as far as the basic concept is concerned, is similar everywhere, although, depending on different legal systems, some differences may exist. The flow of the process always has cases entering the system at one end and moving towards their disposition at the other end. Every agency along the line has the option of moving a case to the next point or dropping it out of the system. Thus, after a crime was committed and reported or detected, the police investigates the crime, arrests the suspect and collects evidence that is written down in a 'docket' or interrogation file. This file is then given to the public prosecutor. It also contains statements from witnesses. The public prosecutor concludes the docket with a decision to prosecute, writes an indictment, charges the accused before court and produces evidence to prove the guilt of the accused beyond reasonable doubt. The court then considers the evidence from the public prosecutor and the accused (and/or his defence) before imposing a sentence upon the accused or dismissing charges. Penalties are imposed with regard to the facts presented in the case and the relevant laws of a country. Penalties may be imposed in the form of a fine, probation, and imprisonment or in some countries, capital punishment. In case of imprisonment, the execution of the court sentence becomes the responsibility of correctional institutions.

All men and women in Namibia are equal before the law. Everyone has the constitutional right to a fair trial with the presumption of innocence until proven guilty. Each person has the right to a lawyer, the right to prepare a defense and to call witnesses, and cannot be compelled to testify against him- or herself or against a spouse. To prevent people from being held in prison unjustly for an indefinite period of time, all trials must take place within a reasonable time. Men, women and children awaiting trial are to be kept separate from each other and other prisoners. However, the current lack of qualified magistrates, other court officials and private attorneys in Namibia has resulted in a serious backlog of criminal cases, which often translates into delays of up to a year or more between arrest and trial, contravening constitutional provisions for the right to a speedy trial. Many of those awaiting trial were treated as convicted criminals.

Access to Justice

The criminal justice system in Namibia was designed to protect the innocent against injustices. Strict requirements of the law exist to maintain fairness in judgement. However, at present there is widespread concern in Namibian legal circles about the standard of justice delivered in some of Namibia's lower courts. Injustices increasingly arise because magistrates' courts fail to meet requirements of the law. A record of proceedings is subject to automatic review and must be submitted to the High Court for review within seven days of the conclusion of the trial. This, however, does not always happen.

Although no official statistics are available in this regard, while doing research in Namibian prisons, the author was well aware that there were few, if any, rich or influential people in prison. One kind of response to law's isolation or alienation is to argue the need for devices, procedures and institutional reforms to make law more accessible; to make the invocation of law easier and more worthwhile for all citizens. From another point of view, however, it could be argued that supplementing legal aid, if provided by formal state institutions, is merely an extension of state control. Legal services are not cheap. For many people, and not necessarily the poorest sections of the community, legal costs would render legal solutions out of the question were there no state- or donor-subsidised systems of financial legal aid. Such subsidised legal aid systems are currently in operation in Namibia. In addition to an existing state-subsidised legal aid system, a non-governmental organisation, the Legal Assistance Centre (LAC) has been active in Namibia since 1989. International donors support the LAC. With only a limited number of offices throughout Namibia, the LAC provides legal services to those who cannot afford it financially, is involved in community-based research and education, gives human rights and para-legal training, assists in law reform and policy design and acts as a human rights watchdog organisation in Namibia.

Although the issues of racism, sexism and classism are essential to understanding the criminal justice system, there is a lot more than economic oppression at work here. Those are just three of the social problems that result from social forces affecting criminal justice. The social forces at play are societal factors, which create events and conditions that influence the way people live. In addition to economic forces, political, religious (or moral) and technological forces affect people's lives. Poverty, unemployment, violence, substance abuse, inadequate education and inaccessible health care are all examples of interrelated social problems or conditions that directly or indirectly influence the control of crime and punishment (Welch, 1996). Many poor people, nevertheless, manage to live a life without clashing with the law, and find a measure of material survival. For most of those in prison, there were more reasons than lack of education and money or a good attorney, for finding themselves behind bars.

Prisons and Corrections

The issue of prisons transcends a number of areas, including women, juveniles, victims of crime, protection of witnesses, health, pre-trial detention, restorative justice and other alternatives to incarceration. Among the dominant features of correctional systems are their size, scope and impact on society. Prisons, in particular prison overcrowding and its financial and inherent human rights problems, remain a world-wide concern.

Currently there are over eight-and-half million prisoners held in penal institutions throughout the world, either as pre-trial detainees (that is, remand prisoners) or as convicted and sentenced prisoners. With a world population of 6.1 billion, this represents an average of incarceration rate of 140 prisoners per 100,000 population. Although this statistic in itself may not be alarming, the worrying fact is that throughout the 1990s, prison populations grew in most countries in all regions of the world. In some developed countries, prison population growth during this period was as high as 40%. This growth cannot alone be explained by increasing crime rates. Rather, there remains a belief that prison is preferable to the alternatives (Tkachuk, 2001). Of special concern is that the increase in imprisonment rates have led to prison overcrowding, which invariably results in a multitude of other problems in prison conditions. Decreased living space leads to poor hygiene and sanitation. In some countries there is insufficient bedding and clothing, and food quality and quantity are compromised. Health care is difficult to administer. There is more tension and violence amongst prisoners as well as violence against staff. Overcrowding results in less supervision, less engagement in constructive programs and restricts activities conducive to reintegration since it leads to a fall in staff-prisoner ratios. Hence the expression: 'prisons are universities of crime'.

Following the criminal justice process, it can be seen that corrections enter the scene early by providing safe custody of pre-trial prisoners on commencement of court proceedings, even though it is also the last resort for the criminal justice system. This puts the correctional system in a position where it inherits inefficiencies that may have occurred in earlier stages of the criminal justice process. To a large extent, the problems of correctional administration can be ascribed to problems arising from other criminal justice agencies. These problems can only be addressed if all key players in the criminal justice system co-operate. Key players include policy makers and legislators, the judiciary, police and prosecuting authorities as well as the media and general public.

The Namibian Prison Service in Context

The current crime situation not only put enormous pressure on Namibia's justice system but also introduces serious constraints on the proper functioning of prisons and correctional services in Namibia. Lack of money, facilities and skills hamper rehabilitation activities and reform in Namibian prisons.

The penal systems in Africa were largely inherited from the colonial powers and the legislative framework, as well as the infrastructure, remains largely unaltered. Although attempts have been made in several countries to improve their prison conditions, they are still inadequate in most prisons. Many prisons in Africa are also characterised by severe overcrowding. In most cases the prison capacity remains limited because it has never been expanded over time. Although the inmate population ratios may seem small, the impact of overcrowding on inmates is severe. Many facilities are either dilapidated or rudimentary in nature, and there are shortages of food, bedding, medical supplies and treatment, and a total absence of recreational facilities. Ill-treatment or torture of inmates is also reported for many countries (Dissel, 2001).

Until independence, the Namibian Prison Service (NPS) was for all purposes part of the South African Prison Service. All staff members were trained in South Africa where apartheid was rigorously enforced. Black and Coloured staff members received little management training, had limited promotion prospects, were not expected to demonstrate initiative and, apart from receiving orders, rarely spoke to white staff members. Their overriding objective was to keep prisoners in custody. Little attempt was made to rehabilitate prisoners, especially if they were non-white. White prisoners were kept separate from other ethnic groups, and workshops such as those of high standard at Windhoek Central Prison were exclusively for white prisoners. The use of corporal and capital punishment was common. For the purpose of capital punishment, there were gallows at Windhoek Prison that could execute four prisoners simultaneously. Apartheid laws strictly controlled the movement of people. The armed struggle was concentrated in the North, and despite the relatively high population density in northern Namibia, only a few police stations were built there. Prisoners were subsequently kept in prisons located elsewhere in Namibia, often hundreds of kilometres from their homes and family members.

There are 13 prisons throughout Namibia at present. The current Namibian

Prison Service resorts under the Ministry of Prisons and Correctional Services. It was established under an Act of Parliament (17/1998) prescribing powers, duties and procedures. Before the Ministry of Prison and Correctional Services was eventually established in 1995 as an independent Ministry, prison services first resorted under the Ministry of Justice, then under the Ministry of Home Affairs. With the establishment of the Ministry of Prisons and Correctional Services, the government made a public commitment to the rehabilitation of prisoners. President Sam Nujoma emphasised the importance of rehabilitation work in Namibian prisons and this resulted in a new mission statement and policy document for the prison service. The following Mission Statement currently serves as the guiding principle in the administration of prison services in Namibia:

> The Namibian prison Service as an integral part of the Justice system contributes to the protection of society by providing reasonable, safe, secure and humane custody of offenders in accordance with universally acceptable standards, while assisting them in their rehabilitation, reformation and social integration (Namibian Prison Service, 2001).

Following its new policy on rehabilitation, the Namibian Prison Service is gradually changing from a punitive to a corrective approach in rehabilitation practices. There are major plans underway to introduce effective treatment programmes for offenders. These programmes will include life skills, education and other treatment programmes relevant to specific offences.

The Namibian government is currently focusing on the Constitutional requirement of achieving a balanced prison service structure. Before independence, all prison personnel was trained in South Africa. At present, the Namibian Prison Service is sharing the Patrick Iyambo Police Training College with the Police. The lack of training, especially for senior members has detrimental repercussions for professionalism. The prison service management lacks experience and needs training to cope with the ever-increasing prison population. To remedy the situation, a working relation was established with institutions of higher learning in South Africa and the correctional services of Canada. These institutions agreed to future co-operation in an attempt to improve correctional practices in Namibia appropriate to the new Namibian Prison Service mission statement.

Prison Conditions

Although the United States (US) Country Report on Human Rights Practices, published in 2000, describes prison conditions and conditions in military detention facilities in Namibia as 'spartan', it mentions that the International Committee for the Red Cross (IRC) and foreign diplomats found conditions in Namibian prisons to be clean and orderly. However, human rights organisations continue to complain about prison overcrowding in Namibia. The overcrowding rate of 33% in Namibia does not compare favourably with overpopulated prisons in South Africa, where the rate is 25%. The authorised capacity of all the prisons in Namibia is

3822 while the average total prison population is 5085 thus exceeding the limit by 1263. South African prisons were designed for 88000 prisoners but hold a daily average of 110 000 (Giffard and Dissel, 1996).

The Namibian Prison Service staff for 13 prisons included 9 social workers, 4 vocational instructors, 6 nurses, one medical officer and 1090 prison officers at the end of 1999. During 1998 and 1999, a total of 597 ex-combatants were added as prison staff in Namibia. By the end of 2000, 372 of 1565 posts were vacant. These numbers reflect severe staff shortages at the prisons in Namibia. At one warden to every 5.7 prisoners, Namibia has a far lower staff to prisoner ratio than exists in first world countries such as the United States where the prisoner-staff ratio was 1 officer per 3.9 inmates in 1990 (Welch, 1996). Similar to Namibia, however, is the staff to prisoner ratio in South Africa, which is 5.5 prisoners to one warden (Dissel, 1995). In total, there are four social workers that have to deal with the administration and problems of approximately 1200 prisoners at Windhoek Central Prison. In 1998, there were only 175 members doing the actual guard duties, 58 administrative staff and 34 specialised functionaries including the 4 social workers.

Windhoek Central Prison, Namibia's largest maximum-security prison, accommodated 1159 lock-up prisoners by the end of 2000. This included 1098 men and 61 women from various ethnic backgrounds, foreigners, juveniles and mentally ill criminals. New forensic facilities were made available for mentally ill prisoners in Namibia at Windhoek Central Hospital at the beginning of 2000 but are not fully used yet. The classification of prisons and that of offenders in Namibia have been questioned for some time. The faulty classification of institutions and that of offenders is regarded as one of the major reasons for overcrowding in Namibian prisons. Currently more than half of inmates are placed in maximum security prisons without considering their behaviour, attitude or personal details (Ministry of Prisons and Correctional Services, 1999). By the end of 2000, there were a total of 5432 prisoners in Namibia: 5162 men and 270 women. Men and women are separated and are not allowed to mix. There were 651 prisoners awaiting trial in Namibia of whom 311 were at Windhoek Prison by the end of 2000 (Ministry of Prisons and Correctional Services, 2001). Although efforts are made to separate youthful offenders from adult criminals, juveniles continue to be held with adults in many rural areas. There are several pilot programmes that provide alternatives to the incarceration of juvenile offenders. In addition, a juvenile centre is currently under construction in the Kavango region of Namibia, about 700 km from Windhoek. Female prisoners are held separately from male prisoners. There have been, however, allegations that female prisoners sometimes are abused by prison guards. Several cases of police officers raping females in custody have been reported.

The Prison Population

The total number of persons committed to all prisons for various reasons in the year 2000 was 5432 compared to 5712 in 1999 while a total number of 651 people in prison were awaiting trial. The downtrend for convicted prisoners does not reflect the decrease of crime but 'may confirm several scenarios which may need to be researched' (Ministry of Prisons and Correctional Services, 2000).

According to the Ministry of Prisons and Correctional Services, the composition of the prison population in Namibia is changing. A much higher proportion of offenders is serving longer sentences or life sentences for violence or rape and drug related offences. The population is becoming younger, more violent and volatile. Towards the end of 2000 there were 441 offenders under the age of 18 in Namibia's prisons. No official statistics for ethnic distribution of prisoners in Namibia are available but it is assumed that these represent the general ethnic distribution found in the total population of Namibia. Data on crime distribution, drawn from total convictions in 2000, indicate that the majority of offenders in Namibian prisons were convicted of house breaking (766) and stock theft (725) by the end of 2000. Drug related offences (194) replaced rape (163) from previous years as the third highest crime in 2000. Prisoners convicted of the crimes of murder and culpable homicide totalled 133 whereas 122 were convicted of robbery (Ministry of Prisons and Correctional Services, 2001).

These figures are an indication that crime incidents in Namibia are mostly poverty related. Incarceration for drug related offences has gradually increased since independence and is an indication of Namibia's growing drug trade problem. Rape was the highest violent offence represented in Namibian prison statistics, which indicates increasing violence against women and children in the country as well as stricter sentencing for the crime of rape. It is, however, assumed that the majority of murder and culpable homicide victims in Namibia are men. Windhoek Central Prison accommodates the majority of violent prisoners (2.15%) together with Oluno Rehabilitation Centre (2%) of the total Namibian prison population.

The Namibian Prison Service makes provision for specific categories of prisoners in its 2001 policy document where it states 'offenders must be treated as individuals'. In addition, the African Charter on Prisoners' Rights provides for specific categories of prisoners such as awaiting trial prisoners, female prisoners, foreign prisoners, juveniles, mentally disordered prisoners, civil prisoners, prisoners facing the death penalty, aged or disabled prisoners and prisoners with HIV/AIDS. There is no special category for political prisoners. The rights and specific conditions of treatment for prisoners in these categories are outlined in the African Charter. In protecting the rights of offenders in Namibian prisons, the prison service states in its policy document that it will 'build on the base of established international standards'. Important categories of prisoners in Namibian prisons include maximum-security prisoners, female prisoners, juveniles and awaiting trial prisoners.

Maximum-Security Prisoners

The maximum-security prisoners are those who have committed serious offences and who still have long sentences to serve. They are usually kept at maximum-security institutions such as Windhoek Central Prison, Oluno Rehabilitation Center or Walvis Bay and Hardap Prisons. Male maximum-security prisoners at Windhoek Central Prison are kept at the prison's F section, the largest section at Windhoek Central Prison, or in single cells. Some prisoners at Windhoek Central Prison's F section are serving multiple sentences of between 12 and 53 years while others are serving shorter sentences for fraud. Those who have committed violent offences are kept together with others who have committed economic offences. Sex offenders, homosexuals and former police officers who are generally regarded as vulnerable prisoners are no longer separated from the rest at Windhoek Central Prison. Although rape and other forms of violence do occur at Windhoek Central Prison, no incidents of inmate-on-inmate violence had been reported thus far because of this arrangement.

Prisoners in the maximum-security sections of Windhoek Prison have nothing to do all day. This situation remains unchanged for the duration of their imprisonment. Maximum-security convicts are seen as of too high a risk to be involved in any outside prison activities. Outside activities involve working outside of prison in a prison working team somewhere in Windhoek city, on the prison grounds or in the prison workshops. Currently, more than half (59%) of Namibia's prisoners are in maximum-security institutions.

Women in Prison

By the end of 2000, 270 of the 5432 prisoners incarcerated in Namibian prisons were women. Out of a total of 418 convictions for the violent crimes of rape, murder, culpable homicide and robbery in 2000, only 8 women (no women were convicted of rape in 2000 although one was convicted in 1998) were convicted. In contrast, 410 men were convicted for the same crimes in 2000 (Ministry of Prisons and Correctional Services, 2001).

Women are usually convicted of the crimes of drug trade, fraud and housebreaking. Women convicted of murder or culpable homicide in Namibia are either serving sentences for killing a spouse or partner in self defence, infanticide or killing another woman in a quarrel about love or money. The percentage of female prisoners of the total Namibian prison population was almost 5% by the end of 2000. Although the total Namibian prison population has slightly decreased from 6223 in 1999 to 5432 in 2000, the percentage representing female prisoners of the total prison population remained relatively constant. By the end of 1999, females represented 5.1% of all prisoners in Namibia and by the end of 2000, they represented 4.9%. Women represent the fastest growing segment of the correctional population in many countries of the world, and more and more women go to prison for violent crimes such as rape and murder (Welch, 1996). Currently one woman is serving a seven year prison sentence at Windhoek Central Prison for inciting three men to gang rape a woman near Rehoboth in 1997. Another woman is awaiting trial for raping a boy of 13. Since the introduction of the Combating of Rape Act in Namibia in May 2000, women can also be sent to prison for raping men.

There were 61 female prisoners at Windhoek Central Prison by the end of 2000. The majority of women in Namibian prisons are above the age of 20. Most of them are mothers of young children. The number of female prisoners under the age of 20, however, has increased significantly from 47 in 1998 to 129 in 1999 but dropped to 57 in 2000. Although female prisoners closely resemble male prisoners in terms of race, ethnic background and age, women are more likely to serve time for economic offences and less likely to be incarcerated for violent offences. Violent offences, therefore, may primarily be gender determined (Welch, 1996).

Juveniles

Offenders of 18 years and younger are classified as juvenile offenders. The number of juvenile offenders committed to Namibian prisons during 2000 decreased from 433 in 1998 to 384 in 2000. Most young people incarcerated in Namibia by the end of 2000 were convicted of either housebreaking or stock theft. Eighty-two juveniles were convicted of housebreaking in 2000 in comparison to 87 in 1998. In the year 2000, 58 juveniles were convicted of stock theft in comparison to 88 in 1998. In comparison to 23 in 1998, only 3 juveniles were imprisoned for drug trade in 2000 (Ministry of Prisons and Correctional Services, 1999, 2001). There is nevertheless evidence of growing drug abuse among the Namibian youth. By the end of 2000, 80% of pupils in Windhoek schools admitted to either using or having experimented with illegal drugs. With the exception of rape, Namibian prison statistics for 2000 show a decrease in the incarceration of violent offenders under age 18. Robbery seems to be decreasing among juvenile offenders. In comparison to 66 in 1998 only 17 juveniles were convicted of robbery in 2000 (ibid.).

However, even though it seems as if only a small number of juveniles aged 18 and under are imprisoned for violent crimes every year, the number of younger people imprisoned for the violent crime of rape is increasing. In comparison to 18 juveniles convicted of rape in 1998, a total number of 21 were convicted of rape in 2000 (ibid.). Most offenders imprisoned for violent crimes are between the ages of 18 and 30. In relation to sex composition, young male convicts outnumber young females significantly. During 2000, only 57 women under the age of 20 were imprisoned in comparison to 884 men in the same age group. The highest male and female offender rates are found in age category 20-39 years, composed of 2740 males and 143 females (Ministry of Prisons and Correctional Services, 2001).

As already stated, there were only 384 juveniles under the age of 18 in Namibian prisons by the end of 2000. They were mostly incarcerated at Elizabeth Nepemba Juvenile Centre in Rundu. Of the 384 incarcerated juveniles, 18 were females accommodated in prisons elsewhere in Namibia. At the end of 1998 there were no female offenders under the age of 18 in Namibian prisons. Although the Prison Act defines a juvenile as a person of 18 years or younger, offenders up to the age of 20 are often kept in juvenile sections. The youngest offender the author encountered at Windhoek Central Prison was a hyperactive 12-year-old who probably needed medication rather than imprisonment. Like women, juveniles are regarded as vulnerable and kept separate from other prisoners. Nevertheless, it sometimes happens that adult prisoners are placed at Windhoek Prison's juvenile section. Among them are violent problem prisoners, adult male prisoners who are victimized by fellow prisoners, and prisoners accused of treason and who are awaiting trial since 1999.

Indications are that the number of juveniles incarcerated in Namibian prisons is dropping. The Namibian courts are trying to keep juvenile first offenders out of prison as far as possible by means of alternative sentencing. In Windhoek, CALS (Change of Attitude and Life Style) is a halfway house that accommodates a limited number of juveniles who are awaiting trial. In Mariental, a small southern Namibian town, a Non-Governmental Organisation (NGO), The Bridge, assists Hardap Prison with juvenile programs. Although most juveniles are first offenders and are in prison for theft or cattle theft, an increasing number of juveniles go to prison for drug related or violent offences such as rape or gang rape, murder and armed robbery. Although their general living conditions are significantly better than those of adult prisoners, juveniles also belong to those who have nothing to do all day. Most juvenile offenders at Windhoek Central Prison play games, experiment with drugs and are initiated into the world of crime by fellow prisoners. Juveniles are generally considered to be at high risk of becoming rape victims behind bars and are kept separate from older prisoners. Some young prisoners, however, do try to improve their academic qualifications through correspondence courses or are taught by qualified older prisoners. At Windhoek Central Prison a few juvenile offenders are successfully engaged in a candle-making project. Young offenders are encouraged to develop their own creativity through a variety of art forms. They are also periodically exposed to guest speakers who address drug abuse as one of several personal growth topics.

Awaiting Trial Prisoners

The total number of people awaiting trial by the end of 2000 was 651. Awaiting trial prisoners are segregated from convicted prisoners if possible and may wear their own clothes as far as these are regarded as suitable. The highest number of awaiting trial prisoners recorded since 1994 was 1729 in 1996 and the lowest, 284 in 1998 (Ministry of Prisons and Correctional Services, 2001). While fewer people were imprisoned every year since 1997, the number of awaiting trial prisoners during 2000 was the highest since 1997.

The slow process of the courts and the backlog of many cases frequently result in prisoners being held awaiting trial for many months, in some cases even years. Efficient co-ordination of the criminal justice system might prevent this from happening. Stated as a joint objective in the 2001 policy document of the Namibian Prison Service is that the Service is to 'foster close collaboration with the other organs of the Justice System'. Theoretically, conditions for awaiting trial prisoners should be better than for sentenced prisoners, as they have not yet been convicted of any offence. Despite having access to a greater number of visits, receiving food from outside and being able to wear their own clothing, conditions for awaiting trial prisoners are grim, especially for awaiting trial political prisoners who are not always sure that they will survive their prison experience alive and unharmed. Namibian newspapers have reported that eight awaiting trial Caprivi secessionists, accused of treason, have died of 'natural causes' since 1999 at the Grootfontein prison. The eighth Caprivi secessionist died in custody of 'natural causes' by October 2002. At present, 128 political prisoners from Namibia's Caprivi region in the North are detained in Namibian prisons after their attempt to secede from The Republic of Namibia at the beginning of August 1999 failed. By the end of 2002, these men were still awaiting trial since the Namibian government was unable to provide state subsidised legal aid to the accused as required by law.

The days of awaiting trial prisoners are also characterised by monotonous routine and idleness. Although the African Charter on Prisoners' Rights specifies otherwise, awaiting trial prisoners are not allowed to work in Namibian prisons neither can they officially make use of social workers and their services. At the time of research, an awaiting trial prisoner whose wife wanted to divorce him committed suicide at Windhoek Prison after his endless requests for a social worker were ignored. During the author's visits to the Awaiting Trial Sections at Windhoek Central Prison, some awaiting trial prisoners were playing soccer in front of their cells while others just lay in bed sleeping or reading, not making use of the few hours permitted outside in-between lock-up times. Most awaiting trial prisoners, however, were outside, sitting on the ground, chatting to cell mates, or standing around in small groups, discussing and smoking.

Conclusion

Imprisonment is used as the main strategy for crime-control and prevention in Namibia. Consequently, prison reform is commonly viewed as a solution to the correctional crisis. Yet, corrections cannot be improved unless the social problems underlying crime are addressed. The critical approach to corrections is similar to the way many other social problems are analysed. Taking the critical approach implies that the criminal justice system is a mechanism of social control which has to deal with the social problem of crime. The critical approach considers interrelated social factors and is therefore different from other approaches to corrections such as the systems approach. The systems model only describes corrections within the context of the criminal justice system and mainly focuses on the interconnection between corrections, the courts and the police. Although punishment practices are expanding rapidly all over the world, the question remains why corrections have not succeeded in meeting the goals of rehabilitation. The answer probably lies in the fact that external forces of crime, which are both expensive and self-defeating, are neglected.

Crime statistics for Southern Africa and Namibia show that acts of criminal interpersonal violence are increasing. This strains development efforts in the region. In contemporary Namibia, the emphasis of crime prevention is increasingly falling on heavier sentences for violent offenders. The rate of released prisoners being incarcerated again for another; often-violent crime is on the rise. A much higher proportion of offenders is serving longer sentences or life sentences for violence or rape and drug related offences. The major concern is to remove violent offenders where they are 'safely locked up in prison'. An important consequence of this approach is that the individual offender and his realities are ignored. Violent offenders currently admitted to prison become increasingly younger and often repeat their offences in and outside prisons after their release, indicating that imprisonment alone is an ineffective form of punishment for this kind of offence. Nevertheless, society continues in its attempts to protect itself against violent offenders by imprisoning them. Although the new Namibian Prison Act of 1998 takes a more philosophical approach to prison rehabilitation, inadequate funds, staff shortages and lack of skills hamper efforts to treat violent offenders in an attempt to combat violence in society.

In the author's 1998-2000 study of violent offenders in Namibian prisons, she identified the critical approach to corrections as the most suitable for interpreting corrections in Namibia since it offers alternative views and solutions to existing approaches of crime intervention. This approach is opposed to looking at corrections as one-dimensional and emphasises the interrelationship between social forces, social conditions, social problems and the social responses to crime intervention problems. Although political and economic policies create favourable social conditions for some members of society, they simultaneously create adverse living conditions and social problems for others. Social problems themselves are interrelated. Inadequate education, for instance, may lead to unemployment and poverty; family disintegration may lead to substance abuse and violence; and poverty and substance abuse may lead to street crime. Social problems in turn elicit social responses such as criminal justice which comprises law enforcement, courts, corrections and other forms of intervention (Welch, 1996).

The author therefore strongly suggests that, in addition to the new Prison Act, Namibia invest time and effort to formulate and implement a more holistic crime prevention strategy to strengthen community morality countrywide. In addition, programs to alleviate poverty as well as addressing the current countrywide alcohol abuse should be implemented in broader society.

References

Bukurura, S.H. (2000), *Criminal Justice and the Namibian Constitution: Experiences and Predicaments of the Past Ten Years*, unpublished, Windhoek, Namibia.

Dissel, A. (1995), *Report on Correctional Services Tour to Denmark, Holland and Britain*, Center for the Study of Violence and Reconciliation, South Africa.

______ (2001), *Prison Conditions in Africa*, Center for the Study of Violence and Reconciliation, South Africa.

Giffard, C. and Dissel, A. (1996), 'Transforming Correctional Services: The Need for a New Vision', *Track Two*, vol. 5, no. 1, March.

Inamboa, C. (1998), 'Parliament Debates Crime Concerns', *The Namibian*, July 22, Windhoek, Namibia.

Lombard, C., Odendaal, A. and Rose-Junius, S.M.H. (1995). *Worldwide State of the Family*, Professors' World Peace Academy, Seoul, Korea.

Ministry of Prisons and Correctional Services (1999), *Annual Report for the Year Ending 1998*, Namib Graphics, Windhoek, Namibia.

______ (2000), *Annual Report for the Year Ending 1999*, John Meinert Printing, Windhoek. Namibia.

______ (2001), *Annual Report for the Year Ending 2000*, Namprint, Windhoek, Namibia.

Namibian Economic Policy Research Unit (NEPRU) (2002), *Quarterly Economic Review-June-2002*, http://www.nepru.org.na.

Namibian Prison Service (2001), *Policy Document and Mission Statement of the Namibian Prison Service*, NPS, Windhoek, Namibia.

Newham, G. (1999), *The Relevance of the National Crime Prevention Strategy for Sustainable Development in South Africa*, Center for the Study of Violence and Reconciliation, South Africa.

Tkachuk, B. (2001), *World Prison Population: Facts, Trends and Solutions*, Rapporteur's Report, Conference of the Eastern, Southern and Central African Heads of Correctional Services, Windhoek, Namibia.

United Nations Development Programme (UNDP) (1999), *Alcohol and Human Development in Namibia*, Namibia Human Development Report 1999, UNDP, Windhoek, Namibia.

______ (2000), *Challenges and Opportunities for Regional Integration*, SADC Human Rights Development Report 2000, SAPES Books 2000, Harare, Zimbabwe.

Welch, M. (1996), *Corrections: A Critical Approach*, McGraw-Hill, USA.

5 Criminal Fraud and Developing Countries

UDO C. OSISIOGU

Introduction

Adopting several theoretical explanations, this chapter addresses aspects of the impact of fraudulent activities on the image of citizens and their country in general. Plausible causal explanations are also identified. Other attributes of the offence such as ethnic background, class and gender are also highlighted. With few empirical studies on fraud carried out in developing countries in particular, attention is drawn to certain findings in other countries that can be regarded as universal. The importance and impact of fraud on the society as a whole has been noted. For instance, economic crime is regarded as a high-reward and comparatively low-risk criminal activity with the unlikely possibility of effective law enforcement action (Rider, 1990). This situation applies to both the developed and developing countries.

What is Fraud?

Fraud is a generic concept, which covers a wide range of activities, some of which may not be criminal as defined by the law. The usage of the term 'fraud' is associated with illegal actions or practices that are dishonest and deceptive. First, from a broader perspective, Sharpe's (1984) definition of crime is any activity, or action that violates the criminal law, and if detected, would lead to prosecution in a criminal court of law or an accredited law enforcement organ. Fraud definitely falls into this category. For Page (1997), a fraud is committed when a person is intentionally deceitful, by commission or omission, with a view to gain for themselves or another, in connection with: entering into a binding promise, or performing or failing to perform a binding promise. Certain activities or behaviour regarded as fraudulent are known to differ and change over time and space or geographical areas. In addition, the broad nature of 'fraud' makes it difficult to identify a precise definition. Thus, legal definitions of fraud tend to contain elements of flexibility with regard to activities that are classified as fraudulent. No definition can adequately comprehend fraud and the nature of fraud varies according to the context in which it is used (Leigh, 1982). Similarly, since fraud has no specific definition, the boundaries are always changing (West, 1988). West notes that criminal and civil laws both involve offences of fraud. Civil law relates to disputes between individuals, groups or organisations affecting only themselves, whilst criminal law is concerned with acts and omissions affecting the community at large or activities that are harmful physically or otherwise.

In this chapter, the particular offence of fraud of interest to the writer is that involving the obtaining of money, goods and services by false pretences. The concept or term 'upfront' is central here, and involves the collection of benefits in anticipation that an agreed transaction or business will be fulfilled. For instance in Nigeria, the relevant legislation is that of Section 4 (19) of the Nigerian penal code, hence the alias '4-1-9' associated with deceptive schemes and practices known as advance fee fraud. In an attempt to expand its reach and make it more focused, the Nigerian government at the time put forward the Advance Fee Fraud and Other Related Offences Decree No. 13 (1995) 'AFFAOFRO'. In Section 1 (1) of the decree:

> ...any person who by any false pretence and with intent to defraud obtains from any other person in Nigeria or in any other country, for himself or any other person in Nigeria or any other country, to deliver to any person any property whether or not the property is obtained or its delivery is induced through the medium of a contract induced by false pretence; is guilty of an offence.

The decree stipulates sanctions of imprisonment of between 5-10 years or more (at the trial judge's discretion) without the option of fine (Osimiri, 1997, p.271).

Historical and Contemporary Practice of Upfront Payments and Fraud

The practice of obtaining by false pretences is not new. A typical aim of obtaining by false pretences is via the collection of advance fees. Demanding for upfront payments or money, goods and services occurs in virtually all arenas of human endeavour such as in business, investments, religion, charitable courses, medical services and products, relationships, and education and training (Osisiogu, 2001). The essence of this review is to buttress our understanding of the nature, pattern and extent of fraud from a historical perspective using some examples.

Historically, central to successful advance fee frauds is the 'confidence trick' exhibited by the fraudster. This encourages the victim to trust the criminal. In the words of Schur (1958), another term associated with confidence is 'confidence game' or 'con game' or trick. Schur observed that from a sociological view, almost all fraud can be seen to involve some confidence trick: a procedure that entails the creation or portrayal through whatever means a relation of confidence, through which a swindle is carried out. Tracing the history of English Criminal Law and its administration from 1750 Radzinowicz and Hood (1986) made certain observations. They note that between 1860 and the First World War, several new crimes were created relating to fraud, embezzlement, larceny, bribery and corruption, the use of explosives, perjury, trade unions, public order, and a wide range of other offences against what was then described as 'good morals'. They state that with regard to the Victorian era, the nature and extent of crime should be assessed against the ever increasing population, high rate of urbanisation, and its antecedent social inequalities or socio-economic disparities. This is in addition to a visible class of the affluent or wealthy individuals who are seen to be 'having a better life'. In his study of long-firm fraud, which is a pattern, or method of obtaining goods by false pretence, Levi (1981) identified early literature and occurrences of this practice. Levi was able to trace the term 'long-firm fraud' to a periodical called *The Orchestra* dated 2 January 1869. The article referred to 'the doings of the "long-firm", a body of phantom capitalists who issue large orders to supply an infinite variety of goods'. Levi (1981: 12) also mentions that in *The Slang Dictionary* (Hotten, 1874), Hotten defines the long firm as 'a gang of swindlers who obtain goods by false pretences. They generally advertise or answer advertisements'. For Levi, documentation shows that the term 'long firm' has been around since the late 1860s, and adds that at the time, it was defined as a class of individuals rather than as a class of activity. In addition, the activity of obtaining goods by false pretence can be traced to the time of Henry VIII, during which an Act concerning this practice was passed in 1543, and more frauds of this nature can be found in the archives.

In America, the scam was first recorded around 1820 (Morton, 1992). In a case involving a Spanish prisoner who had $3million in Latin America, Morton notes that six people were employed full time to write hundreds of letters of offer. By 1900, postal authorities had seized over 1,400 letters – most likely a small fraction of the total number of letters sent out. Morton states this type of scam is operating perfectly well in Britain today, albeit in a slightly different form. Today, businesses receive letters explaining how the fraudster has come across an unaudited amount of money in the bank or government department where he works. The addressee must send details of his bank accounts so that the money can be transferred. Also, for example, in the 1930s it was Jewish prisoners in Germany who were seeking a way out. Morton remarks: 'who dares say that history does not repeat itself' (Morton, 1992, p.115). People have always practised fraud for material gain, and early records of the Middle ages tell of coin-clippers, forgers cases of impersonation, false promises made under contract, sale of other people's land, and exploitation of charity through fraudulent begging were among tricks used (Vallance, 1955).

Finally, a discussion about the history of scams will not be complete without mentioning the role of one of the 'masters', Charles Ponzi, an accomplished swindler, reputed as being the originator of the pyramid scheme and other methods of obtaining money by false pretences. Knutson (1996) has developed a website titled *Charles K. Ponzi*. According to Knutson, in the summer of 1920 Ponzi's scam became very popular. Before his investment scam was exposed Ponzi had collected $9,500,000 from 10,000 investors by selling promissory notes paying

'50% profit in forty-five days'. Ponzi claimed he was giving investors just a portion of the 400% profit he was earning through trade in postal reply coupons. Investigations later revealed that there were no coupons or profits. The truth was that earlier notes were paid at maturity from the proceeds of later ones. It was another instance of robbing 'Peter to pay Paul'. The simplicity and grand scale of his scheme linked Ponzi's name with this particular form of fraud. Knutson notes that Ponzi's operation expanded dramatically as satisfied investors spread 'the good news'. After a few months he was taking in about $1,000,000 a week. He then expanded to several other cities. Federal, state, and county officials suspected Ponzi's business but could not identify concrete evidence of illegality. Apparently, all investors were fully paid promptly. However, the Massachusetts District Attorney convinced Ponzi to quit accepting deposits from new investors until an auditor could verify the soundness of his operation. It was noted that during the run on Ponzi's scheme, he had hot dogs and coffee served to the thousands crowding outside his office to get their money back. Some were so impressed with this gesture that they had a change of heart and went home. He assured nervous investors, claiming that he had $12 million in assets: $4 million in America, and $8 million overseas. Ponzi finally ended up in jail.

To sum up, over time, fraudsters have been observed to possess certain attributes especially that of confidence. Discussing the 'craft' of the long-firm fraudster, Levi (1981) emphasises that these skills entail two principal categories. First, to obtain goods on credit and second, to avoid conviction and imprisonment. The highly rated fraudster succeeds on both; the middle-range crook succeeds on the first and fails in the second. The incompetent fraudster fails on both. Fraudsters also employed various strategies to avoid arrest and conviction. This can be regarded as the ultimate test of the fraudster's skills. According to Levi, ways of handling this include providing appropriate inducements to front men to deter them from squealing to the police and to travel to a different continent or country adopting new identities if necessary. For Levi, important factors that determine movement include language, extradition laws, and police corruption. In contemporary fraudulent practice, it has been observed that technological changes can facilitate certain crimes. This could further complicate or make their investigation difficult. Examples include fraud involving the use of computers, international direct-dialling telephones, telexes, computer-aided despatch systems and facsimile senders, which all enable fraudsters to distance themselves geographically from their targets. The spread of offshore banking and investment schemes has been of benefit to multinational corporations and fraudsters (Levi, 1987). Thus, business/economic activities have played their role in altering the pattern/method of fraud. For instance, in the mid-1980s, documentary fraud became more popular than insurance claims for 'lost' cargo and claims for 'sunk' vessels. 'The reason being that due to the excess of supply and demand in the market, ships themselves became so cheap that they were worth less than their cargoes' (Levi, 1987, p.3).

Fraud, Impact and Explanations: A Case Study of Nigeria

In this section, Nigeria is used as the main example to discuss this matter. This stems from several factors, some of which include that it is a developing country, and has been associated with various scams especially those involving advance fees by the print media, the police and Intelligence especially in the UK and the US. As a consequence, the Nigerian government and citizens have embarked on deliberate image-building programmes and activities to show that this negative publicity is the result of a negligible number of people. It is not unusual for stereotypes to develop where certain citizens or countries have been associated with particular types of criminal activities. It is not possible to measure or quantify in precise terms the impact of such negative publicity. Stories of personal experiences and the attitude of the business and tourist communities are pointers to this development. On the other hand, the historical development of Nigeria, which is similar to that of other developing countries show signs or characteristics that are capable of inducing certain individuals to engage in fraud and criminal activity. Developed countries also experience various forms of fraud including advance fee fraud perpetrated by its citizens. Other crimes such as grand corruption and embezzlement have created the bulk of the social, political and economic problems experienced in developing countries. However, advance fee scams or frauds are mostly associated with Nigerians as reflected in various reports.

The impact of the 'image' problem can be seen in a speech by Ihode (1998), the National President of the Nigerian-American Chamber of Commerce, in which he stated that Advance Fee Fraud (alias 4-1-9)

> ...has so badly dented our national image that Nigerians travelling abroad to transact business cannot but recall with palpable consternation at the cynicism and spite with which this nation and its nationals are regarded particularly in Europe and America.

Further, going by the campaign of calumny, the word Nigerian is regarded as synonymous with criminality in some parts of the world. The fact that Transparency International (TI) (2001) has placed Nigeria as one of the most corrupt countries in the world best describes the image problem in the light of their 'survey'. According to TI, they carried out an opinion poll with certain people believed to have been or are in a position to make comments on the issues identified in their research. Thus, the outcome of their findings is regarded as 'the collective opinions of the business and tourist community'. It should be noted that some respondents could have resorted to illegal activities for their business interests. For TI, fraud is an integral part of corruption. They acknowledge that corruption can be found in virtually all countries of the world. The agency's Corruption Perceptions Index 2001 ranked 91 countries. The 2001 Corruption Perceptions Index (CPI) is said to reflect the degree to which corruption is perceived to exist among public officials and politicians. The impact of 'corruption' analysis cannot be overemphasised. The Nigerian government's Special Adviser on Drugs and Financial Crimes (Mohammed, 1998) remarked that some countries have found some International Non-Governmental Organisations (NGOs) useful instruments of foreign policy. While acknowledging the constructive contributions of most of these organisations, the role of the NGO Transparency International (TI) in 'blackmail' was stressed. He also noted that the officials of TI have never visited Nigeria, thus, he notes that the criteria adopted in their assessment are questionable, unjustified and dishonest.

Nigeria is located in the western part of Africa, with a population of about 127 million. According to the 2001 worlds Population Data Sheet (*The Nigerian Guardian*, August 13, 2001), Nigeria is the 10th most populous country in the world. The 1996 population was estimated to be 115 million, with a GNP per capita of US$240. It is also one of the most ethnically diverse countries comprising of about 250 ethnic groups and over 200 languages. In general employment and unemployment figures are said to be erratic. According to the 1999 Commonwealth Yearbook, basic infrastructure is not adequate and where it exists is not properly maintained. As observed in the 1998/9 World Economic Factbook, Nigeria has other natural resources, but a substantial part of its income is from oil production. Nigeria gained its independence from Britain in October 1960 and the Federal Republic was proclaimed in 1963. The country survived a civil war between 1967 and 1970. Since independence, the country has experienced political and economic instability, with successive military dictatorships. From May 1999 to present, a democratically elected government has been governing the country.

In the course of its turbulent history, crime has been on the increase. Especially after the civil war (1967-1970), the spate of property and violent crimes increased. On the political side, corruption, mismanagement and nepotism were prevalent. These are some of the conditions that are capable of creating fraudulent activities, and advance fee fraud in particular. Certain dishonest individuals have decided to take advantage of the global business environment to carry out all sorts of fraud. In examining the historical background of advance fee fraud in particular, the Nigerian government's Special Adviser on Drugs and Financial Crimes (Mohammed, 1998) noted that before the introduction of stringent economic measures such as the Structural Adjustment and Deregulatory programmes in the 1980s, trust and confidence in business internationally and locally was common. In addition, the national currency was strong and stable compared to those of other countries. Liberalisation of the economy was a pre-condition for the successful implementation of the programmes. With privatisation and commercialisation government subsidies were withdrawn from certain essential services such as petroleum pump price and electricity. Unfortunately, these changes did not result in increased productivity since one of the consequences was the depreciation in the value of the national currency (the Naira) against other currencies. This created difficulties for citizens. The economic advantage of possessing foreign currencies within the country became evident. This probably led to the exploitation of would-be foreign investors by criminals who demanded advance fees for business and other commercial arrangements.

In a study of crime from the Nigerian perspective, Marenin and Reisig (1995) assessed the validity of the General Theory of Crime proposed by Gottfredson and Hirschi (1990). They argued that cultural variability is not important in the causation of crime and that we need to look for consistent causes of crime. Further, one theory of crime can adequately explain cross-cultural differences in crime rates. These include the concepts of pain, pleasure and self-interest calculations as important considerations for the offender. Also, individuals who commit crimes including frauds are characterised by low levels of individual restraint or self-control that ought to have been implanted during childhood or during the socialisation process of the individual. In addition, low levels of self-control alone do not explain crime. Opportunity and situational conditions (e.g. vulnerability of the victim) are significant factors. Thus, developed and developing countries have similar causal explanations for fraud and crime.

For Marenin and Reisig, in Nigeria crime is committed within specific contexts. Factors that are contributory to crime include the presence of a large and growing population, a small and declining per capita income, the development of glaring differences in wealth and lifestyles, which create possibilities for large-scale corruption. Others are political instability, ethnic distrust and uncertainty among the public about the future. Little trust in government, its leadership and with much of public and private life consumed by the struggle to 'survive' further compounds the problem. Property offences constitute about one-half of all reported crimes. The dependence on importation opens the doors for corruption and fraud: ranging from white-collar crimes carried out by Nigerians and foreigners (e.g. importation of second-hand and shoddy goods). Government contracts are very lucrative and performance standards are seldom enforced. Other economic crimes include the sale of foreign currencies in the black market and smuggling in and out of the country. Finally, Marenin and Reisig (1995), note that with regard to the occurrence of crime and fraud in particular, the key findings from Nigerian based research are threefold. First, Oloruntimehin (1992), explained trends in crime rates by citing the social dislocation and economic pressures brought on by political instability, uneven development, high unemployment, white-collar fraud and corruption, rapid migration to the cities with a consequent lack of amenities, and high degrees of anonymity in urban areas. Odekunle (1978, 1986), noted that the causes of crimes cannot be found in peculiarities of individual character or general normlessness, and that the (corrupt) norms are quite clear and enforced in favour of those in power. According to Adeyemi (1990), only an organised, deliberate and integrated (e.g. public and private sector input) effort to understand, and react to all the problems mentioned above will be able to prevent crime.

It has been adduced that the reasons for elite corruption and political-economic crimes in Nigeria are associated with individual traits such as greed, selfishness and lack of moral integrity. Other explanations or probable reasons given for crime in Nigeria include the attractiveness of quick financial gains. It has been noted that this occurs within general conditions of poverty, uncertainty, social and political instability; a pervasive belief that everyone else is doing it; and a capitalist economic system that values individualism, competition, acquisition, and wealth (Marenin and Reisig, 1995). In addition, in the absence of support from the state, the extended family system whereby the more successful and employed family members are culturally bound to take responsibility for the general well-being of their kin are also contributory. Similar views were noted by Abba et al. (1993), Achebe (1983), Adamolekun (1985), and Watts (1985). In addition, certain problems experienced in developing countries tend to have an impact on crime control. For instance, in Nigeria, police/public co-operation is poor. Public attitudes exhibited are that of distrust, misunderstanding, fear, and fear of arrest after police questioning. Police studies in Nigeria show that police officers living in barracks (an offshoot of the Colonial era) puts them in a particular class and reduces their social status. This obviously affects interaction and good relationship with the public (Clinard and Abbot, 1973).

Jones (1993) researched into the activities of Nigerian crime networks in the United States. While noting that it is difficult to assess the quantity of crime committed by Nigerians, he states that certain patterns seem to have emerged. He mentions Senator Roth's subcommittee report, which identified elements of the 'Nigerian' crime network. The most common element is the individual who learns how to commit fraud from another Nigerian, sometimes for a fee and puts the information into practice for a living. It was mentioned that in a Secret Service raid conducted in Atlanta, agents recovered what they named a 'Nigerian Handbook'. The document is said to be 'a well-crafted instruction guide explaining how to commit various types of fraud'. However, there was no confirmation that Nigerians prepared the document, but they claimed that it was distributed to Nigerians entering the country (Jones, 1993, p.63).

The easy flow of paper or stationery, the relative ease in obtaining credit, bank loans, insurance policies and so forth, the laxity on the part of institutions that administer these services and their profit making interests, all contribute to and facilitate these activities (Jones, 1993). With reference to the stained business image of Nigerians, Jones observes Imasa's (1991) remark that the Nigerian government should make it compulsory for her businesses to belong to a government-sanctioned organisation. To Jones (1993), the problem of Nigerian crime networks in the United States must be addressed at its source, Nigeria, through the enactment and implementation of relevant policies.

The Media and Crime Reports

Apart from reports about Nigeria's previous military dictatorships and in Nigeria's involvement in crime or advance fee fraud in particular, the objectivity of media reports and other publications are questionable. For instance, on the Internet certain websites are dedicated to *Nigerian crime.* A website, *Nigeria - The 419 Coalition Website* (2000) is devoted to this as their name implies. In this site, various pages contain advisory information on the scam. Samples of scam letters are also made available. In a nutshell, the coalition group claim that the Nigerian government officials are directly involved in advance fee fraud scams. The Nigerian government is also accused of doing little to address these problems, but would rather apportion blame to victims. On the other hand, Nigerian readers responding to this website blame the situation on greedy individuals who are ready to earn huge profits from illegitimate transactions.

Looking at the print media in the UK, certain articles have been written and responded to by Nigerians on the subject of 'Nigerian' crime. For instance, in a front-page article in The *Independent* newspaper (February 2, 1998) titled 'Nigerian crime poses serious threat in Britain', it was stated that criminals, mainly Nigerians have been discovered working inside government departments and that the National Crime Intelligence Service (NCIS) was of the view that the cost of their fraud amounted to £3.5 billion a year. The fraudsters were said to concentrate on con-tricks, benefit fraud, drug-trafficking mainly cocaine, and illegal immigration. In another UK newspaper, The *Observer* (September 13, 1998) one article was titled 'Nigerians fight "crook" image: They're pushers, charlatans and swindlers...aren't they?' Cal McCrystal debunked the stereotype. McCrystal noted that the image of Nigerians has never been worse. 'In Britain they are regularly depicted as swindlers, drug traffickers, impostors, quacks and charlatans'. In this article, Professor Muhammed Anwar of Warwick University's Centre for Research into Ethnic Relations is quoted to have said 'the Nigerian image thing has been created mainly through the media – that people from Nigeria are always doing something wrong. This process is getting worse'. According to McCrystal, among government agencies in London, the Nigerian profile is murky. For instance, he notes that an internal Customs and Excise memo stereotypes Nigerians as likely drug runners.

Nigeria is not the only country or community that has been labelled with a given type of criminal activity. Though exaggerations are commonplace, this is probably an outcome of the ethnic origins of the offenders. In turn, media reports are capable of creating stereotypes through emphasis on the offender's background. For instance, in the UK, in The *Independent* and *Guardian* newspapers (both of August 3, 2000), an article titled 'Organised crime costs UK £50bn in a year' discussed the impact of various crime groups. The newspaper information was culled from *The Threat from Serious and Organised Crime*, a National Criminal Intelligence Service (NCIS) report. In the NCIS (October 19, 2001) website, it can be observed that some crimes were strongly associated with certain nationalities probably based on the frequency of occurrence of the offence(s) in question. The *Independent* newspaper of August 3, 2000 summarised the NCIS report concerning the variety of nationalities-based gangs. It noted that the 'British Caucasian' criminal (represented as white working class) make up by far the majority of organised crime groups in the UK. Colombians and West Indians were more involved in drug crimes; the Turkish and the Former Soviet Union in money laundering, prostitution, excise fraud of cigarettes and vehicle smuggling. The Albanians and Chinese are noted for smuggling involving organised immigration crime, trafficking in women prostitutes, heroin and arms trafficking. West Africans mainly engage in fraud crimes, for example benefit, mortgage, credit card fraud, and cocaine smuggling via couriers. For South Asians, wholesale drug dealing particularly heroin, cocaine and cannabis; immigration smuggling; counterfeit clothing and credit card forgery; large-scale mortgage fraud and cloning of mobile telephones are common crimes. Finally, crimes involving the use of firearms were associated with British Caucasians and Motor Cycle Gangs (e.g. drugs, armed robbery, fraud and bootlegging, some of which involved families and associates).

The idea of labelling certain activities, as 'Nigerian crime' or crimes of other countries is an issue that needs to be examined closely. This is probably due to the tendency of looking for a scapegoat in explaining societal evils or simply associating countries with criminal activities of a few citizens. Obviously, the effects of generalisations are taken for granted. In the UK *Times* of January 10, 1997 a Detective Inspector David Crinnion of the Metropolitan Police Fraud Squad stated that in relation to non-existent money, scam letters could readily be translated as follows:

> Dear Sir or Madam, I am a thief who has stolen a lot of money from the Government and would like your help to get it out of Nigeria.

In a response to an article regarding letters from Lagos in the UK *Times* newspaper of August 20, 1999, Dele Ogun, a Nigerian lawyer based in London challenged the accuracy of the publication. He also notes that the article was misleading in the sense that it did not explain the origins of the scam industry. For Ogun, this practice can be traced back to the early 1980s when Nigeria was 'awash with oil boom money'. At this time crooked Nigerians, especially politicians, colluded with fraudulent western business contractors and inflated tender prices for government contracts. It became the practice for contractors to demand upfront fees or 'mobilisation fees' to cover initial costs of the project. Usually, the contracts were not executed and the advance fee retained or shared by the politician and his foreign partner. Ogun concludes that westerners became the victims of 'Nigerian' fraudsters when the economy collapsed.

Some Anti-crime Initiatives in Nigeria

The Nigerian government and citizens have consistently made efforts to address crime/fraud. For instance, the law referred to as the Advance Fee Fraud and Other Related Offences Decree No. 13 of 1995, which criminalised any attempt to obtain any benefit under false pretences was created to intensify this fight. In 1998, an international seminar was organised by the Nigerian-American Chamber of Commerce in conjunction with the Nigerian Police Force on Advance Fee Fraud and other financial crimes. The Governor of the Central Bank of Nigeria (CBN) (1998) highlighted that an International Financial Transactions Surveillance Office in the Foreign Operations Department of the CBN was established in 1997 to target advance fee fraud at the global level by routinely verifying and replying to enquiries relating to scam letters, telefax and so forth. The CBN also carries out extensive publicity campaigns through seminars, workshops and press statements. A Money Laundering Surveillance Unit was established in the Examination Department of the bank in 1994, which helps to implement guidelines in the Money Laundering Decree of 1995.

Furthermore, since 1990, the CBN has placed advisory advertisements in over eighty newspapers and magazines in twelve languages in thirty-six countries. The publications usually stress that the CBN and the Nigerian government cannot and should not be held responsible for bogus and shady deals transacted with criminal intentions, and that there are no contract payments trapped in the bank's vaults. Documents presented by the fraudsters are all forgeries, bogus and fraudulent (CBN, 1999). This is all in addition to co-operative efforts with investigative, financial and regulatory establishments in various countries. Other developments include the creation of a National Drug Law Enforcement Agency (NDLEA) in 1989, established with powers to address issues associated with drug trafficking and money laundering.

Recently, a preliminary report of advance fee fraud investigators led to the creation of a National Committee on Advance Fee Fraud (NCAFF) in 2001. NCAFF is expected to formulate an effective strategy against fraudsters locally and internationally. In other words, aims to work towards the prevention, investigation and prosecution of advance fee fraud cases. Setting up a comprehensive database for the storage and analysis of information concerning the offence(s) and offenders is also an objective. Its membership is drawn from related security (the police and security services) and associated agencies such as the justice departments, the central bank, postal services and Internet service providers. Also, in a similar development, the Central Bank of Nigeria issued fresh directives to check the activities of fraudsters such as the Customer Identification Procedure, aimed at ensuring that banks and financial institutions take stipulated steps with a view to knowing their customers in detail (*The Nigerian Guardian*, December 5 and 20, 2001).

Public Image and Crime

Some researches have addressed issues of public image and crime. Hills (1971) noted that in general, public perceptions and definitions of crime or what the crime problem is could affect the enactment and enforcement of criminal laws. He points out that the content of media reports conveying these feelings are not well researched. He notes that the media play an important role in shaping views. Television, radio, magazines and newspapers have become major public forums for information on crime events, sanctions and policies. Thus it is common for various interest groups to manoeuvre these communication outlets to mobilise political support for their conception of the crime problem. Methods in which this can be achieved include selective coverage, emphasis, omission, and mode of presentation.

It is also common to find highly dramatic, publicly visible and violent crimes receiving greater media coverage. Hills notes that in the United States certain studies showed that people's estimates of how much crime increase had occurred were related to the rise in newspaper coverage of crime news rather than with the actual rise in the amount of crime. For Hills, other visible non-violent crimes such as fraud, embezzlement and other forms of white-collar crime especially by corporate offenders represent far greater economic losses but are not generally pursued with great zeal by the media. A probable explanation would link this trend to factors such as social class, celebrity status, and control of the media.

Quinney (1974) looked at the public opinion-crime issue from an ideological perspective. He notes that in order to control crime and its perception by the public, the government applies criminal sanctions at times needed to convince the public that its own interests are being endangered. In every society, the official ideology accepted by the public stresses and rationalises the concerns and reactive policies of the ruling class in a given society. With this, the public is prevented from developing critiques and solutions that can threaten the existing order. Then public consciousness is avoided. Quinney states that with the appropriate public opinion, official policies can be instituted without the appearance of exploiting the public and serving the narrow interests of the ruling class. For Quinney, the media are not explicitly engaged in the transmission of an official ideology. This may not be the same for all countries. It is important for an understanding to exist between a government and the media although this does not have to be overtly expressed in addressing the crime problem. 'Inappropriate' crime stories are capable of creating 'crime panics' which will not be helpful to social and business life.

According to Edwards and Gill (2002) it is common in the literature to find that organised criminals are regarded as external threats to western economies as indicated in the National Crime Intelligence Service publications (NCIS, 1993, 1999). It is also common to find assertions made about the impact of these groups on national economies. For instance, three Chinese organisations are said to pose the most potent threat to global security (Myers, 1996). Voronin (1996) estimates that 40-50% of the Russian economy is controlled by organised crime. Thus, the notion of security from these perspectives is defined in opposition to external alien actors, cultures and organisations (Edwards and Gill, 2002). With regard to this viewpoint, Edwards and Gill (2002), Block (1991), Hobbs (1998) and Rawlinson (1998) have challenged this image and its consequent reduction of the complexity of organised crime to a crude conception of alien conspiracy. Further, 'from this perspective, organised crime is understood in one sense as a response to the demand in western societies for illicit services and, in another, as an indication of the limits encountered by nation-states in exercising sovereign authority over their domestic populations. The common theme here is that the source of organised crime is endogenous' (Edwards and Gill, 2002). An example of the interdependencies between legitimate and illegitimate entrepreneurs from Edwards and Gill's paper is that noted by Block (1991) who identified the services provided by criminal organisations to 'upperworld' businesses in dumping toxic waste. In another example observed by Ruggiero (1998, p.121) 'money laundering can be regarded as a service provided by the financial sector to conventional organised crime'.

In addition, the use of 'alien conspiracy' theories has been identified as excuses for the crime problem in general. Hobbs and Dunnighan (1999) noted that the persistence of 'alien conspiracy' theories has not been limited to academic debate. Threat assessments contrived by NCIS have concentrated upon a range of exotic criminal organisations (NCIS, 1993, 1997), and the identification of aliens as the principal organised crime threat to British society, is a device that conveniently excuses British society from taking responsibility for its own maladies. Identifying aliens as the principal organised crime threat to the state, however, constitutes rather than the mere scapegoating of minorities (1999, p.69). The NCIS reports reveal that new criminal markets exist alongside legitimate businesses. They also show that crime networks are locally constituted, and that it is possible to find similarities between local and international crimes in areas such as immigration, emigration, employment, and work in leisure cultures. It is important to add that Hobbs and Dunnighan (1999) rightly state that certain crime networks have some kind of international connection, and provide evidence of the impact of foreign cultures on indigenous markets, or new trading arrangements that do not ignore, but utilise national boundaries. For the criminal or fraudster, there are advantages of global activity such as avoiding prompt detection and prosecution. More so, it makes the computation of the extent of crime more difficult. At any rate, examples of known cases are indications that the economic impact is considerable in all areas with some connection to the activity.

Victims and Fraudsters

Victims and fraudsters are known to come from all walks of life. In the author's study of various fraudulent scams perpetrated between 1994 and 2001, particularly in the UK, the average age of offenders was shown to be about forty-three years (Osisiogu, 2001). As with other research, this is within the average age of fraudsters. Male offenders were higher in number (about 80%), and some fraudsters operated as couples. Very few female fraudsters operated independently. Given that the research was not a survey, findings cannot be generalised.

With regard to victimisation, studies on victims of fraud are few. In certain types of crime, according to Levi:

> It is an analytical truth that all victims bear some responsibility for their victimisation. In the case of long-form fraud, the degree of 'victim participation' is greater and more positive than it is in most types of property crime, because the victim parts with his property voluntarily to the offender (Levi, 1981, p.126).

For instance, in Canada, the National Task Force on telemarketing fraud called Project Phonebusters notes that victims of fraud could be individuals, groups, corporations or all the above independently or jointly. Project Phonebusters (1997) reported that between January and May 1997 over half (51%) of the victims of telemarketing scams that paid out money were over 60 years old and this age group represented 73% of those victimised for scams worth over $5,000 (Janhevich, 1998).

Currently, issues concerning the victim's plight receive a lot of attention especially from the media. According to Churchil (1997), in cases of advance fee frauds, victims normally do not report the fraud to the police. They would rather put aside the event as an experience. This is because the amount of money lost may be regarded as small or because they fear looking foolish for falling for the fraud. This situation is perfect for the fraudster, who is likely to repeat the scam. In Levi's (1985) study, it was revealed that large frauds typically involved more social interaction between victims and offenders and were mainly carried out by white-collar males. Family and (former) friends were the main culprits in cases of fraud on private individuals. Further, individuals who are not necessarily wealthy are more likely to be the victims of mail order and investment frauds (Levi, 1988). Businesses are the prime victims of credit and computer frauds. With regard to the number of offences, the most common frauds involve the use of plastic money. This is attributable to the 'cashless' methods of economic transactions today. Going by these developments, Levi states that the financial sector (banks, building societies, and insurance companies) accounts for a substantial part of the costs of fraud recorded by Fraud Squads.

In Osisiogu's (2001) research, most of the victims were the elderly. Interviews with investigating officers reveal that fraudsters target them because it is assumed that they have accumulated some savings over the years. Most are also retired and would probably pick up interest in 'new commercial' activities. In addition, unless the loss is extremely large, most elderly victims would rather forget the incident because of the anticipated stress and time involved in pursuing the matter. The total number of victims from a particular scam can be quite large and peculiar attributes depend on the type of scam or product involved. For instance, in scams involving emotional relationships, most of the victims are women who are either single or divorced and middle-aged or over. In some cases men have also been exploited. The fraudster manipulates the vulnerability of the victim's circumstances or situation. In charity scams all categories of victims are exploited, especially those within the older age brackets who have and are willing to make donations in cash or kind. Victims of investment frauds are generally naïve, and are quick to cash in on supposedly lucrative deals (Osisiogu, 2001). Further, in some cases, honest victims are exploited especially when the scam in question has been created in line with conventional practices or where the victim is familiar with the fraudster. The highest number of victims is usually associated with investment scams and frauds involving general goods and services. Unemployed people are mainly the targets of educational training scams. Those already in industry also fall prey to fake courses. In religious scams, the victims selected from all walks of life especially via the family, and are so immersed in the 'cult'. To sum up, it should be noted that victims of fraud involving the manipulation of trust come from all spheres of human endeavour, and are of different ages. With the Internet today, it is possible for children less than ten years old to fall prey. In some cases the very educated have been conned. This is so because trust is an important ingredient in social interaction and the fraudsters exploit this fact.

With regard to fraudsters, the usual offender within the commercial context or environment is privileged, of high status, well educated, male, and in a position of respect in society (Nightingale, 1996). For Janhevich (1998) fraud is not a homogeneous category of crime as it ranges from the simple to the complex. Exposed individuals will obviously carry out the more complicated frauds that also require reasonable investment. In other words, 'a typical offender' category will be difficult to substantiate. In Levi's (1985) study, most of the fraudsters were blue-collar, described as typical males and unemployed at the time of the offence, and in general, was without educational qualifications and likely to be unmarried. He was also likely to be a solo offender with very modest socio-economic status, who makes use of deception to obtain cash or goods from organisations such as banks, government agencies and employers. The blue-collar offenders were not likely to use their own business or profession as a tool of fraud. On the other hand, the white-collar male fraudster was typically older, employed at the time of the offence, educated to a reasonable standard, and married with children. The white-collar fraudster typically used his organisation as one of his tools in manipulating the fraud. Levi's research revealed that 'blue-collar frauds' were dealt with far more rapidly than other frauds especially those that involved private victims. This can be attributed to their relatively simple or less complicated nature and the ease in which victims identified them.

Walters (1995, 1999) addressed the problem/implications of advance fee fraud from the perspective of the legal profession – a respectable career exploited by certain individuals to perpetrate fraud. According to Walters (1995), advance fee fraud is becoming increasingly sophisticated and is still claiming victims who lose large sums of money, which are rarely recovered. He notes that the legal profession is affected in some of the following ways:

1. In the case of 'Nigerian' letter type frauds, solicitors targeted by fraudsters may be tempted to use their clients' money for the sham investment. This can be used to make any initial payment requested by the fraudsters to cover expenses such as airline tickets and hotel accommodation, or the solicitors may give details of the clients' bank account to the fraudsters. In this scenario, the solicitor may be oblivious of the actual intentions of the fraudster to permanently withhold deposits.
2. Solicitors can also be used as 'custodians'. Here, the investor is told that the 'refundable' fee will be held by a lawyer in an 'escrow' account (a separate account independent of the transaction in question) for safety

reasons. In this case, the solicitor is part of the scam, as he is the only one with access to the funds.

3. Solicitors help to write letters, with the aim of persuading the victim and authenticating the proposed transaction.
4. Solicitors are giving undertakings to third parties in relation to the holding and release of money in the likelihood of non-compliance with the terms of the agreement.
5. Solicitors may be actively looking for investors to introduce to supposed investment schemes.
6. Solicitors may themselves be the fraudsters, stealing advance fees from investors who have entrusted their savings with their 'consultant'.

Walters concludes that the solicitors involved may be fraudsters. They may deliberately or negligently ignore the risks of the transactions and are ignorant of the risks and warnings on such practices given by their Law Society and the press at large. He notes that there is no excuse for the current failings of the legal profession and those of its regulators. Such malpractice or frauds damages the reputation of the legal profession and other professions associated with the transactions and the financial world in which it operates in general (Walters, 1995, 1999). However, it is important to note that solicitors could also be victims. They could genuinely be misled to endorse a given transaction or attest to an individual's character based on the information accessible to them, thereby risking their client's funds. They could be directly affected if they invest privately in fraudulent schemes. Situations could also change as a result of unforeseen circumstances especially on the part of those running the 'business', which could embarrass the solicitor. Thus in some cases, solicitors are not immune to scams even when the appropriate precautionary steps are taken. In a nutshell, the legal profession could be used as a convenient avenue to collect deposits from victims. In our society, this is as a result of the level of trust and integrity associated with the profession and upheld by the majority of solicitors. Similar professions among others that have relatively high degrees of trust are the accounting/banking and medical professions. Damage can be done to any profession or occupation when their associated positions of trust and confidence are used or manipulated for deception or criminal fraud.

In support of the arguments above, Hoogenboom (2001) in his discussion on illegal financial services and the offshore industry notes that professional money laundering specialists sell high-quality services, contacts, experience and knowledge of money movements. These services are supported by the latest electronic technology, and made available to the trafficker or criminal willing to pay their lucrative fees. Furthermore, this practice makes enforcement more difficult, especially in cases where legitimate and illegitimate funds are deliberately combined from different sources. In the case of advance fee frauds, the criminal consultant diverts fees paid for certain services. Thus, it is possible for legitimate and illegitimate business transactions to fall prey to the crooked professional. In an analogy of financial crimes, Hoogenboom (2001) developed the concept 'market for illegal financial services'. In this market approach towards economic crime he notes that a distinction can be made between individuals or players in the supply, demand and product lines. On the supply side, the following groups or categories are involved: lawyers, accountants and other professional financial service providers; correspondent banking; offshore banking; private banking; insurance companies; onshore banking; fiscal advisors; and stockbrokers. He notes a prominent example of fraud by mainly accounting professionals – the Bank of Credit and Commerce International (BCCI) fraud where a bank supposedly worth $20 billion became worthless despite the involvement of auditors over the years.

As noted earlier, of relevance to the role of certain individuals or professionals is the nature of 'contract' and its facilitators or 'custodians'. According to Fukuyama (1995), rules and contracts have not eliminated the need for trust in all spheres of human endeavour. For example, professionals like doctors, lawyers, or university professors, having received the required training for accreditation and practice, are expected to use their judgement and initiative in practice. The nature of their judgement is too complex to have all the details spelt out in black and white. Thus, professionals are in the position to go about their business relatively unsupervised and as such, are generally more trusted than non-professionals. The concept of 'professional' is associated with integrity and good conduct. In this regard, it is possible for the professional to betray the trust placed on him or her. Unfortunately, all commercial activities are based on some financial risk either on the part of the seller or provider of a product, or on the service or the consumer.

Conclusion

The theories of rationality or rational choice (with a strong bias for economics/cost/benefit analysis of the offence *vis-à-vis* sanctions); culture (as it concerns the image of corruption in business especially in developing countries and the role of material possessions in personal status); and opportunity (as presented by the nature of trust and risks in human relations and commerce – the central elements required for advance fee fraud), all provide plausible explanations for criminal fraud.

To the extent that the majority of citizens are law abiding, the explanation for criminal activity is located within the individual and his 'rational'/economic responses to socio-economic, and probably political conditions. The prestige attached to material possessions globally is also a contributory factor. More so, the fact that many governments in developing countries have not been able to satisfy and meet the basic needs of their citizens may persuade some people to resort to crime/fraud thereby tarnishing the image of responsible citizens and their countries at large. It is the responsibility of a country to address its crime problems. In the final analysis, the cause of whatever social, economic and political problems lies within the polity. For instance, post-independence developing countries are in position to take and make good judgements on behalf of their citizens. Where the contrary is the case, then the policy makers and administrators are to blame for unpatriotic decisions especially as they concern developmental projects, investments and the provision of basic needs. The implications of crimes and financial crimes in particular are grave. Apart from reducing the level of confidence, trust and credibility internally and internationally, the continued activity could and has undermined respectability, social, political and economic development.

Researchers have suggested various strategies of dealing with or preventing fraud. These include theories of deterrence such as shaming, confiscation, imprisonment, prompt investigations and prosecutions. While private organisations can play an important role to ease the burden on government agencies, the state still determines the seriousness in which certain offences or fraud cases are regarded. The media can influence this decision, and at the same time put pressure on the bodies responsible for certain investigations. Publicity is capable of putting fraudsters out of business and the threat of publicity is known to have led to refunds to aggrieved customers. On the macro-economic level, there are multiplier effects of illegal economic activity concerning the creation of wealth and employment opportunities in 'licit' economies (Edwards and Gill, 1999). This condition is often ignored when computations are made about the cost or value of economic crime. Thus, for Edwards and Gill (2002) viewing crime as enterprise raises questions about the role of illicit entrepreneurs in boosting macroeconomic growth, and providing employment opportunities. This is so especially where enough legitimate opportunities do not exist and avenues for alleviating severe poverty are minimal, such as in developing countries including those in Eastern and Central Europe (Rawlinson, 1998). Therefore, the social as opposed to the narrow notion of emphasising aspects of criminal justice in the control of fraud and other economic crimes should be emphasised.

Frauds are not only common in periods of economic depression. In fact, during times of economic boom the criminals are successful in getting savings from prospective investors and spenders. Informants attributed crime to pure greed. This is contrary to certain beliefs that people who usually commit economic crimes are responding to disadvantageous and desperate needs. For instance it is not surprising to learn that most tax crimes are committed by the well-to-do, and shoplifting offenders for instance cut across all segments of society. Unlike the desire to meet one's basic needs, greed is by definition insatiable (Gabor, 1994). The author shares Gabor's (ibid.) view that fraudsters are known to acquire expensive clothes, luxury cars and to entertain themselves at choice holiday locations and hotels. The more a culture glorifies the unfettered accumulation of wealth and consumption, the more likely it is that people will be prepared to act criminally and unscrupulously, regardless of their employment opportunities and economic situation. In addition, wealth, after all, is a symbol of status and power.

The victim and the police will have to be determined to bring offenders to book, as the typical conman collects small sums from several or hundreds of victims expecting to reduce police and public interest in the scam. However, as long as fraudsters emulate the practices and psychology of legitimate enterprises, it is unlikely that the crime will be completely eliminated. The ideal approach to fraud is to minimise risk to victims (e.g. enlightenment programmes and information), and maximise risk to offenders (e.g. proactive policing – involving the private and public sectors, media coverage and warnings, leaflets of advice in bank statements etc., and stiffer sanctions especially with regard to victim compensation and the forfeiture of ill-gotten gains) (Osisiogu, 2001).

References

Abba, A. and Associates (1993), *The Nigerian Crisis: Causes and Solutions*, Academic Staff Union of Universities of Nigeria, Nigeria.

Achebe, C. (1983), *The Trouble with Nigeria*, Heinemann Educational Books, London.

Adamolekun, L. (1985), *The Fall of the Second Republic*, Nigeria: Spectrum Books Limited, Ibadan.

Adeyemi, A. (1990), 'Crime and Development in Africa: Case Study of Nigeria', in Zvekic, U. (ed.), *Essays on Crime and Development*, United Nations Interregional Crime and Justice Research Institute, Rome.

Block, A. (1991), 'Organized Crime, Garbage and Toxic Waste: An Overview', in Block, A. (ed.), *Perspectives on Organized Crime: Essays in Opposition*, Kluwer, Amsterdam.

Central Bank of Nigeria (1999), 'Press Statement on Advance Fee Fraud: Don't be fooled! Many have lost money, if it is too good to be true then it is not true', Downloaded on February 8, 2001 from http//www.nopa.net/Useful_Information/419/cbn.html.

Churchil, D. (1997), 'Money for Nothing', *Police Review*, vol. 105, pp.23-4.

Clinard, M.B. and Abbot, D.J. (1973), *Crime in Developing Countries: A Comparative Perspective*, John Wiley and Sons, London.

Edwards, A. and Gill, P. (1999), 'Coming to Terms with Transnational Organised Crime', paper presented to the inaugural meeting of the UK Economic and Social Research Council's Research Seminar Series on Policy Responses to Transnational organised Crime, University of Leicester, United Kingdom, 8th September 1999.

______ (2002), 'Crime as Enterprise? The Case of Transnational Organised Crime' *Crime, Law and Social Change*, 37/3: 203-223.

Fukuyama, F. (1995), *Trust: The Social Virtues and the Creation of Prosperity*, Penguin Books, London.

Gabor, T. (1994), *'Everybody Does It!' Crime by the Public*, University of Toronto Press, Toronto.

Gottfredson, M. and Hirschi, T. (1990). *A General Theory of Crime*, Stanford University Press, Stanford, CA.

Governor of the Central Bank of Nigeria (1998), 'The Efforts of the Central Bank of Nigeria (CBN) in the Fight Against Advance Fee Fraud', Paper presented at the Nigerian-American Chamber of Commerce International Seminar/Workshop on Advance Fee Fraud (419) and Other Financial Crimes, Lagos, Nigeria, March 25-26.

Hills, S.L. (1971), *Crime, Power, and Morality*, Chandler Publishing Company, London.

Hobbs, D. (1998), 'Debate: There is a Global Crime Problem', *International Journal of Risk, Security and Crime Prevention*, vol. 3, pp.133-7.

Hobbs, D. and Dunnighan, C. (1999), 'Serious Crime Networks: The Police Response to a Local Problem', in Carlen, P. and Morgan, R. (eds), *Crime Unlimited? Questions for the 21st Century*, Macmillan, London.

Hoogenboom, B. (2001), 'The Market for Ilegal Financial Services: The Offshore Industry', Draft Paper, Nyenrode University, The Netherlands, May.

Hotten, J.C. (1874), *The Slang Dictionary*, Chatto & Windus, London.

Ihode, M. (1998),'Advance Fee Fraud, a.k.a '419', and Other Financial Crimes, Searching for a Solution to the Problem', paper presented at the Nigerian-American Chamber of Commerce International Seminar/Workshop on Advance Fee Fraud (419) and Other Financial Crimes, Lagos, Nigeria, March 25-26.

Imasa, P. (1991). 'Business Fraud Surges', *The Nigerian Economist*, October 14, pp.9-10.

Janhevich, D.E. (1998), 'The Changing Nature of Fraud in Canada', *Juristat*, Catalogue no. 85-002-XPE, vol. 18, no. 4.

Jones, M. (1993), 'Nigerian Crime Networks in the United States', *International Journal of Offender Therapy and Comparative Criminology*, vol. 31, no. 1.

Knutson, M.C. (1996), The Remarkable Criminal Financial Career of Charles K. Ponzi "The 'Ponzi Scheme" and "Denouement and Epilogue", Downloaded on February 6, 2001 from http://www.mark-knutson.com/-Charles K. Ponzi Website.

Leigh, L.H. (1982), *The Control of Commercial Fraud*, Heinemann, London.

Levi, M. (1981), *The Phantom Capitalists: The Organisation and Control of Long-Firm Fraud*, Heinemann, London.

______(1985), *The Victims of Fraud*, (1st edn.), Economic and Social Research Council, Swindon.

______(1987), *Regulating Fraud: White-Collar Crime and the Criminal Process*, Tavistock Publications, London.

_______(1988), *The Prevention of Fraud*, Crime Prevention Unit, Paper 17, Home Office, London.

Marenin, O. and Reisig, M.D. (1995), 'A General Theory of Crime and Patterns of Crime in Nigeria: An Exploration of Methodological Assumption', *Journal of Criminal Justice*, vol. 23, pp.501-518.

Mohammed, A. (1998), 'Nature, Types and Manifestations of Financial Crimes in Nigeria', paper presented at the Nigerian-American Chamber of Commerce International Seminar/Workshop on Advance Fee Fraud (419) and Other Financial Crimes, Lagos, Nigeria, March 25-26.

Morton, J. (1992). 'The Spanish Prisoner Swindle', *Criminologist*, vol. 21, pp.112-15.

Myers, W.H. (1996), 'The Emerging Threat of Transnational Organised Crime from the East' *Crime, Law and Social Change*, vol. 24.

NCIS (National Criminal Intelligence Service) (1993), *An Outline Assessment of the Threat and Impact by Organised/Enterprise Crime Upon United Kingdom Interests*, NCIS, London.

_______(1997), *Annual Report*, Home Office, London.

_______(1999, Service Plan 1999-2000, NCIS, London.

_______(2000), *Annual Report 1999/2000*, NCIS Corporate Communications Branch, London, Downloaded on September 28, 2001 from http://www.ncis.gov.uk.

_______(2001), '£150 million annual loss across Britain feared as NCIS warns of surge in advance fee fraud letters', Press Release, July 10, Downloaded on September 30, 2001 from http://www.ncis.gov.uk/press/24_01.html.

Nigeria – The 419 Coalition Website (2000), 'We Fight the Nigerian Scam', Downloaded on April 19, 2000 from http://home.rica.net/alpae/419coal.

Nightingale, B. L. (1996), *The Law on Fraud and Related Offences*, Carswel, Toronto.

Odekunle, F. (1978), 'Capitalist Economy and the Crime Problem in Nigeria', *Contemporary Crises*, vol. 2, pp.83-96.

______(1986), 'The Legal Order, Crime and Crime Control in Nigeria: Demystification of False Appearances', *Nigerian Journal of Policy and Strategy*, vol. 1, pp.78-100.

Oloruntimehin, O. (1992), 'Crime and Control in Nigeria', in Heiland, H., Shelley, L. and Katoh, H. (eds), *Crime and Control in Comparative Perspective*, Walter de Gruyter, New York.

Osimiri, U. (1997), 'Nigeria: An Appraisal of Advance Fee Fraud Legislation', *Journal of Financial Crime*, vol. 4, p.271.

Osisiogu, U.C. (2001), *Criminal Fraud: An Investigation into the Manipulation of Trust and Deception*, Ph.D. Thesis, University of Hull, United Kingdom.

Page, F. (1997), 'What is Fraud ?', *New Law Journal*, vol. 147, pp.321-2.

Project Phonebusters (1997), *A National Task Force Combating Telemarketing Fraud*, Ontario Provincial Police, Ontario.

Quinney, R. (1974), *Critique of Legal Order: Crime Control in Capitalist Society*, Little, Brown and Company, Boston.

Radzinowicz, L. (Sir) and Hood, R.G. (1986), *A History of English Criminal Law and its Administration from 1750*, vol. 5, Stevens and Sons, London.

Rawlinson, P. (1998), 'Mafia, Media and Myth: Representations of Russian Organised Crime', *The Howard Journal*, vol. 37, pp.346-58.

Rider, B.A.K. (1990), 'Organised Economic Crime', Eight International Symposium on Economic Crime, Jesus College, Cambridge.

Ruggiero, V. (1998), 'Transnational Criminal activities: The Provision of Services in Dirty Economies', *International Journal of Risk, Security and Crime Prevention*, vol. 3, pp.121-9.

Schur, E.M. (1958), 'Sociological Analysis of Confidence Swindling', *The Journal of Criminal Law, Criminology and Police Science*, vol. 48, pp.296-304.

Sharpe, J.A. (1984), *Crime in Early Modern England 1550-1750*, Longman, London.

The Nigerian Guardian Newspaper (2001), Downloaded on August 13, December 5 and 20, 2001 from http://www.ngrguardiannews.com.

Transparency International (TI) (2001), Downloaded on July 13, 2001 from http://www.gwdg.de/~uwvw/icr.html.

Vallance, A. (1955), *Very Private Enterprise: An Anatomy of Fraud and High Finance*, Thames and Hudson, London.

Voronin, Y.A. (1996), 'The Emerging Criminal State: Economic and Political Aspects of Organised Crime in Russia', *Transnational Organised Crime*, vol. 2, pp.53-62.

Walters, A. (1995), *A Practical Guide to Identifying Advance Fee and Prime Bank Instrument Fraud*, Sweet and Maxwell, London.

______ (1999), 'The UK, The Advance Fee Fraudster's Paradise', *Advance Fee Fraud*, Accessed on February 15, 1999 on, http://www.demon.co.uk/walker-martineau /Article%20%20Advance%20fee%20 fraud.html.

Watts, M. (1985), 'Visions of Excess: African Development in an Age of Market Idolatory', *Transition*, vol. 51, pp.124-41.

West, H. (1988), *Fraud: The Growth Industry*, Kogan Page in association with The British Institute of Management, London.

6 Transnational Crimes: The Case of Advanced Fee Fraud in Nigeria

IHEKWOABA D. ONWUDIWE

Introduction

This chapter provides a criminological perspective on advanced fee fraud (419) in the Nigerian context. While it condemns 419 in Nigeria, this analysis reveals that economic swindling is not unique to Nigeria. The chapter also scrutinizes the nature of 419, investigates the cruelty of the criminality of advanced fee fraud as a form of economic fraud, articulates the reasons behind 419, and reviews its detrimental effects on Nigerians and gullible victims of the international community. Although few studies have peripherally examined 419, this study offers a theoretical explanation of this form of fraud. Specifically, it employs Robert Merton's anomie theory to argue that like their American and European counterparts, some Nigerians have unfulfilled material needs which predispose them to criminality.

The global society today experiences some aspects or elements of transnational crimes. Currently, advanced fee fraud, which has been part of history, is endemic in Nigeria. Not only has this form of fraud ruined Nigeria's image, it has also devastated the economic well-being of gullible foreigners who have been duped by greedy Nigerian fraudsters. The author will also advance the unpopular view that these gullible foreigners were also greedy to have engaged in such dubious financial ventures. While we empathize with the innocent foreigners, this paper illustrates also that this form of fraud is not limited to Nigerian fraudsters.

Not much has been written about this crime and its impact on society. However, Ebbe, in his *The Political Criminal Nexus: The Case of Nigeria* (1999) examines 419 as a scam carried out in collusion with Nigerian politicians and con artists, and aimed at defrauding the Nigerian government and foreign nationals. The Nigerian brand of 419 includes 'a variant of the Nigerian advanced fee scheme and has been used to defraud anyone in the world who is willing to succumb to the temptation offered to make some quick money' (Smith et al., 1999, p.1).

Nigerian 419 can be defined as an advanced fee fraud recognized under section 419 of the Nigerian Penal Code, which addresses fraud schemes. The felony involves a perpetrator impersonating a government official writing a letter, which offers a 'greedy' victim the opportunity to make millions of dollars from the illegal transfer or deposit of Nigerian funds abroad which the Nigerian government allegedly overpaid on a contract. The scheme relies on the willingness of victims who possess the predisposition to violate the law by responding to such illegal offers and by providing business and personal information such as letterheads and bank account numbers for the completion of the contract. Victims of such schemes are also pressured to wire money for some unforeseen taxes, fees to the Nigerian government, attorney fees, and bribery fees supposedly to be paid to officials for a swift deal. In reality, the victims will lose their money because the funds are not available in Nigeria for illegal transfer (Smith et al., 1999; de Beer, 2002; US Secret Service, 2002; US Department of State, 2002; Nigerian 419 Coalition, 2002). The US Secret Service (2002) estimated that at least $5 billion (US dollars) have been lost to the fraudsters in the last 12 years. Below we review the methodology employed in this study and examine 419 or advanced fee fraud and how it actually works.

Methodology

In this study, the methodology used relies on content analysis of Nigerian newspapers and magazines, and internet resources. Content analysis is a scientific tool utilized to gather and analyze the content of text. The text consists of written words, meanings, and symbols that serve as a medium for communication (Neuman, 2000). Ebbe (1999) used content analysis in examining organized crime in Nigeria. Others have used this qualitative approach in investigating national anthems (Cerulo, 1989) or exploring public speeches (Seider, 1974). Content analysis is useful when a subject is to be studied from a long distance and for the examination of historical documents (Neuman, 2000).

Data were collected from Naijanet.Com, which is a Nigerian internet news website. It disseminates information on Nigeria and makes it possible for anyone to read Nigerian magazines and newspaper articles. Naijanet.Com publishes news from *This Day*, *Newswatch*, *The Guardian* and many other news outlets. Naijanet.Com also maintains an archive of historical and contemporary documents about Nigeria. It has data on 419 that includes old and new developments on advanced fee fraud. In addition, data was also collected from the Nigerian 419 Coalition website. The 419 Coalition maintains an archive of news on 419 since 1996. It also has stored samples of the letters written by 419 syndicates. The 419 coalition has specific information on advanced fee fraud in various countries. Moreover, it maintains a linkage to other websites dealing with the issue of 419 that the researcher found very useful.

Although the author had been collecting information since 1993 about 419, in this study he relies on the archives of Naijanet.Com, the Nigerian 419 coalition, the US Department of State websites, other countries and particularly the information and advertisements of the Nigerian government and the Central Bank of Nigeria (CBN). Finally, this study focuses mostly on the Nigerian Criminal Code, which defines the crime of 419 and the abundant literature on corruption in Nigeria.

Definition and Characteristics of Advanced Fee Fraud (AFF) or 419

Due to the numerous letters Nigerian fraudsters send abroad soliciting business partners, many nations have awakened to the task and presently warn their citizens about 419. Their websites begin by explaining 419 as an advanced fee fraud outlined in Section 419 of the Nigerian Criminal Code. The scheme is designed and operated by a fraudster, along with an organized gang, with the intent of obtaining money, by deception, from individuals and corporations (419 Coalition 2001). This paper provides the complete definition and provision of this fraud as prescribed in the Nigerian Criminal Code Act. Section 419 of the Code refers to it as the AFF. Indeed, AFF is a kind of confidence game (fraud by deception) perpetrated by greedy Nigerians against gullible and equally ravenous foreigners with the intent to make quick and gigantic sums of money. 419 is a hoax. A hoax is an act intended to deceive, trick, or dupe an individual based on fraud or fabrication. 'Most hoaxes work because somebody somewhere is ready and willing to believe the less than believable' (MacNee, 1995, p.xi). Chapter 38 of the Nigerian Criminal Code Act deals with obtaining property by false pretenses and cheating. Section 418 of the Code specifically defines what constitutes a false pretense. It reads as follows:

> Any representation made by words, writing, or conduct, of a matter of fact, either past or present, which representation is false in fact, which the person making it knows to be false or does not believe to be true, is a false pretense (Nigerian Criminal Code Act 1990, p.165).

While Section 418 provides the definition of obtaining items by false pretense, governments who warn their people about this brand of fraud have alluded to only section 419. This may be because Section 419 refers to the individual obtaining goods by a false pretense and the sanctions imposed by Nigerian law. According to Section 419 of the Criminal Code Act:

> Any person who by any false pretence, and with intent to defraud obtains from any other person anything capable of being stolen, or induces any other person to deliver to any person anything capable of being stolen, is guilty of a felony, and is liable to imprisonment for three years. If the thing is of the value of one thousand naira or upwards, he is liable to imprisonment for seven years. It is immaterial that the thing is obtained or its delivery is induced through the medium of a contract induced by the false pretense (1990, p.165).

This section of the Nigerian law is explicit about the illegality of 419 and for any Nigerian to engage in theft of money through bogus contracts and empty promises of millions of dollars to be gained by naive partners. It is hard to argue that there is a criminal nexus between the 419 loose union of organized syndicates and legitimate government employees. Although history demonstrates that in every nation there are dubious people who are prone to criminal behaviour, the Nigerian law is unambiguous about fraud. Advanced fee fraud constitutes a felonious act punishable by possible incarceration. Therefore, any government official in collusion with 419 syndicates is participating at his or her own peril. Such a greedy employee is not representing the government of Nigeria but rather, his or her own egocentric economic interests.

In addition to 419, the global society, including the United States, Australia, England, and South Africa, is also going after Nigerian heroin and cocaine traffickers (Hammer et al., 1991). These countries also target other financial crimes such as insurance fraud, credit card fraud, and money laundering, Nigerian counterfeiting and false documents, trafficking in persons, including alien smuggling and prostitution, and Nigerian corruption (Ebbe, 1999). Efforts against these crimes require the cooperation of the Nigerian government, foreign governments, businesses, victims, and the Nigerian people (Winer, 1996). While all these brands of fraud deserve some adequate space in this present work, the hoax that eats at the fabric of the Nigerian polity today is Advanced Fee Fraud.

Its characteristics involves tricking potential victims into parting with their money by convincing them that they will receive more benefits in return if they send tax levies on the frozen amounts they will collect. This particular type of dupery has been used in Australia in the 1840s (Smith et al. 1999) and in the United States in the 1930s (Klein 1956). In the Australian case, Mr. Monies, a rich and powerful man parted with funds to one Mr. Mick Bell noted as 'one of the most cool, impudent vagabonds in Sydney', to carry out his financial deals. Mr. Bell was to sponsor the transportation and shipment of a 'mythical 20,000 pounds worth of items'. Mr. Monies financed the business proposition and later realized that Mr. Bell was a fraud and reported the deal to the Sydney police. Bell was convicted and sentenced to two months imprisonment (Smith et al., 1999; Hall, 1993).

The US case involves a supreme fraudster, Oscar Merill Hartzell, who once resided in Madison County, Iowa. Hartzell swindled seventy thousand Americans for at least $2 million and was incarcerated for his fraud 'over the screaming protest of all seventy thousand suckers' (Klein, 1956). His fraud resembles the Nigerian 419 in that Hartzell demanded secrecy from his victims. The scheme was based on letter writing to Iowa residents from England claiming that he has made an extraordinary discovery. He insisted that he had proof that Sir Francis Drake (a deceased wealthy man at that time) had an illegitimate son who was put in prison to avoid scandal. According to Hartzell, the true heir to this son, whom he, Hartzell can only reveal, was entitled to $22,000,000,000. As in the Nigerian 419, Hartzell insisted that the problem was to raise the money to fight England to release this money to the proper Iowa heirs. He solicited $500 contributions from people in Iowa who are related to Mr. Drake because when the money is finally released in England, it can only go to those with blood relations to Drake or those that answer the Drake name. The ruse worked, and some people even lost their homes in the process (Klein, 1956).

In Nigeria, the 419 ruse takes on different characteristics. The scam usually entails the fraudsters initiating contact, either by mail, telephone, or now, by email with a company or an individual suspected of having considerable amounts of money. A Nigerian 419 syndicate forwards a business proposal in the form of a typed or hand-written letter. The syndicate claims to be representing an important governmental official. In the letter, the fraudster claims to have access to large sums of money, usually millions of American dollars. The letter promptly informs the potential victim of the immediate need to disburse the over-budgeted amount to an overseas bank account. This urgency requires that the company or individuals release a bank account where the con-artist will wire the money. As one of the letters included in this work demonstrates, some of the fraudsters have not benefited from their Nigerian education. However, their letters appeal to the gluttonous part of the targeted victims' brain (419 Coalition, 2001; US Department of Justice, 2001).

The potential victim is told in the letter that as a commission for providing a bank account, he or she will receive at least 25% to 30% of the money that will be transferred to the foreign account. Victims are also warned that in order to maintain a high level of secrecy, they must allow for smooth transactions of the ruses. However, this is not the end of the scheme. The prospective foreign partners are also required to provide documents such as signed blank company letterheads, blank invoices, telephone and fax numbers, and bank account details. These documents are essential in enabling fraudsters to transfer money into intended victims' accounts. Fraudsters realize that anyone credulous enough to accept such a ruse may be unwilling to report the matter to the police for fear of being accused of criminal activity. This is perhaps why 419 has been successful for many years (however, there are some instances in which victims become wise to the hoaxes and report them to the appropriate authorities). The progress and achievement of 419 syndicates are predicated upon the gluttony of victims' illegal complicity. In short, offenders are able to engage repeatedly in the fraud because the police are frequently unable to secure credible witnesses due to victims' involvement and ignominy.

As the author writes this paper, a new form of 419 has emerged. Oyedoyin (2002) writes about how 'suspected conmen lure Nigerians abroad with $31m deal'. It appears that the publicity mounted by the 419 coalition and international governments, as well as by strict law enforcement efforts of the Nigerian government, are yielding dividends. Foreign companies and individuals are being educated about 419, thereby making it difficult for the syndicates to continue acquiring their ill-gotten wealth. This new form of 419 is about fraudsters seeking to establish business relationships with Nigerians in London. They promise to transfer about $31 million into the bank accounts of their intended victims. This time, the late Abacha (Nigerian former Head of State) is blamed because the fraudsters claim that prior to his sudden demise, he over-budgeted money for different projects. This money is trapped in the Nigerian Central Bank and there is an urgent need to free the funds and transfer them into foreign accounts. The fraudsters go as far as providing the revenue sharing formula between them, the government officials involved, and their European-Nigerian victims. In this particular case, the intended victims are Nigerians living abroad, not Europeans, which has been the case in the past when most victims had been foreigners.

Another troubling type of 419 consists of a group of Nigerian expatriates who are believed to be maintaining operational cells in the United States, Europe, and Asia. Because Nigerian law enforcement activities are difficult to evade, some Nigerian 419 syndicates and fraudsters from other nations have moved their illegal practices to different countries. Since offenders and victims are now located in every corner of the world, Smith et al. (1999) argue that it may not be accurate to refer to the advanced fee fraud as the Nigerian advanced fee fraud. Expatriate Nigerians are intermediary con-artists who work in conjunction with 419 fraudsters in Nigeria and who sometimes masquerade as representatives of the Central Bank of Nigeria or as agents of the government. Usually, Nigerian 419 syndicates appear, on the surface, to be authentic organizations, making it unlikely that victims will doubt their legitimacy. Nigerian 419 artists have the necessary resources to provide the appropriate environment (e.g., executive offices) and people (e.g. government or CBN officials) for any transaction that requires convincing victims about their legitimacy. They go to great lengths to persuade victims to accept the validity of their ventures, even if it means borrowing symbolic offices to accomplish an intended fraud. Although Nigerians face the danger of both macro- and micro-aggressions (racial profiling tactics such as selective enforcement of the law) in South Africa, they are not the only groups that partake in 419 activities. South Africa has its own home-grown 419 scam artists. The South African Police Department has summarized the method used to secure money from the victims:

1. Asking the victim to deposit money into a specific bank account to help cover expenses for completing the deal, which may include paying bribes to other parties in Nigeria.
2. Once the original fee has been paid, 'complications' may arise which necessitate the payment of other fees.
3. Organizing a meeting in Nigeria and once the victim is in Nigeria, his passport is confiscated and he is detained until sufficient payment is received.
4. Using the bank details and official letterheads to transfer money out of the victim's bank account and into an account under the control of the criminals.
5. Once the money is lost, an "official" may contact the victim on the pretext of helping the victim retrieve the lost money that, in turn, also cost money (de Beer, 2002).

It is a recurring dupery that saps the resources of the victim until it runs out. 419 fraudsters lack moral conscience and indeed have no remorse in their dealings with foreign victims. What historical facts may have impacted on this phenomenon? Have Nigerians always been engaged in 419, or are there certain changes in Nigerian political and economic epochs that will explain this heinous dupery?

Historical Background

To understand Nigeria and 419, it is crucial to have knowledge of the historical factors in terms of the political and economic situations that have shaped the nation. Nigeria is the paragon of Africa (Onwudiwe, 2000) and the most populous black nation in the world, with over 125 million people (World Almanac and Book of Facts, 2000). Today, the Nigerian federation consists of 36 states and is governed from the capital city, Abuja, by President Olusegun Obasanjo. Nigeria is made up of many ethnic groups with different dialects and languages (Ebbe, 1999). Lagos, aptly referred to as the largest city in Africa, is the commercial center of the country.

Peter Ekeh (2001) suggests that forty years after the demise of colonialism, Nigeria's legacies still dominate the lives and administrative affairs of the nation in very destructive fashions. It was colonialism that ushered in military rule in Nigeria. Together, British imperialist governance and native military rule have created innumerable and unmanageable political problems for Nigeria. Ekeh notes that colonialism created intellectual barriers between the natives and their traditional past. Imperialism, he argues, distorted traditional systems of governance while it magnified its presence and offered its own methods of supremacy.

Britain took control of Lagos in 1861 following the abolition of the slave trade and gradually extended its dominance to other parts of Nigeria until 1900. Ebbe (1999) demonstrated that colonial administration lasted from 1849-1960, while direct management of Nigeria by Britain lasted from 1900-1960. Nigeria regained her independence from imperialist Britain on October 1, 1960 and became a republic on October 1, 1963 (World Almanac and Book of Facts, 2000). Since Nigeria regained control of its sovereignty from Britain in 1960, it has been ruled by a series of tyrannical military leaders, intermingled with short spans of rule by civilian governments. The recently deceased leader, General Sani Abacha, assumed the status of Head of State in 1993 after declaring democratic elections invalid that year. Mr. Moshood Abiola, who was projected to win the 1993 presidential election, was arrested and imprisoned for treason when he claimed, rightfully so, to be the legitimate president of the country in 1994. Both men died mysteriously of a heart attack in 1998 (Naijanet.Com, 2001).

The death of Abacha terminated the reign of a brutal oppressor. Immediately after his death, General Abdulsalam Abubakar promised and delivered a new democratic election on February 27, 1999. Olusegun Obasanjo, a former military ruler, won the presidential race and became the first civilian president in fifteen years. He took the Oath of Office on May 30, 1999. President Obasanjo promised to eradicate Nigeria of the corruption that had characterized previous military authoritarian regimes and which had crippled the governance of the country for twenty-nine years of the thirty-eight years of self-rule since Nigeria gained its independence (Naijanet.Com, 2001).

Because of the military rulers' greed and insatiable desire for wealth, the economic condition of Nigeria was rendered dormant and useless with utter impunity. More than any other military looter, General Sani Abacha was responsible for emptying the country's treasury. Abacha stole billions of dollars and expropriated the funds overseas. After his death, Abacha's family gave back $750 million to the Nigerian authorities (Naijanet.Com 2001). The Reuters news Agency reported on January 28, 2002 that Switzerland would give Nigeria the bank records that will help Nigeria recover money that had been stashed abroad by the late Abacha and his cronies (Naijanet.Com, 2001). Nigeria has also requested that Britain, Germany and the United States help in the investigations. While the Geneva investigators have already resulted in the freezing of about $535 million related to the Abacha case, Nigeria claims that the late dictator and associates stole more than $2.2 billion between 1993 and 1998 (Naijanet.Com, 2001). The corruption the country has witnessed throughout its history due to despotic leadership is beyond reproach and is the precursor to 419.

Corruption and Despotic Leadership

Corruption in Nigeria can be linked to Nigeria's colonial legacy. The slave trade was a corrupt, immoral, and illegal enterprise executed by greedy Europeans who milked the human and natural resources of the country. Contrary to some pseudo-assumptions surrounding the termination of slavery, Ekeh (1998) points out that the slave trade was not abolished to benefit Africans. It was indeed terminated in the 19th century for the welfare of Europeans themselves in order to secure raw materials for its industrial production. Europe no longer needed the slave trade that had helped develop its mercantile capitalism. That is because by the 19th century the growth of industrial capitalism was no longer dependent on slave labor. Suffice it to say that African leaders battled firmly to end slavery through various means such as rebellion, theological communications as was the case with Bishop Ajayi Crowther, the Haitian revolution, and the contributions made by black people in the American civil war. Colonialism succeeded the slave trade in Africa in the last decades of the 19th century purely to maintain European economic interests, not to secure individual African freedoms. Corrupt Europeans taught their trade to the comprador bourgeoisie that took over power after the flight of euro-hegemony (Rodney, 1982; Fanon, 1968; Onwudiwe, 2001).

It is a well-documented fact in the literature today that Europe drastically underdeveloped Africa and that both colonialism and neo-colonialism are still destroying the continent, including Nigeria (Rodney, 1982). Most African economies are still twisted in part by their past experiences as European colonies. Corruption was easy to ascertain since under the system of colonialism, Nigeria exported its raw materials to Europe where the raw materials were changed into manufactured products. Some of the items were then returned to the colony for sale, and the profits were expropriated back to the metropolis. The same cyclical nature of unbalanced trade relationship existed in other African countries. Latin American dependentistas (Frank 1969, Cardoso, 1977; dos Santos, 1970) have written voluminously about it. This symbiotic relationship has been dubbed neocolonialism that has continued the process of colonial exploitation (Palmberg, 1983).

In fact, Wallerstein (1979) demonstrated that the capitalist system of economic production started in Europe in the 16th century and led to the huge capital accumulation and the transfer of surplus from the poor nations to the rich countries. The reorganization of production structures involved the development of both cash crops and of mining operations for export in the world market (Ake, 1978). It is this reorganization of political and production structures that created new nations and new classes of oppressors as well as new classes of the oppressed. Colonial authorities, through classic divide and rule policies (as in the case of Nigeria), deliberately miked the economies of the colonies (Wallerstein, 1979). It is within this framework and against this economic realism and the consequential global inequality that the poor economic conditions for peripheral countries have been sustained.

The argument is made that after independence native colonial leaders later adopted the specific method of accumulation utilized by colonial countries for economic repatriation. As noted below, through various dubious means, these leaders expropriated billions of Nigerian dollars overseas. Their European counterparts, whose accounts were used to transfer the money, also profited from the pillage. Today's 419 trick is successful because greedy foreigners had already amassed wealth through their transactions with despotic and corrupt Nigerian leaders. What other explanation could account for a victims' willingness to send money to unknown people in another country if such deals had not been profitable in the past? The obvious explanation is greed. Indeed, 419, despite massive campaigns in Europe and America designed to inform the public about the trick, continues to grow because of the predilections of foreigners to acquire illegal wealth and the determination of fraudsters to dupe their naïve victims. The desire of the fraudsters and their victims cannot escape the parameters of colonial legacy.

It was the residual effect of colonial corruption that simply corrupted the Africans, which in my view has engendered 419. This will be made clear by first providing a definition of corruption. In an excellent article, *Corruption in Nigeria: Historical Perspectives*, Osoba (1996) suggests that corruption is a global phenomenon and must be treated in particular reference to a country's social context. Osoba defines corruption as 'anti-social behavior conferring improper benefits contrary to legal and moral norms, and which undermines the authorities' capacity to secure the welfare of all citizens' (1996, p.1).

Corruption occurs because of a person's willingness to subvert rules in order to achieve material success. Osoba (1996) claims that corruption has become a way of life in Nigeria and as the principal means for private accumulation of property during the era of decolonization. It has shaped political and economic activities in Nigeria in the absence of other legitimate opportunity structures after independence. All subsequent regimes in Nigeria, both civilian and military have been inundated by corruption. The culture of corruption has been maintained and sustained by the proliferation of the oil boom in which revenues have led to a deepening crisis of kleptocracy (Osoba, 1996). Currently, crude oil sales in Nigeria account for more than 90% of export earnings and around 75% of government revenue (Osoba, 1996). When world oil revenue declined in the mid-1980s, the wealth of the country experienced a devastating nose dive (Osoba, 1996). Coupled with the endemic evidence of elite corruption, the economy was in a state of tatters, and Nigerians began devising innovative methods of survival. Fraudulent schemes, including 419, became a way of life (Robinson, 1999, Smith, 2000).

The phenomenon of 419 emerged because of the exploitation of the masses. A few politically well-placed individuals acquired wealth with utter impunity at the expense of ordinary Nigerians. Therefore, there is a direct link between 419 and official corruption in the Nigerian context. Although Osoba's analysis was correct, he is not the only Nigerian scholar that has alerted the country to the devastating consequence of corruption.

In his *The Trouble with Nigeria*, Chinua Achebe (1983) cautioned his readers that the problem with Nigeria stems from the dilemma of leadership. He states that the corruption in Nigeria will demolish the country because it has reached a critical threshold of calamity. He asserts that Nigerians are corrupt because the system in Nigeria supports and abets the fertile grounds for corruption to thrive. As Ebbe (1999:5) aptly asks, 'when the Head of State leads the way in corruption and malfeasance, who will control the law breakers?' In short, when those at the top are corrupt, those at the bottom are also bound to be corrupt. Advanced Fee Fraud did not occur in a vacuum. It is part of the environmentally corrupt atmosphere that has clouded Nigeria since colonialism. The pursuit of the 'national cake' (referred to as 'pork' in American politics), is seen by ethnic groups and politicians as the reason for joining politics. Rather than bringing projects and infrastructures to a politician's constituency's welfare, as is the case in the United States, the ruling class cabal in Nigeria has demonstrated to those at the bottom that being honest and honorable does not pay (Osoba, 1996; Ebbe, 1999).

Osoba (1996) demonstrated this in several ways, and Achebe pointed out that Nigeria is perhaps one of the most corrupt nations in the world. An indication of just how corrupt Nigeria is has been documented in the Corruption Perception Index published by Transparency International, a German firm, on September 22, 1998. On a scale of 1 to 10, with 10 representing the highest level of perceived corruption, Nigeria scored 1.9 (Transparency International, 1998; Mukherjee, 1997). Nigeria also topped the list of most corrupt nations with which to conduct business, followed by Bolivia, Colombia, Russia and Pakistan (Mukherjere, 1997). This is not astonishing. Osoba (1996) illustrates that during the Pious Okigbo's Panel of Inquiry into the Central Bank's Accounts in the regime of General Babangida, about $12.4 billion of Nigeria's oil revenue from the CBN account was unaccounted for. He also notes that the first Obasanjo regime could not properly account for about $5 billion supposedly owed by the three branches of government to domestic and foreign contractors. Nigeria was infected by 'squandermania.' However, Osoba insists that no country is immune from the disease of corruption:

1. Corruption was not invented by, nor is it peculiar to Nigerians. On the contrary, it is a global phenomenon with deep historical roots, although it manifested itself with significant similarities and differences in different societies, depending on the peculiar systems of power distribution and the legal and moral norms operating therein.
2. Corruption, like all social phenomenon, is intelligible only in its total social context: its peculiar form, dynamics and degree of social and cultural acceptability or tolerance being critically related to the dominant mode of capital accumulation; income, wealth and poverty distribution; power configuration; and the underpinning moral and ethical values operating in a given society.
3. Corruption in Nigeria is a kind of social virus which is a hybrid of traits of fraudulent anti-social behavior derived from British colonial rule and those derived from, and nurtured in the indigenous Nigerian context (Osoba, 1996, p.2372).

Scholars have recognized that the Nigerian economy has been ruined and squandered by the despotic and brutal leadership that still owes its allegiance to colonial masters. Michael Mann (1993), in his work *The Sources of Social Power*, illustrates a difference between despotic and infrastructural power. While despotic power refers to the oppressive capacities of the state, infrastructural power relies on the state's knack for infiltrating society in order to execute its policies. Employing Mann's disjunction between despotic and infrastructural power, Lukas (1998) examines the relations between the military and the Nigerian civilian elites in Nigeria from 1985 to1993. His study demonstrates that weak and peripheral states are more likely to experience a conflict between despotic and infrastructural power than are strong and core societies. Nigeria is an excellent example of how the military has utilized methods of despotic tactics to maintain control over the political class. Between 1985 and 1993, Nigeria witnessed a ban on politicians (Lukas, 1998), imposition of a corrupt two party system (Osoba, 1996), death of a powerful and intellectual journalist (Ebbe, 1999), the demise of a civil rights advocate (Ebbe, 1999; Amnesty International, 2001), and an annulment of elections that threatened the hegemony of military power (Smith, 1999; Osaghae and Onwudiwe, 2001). Lukas states that although the military was able to silence and imprison some politicians, it was unsuccessful in restructuring in ways that would sustain its own power. Because of the persistent use of despotic strategies to govern, which actually led to the decline of the Nigerian state, Nigeria went through serious hardships (Lukas, 1998).

As Mann (1993) suggests, despotic power is power over society. The Buhari regime, which lasted from 1984 to 1985 (replaced by the Babangida regime), is frequently cited as one of the egregious forms of despotic rule. Under Buhari's reign of terror, the press was censored, civil society institutions were silenced, and outspoken fearless politicians were imprisoned incommunicado (Lukas, 1998). Buhari's style of governance isolated his regime from the rest of the society, making it easy for Babangida's successful coup in August 1985. Although he started by including the political class in his regime, Babangida's administration cannot escape the despotic label, for it was under his watch that Dele Giwa, a newspaper editor, was killed by a letter bomb. It is widely believed in Nigerian circles that the letter bomb was sent by the military (Ebbe, 1999, Osoba, 1996; Smith, 1999; Lukas, 1998). Like Buhari's regime that preceded him, the military under Babangida also silenced politicians, censored the press, oppressed the university traditions, and repressed labor unions, other professional associations and human rights organizations. Babangida was able to last by running a corrupt political patronage system composed of military and civilian millionaires. Joseph (1987a) introduced the term 'prebendal logic' to describe the collusion of the political class and the Babangida administration in that the civilian politicians and the military alike were in politics for the personal enrichment of themselves and their political supporters (Ebbe, 1999). Lukas (1998) asserts that prebendalism in Nigeria is responsible for the massive corruption that has characterized the Nigerian polity, resulting in the appropriation of the Nigerian treasury for personal gains. Under Babaganda, everyone who had the opportunity crudely embezzled the national cake. In short, the prebendal attitude rendered some of the politicians powerless because they relied on selling out or being bought off by the military regime. In Nigeria, to be 'settled' denotes being bribed, a situation that indeed discredited many old and new breeds of politicians (Lukas, 1998).

While efforts are being made by the Nigerian government to fight 419 and to disseminate information across the globe to warn victims of the crime, it is not enough to eliminate the crime altogether. There is massive unemployment in Nigeria, which precludes college graduates from striving for their economic and social well-being. At the same time, billions of dollars in Nigerian oil wealth are been siphoned abroad by greedy Nigerian leaders, who do not invest their equally ill-gotten wealth in the Nigerian economy. In a capitalist society such as Nigeria, where welfare, food stamps, and other government assistance to the poor are hardly available, individuals are compelled to engage in lawbreaking activities in order to subsist. It is contended here that poverty, unemployment, and alienation in Nigeria prepare breeding grounds for criminal activities such as 419. A theoretical explanation of 419 in the Nigerian context is presented below.

Theoretical Explanations

In *Crime and the American Dream*, Messner and Rosenfeld (1997) argue that the Michael Milken's story is an excellent illustration of the contradictions of crime in the United States. Milken illegally earned about $550 million annually in 'junk bonds' and was ordered by the court to reimburse over $1billion in fines and restitution. While Milken swindled individuals for more than a decade, he has since become a consultant, counseling corporate leaders who adore him as a financial guru. He also teaches a business course at the University of California at Los Angeles (UCLA). Messner and Rosenfeld (1997, p.2) assert that Milken's financial and con skills exemplify:

> ...elements of social character rooted in broad value orientations within American culture that help shape both the archetypal American hero and the archetypal American villain.

The savings and loan (S&L) debacle in the US in the 1980s also illustrates how cultural practices can lead to massive financial losses. Charles Keating of Lincoln Savings and Loan was known to have forged documents, shredded documents, and manufactured fraudulent papers in order to deceive government supervisors. Together, the whole of the Savings and Loans scam caused the American taxpayers over $500 billion (Pontell and Rosoff, 2000).

In the US, these types of crimes have generally been explained by employing the strain theory of Robert Merton. The author believes that this theory is also appropriate for an analysis of the 419 debacle that has engulfed Nigeria today. Agozino (2002) states that Merton (1938) grasped his concept of anomie from Durkheim's perspectives and applied it to the American society. Robert Merton's (1938, 1979) strain theory articulates how 'some social structures exert a definite pressure upon certain persons in society to engage in non-conformist rather than conformist conduct'. In this case, there is a disjuncture or a split between societal goals and the acceptable means for achieving those goals. Merton explains that it is this disjuncture that creates a condition called anomie. According to Lynch et al. (2000), people in any given society pursue success and material goals set forth by their own culture. In the US for example, the pursuit of financial success is the overall goal for the majority of the people (Adorno, 1991; Messner and Rosenfeld, 1994; Michalowski, 1985; Herbert, 1962, Agozino, 2002; Zelnick, 1996; Kendal, 1996; Agnew, 1999; Arkers, 2000).

However, Agozino (2002) explains that Merton implied in his work that the members of the lower-class are more likely to choose innovative means in order to achieve the culturally valued goals in the face of unequal opportunities. Agozino's observation is applicable to the situation of 419 in Nigeria since power corrupts and absolute power corrupts absolutely. Although it has been argued that despotic and authoritarian leaders in Nigeria have ruined the economy by expropriating Nigerian wealth abroad, 419 in contemporary Nigeria is the function of individuals inundated by massive elite corruption. Some of the 419 gurus have college and university education but the majority has not received college training. It is not uncommon in the Nigerian 419 environment to witness university graduates working for a 419 *oga* (head/principal con-artist) without a college education. Nigerians, like their American counterparts, experience strain in order to acquire material success. Nigeria is a highly materialistic society, and the culture emphasizes success in terms of wealth and property but not everyone has equal access to the Nigerian dream.

Relative deprivation occurs in industrialized and non-industrialized societies where the lower-class, young males, or ethnic minorities are unemployed and feel discriminated against economically (Shelley, 1981). These conditions can also exist in developing societies where new metropolitan residents seek to acquire material possessions that were never made available to them before (Shelley, 1981). For example, after independence, most African leaders distended their pockets with African money, leading to unnecessary affluence. Those who have the least in such societies may be angry because the society's distribution of wealth is unjust. Therefore, relative deprivation combines economic inequality with feelings of resentment and injustice among those groups who have the least in such a society. Such feelings of resentment, characterized by inequality, unemployment, power and corruption may lead to illegitimate means of acquiring wealth such as 419 by the guilty 419 syndicates in Nigeria and their guilty foreign partners.

It is not perplexing at all to acknowledge the existence of 419 in a materialistic culture where a few individuals are controlling the wealth of the country. The members of 419 syndicates with or without college education are bright and innovative. The pressure to achieve something in Nigeria, coupled with the opportunity created by 419, induces individuals to engage in lawbreaking activities. The Nigerian culture, *inter alia*, emphasizes financial success. Although the culture also emphasizes legitimate means of achieving cultural goals, in the face of corruption by the military and civilian leaders, it is doubtful that a case would be made about equal emphasis being placed on the means to achieve legitimate goals. This view may not be trendy, but it is predicated upon the reality of the looting atmosphere that has characterized Nigerian leadership during and after colonialism.

A corollary position taken in this present work rests on the premise that 419 syndicates may have been the work of wealthy Nigerians who had first-hand knowledge of how despotic leaders exported Nigerian wealth abroad. It is argued here that these leaders tried to get rich, also, by conning their European counterparts into remitting large sums of money to Nigeria before they could receive their illicit funds. The European allies may have complied since, perhaps, many Europeans have become rich due to prior illegitimate transactions with Nigerian leaders (i.e., rogues with legitimate access to the Nigerian wealth). This ferocious cycle may have trickled down to dissident unemployed individuals who, without mercy, exploited their European 'mugus' (easily deceived people). It is not feasible at all to believe that 419 came out of nowhere in Nigeria. Further studies will illustrate that there must have been a collusion between greedy Nigerians in power (similar to

Ebbe's analysis) and equally greedy Europeans who have succeeded in stealing Nigerian money.

The crime known as 419 came to the attention of the world only after innocent Europeans, Americans, and people from other countries became victims of the fraud. One wonders how Abacha and other government officials managed to have billions of dollars overseas. Furthermore, foreign governments and their financial headquarters hoarded illicit Nigerian funds without regard to the massive suffering of the Nigerian people. They are illegal because the transactions were conducted despite heavy opposition from the masses. Sound financial advice would have been the total rejection of banking services and the warehousing of this money in Nigerian banks. Then, the interests alone from that money could have been used to create job opportunities for Nigerians. It seems that innocent people are paying for the ravenous conditions caused by other nations' duplicity. But when 419 crosses over to involve the illegal receipt of money from foreigners and to escalate the killing of innocent people, it behooves rational thinkers, not only to condemn it, but also to try and offer strategies that will ameliorate this ruse as well as criticize any assumptions that can explain the behavior.

Assessing Robert Merton and Anomie

Robert Merton's anomie theory and its application to crime and the American dream do not claim that his analysis could account for all brands of criminal behavior. Rather, in his 1938 essay, *Social Structure and Anomie*, which examines how culture focuses on the individual and how social structure places emphasis on society, Merton attributes crime to a lack of articulation within and between the underlying parts of social organization. Merton assumes that crime and deviance result from the malintegration of rudiments of culture and from an identical lack of fit between culture and social structure (Akers, 2000; Vold et al., 2002; Lynch et al., 1986; Messner and Rosenfeld, 1997). According to Merton, a greater emphasis on goals relative to means leads to even stronger strains on individuals who engage in acceptable modes of behavior, which includes legal parameters in the pursuit of culturally defined success. Also, social organization produces crime by unequally distributing opportunities to attain success goals in society. In a class system, some individuals or groups have primary advantages over others in satisfying their appetites. Merton argues that the pressure to attain success is most acute for members of the lower-class because they face more barriers to the legitimate means of achieving the acceptable goals that are common to most people (Vold et al., 2002).

Before examining the criticisms leveled against Mertonian liberalism, we must reemphasize that, alone, neither cultural conformity nor structural deprivation constitutes sufficient cause for crime in Merton's explanation. As Merton indicates, anomie theory, although not just a simple economic deprivation perspective, maintains that culture conditions the impact of the social structure on crime. This is true in both the United States and Nigeria, which, in fact, possess similar conditions (a culture of greed, unequal access to means, an educated class, a poor class, unequal distribution of wealth and ethnic marginalization, etc.) as its American counterpart. However, researchers have tested anomie theory and have concluded, generally, that it is not a theory of individuals' criminal motivation but rather, as aforementioned, a theory of social organization, which cannot be falsified by a micro-level of analysis (Messner, 1988; Bernard, 1987; Burton and Cullen, 1992; Bernard and Snipes, 1995). Kornhauser (1978), in an extensive criticism of strain theories, dismisses the utility of Merton's analysis. While urging criminologists to abdicate both the theoretical and empirical grounds of anomie theory, she concludes that the theory's assertion that a split occurs between aspirations and achievements, and which, in turn, causes crime and delinquency, lacks empirical and theoretical support. In 1984, Bernard rejected the validity of Kornhauser's claims, while Cloward and Ohlin asserted that delinquents do not possess high aspirations but are, instead, more interested in immediate gratifications, such as owning fast cars. In a related research endeavor, Farnsworth and Lieber (1989) noted that when compared in financial terms, the disjuncture between aspirations and expectations can be associated with delinquency. In his reinterpretation of the strain theories of Merton, Cohen, and Cloward and Ohlin, Cullen (1984) agreed with Kornhauser that at the micro-level of analysis, individuals in situations of social structural strain would experience frustration, which would push them in the direction of lawbreaking. Cullen also suggests that in Merton's societal level of analysis, criminals are not described as pressured or frustrated.

The most conspicuous restriction of Merton's work is that it relies exclusively on inequality (as one aspect of social structure), but at the same it also relies on access to the legitimate means of success without equally explaining how the institutional structure of society plays a role in producing the anomic strains that are amenable to crime (Messner and Rosenfeld, 1997; Agozino, 2002). Messner and Rosenfeld (1997, p.54) have organized the common criticisms of Merton's theory as follows:

1. Merton assumes that value consensus exists in society and that the goal of monetary success is supreme. In fact, other goals are equally important, if not more important, for many Americans, and no single value pattern dominates American culture.
2. Merton's formulation of the crime problem is class biased. His explanation cannot explain the crimes of the rich and powerful. Moreover, the high frequency of such crimes constitutes empirical disconfirmation of the theory.
3. Merton fails to draw out the radical policy implications of his argument; he erroneously implies that liberal social reform (that is, providing greater equality of opportunity) offers a realistic solution to the crime problem in the United States.
4. Finally, Merton does not provide a precise definition of anomie. Alternatively, the conception of anomie that is discernible in his theory

differs significantly from, and is inferior to, Durkheim's original formulation.

Messner and Rosenfeld suggest that criticisms one (1) and two (2) above are based, generally, on the oversimplification of Merton's work. On the other hand, they found merits in the last two criticisms by suggesting that Merton and his followers failed to realize the radical policy implications of the strain theories and that we cannot be able to reduce crime in America by expanding opportunities to the disadvantaged members of society.

Whatever the limitations of Merton's theoretical formulation, anomie theory recognizes the enduring problems that characterize not only American society but Nigerian society as well. Both liberals and conservatives alike view economic growth, competition, and greater equality of opportunity as strategic solutions to crime. Nigeria, for example, is constrained by a lack of economic growth and the problem of ethnic marginalization, which, in turn, stifles competition in all areas of its national economy. The crime of 419 may be a white-collar crime, but it is also seen as a menacing phenomenon, both at the societal level and the street level. Originally, 419 was a crime involving the most privileged class who, as was explained earlier, colluded with foreign nationals at the government (macro) level of analysis in order to expropriate Nigerian wealth abroad. The reality is that the underclass, faced with abject poverty, inequality and massive unemployment emulated the illegal tactics of the corrupt upper-class in Nigerian society by also engaging in innovative means to acquire wealth and material success. Although illegal, the system of innovation labeled 419 was deemed to be reasonable for the pursuit of material success. We also recognize the fact that the 419 ruse and the potential gains that come from it is not easily available to the poor masses. For example, poor school teachers and market traders who abandoned teaching and trading in favor of 419 do not have the means to engage in this scam. They must first serve a 419 *oga* (head/principal con-artist) with the hope of raising the funds needed to fully participate in the trick. On the other hand, the rich are well placed in society, and enjoy opportunity structures, which enable them to make millions of dollars in their 419 ventures.

Conclusion

The efforts of the civilian Nigerian government to stamp out 419 must be applauded and encouraged by the international community affected by the trick. While Nigeria has passed draconic statutes with severe sanctions against 419 syndicates, the ruse will certainly persist if the government does not tackle economic and social ills. It is poignant to conclude in this piece that 419 will go on in Nigeria until such times as the people will be able to succeed, or at least achieve the minimum financial success necessary to care for their families. Crime occurs in every society.

Durkheim (1895) understood this reality a long time ago. There will always be people in Nigeria, regardless of their economic situations, who will still exhibit the proclivity towards criminality. The United States, with all its social amenities for the poor, has not solved the problem of crime. Recently, the Enron energy corporation failed because of the greed of the individuals operating the company. Enron is an energy corporation that operates one of the America's largest gas transmission systems. Headquartered in Texas, its subsidiaries provide gas supply management services to North American consumers and other countries, such as India and Nigeria. Innocent Americans lost their life savings and retirement funds. Credit card fraud, Medicaid fraud, insurance and other tricks are in fact part of the American society. Suffice it to say that crime is not unique to Nigeria.

The problem of 419 is that it cuts across international boundaries to harm innocent people who believe that the proposals sent to them in the mail from Nigeria are authentic. Some people will question this assumption because some 419 syndicates make it explicit that their proposals are, indeed, illegal. In other words, the money in question is unused money that they want to dispatch abroad, illegally. Blame must be apportioned to both the Nigerian scoundrel and the foreign villain equally, because these are rational beings planning to illegally swindle money from the government. Whatever may be the case, 419 has ruined foreign lives and must be condemned. To do that, the Nigerian government must improve the quality of life of the people by providing adequate education, creating jobs, decentralizing governmental functions to enable local areas fill positions such as law enforcement vacancies and mounting an honest effort against poverty and disease. The international community must do their part by educating their citizens about 419 as well as by reducing debt payments against countries such as Nigeria.

References

Achebe, C. (1983), *The Trouble with Nigeria*, Fourth Dimension Publishers, Enugu.

Adorno, T. (1991), *The Culture Industry*, Routledge, London.

Advanced fee Fraud and Other Related Offences Degree, No. 13 of 1995, http://www.house.gov/markey/nigpr.htm.

Agnew, R. (1992), 'Foundation for a General Strain Theory of Crime and Delinquency', *Criminology*, vol. 33, pp.47-88.

Agozino, B. (2002), 'African Women and the Decolonisation of Victimization: Dazzling Crime Figures', *Critical Sociology*, vol. 28, Issue 1-2, pp.123-145.

Ake, C. (1978), *Revolutionary Pressures in Africa*, Zed Press, London.

Arkers, R.L. (2000), Criminological Theories: Introduction, Evaluation, and Application, Roxbury, Los Angeles.

Bernard, T.J. (1984), 'Control Criticisms of Strain Theories: An Assessment of Theoretical and Empirical Adequacy', *Journal of Research in Crime and Delinquency*, vol. 21, no. 4, pp.353-72.

Bernard, T.J. and Snipes, J.B. (1995), 'Theoretical Integration in Criminology', in Tonry, M. (ed.), *Crime and Justice*, University of Chicago Press, Chicago.

Box, S. (1987), *Recession, Crime and Punishment*, Barnes and Nobles, New Jersey.

Burton, V.S. and Cullen, F.T. (1992), 'The Empirical Status of Strain Theory', *Journal of Crime and Justice*, vol. 15, pp.1-30.

Business America (1999), 'Doing Business in Nigeria: Distinguishing Between the Profitable and the Questionable', November, vol. 116, Issue 11, pp.26-27.

Cardoso, F.H. (1977), 'Consumption of Dependency Theory in the United States', *Latin American Research Review*, vol. 12, pp.7-24.

Cerulo, K.A. (1989), 'Sociopolitical Control and the Structure of National Symbols: An Empirical Analysis of Anthems', *Social Forces*, vol. 68, pp.76-99.

Cloward, R. and Ohlin, L.E. (1960), *Delinquency and Opportunity: A Theory of Delinquent Gangs*, Free Press, New York.

Cohen, A.K. (1955), *Delinquent Boys: The Culture of the Gang*, Illinois, Free Press.

Criminal Code Act (1990), CAP 77: Laws of the Federation of Nigeria.

Cullen, F.T. (1983), *Rethinking crime and Deviance Theory: The Emergence of a Structuring Tradition*, New Jersey, Rowman and Allanheld.

de Beer, T. (2002), *Commercial Crime Investigations: Head Office*, http://www.sarnet.co.za/comcrime.

Dos Santos, T. (1970), 'The Structure of Dependence: Papers and Proceedings', *American Economic Review*, vol. 60, pp.231-236.

Durkheim, E. (1895), *The Rules of Sociological Method*, Free Press, New York.

Ebbe, O.N. I. (1999), 'The Political-Criminal Nexus: The Nigerian Case', *Trends in Organized Crime*, Spring, pp.29-59.

Ekeh, P. (2001), 'Nigerian Political History and the Foundation of Nigerian Federation', in Osaghae, E. and Onwudiwe, E. (eds), *The Management of the National Question*, PEFS, Ibadan.

Fanon, F. (1968), *The Wretched of the Earth*, Grove Press, New York.

Farnsworth, M. and Lieber, M.J. (1983), 'Strain Theory Revisited: Economic Goals, Educational Means, and Delinquency', *American Sociological Review*, vol. 54, pp.263-74.

Frank, A.G. (1969), *Underdevelopment or Revolution?*, Monthly Review Press, New York.

Hall, R. (1993), 'Sydney's Original Sins', *Good Weekend*, 20 November, pp.72-5.

Hammer, J., Bartholet J. and Mckelvey, P. (1991), 'The Nigerian Connection: The Newest Link in the Growing Heroin Trade', *Newsweek*, vol. 118, Issue 15, p.43.

Herbert, I. (1996), 'The Coca-Cola Company', in Ohmann R., Averill, G. and Curtin, M., Shumway, D. and Traub, E.G. (eds), *Making and Selling Culture*, Wesleyan University Press, Hanover.

Kendal, D. (1996), 'Warner Brothers Television', in Ohmann, R., Averill, G., Curtin, M., Shumway, D. and Traub, E.G. (eds), *Making and Selling Culture*, Wesleyan University Press, Hanover.

Klein, A. (1956), *Grand Deception: The World's Most Spectacular and Successful Hoaxes, Impostures, Ruses, and Frauds*, Faber and Faber, London.

Kornhauser, R.R. (1978), *Social Sources of Delinquency*, University of Chicago Press, Chicago.

Lukas, J. (1998), 'The Tension Between Despotic and Infrastructural Power: The Military and the Political Class in Nigeria, 1985-1993', *Studies in Comparative International Development*, Fall, vol. 33, Issue 3, pp.90-114.

Lynch, M.J. and Groves, W.B. (1986), *A Primer in Radical Criminology*, Harrow and Heston, New York.

MacNee, S. (1995), *Hoaxes: Dupes, Dodges and Other Dastardly Deceptions*, Visible Inc, Detroit.

Mann, M. (1993), *The Sources of Social Power*, Cambridge University Press, New York.

Merton, R.K. ([1938]1979), 'Social Structure and Anomie', in Jacoby, J. (ed.), *Classics in Criminology*, Oak Parks, Moore.

Messner, S.T. (1988), 'Merton's Social Structure and Anomie: The Road Not Taken', *Deviant Behavior*, vol. 9, pp.33-53.

Messner, S.F. and Rosenfeld, R. (1997), *Crime and the American Dream*, Wadsworth, Belmont.

Michalowski, R. (1985), *Law, Order and Power*, Random House, New York.

Mukherjere, S. (1997), 'Survey on Corruption Points Finger at Nigeria', *Denver Business Journal*, vol. 49, no. 2, pp.36-39.

Neuman, W. L. (2000), *Social Research Methods: Qualitative and Quantitative Approaches*, Allyn and Bacon, Boston.

Nigerian Criminal Code Act (1990), Lagos, *Nigeria.*

Nigerian-419 Coalition (2001), News on Nigerian Scam/419 Operations.

Okenwa, L. (2002), '45,000 Nigerians Trafficked to Europe–Minister', *This Day*, February.

Onwudiwe, I.D. (2000), 'Decentralization of the Nigerian Police Force', *The International Journal of African Studies*, vol. 2, pp.95-114.

Osaghae, E.E. and Onwudiwe, E. (eds) (2001), *The Management of the Nigerian Question*, PEFS, Ibadan.

Osimiri, U. (1997), 'Appraisal of Nigerian Advanced Fee Fraud Legislation 1995', *Journal of Financial Crime*, vol. 4, pp.271-277.

Osoba, S. (1996), 'Corruption in Nigeria: Historical Perspective', *Review of African Political Economy*, vol. 23, pp.371-387.

Oyedoyin, T. (2002), 'Suspected Conmen Lure Nigerians Abroad with $31m Deal', *The Guardian*, Wednesday, January 23.

Palmberg, Mai. (1996), *The Struggle for Africa*, Zed Books, London.

Pontell, H.N., Rosoff, S.M. and Lam, J. (2001), 'The Role of Fraud in the Japanese Financial Crisis: A Comparative Study', in Pontell, H.N. and Schichor, D. (eds), *Contemporary Issues in Crime and Criminal Justice: Essays in Honor of Gilbert Geis*, Prentice Hall, New Jersey.

Robinson, S. (1999), 'Hands up for Democracy', *Time*, 15 March, Issue 1, pp.36-38.

Rodney, W. (1982), *How Europe Underdeveloped Africa*, Howard University Press, Washington, D.C.

Seider, M.S. (1974), 'American Big Business Ideology: A Content Analysis of Executive Speeches', *American Sociological Review*, vol. 39, pp.802-815.

Shelley, L.1. (1985), 'American Crime: An International Anomaly?', *Comparative Social Research*, vol. 8, pp.81-96.

Shumway, D. and Traub, E.G. (eds) (1996), *Making and Selling Culture*, Wesleyan University Press, Hanover.

Smith, R.G., Holmes, M.N. and Kaufmann, P. (1999), 'Nigerian Advanced Fee Fraud', *Trends and Issues in Crime and Criminal Justice Issues: Australian Institute of Criminology*, vol. 121, pp.1-6.

Transparency International (1998), 'Corruption Perception Index', *TI Newsletter*, December: 2.

United States Department of State Bureau of International Narcotics and Law Enforcement Affairs (2002), *Tips for Business Travellers to Nigeria*, United States Department of State Bureau of International Narcotics and Law Enforcement Affairs, USA.

Vold, G.B., Bernard T.J. and Snipes, J.B. (2001), *Theoretical Criminology*. Oxford University Press, Oxford.

Wallerstein, L. (1979a), *The Capitalist World Economy*, Cambridge University Press, London.

Winer, J. (1996), 'Statement Before the Subcommittee on Africa of the House International Relations Committee', Congressional Hearings, September 11, Washington D.C.

World Almanac and Book of Facts (2000), *Nations of the World: Nigeria*.

Zelnick, S. (1996), 'Twentieth Century Fox', in Ohmann, R., Averill, G., Curtin M., Shumway, D. and Traub, E.G. (eds), *Making and Selling Culture*, Wesleyan University Press, Hanover.

Internet Websites

The Guardian Online-http://www.ngrguardiannews.com, December 20, 2001

http://memory.loc.gov/cgi-bin/uery/r?frd/cstdy:@field (DOCID+ng0167

http://www.expdisc.com/cbn.htm

http://www.superhighway.is/iis/access.html

http://home.rica.net/alphae/419coal/

http://www.house.gov/markey/nigpr.htm

http://www.naijanet.com

http://www.ustreas.gov/usss/financial_crimes.shtml#Financial

http://www.usdoj.gov

http://home.rica.net/alphae/419coal/Extortionsamples.htm

7 Women Faced with Violence: A View on Skin Colour in Brazil

ALICE ITANI and WAGNER VOLPE

Introduction

This chapter should contribute to the debate on violence involving women in medium-sized Brazilian cities. On the basis of evidence that women were considered an agent of violence in the 1990s and in great urban centers, an attempt was made by the authors to verify if this was the case in the 1980s and in medium-sized Brazilian cities. This chapter is based on a study of women who died as a result of factors not related to illness, in Rio Claro from 1980 to 1991. In analyzing those cases, four questions were posed: What do women die of? When do women kill? Are there similarities between women and men's violent behaviours? What distinguishes black women's involvement with violence from those of their white counterpart?

The authors observed an increase in rates of women's presence in homicide, suicide and car crash. Furthermore, men and women differ in their behaviour when faced with violent situations involving death. Men's involvement in homicide often occurs in public places such as bars, usually under the influence of alcohol, and through the use firearms at home events. In contrast, women's involvement in homicide is likely to take place in domestic locations where domestic utensils are used as weapons. Unlike men, women involved in homicide are likely to be sober. It was interesting to observe that contrary to popular perceptions, black women, even when experiencing adverse labour conditions, are not significantly involved in situations of violence.

Women are among the highest homicide risk group, alongside children and teenagers. Studies on violence have been based on figures from large cities and metropolis while only few are from medium-sized cities. Popular notions regarding such violence have included the view that violence in great cities and metropolis is more frequent than in medium-sized cities, and that the black population is more frequently involved in violence than the white population.

Through the authors' study of violence-related death cases in Rio Claro, this chapter hopes to contribute to the debate on violence involving women in medium-sized cities. Rio Claro, a city of 130,000 inhabitants, lies in São Paulo's northeast region, which was essentially dependent on slavery in the 19th century (Dean, 1976). The period of focus, 1980 to 1991, refers to two demographic censuses performed by the Brazilian Foundation Institute for Geography and Statistics (*Fundação Instituto Brasileiro de Geografia e Estatística* (FIBGE)). The study shows a change in the main characteristics of female deaths as well as alterations in women's behaviour in situations of physical violence. Having observed an increase in female mortality caused by violent deaths, the study analyzed the data in order to identify the social characteristics of these women. Given that the Brazilian population is composed of 51% female and 49% male, and that the black population represents almost half of it, *a view on skin colour* embarks on identifying distinct attitudes both in terms of gender (i.e. men and women) and color (i.e. black and white). We consider black as all Afro-Brazilians and all their mixed birth descendants. We also consider age groups and labour activities in order to locate the role of violence on women's lives. Since women are significantly leaving home to enter the labour market, this transition seems to have a great impact on family behavioural patterns. However, it should be noted that violence towards women occurs at many levels, ranging from experiences of violence at home to unequal conditions in the labour market and in their rights as citizens. In addition to that, the Brazilian government gives very low priority to family welfare, especially to women as housewives and mothers taking care of their children. Before analyzing data on women in an urban violence context, we will point out some aspects of women's lives to enable readers to define their presence in the Brazilian society.

Women in the Process of Change

As women have had a significant presence in the labour market since the 1960s, their departure from home has had a great impact on the patterns of family life, as evidence in other countries has shown (Lasch, 1977). This transition from being a housewife to participation in the labour market may have helped them see a possibility of survival, whereas in the past their only other alternative was marriage. However, if a professional career has become 'allegedly' an aspect of choice, one must also examine the data to trace where women are in the labour market, in terms of age group and color as well as their work activities in order to unveil how violence occurs in their lives. To illustrate this point, we briefly draw upon data reported from the 1960s to the 1990s to show the evolution of female behaviour, firstly, in terms of political participation and secondly, in terms of their participation in the labour market. These two aspects of women's presence in Brazil sheds light on their encounters with urban violence.

Women Fighting for Their Rights

Brazilian women represent more than half of the total Brazilian population, although their political influence is not in the same proportion. Nevertheless, their presence has been growing markedly over the past few decades. Women's political participation has been visible since the 1960s in Brazil, through their fight for their rights and their public actions within politics. In fact, studies have shown that this political visibility has been largely influenced by women from the lower-class. During the 1960s, lower-class women moved to greater cities and took on new urban living habitats and culture. In the same period, studies on the contribution of black population to Brazilian society also started to develop, for example a research study conducted by the Florestan Fernandes's team of the Universidade de São Paulo. Furthermore, since the 1960s, a new statistical methodology has been developed, which considers male and female numbers in the population and in the labour market. Black women started to be part of the demographic census after 1980.

Women from the higher classes and intellectual spheres, although more institutionally controlled, have been part of the public life since the 1930s. Since the end of the First World War, women's presence has been expressed through several social movements geared toward defending women's rights in Brazil. These have included The League for Intellectual Emancipation of Women and The Federation for Female Progress under the distinguished leadership of Bertha Lutz. The permission for female students to study at public high schools was obtained through such movements, as well as other achievements including a revolution in customs.

At that same time, Brazil celebrated its Independence Centenary, with extensive economic and political transformations such as the collapse of the former oligarchy and the birth of a new power represented by the industrial bourgeoisie. Other transformations included a cultural revolution illustrated in changes in the aesthetic perspectives towards viewing, painting and reciting that resulted in the Modernist movement, the Pau Brasil movement and the Week of Modern Art of 1922, which had as its symbol a woman painted by Di Cavalcanti.

Between the two World Wars, women achieved the status of citizenship. In 1932, women achieved the right to vote at elections. It is also in this period that the Brazilian Constitution of 1934 attributed equal rights to all under the law and thus prohibited discrimination on the grounds of sex, race and class. The item 'equality of sexes' is, nevertheless excluded from the 1937, 1964 and 1967 constitutions even though the text 'equality of all in the name of the law' was maintained. It was only in the Constitution of 1988 that the text on equality of sexes in terms of both rights and obligations was explicitly written in the law (Bicudo, 1994). This was as a result of women's struggles in the political arena.

Since the 1970s women have become an active presence in social movements such as in the remarkable movement against the increase in costs of living. Women are present in such movements as they are the main victims of financial problems in the domestic economy; they are also present in public politics where they make demands for facilities such as nurseries, public transport and schools. The sphere of such political involvement includes neighbourhood associations, clubs for mothers, demonstrations and picketing on the streets. Women are also present in movements demanding amnesty for political prisoners and for the end of military dictatorship. They were active in demonstrations and picketing against the military dictatorship in the 1970s, and were strongly repressed by the military government. In the case of black women, the 1988 Brazilian Constitution as well as the debate on the 100 years of the Abolition of Slavery in 1989 provided a platform for their voices to be heard, and for public acknowledgement of the various movements organised in the defense of black women's rights.

The victory achieved by Lula from Partido dos Trabalhadores PT in the 2002 elections for the President of the Republic can also be considered a female victory, due to women's active presence and outstanding strong voice in their militancy for the left. While female leadership is still limited in political positions, there has been a growth in the number of women candidates for political representative positions at both executive and legislative levels. The number of female candidates increased from 786 in 1994 to 2647 in 2002. Besides, even though there are no data on female votes, Lula was elected on 53.7 million thus representing 61.3% of the total number of electors, which stood at 115 million out of which 58.6 million were women.

Women in the Brazilian Labour Market

Women were established in the urban labour market after the 1960s and since then, their number in the labour market has increased significantly. In the 1960s, they were employed in manual and unskilled positions often in domestic services as cleaning ladies, house-maids and so forth. This level of employment accounted for approximately 92% of the women in employment.

Women made great progress in the 1970s and 1980s. They moved to other levels of employment, leaving unskilled employment for clerical positions. In 1980, women were mostly in clerical positions. However, figures show a great difference according to skin colour. The most significant progress was made by black women who began to take qualified manual work and in 1980 represented 22% of the blue-collar labour force (FIBGE, 1990, 1995). While black women's participation in the labour force rose by 22% from 1960-1980, that of white women rose by 15%. Overall, women not only began to gain access to well-paid jobs in professional and technical fields, they also gained new levels of socio-economic status. This distribution of labour resulted from women's access to education that led to better educational improvement, enabling them to occupy qualified positions. It was mostly due to an increasing urbanization process since the 1960s. The growing economy and relatedly the increase in the availability and variety of jobs as well as the increase in the demand for workers has enabled women to take part in the formal section of employment and consequently increase their presence significantly in the labour market. From 1960 to 1980, urban workers witnessed increased job opportunities and an absolute increase in their wages (Seade, 2002).

The 1980s were decisive for women in the labour market. Women made up almost half of Brazilian active population. In the beginning of the 1980s, they represented 31.3% of the active population and in 1990 the figure rose to approximately 36% (FIBGE, 1980, 1991). By the end of the 1990s, it increased to 41.4%. The profile of the female working population was also modified. In the 1970s, young, single women in the 20 to 24 age group ranked highest in the female working population; in the 1980s, this shifted to the 20 to 30 age group who were mostly married or had other marital statuses. At the end of the 1980s, the 30 to 40 years age group became dominant.

Despite the age variations in female participation in the labour force from the beginning of the 1970s to the end of the 1990s, there was an increase in the number of women in each age group. In the 1980s there was a larger distribution of female participation by age group. Data also show a reduction in the rate of female child labour in the 10 to 14 years age group but an increase in the 15 to 17 years age group. The labour market has been absorbing a larger number of women of different ages. It not only benefits young and single women but has also moved beyond to accommodate older women.

As noted in the 1996/1999 *World Development Reports* published by the World Bank, there is a worldwide increase in the number of women occupying positions that used to be essentially male. Women now work in male-linked occupations such as computing and piloting related jobs for example as train and underground conductors, bus and taxi drivers. However there is still limited participation. In Brazil, we found that in 1990, 9% of female workers were in factories as opposed to 27% male participation. Domestic work was still a great part of female employment, representing 17% of Brazilian female labour force, but in the Metropolitan Region of São Paulo, the figure for women in domestic employment was 45%. In terms of skin colour, 31% of black female workers in the Metropolitan Region of São Paulo were in domestic work as opposed to 14% white female workers. In contrast, 13% of white women were in public employment as opposed to 9% of black women.

Despite the improvement in the educational achievement of women, not all women are in prestigious positions and earn higher wages; at least not in the same proportion of gender employment distribution. It is true that there have been advances. However, studies have already shown that segregation persists in various occupations in relation to sex and race (Hirata, 2002; Bruschini, 2002). Women in employment are mostly in female-linked occupations ranging from reception, secretarial, tailoring, primary and middle school tutoring activities to nursing. We also observed that management and administration positions continue to be dominated by men. Inequality is still greater for the black women. In the 1990s, only 34% of black women in employment had accessed positions with better wages as opposed to 63% of their white counterparts (FIBGE, 1999; Seade, 2002).

There is also wage discrimination. In almost all occupation categories, white males are paid higher salaries. Women are paid lower salaries even when women have higher levels of education than their male colleagues. The salary difference also increases mostly in the white-collar occupation category. The greater salary gap is evident for qualified occupations and highly qualified employment. In six professional occupations analyzed, we observed that male wages were higher and practically double those of their female counterparts (FIBGE, 1999; Seade, 2002). In those occupations, women's qualifications were reputedly higher. This shows that sex discrimination is so significant in the labour market that women need higher qualifications to gain access to equal positions. We also observed that among women that are head of the family, 20% of them had 14 years of educational background but they were also paid lower salaries compared to men in the same position. Their salaries were, on average, 47% lower than those of their male colleagues.

As observed, women's participation in the labour market was responsible for other aspects of Brazilian family life. There was an increase in the number of women as head of the family, reaching 52% of the total number of Brazilian working women by the end of the 1990s (FIBGE 1990, 1995). This phenomenon is also observed in other countries according to data from the 1996/1999 *World Development Reports*. The increase in the number of women supporting the home has meant that by the end of the 1990s, women supported one-quarter of Brazilian families (FIBGE, 1999; Seade, 2002).

However, it is important to note that inequality is prevalent in the history of Brazilian women. There is a significant difference between the living conditions of poor women as compared with those of the middle- and upper- classes. Poor women had already achieved independence by the end of the 19th century; they were earning wages although precariously. They performed domestic services such as washing and starching, seaming or embroidering, cooking or making sweets and appetizers, and working as housemaids (Soihet, 1997). Furthermore these women managed to make a living selling handicrafts in cities, and selling sweets and food. Such activities rendered them targets of public criticisms. Survival strategies developed by poor black women have been in existence since the colonization period when they worked as street vendors, selling sweets and appetizers in the mining areas (Soihet, 1997). These aspects of the history of poor women may impair studies of the increase in the number of women as the head of families and such studies should bear in mind that they may not really be new facts but only new discoveries of situations that already existed.

It is important to emphasize that discriminatory practices and racism are now criminal contraventions. Since the 1988 Constitution, such practices are considered crimes with no right to bail or to prescribing, and are liable to penalties of reclusion. In fact, several laws (such as the Laws 7716/89, 8081/90, 9029/95 and 9459/97) were passed in the last decade aimed at preventing discrimination against women and on the bases of colour, age and civil state in relation to access to employment.

Violent Death as Ultimate Violence

Violence against women cannot be denied. Among levels of violence are cases of violence against physical integrity, ranging from physical aggression to those extreme cases involving homicide, which is considered to be a violent death. In the case of extreme violence whereby the value of life is involved, the role of the state and society as a group in the social institution process is questioned. In this sense, the study of female death by external factors can also contribute to the assessment of Brazilian social institutions (Elias, 1978).

In the study conducted in Rio Claro, we initially observed female mortality rates between 1980 and 1991 from census data. All cases reported from 1980 to 1991 were taken in order to examine how women were involved in violence in the 1980s. Nevertheless, data was initially confusing and contributed very little to our comprehension of the violence question. In the light of this, the data were complemented with data from local registers. In studying cases of female mortality and cases involving women in deaths by external factors (i.e. other causes except disease), the study in Rio Claro showed different aspects from what was expected and led us to seek more specific data on how the cases occurred. Cases registered at police stations were also counted as well as those at specialized police stations and registers. We also identified and followed trials in criminal courts. Furthermore, materials in town hall files of local newspapers and journals were included and we conducted interviews and collected witness evidence from people who lived close to victims. Thus, we made an attempt to search data from distinct sources as well as different points of view in order to understand each event involving women in homicide.

Therefore, our study analyzed circumstances in which women were involved in violent cases. We analyzed only cases registered and reported in the town forum in criminal lawsuits from 1980 to 1991 in order to assess how women were involved in violence in the 1980s. Since the worst violent cases against women are those affecting their physical and mental integrity, the study also tried to understand how or in what manner aggressions and death involved women.

What do Women Die of?

The major violence affecting women's physical and moral integrity lies in death by external factors and notably violent death. Male mortality predominates over female mortality. This is a fact that is acknowledged not only in our study in Rio Claro but also in all state and country regions. In São Paulo State, female mortality is at an average of 39% of all cases of death registered (Berquo, 2000). The female mortality rates tend to decrease. Nevertheless, young women alter this scenario. Deaths of women between 20 and 29 years old have increased considerably over the past decades (Berquo, 2000).

The study conducted in Rio Claro showed that the greatest cause of death among females was due to cardiovascular diseases. This is also the case in other regions of the country. In the State of São Paulo, the main causes of female death are also heart diseases and brainvascular accidents (Berquo, 2000). A marked phenomenon is that these causes predominate over breast cancer. However this change does not mean that there is a decrease in female death due to cancer. What is happening effectively is an increase in death due to other causes. However, it is necessary to note some particularities. When the study data of Rio Claro observed age groups, death due to 'external factors' ranked highest in female death rates among women up to 34 years of age.

In general, we noticed two main factors in young women's death. The first is that traffic accidents appear to be the main cause, especially when more recent periods are analyzed. It is true that men die more than women in traffic accidents. Nevertheless, we deduce that there has been a noticeable increase in women's mortality as a result of traffic accidents, mostly in the last decade. If at the beginning of the 1980s, the mortality rate between women and men was 8, representing one female death to every eight male deaths in traffic accidents, this rate changed considerably in the 1990s (Berquo, 2000). During this period, the rate between the sexes became 2 male deaths to one female death. This means that a significant increase in violent deaths due to traffic accidents has occurred and has been increasing, most notably among women since the beginning of the 1980s.

However, three aspects to these changes must be considered. Firstly, the statute with regard to culpability of traffic accidents has been altered. Because the causing of traffic accidents is considered a crime since the 1988 Constitution and the new traffic code, it now attracts greater criminal sanctions especially when it involves negligence and speeding or driving under the influence of alcohol or drugs. Secondly, women are not always guilty of traffic accidents. Data on traffic accident show that most drivers involved in accidents are young males between 20 and 29 years of age. Thirdly, female victims of traffic accidents are recorded as accident at work, especially when most of these accidents happens on their way to work (Beraldo, 1993).

In Brazil in general, data also show that women have died more in traffic accidents since the 1970s. However, data for Brazilian capitals demonstrate an increase in female mortality coefficients and has been reaching male mortality levels since the 1980s. Traffic accidents, to and from work, are also considered the main cause in accidents at work (Beraldo, 1993), leading us to conclude that working women are among the accident victims. However, the Rio Claro study shows that at the beginning of the 1980s all women victims of traffic accidents were classified as 'housewives'. In the 1990s however, of all female traffic accident victims, only 50% were classified as housewives, which means that those women were not involved in professional activities outside the home. The others had distinct occupations including photography, clerical, secretarial or mill work.

A second new fact of mortality among young women in Brazil is AIDS. It appears as the second cause of death, mostly among those between 15 and 34 years of age. While the numbers of death from abortion or pregnancy-related hypertension have decreased significantly (Berquo, 2000), death among young women from 25 to 29 years old from AIDS has increased significantly.

The data shows, yet, that women are not very prone to commit suicide. The tendency to commit suicide occurs among men. Studies have shown a higher suicide rate for males although there is a higher rate of suicide attempts by women. For men most suicide attempts are fatal (Cassorla, 1994). In Rio Claro, the number of suicides increased in some periods, as in 1990, 1991 and 1996. There is also a coincidence of increased numbers in suicide mostly in the years of new economic plans established by the government, which leads us to hypothesize that these plans have had negative impacts on people's living conditions or their emotional stability.

With regard to black women, if there were a supposition that they were more involved with violence that would be a mistake. Data shows that white women are more involved in distinct causes of violent death such as homicide, suicide and traffic accidents. The figures are 80% for white women and 20% for black women. However, skin color is still a factor in terms of socioeconomic distinction in Brazil. Thus, black women may be protected from traffic accidents because the number of black female drivers is lower than that for white female drivers. Another aspect that appears in the analyzed cases is that black women involved in these deaths are essentially young, from 19 to 28 years old. However, what is new in the Brazilian scenario is that women start to signify in cases of death due to homicide. It is a fact that women are not predominant. While homicides in large cities are one of three main causes of male death, it is the 12th cause of death among women (Drumond Jr., 1999). Nevertheless, when analyzed by age, we should consider that in São Paulo homicides are already the main cause of death for young women from 10 to 39 years of age.

There are also differences by social group and professional occupation in São Paulo. Among women in personal services such as maids and cleaning ladies, homicide appears as the main cause of death mostly among young women. In São Paulo, among violent deaths of black women, homicide is also the main cause of death (Drumond Jr., 1999).

We may consider that the change of urban life styles since the 1970s has had an impact on female mortality. An aspect that we can relate to cardiovascular diseases is the change in women's life styles. One fact is the increased engagement of women in the labour market since the 1960s. In fact, data shows an increased participation of women in the Brazilian working population. We verified the presence of women in the labour market as being mostly in services. Another notable fact in the Brazilian case is the growing increase in the number of families supported by women who are head of the home (FIBGE, 1999; Seade, 2002). This has also been observed in various countries as the 1996/1999 World Development Reports show.

However, it is worth considering that female deaths that appear in the study in Rio Claro show that they are not directly related to professional activity. Among women that die of cardiovascular disease in the Rio Claro's registers, most were classified at housewives. The increase in traffic accidents and deaths due to AIDS is more related to the changing patterns of urban life and the sort of activities in which women are involved. It is incontestable that there is an increase in personal car use for women and families as a means of transport. If on the one hand, women are more present in the labour market, they are also being required to perform more sophisticated housework activities such as taking kids to school and other recreational activities, going shopping and so forth. Female stress starts to be a cause for concern among females in the labour market due to the doubling of obligation since they will go home at the end of the day to face more work at home. Women in full-time domestic work also deserve attention considering new demands of current urban life style.

Who are the Aggressors?

The aggressor in homicide cases is mainly male in the Rio Claro study. Cases of violence involving drunken male aggressors are a current and dominant fact. It can be stated that they result from high alcohol consumption, which is a strong component of male behaviour. Deaths from drug consumption are more likely among men than women. This also can come from high consumption of drugs such as marijuana, cocaine, crack and heroin among men than among women. There is effectively an increase in regular drug use, which is an important fact in medium-size cities.

The scene of male crime is on the streets. More than half of the cases presented in our study, in which the aggressor was a male, took place in a public place. In our Rio Claro study, bars appear as a privileged place for male crime. Two causes appear to trigger off conflicts: drink and women. These conflicts center around disagreements on questions of moral order, which may be financial debts or misunderstanding over what has to be paid and how a certain object or merchandise must be bought. The disagreement lies in how the question such as a debt or honour is morally handled.

Male violent deaths have doubled since 1988. In the 1980s, there were high numbers of male homicides, especially for the period 1980-88. We noticed an increase in homicides among young people. In Rio Claro, violent deaths increased by 94% for the 10 to 14 years age group and by 43% among those aged 15 to 19 years old. This increase is noticeable in the rest of the country too. In Brazil, major increases were for groups between 10 to 14 years old, which means 80% of homicides for those in their early teens and 45% for those aged 15 to 19 year old (Souza, 1994). For teenage women aged 10 to 14 years, death due to homicide also showed a dramatic increase of 44%. Data show that in this period a very significant number of Brazilian children and adolescents were victims of homicide, a situation which called for greater attention from state educational authorities.

In Brazil, young women are prone to diverse forms of aggression and acts of violence for which the aggressors are mostly male. This is particularly evident among women who make their living on the streets or who are exposed to violent situations on the streets. Young black women make up of the majority of this category of women. This observation leads us to the conclusion that this violence is the consequence of the violent features of social and economic deprivation that they are primarily exposed to. They are more likely to be marginalized in Brazilian society since they are located in all the three positions of 'social disadvantage': being women, being economically deprived and being black.

One point to note is that it was difficult to analyze cause of death in the case of female victims of violence. The death certificates were inadequately completed; they tended to be filled in more adequately when the victim was male. For instance, the description 'undefined causes' was more frequently used for female victims. In such cases, the examination of the victim was enhanced while the lack of information tended to obstruct the examination of the aggressor. In our study in Rio Claro, it was possible to examine the aggressors due to the fact that collaborators facilitated our access to court reports.

Home as a Place of Violence

Women are victims of homicide and most frequently in environments of domestic violence. In fact, data shows that 70% of reported violence towards women occurs at home. It also shows that 50% of female homicide victims were described as housewives who were mostly attacked by their own husbands (Berquo, 2000; Deslandes, 2000).

The fact that the number of homicide cases involving women is growing, mostly in large cities, led us to conduct a detailed study of cases concerning women as victims in Rio Claro between 1980 and 1991, using data from lawsuits and reports. Homicides involving women in Rio Claro during this period had four aspects. The first is the place where they occurred. The analyzed cases showed that 90% occurred at home. A second aspect is the alleged cause. Seventy per cent of the analyzed causes were considered crimes of passion. A third aspect is the crime perpetrator. On the basis of the analyzed cases, the perpetrator of the crime of homicide was in most cases a man, and in cases of crime of passion, the husband. The fourth aspect is the instrument used in the crime. The analyzed cases showed that firearms appeared in 50% of the cases as the instrument used for the crime while knives appeared in 40% of the cases.

However, women have been appearing as aggressive perpetrators as well. Out of 180 homicide cases in the period 1980 to 1991, women appeared in 8 cases, which means that in 4% of all cases, they were the perpetrators of homicide. In all these cases, the location of the crime was the home. Sixty-five per cent of the cases were classified as crimes of passion and 90% classed as a reaction to maltreatment or in self-defense.

The findings of the study show women are rarely homicidal in street situations or in other places. Secondly, the home is the scene of the crime, which results from a family conflict with their husbands. Thirdly, women turn to homicidal impulses when reacting against maltreatment. Fourthly, the most used instruments are knives, meat boards and crowbars. The women in the study were domestic workers, which can explain their use of mostly kitchen implements with which they are most familiar. Among the female cases, a black woman appeared only in one case. In this case, the woman acted in self-defense with the help of others.

Such findings have been observed in Mexico where women often commit homicide in a family environment and in most cases as a response to previous aggressions of which they were victims (Lopes, 1996). It is interesting to mention a study conducted in São Paulo based on registered cases by CRAMI (Centros Regionais de Maus Tratos à Infância), a state Institution responsible for the welfare of children in Brazil. In the study women appeared as main child abusers. In fact, data obtained from CRAMI reports show the mother as the most common child abuser. The spotlight on the mother as an agent of child abuse is present in many studies (for example, Gil, 1978; Gelles, 1979; Meyer 1988) where it is acknowledged that the mother spends most time with the children and is responsible for disciplining and teaching them social rules.

However, it has been shown that when the father spends the same amount of time as the mother does with the children, he is also a frequent abuser. But, data shows a variation in this violent situation. When the father is the child aggressor, he is usually employed. When the mother is the abuser according to the data, she is usually unemployed and she is responsible for housekeeping. She is usually in a low socio-economic situation of an underprivileged class, getting by on a low income in situations of extreme insecurity. The mother's aggression, in these cases, can be considered as resulting from stress caused by workload associated with insecure conditions of life and from financial problems involved in supporting their children. On the basis of this data, the state needs to give significant consideration to the provision of relevant support to women in their role as mothers.

Conclusion

Our study conducted in Rio Claro showed that violent death is not limited to large cities but is also present in medium-size cities, although not on the same scale. In addition, data shows a current reality, that is, the increase of violence against women in their home environment, and which affects mostly young women and has great impact on their reproductive age. The data seemingly confirm an increase in the number of women involved in violent death cases. In the period between 1980 and 1991 there was an increase of female presence in rates of homicide, suicide and traffic accidents. Nevertheless, the increase in the number of traffic accidents results not only from their participation in the labour market but also from the increase in the number of women as car drivers and in their increased engagement in activities outside the home.

We could also conclude that home is the predominant place for female violence. The study also shows new behaviours by women who are revealed as being responsible for aggression with the husband as the common victim and whose homes are the predominant locations for homicide. However, we observed a difference between male and female violent behaviours. While the male aggressor acts with a fire weapon and under the influence of alcohol, women move from being the victim to being the perpetrator, often in reaction to aggression. This leads us to conclude that homicide is not a typical female practice but appears as a defense mechanism in response to aggressions in which they were originally victims.

Another finding is that this new female behaviour occurs within other broader contexts. The first one is that their engagement in the labour market has provided a certain degree of financial independence to women, enabling them to take some distinguished action towards the new possibility of breaking their marriage vows. A second aspect, which also results from the first, is the increase in the number of women as providers for the family. We are led to believe that there are more women supporting their families and this can form one of the conflicting points of a marriage relationship. A third aspect is the attitude that women are taking in defense of their rights and actions in public politics, which may also be a contributory factor to this new defense attitude in the family environment. A fourth aspect to be considered is the installation of specialized police stations to attend to women victims of violence since the 1980s.

Another aspect to be emphasized is that the percentage of black women involved in violent death is significantly lower than that of white women. This means that violent death is not among the main causes of death for black women in Rio Claro. However, we recommend further study on causes of deaths in the city of São Paulo where homicide appears as the main cause of death among young black women, especially since the official records are more likely to indicate that the cause of the death of a black woman was unknown.

Women are also victims of limited support by the government. First of all, we mention the limited state support given to education and family care, and notably to children. There is a lack of financial support to women in their role as agents of reproduction, which otherwise would contribute effectively to better standards of living for children. This observation sustains our supposition that the lack of stability in standards of living will lead to family conflicts. A second observation is that there is a lack of support by the government for women as citizens.

Although Brazilian women have managed to achieve progress in terms of Brazilian legislation, they still experience discrimination. Impunity and discriminatory treatment still rule in the judicial system as shown in the studies by Comissao Teotônio Villela and Nucleo de Estudos da Violência USP in the Americas Watch (1991). Female victims of violence do not always have the courage to report incidents of violence, especially when the violence is within the domestic sphere. When the aggressor is their own husband, the women fear that retaliation is out of their control. Criminal justice practices also show that in Brazil, men that kill their wives under suspicion of infidelity can be acquitted by the court under the argument that they acted in 'self-defense of their honour' (Soihet, 1997;

Bicudo, 1994). In the case of black women, they are still marginalized in the social, economic and political spheres. However, they are organizing and fighting for their rights.

We must stress that there are some limitations in this kind of research on violence towards women. One of the limitations relates to the fact that cases are not always effectively recorded. Invariably, one might ask if there has been an increase in cases or only an increase in their registration. The increase in the number of cases of violence towards women may not be related to an effective increase in the number of violent cases but to an increase in the numbers reported and registered over the past few years. Recent conditions of living standards for women may have encouraged violent situations or they may have facilitated the reporting/recording of violent incidents, which in the past would have been unreported. We also wish to stress that this kind of research may also be affected by the manner in which the lawsuits are handled in court as some defense arguments may not always reflect the actual cause/s of violence.

References

Americas Watch (1991), *Violência no Brasil*, São Paulo, Nucleo de Estudos da Violência da USP, Comissão Teotônio Vilela.

Beraldo, P.S.S. (1993), *Mortalidade por acidentes de trabalho no Brasil: uma análise das declarações de óbitos, 1979-88*, *Informe Epidemiológico do SUS*, vol. 2, pp.41-59.

Berquo, E. (2000), *Morbimortalidade,* Campinas, Editora Unicamp.

Bicudo, H. (1994), *O Brasil cruel e sem maquiagem*, São Paulo, Moderna.

Bruschini, C. (2002), *Gênero, democracia e sociedade brasileira*, São Paulo, Editora, 34.

Cassorla, R.M.S. (1994), *A autodestruição humana*, *Cadernos de Saúde Pública*, Rio de Janeiro, Fundação Osvaldo Cruz, vol. 10, pp.61-73.

Dean, W. (1976), *Rio Claro: A Brazilian Plantation System, 1820-1920*, Stanford University Press, Stanford.

Deslandes, S.F. (2000), *Caracterização dos casos de violência doméstica contra a mulher atendidos em dois hospitais públicos do Rio de Janeiro*, *Cadernos de Saúde Pública*, vol. 16, no. 1, pp.129-137, jan/mars.

Drumond Jr., M. (1999), *Homicidios e desigualdades sociais na cidade de São Paulo: uma visão epidemiológica*, *Saúde e Sociedade*, vol. 8, no. 1, pp.63-81.

Elias, N. (1978), *Civilizing Process*, Basil Blackwell, Oxford.

FIBGE, (1980), *Anuário Estatístico do Brasil.*

______ (1991), *Anuário Estatístico do Brasil.*

______ (1995), *Anuário Estatístico do Brasil.*

______ (1999), *Anuário Estatístico do Brasil.*

______ (1990), *Brasil: Pesquisa Nacional por Amostra de Domicilio.*

______ (1995), *Brasil: Pesquisa Nacional por Amostra de Domicilio.*

______ (1999), *Brasil: Pesquisa Nacional por Amostra de Domicilio.*

Gelles, R.J. (1979), *Family Violence*, Sage, London.

Gil, D. (1978), *Violence against Children: Physical Child Abuse*, Harvard University Press, Cambridge.

Hirata, H. (2002), *Nova divisão do trabalho*, São Paulo, Boitempo.

Lasch, C. (1977), *Heaven in a Heartless World: The Family Besieged*, Basic Books, New York.

Lopes, M.V. (1996), *Muertes por homicidio, consecuencias fatales de la violencia. El caso de Mexico 1979-92*, *Revista de Saúde Publica*, vol. 30, no. 1, pp.46-52.

Meyer, M.P. (1988), *Violência contra a criança: Uma questão emergente*, Master's thesis presented to PUC-RJ, Rio de Janeiro.

Seade, (2002), *Inserção das mulheres negras no mercado de trabalho na Região Metropolitana de São Paulo 1995-2000*, São Paulo.

Soihet, R. (1997), *Mulheres pobres e violência no Brasil urbano*, in Mary del Priore (org.), *A história das mulheres no Brasil,* São Paulo, Contexto/Unesp.

Souza, E. (1994), *Homicídios no Brasil: O grande vilão da Saúde Pública na década de oitenta*, *Cadernos de Saúde Pública*, Rio de Janeiro, Fundação Osvaldo Cruz, vol. 10, pp.45-60.

8 Working from the Inside/Out: Drama as Activism in Westville Female Prison

MIRANDA YOUNG-JAHANGEER

Introduction

> If you have come here to help me,
> You are wasting your time.
> If you have come here because
> Your liberation is bound up with mine,
> Then lets work together.
> (Lilla Watson, Aboriginal ex-prisoner, cited in Faith, 2000, p.167.)

Freedom is acquired by conquest, not gift. It must be pursued constantly and responsibly. Freedom is not an ideal located outside of man [sic] nor is it an idea, which becomes a myth. It is rather the indispensable condition for the quest of human completion (Freire, 1972, 2000, p.47).

Prison Theatre, and specifically Women's Prison Theatre in South Africa is a new and fragile area of activity. In embracing the spirit of the new constitution, which transferred Correctional Services out of the jurisdiction of the army, recreational activities were introduced into the prisons in 1996 for the first time. This opened new doors of possibility for practitioners and in 1999, Chris Hurst and Beki Nkala of the Drama and Performance Studies (University of Natal, Durban, South Africa) were invited by the Westville Prison Complex to assist in the staging of a play with Medium B inmates.

Westville Prison Complex is an urban prison located near one of Durban's more prestigious suburbs. It consists of four prisons: Female Prison, Youth Centre, Medium B – male maximum-security and Medium A – male-minimum security. Approximately 12,000 prisoners are housed here. The play, Shibobo (Zulu term for an act of skilled manoeuvring in football) written by Kaba Mkize was a great success and inmates were invited to perform at a local theatre to much acclaim. The success of this collaboration resulted in a first year University course entitled Theatre for a Developing Nation (TFD) being established in 2000 by Hurst and

Nkala, which aims to introduce participatory theatre skills to both students and inmates from Westville's Medium B, Youth and Female Prisons. The practical element of the course culminates in a day of play exchange akin to Eugenio Barba's (1985) notion of 'bartering' or points of contact between cultures. 'In any barter the "micro-culture" (...) [the inmates] of one group meets the "micro-culture" of the other [the students]. This meeting is realized through an exchange of performances, that is cultural products, but these products are not as important as the exchange itself' (Barba, 1985a cited in Watson 2000, p.245).

Methodologically the work conducted in the Prisons[1] by Hurst, Nkala and myself, has been directly informed by Paulo Freire's liberatory pedagogy of the oppressed (1972, 2000), whose emphasis on praxis as 'action and reflection upon the world in order to transform it' (2000, p.51) has been regarded as particularly appropriate since it encourages disempowered communities to view change as possible (Mda, 1993). Augusto Boal's Theatre of the Oppressed (1979) which grew from Freire in his focus on an active dialogic methodology in the practice of liberation, specifically Boal's Forum Theatre (see Playing for Real for a fuller description) has also informed our theatre work in the prisons.

The notion of 'the oppressed' as applied by Freire (2000) and Boal (1979) is not used uncritically here, for while their theory is useful on a number of levels it fails to deconstruct the ways in which social relations (gender, race, class) articulate (Agozino, 1997). For it is an understanding of the interplay of power dynamics upon the individual that is crucial in challenging a monolithic conception of women (or blacks) as 'the oppressed' while at the same time maintaining an understanding that patriarchy is pervasively experienced by all women – at some level – and should be passionately fought against.

In focussing specifically on theatre with women inmates, the notion of what constitutes 'the oppressed' is taken even further. The triple oppression that characterises the majority of women in South Africa in terms of the interconnections of gender, race and class (Davis, 1984; hooks, 1989) here includes being stripped of civil liberties (while I am aware of the multiple categories of power that exist such as sexual orientation, age and literacy, I shall for the purposes of this paper be dealing primarily with these three). However, in embracing the Foucauldian (1984) conception of agency as always present (barring instances of torture or execution) and resistance as possible, one might ask as Anne Worrall (1990) does: Who are these women who have deviated from the patriarchal conception of what a woman should be? Are they martyrs to the Radical Feminist cause or are they the embodiment of the extremity of powerlessness and voicelessness?

Women inmates are widely regarded by theatre practitioners, primarily in the West as being more 'resistant, volatile and less predictable' (Hughes, 1998, p.49) than men. In my experience of working in Westville Female Prison as a drama facilitator, it was resistance which initially characterised many of these women who 'defy description' (Worrall, 1990, p.1). This resistance was typically characterised by inaction and passivity rather than volatility. The women had chosen to be there yet many refused to get up into the space or found ways to stall the projects, often sabotaging it for others who did wish to participate. As the relationship has developed between the inmate participants and myself and as inmates have taken greater ownership of theatre in Westville Female Prison, this has changed. Nevertheless the oppressive structure and functioning of the prison combined with external stress such as concern for children on the outside, which create feelings of powerlessness and lack of autonomy do tend to impact in a way that is unpredictable. They must respond to these conditions through the limited choices available to them, absenteeism for example. This would seem to indicate that while the idea of 'volatility' is in question the overriding context of prison, as an oppressive overcrowded space (Westville Female Prison houses around five times its intended capacity) where power is so overtly exercised, seems to effect similar possibilities of 'resistance, disobedience and oppositional groupings' (Foucault, 1984, p.162) irrespective of the wider geographic location.

It is certain that powerlessness is rarely absolute. Internalised powerlessness may not correspond to an external reality and external curtailments of freedom and agency, however extreme may not be internalised. Nevertheless, in considering the relative nature of power, black women inmates, particularly those who were incarcerated during apartheid were extremely limited in the degree to which they were able to exercise their own will unless it corresponded to the will of the institution (personal conversation with Female inmate previously on death-row). More recently, inmates have had more institutionalised power. South African prisoners, unlike in the United States for instance, are now allowed to vote. Inmates now have a right to education, and telephone numbers for human rights organisations are visible on the walls. Despite this, inmates often choose to portray themselves as 'powerless' and 'persecuted', describing themselves as 'slaves' for instance (personal communications, 2002). The fact that they are able to communicate such opinions to me, without fear of torturous punishment as during apartheid, indicates that this is not entirely so.

The fall of apartheid had a profound effect both institutionally and on the consciousness of the people. These changes impacted the possibilities for expression and resistance as discussed in this chapter. This is particularly evident in the transformation of a resistance characterised by inaction typically practiced by women offenders, into a form of conscientised positive activism where theatre was chosen as the tool with which to articulate patriarchal injustice to government and media. In keeping with Boal's conception of theatre as 'a rehearsal for revolution, (1979, p.155) it is proposed that this 'revolution' was able to occur through the exercise of Freirean pedagogy (praxis, dialogue) as theatre (participatory issue-based plays). In a recent event (December 2001) held at Westville Female Prison for the Justice for Women Campaign, women used popular theatre to highlight the patriarchal bias of courts in sentencing in cases where there has been abuse. An invitation was extended to the Justice Department, Gender Commission and representatives of the media to hear their stories. Popular performance was the medium of expression, rearticulated by the media for the public. While both broadcast and print media were present, I will refer specifically to the articles that appeared in the local press (*Sunday Tribune*) the following day. While I am aware that a fuller study could include analysis of reportage across the media, the local print media is particularly relevant, as this is the media that the inmates themselves were exposed to. The responses/feelings of inmates are regarded as paramount.

In the course of this chapter, I hope to describe and theorise this chain of events that I have been a part of and which feed into a larger narrative of oppressed/oppressor and ultimately the fear of freedom (Freire, 2000).

Playing for Real

What characterises Prison Theatre, as a dramatic form is that unlike other community theatre such as South African 'Worker Theatre' for example, it is defined not by the community who is involved in its creation, but rather by the space/place it occupies (Thompson, 1998). This emphasis on defining space, both indicates the power of space to shape the nature and experience of the interaction that occurs within it. It offers practitioners and participants alike the freedom and flexibility to respond creatively to the specific conditions and contexts that they find themselves in, not just as inmates but also as individuals with histories and cultures, who experience the interplay of power at a personal and political level. Thompson (1998, p.15) writes: 'the identification of our work as theatre in prisons, rather than theatre with offenders… alters both its scope and how it is practiced… "Theatre in Prisons" suggests that the practice can be as wide and as inclusive as possible'.

Prison Theatre as it has evolved in Westville Prison has been a convergence of traditions with a common ambition: liberation, conscientization resistance and the underlying belief in the power of cultural action to transform society (Freire, 2000). As the intervention was collaborative, the idea was not to impose an existing form, but rather to negotiate a new form by embracing the influences of African popular culture (Barber, 1997): 'traditional' song, and counter-cultural forms such as Protest Theatre (Kerr, 1995; Simon, Ngema and Mtwa, 1983), which informed the experiences of the inmates with other more openly didactic forms such as Theatre for Development (Mda, 1994), which grew from University Travelling Theatre (Kerr, 1995) and Boalian Forum Theatre in an eclectic mix. The result: plays, which in both form and content sought to challenge mainstream cultural practices that exist to reinforce the *status quo*. Although it is not the focus of this paper to analyse in detail the influences of South African Prison theatre, it is relevant in the context of resistance and activism to highlight the fact that the existing influences that have been drawn on by the inmates when workshopping their plays have been largely grounded in counter hegemonic cultural expression.

Where the plays depart in form from University Travelling Theatre is that where this form used drama as a mode of active explanation to initiate dialogue between two groups external to the actors (Kerr, 1995), in our brand of Prison Theatre the play is central to the dialogue – it is the dialogue. In this way it is more similar to

Forum Theatre, which is described by Boal (1992, p.xxi) as 'a theatrical game in which a problem is shown in an unsolved form, to which the audience…is invited to suggest and act solutions'. The form thus empowers the audience to transform the course of action of the play through the devise of the 'spect-actor' (Boal, 1979) which was conceived 'to change people – "spectators", passive beings in the theatrical phenomenon – into subjects into actors, transformers of the dramatic action' (1979, p.122). However, the prison plays depart from Forum Theatre through a reformulation of the 'spect-actor' with the reconceptualising of 'performance space'. An enduring feature of the Westville Prison Plays is the fluidity of the performance space (scenes and dialogue/discussion with 'audience' can occur anywhere in the room). Thus, the 'spect-actor', need not approach the playing area and shout 'Stop!' in order to 'intervene and change the vision of the world' (Boal, 1993, p.335) since all the space is performance space. This inclusive staging effectively also transforms spect-actors and actors alike into performers, coupled with the fact that the form of the play, informed by liberatory pedagogy, empowers all participants to engage participatorily.

In addition, where Theatre for Development and University Travelling Theatre are used to offer solutions and solve development issues, the issue-based prison plays' ambition is not to provide the right answers, but to provide the right questions, which raise awareness and ultimately the consciousness of all participants. This distinguishes it from other forms of Prison Theatre in the United Kingdom and America (Thompson, 1998), which tend to sway towards psychodrama in their focus on rehabilitation. This focus on the personal psychological processes, which lead to crime, has not been our motivation. Due to the historical processes at work in South Africa: post-colonialism, post-apartheid, a focus on individual psychology has not been thought useful.

Prison Theatre in Westville Female Prison takes as its narrative the experiences of oppression (predominantly patriarchal) of the women who workshop the plays. They are powerfully autobiographical and provide a much-needed platform for the representation of women's lives in a way that is both tragic and comic. As it is 'silence' which characterizes 'the oppressed' (Freire, 2000) and silence that is regarded in feminist circles as 'submission to the patriarchal authority' (hooks, 1989, 6), the speaking out around these issues is the first crucial step in gaining a increased sense of agency/authentic power; it is the first step to being heard.

Articulating Power Dynamics: Gender/Race/Class

Women the world over are being incarcerated for longer and for more minor crimes than ever before (Faith, 2000). This trend towards female imprisonment, which shows an increase of women prisoners in the United Kingdom of 100% since 1970 (Hughes, 1998) is not so much indicative of an increase in crime, but it is sadly symptomatic of pernicious patriarchy. Extensive work has been done by feminist criminologists to expose the way that the criminal justice operates as a mechanism for the reinforcement of (white) patriarchal authority. Women who find themselves caught up in it are 'assessed, judged, treated, punished – not because they are understood but because they are not' (Worrall, 1990, p.2). As stated by O'Dwyer et. al (1987 cited in Hughes 1998, p.47), the prosecution of women is often based on patriarchally defined deviance such as 'their own refusal to comply with culturally conditioned female gender stereotype requirements [which] have resulted in it being denied that they are real women [my italics]'. This is not only prejudicial, but effectively disqualifies certain women from being able to speak about their own condition with any agency. It is with this understanding that participatory, workshopped drama as a methodology is considered an appropriate and effective way of attempting to counteract some of the damage done to offending women.

In justifying the study of female inmates and the social/historical conditions that land them behind bars, Worrall (1990, p.4) states, 'The conditions and processes that over-determine the fate of this group of deviant women are intrinsically no different from those within which 'conventional' women are also controlled'. This necessarily implies a shift in focus away from individual offender as solely accountable, towards an awareness of social structures that perpetuate crime – 'such as imperialism, racism, capitalism and sexism, because they promote inherently repressive relationships and social injury' (Klein and Kress, 1976 cited in Worrall, 1990, p.3). This is particularly pertinent in South African society, which has been, and continues to be the playground for all these oppressive systems to flourish. Freire's (2000, p.174) methodology of dialogical action, which informs our work, strives 'to make it possible for the oppressed, by perceiving their adhesion [their relationship to oppressive structures], to opt to transform an unjust reality', thus operating at the level of the individual in order to conscientize about larger processes of domination.

Within the area of women and crime, the feminist movement has on the whole been more concerned with women as victims of crime than as victims of criminalisation (Sudbury, 2001, p.144). This demonstrates a failure to make the connection generally between crime (violence) and oppression (Fanon, 1965; Freire, 2000) and specifically women's crime as by and large a consequence of patriarchal oppression. Studies show (Faith, 2000, p.164; personal communication Ms. L. Dlamini social worker Westville Female Prison) that over 80% of imprisoned girls and women have been physically, sexually or emotionally abused by men. This is significantly higher than women who have not committed crime (Faith, 2000). While a closer reading of Fanon (1990) explains why there is a rise in criminal activity amongst both men and women in postcolonial/oppressed societies generally, it is the 'crime' that has been directed specifically at abusive men – the embodiments of patriarchy, that is of interest here. Due to the relative nature of crime (Mead, 2000, p.13), which tends to be defined according to the class/gender/race articulations of the existing social order, what could conceivably be interpreted as self-defence in these cases has been regarded by the criminal justice system and media as heinous crime committed for material gain (Sowetan, March 27, 2002, p.3). These women typically receive maximum sentences (statistics provided by Correctional Services). This is indicative of how patriarchy, at every turn – within the criminal justice system and the media, have undermined, undercut and attempted to disempower and punish women who would dare to strike back or talk out.

However, patriarchal domination, as bell hooks (1989, 1993) demonstrates shares an ideological foundation with racism and other forms of group oppression, thus we cannot fully understand the way in which women are perceived and treated in society (of which the criminal justice system is part) without acknowledging these interconnections. Indeed, in South Africa where race (and to some extent class) was hierarchically institutionalised, it becomes impossible to look at gender without acknowledging how these power dynamics articulate. It is the position of this author that "although race, class and gender relations are different, they are not separable in theory or in practice" (Agozino 1997, p.17). The model of articulation is thus employed here (Agozino, 1997; Hall, 1996; hooks, 1993).

Drawing on Franz Fanon (1965, 1990), Angela Davis (1984, p.36) makes the parallel between 'sexual violence' against individual women and neo-colonial violence against people and nations since the conditions, which spawn racism, and racist violence, are the very same conditions which encourage sexism and sexist violence. Violence against women stems from a need to exert power over the less powerful, in a racist/classist society such as South Africa. It is black women who are the most disempowered and fall prey to the most abuse, privately and institutionally. We therefore cannot isolate gender or racial issues, when attempting to understand the interplay of oppression within a society and within an individual.

An analysis of sentencing, as a reflection of this articulation of power in relation to class/race in the group of women the author works with, revealed some interesting information. While only a small study, the outcomes do confirm perceptions held by the inmates themselves (Hurst, Nkala and Young, 2002) as well as feminist criminology studies abroad (Worrall, 1990; Carlen, 1990; O'Dwyer et al., 1987 cited in Hughes, 1998). In my group of 21 women 77% are convicted for murder, 70% for straight murder, 7% for murder and robbery. The remaining 23% is split between fraud, housebreaking, assault, possession of weapons (political crime) and interestingly one woman convicted for rape. The demographics of those 21 women are: 76% black, 9.5% coloured, 9.5% Indian and 4.7% white. The spread across race/class groups in the female prison is far more representative of the South African population than in the Medium B (male) and Youth Prisons, which are almost 100% black. This seems to indicate that the conditions, which propagate crime amongst women tend to cut across boundaries of race and class. A lot of serious crime in women tends to be retributive rather than indicative of a cycle of arbitrary criminal behaviour, although this is also increasing for the reasons discussed above (Fanon, 1965; Freire, 2000).

Averaging the sentences across race groups, the disparity between the black and Indian sentencing for murder is not significant, besides the fact that it is high: black: 20 years; and Indian: 22.5 years. What is significant is that the coloured women's sentencing averaged 31 years, notably higher; and the only white woman who was convicted for murder in my group received only seven years, the lowest sentence for murder by far.

A look at class/education proved even more interesting. The statistics revealed that the less educated women, (below grade 10 education) who come from a predominantly rural background received significantly shorter sentences for murder – an average of 15 years as compared with better educated (urban) women – above grade 10 education, who received an average of 20.6 years. Class is acknowledged as an interconnected power dynamic that influences the treatment and perception of women in society (Davis, 1984) and consequently has the potential to influence sentencing (Sudbury, 2000); however in this instance, it seems cultural stereotyping has played a stronger role. Stereotypes around rural women tend to be passive, dutiful and long suffering while those around educated (urban), particularly black women tend to be that she is sophisticated, manipulative and opportunistic.

Since a detailed knowledge of their individual cases is not available, other than what has been revealed to me personally, we cannot state conclusively that there has been blatant prejudice here. But an understanding of stereotypical perceptions of race/class (for example that coloured people are violent gangsters) propagated by the media and which feed into the interplay of power dynamics, particularly as it concurs with the perceptions of those who have experienced it first hand, makes it worth noting.

It is an awareness of these dynamics (class/race/gender), which informs the work done in Westville Female Prison. The work expressed the need for gender sensitivity and the importance of providing an opportunity and skills for the most oppressed people in our society to learn how to speak up and speak out through cultural action. However, as Loots (2001, p.12) points out 'it is not enough to be "allowed" to create cultural products unless these products are given the space to be seen and heard; in short have agency within a society'. The extent to which they are or are not listened to seriously (Spivak, 1990) will be discussed in the second half of the chapter. However there is much to be said for the 'soft' effects of creative action done in obeisance of the pursuit of authentic freedom.

Social Impacts of Drama in Westville Female Prison

Working within the prison system presents many challenges and dilemmas to the drama facilitator in terms of her own subject position (negotiating across class and race) and the nature of the intervention. Too often the 'punitive ideology and practice of the prison regime' (Hughes, 1998, p.52; Faith, 2000) impacts the intervention in a way that is domesticating. However, in attempting to understand the potentially problematic role of drama in prisons, Thompson (1998, p.17) asks, 'what should we be doing? Are we playing the disciplinary role of the prison or are we inciting rebellion? Can we comfortably define and find a blurred edge between the two? Are we content to liberate a person's imagination because we cannot liberate their body?'

There are no hard and fast answers to these very real questions; however, Karlene Faith (2000) suggests that what the practitioner must ultimately ask herself is 'Who benefits?' Motivating for permission to work in the prison system requires that there are benefits to the prison; however these benefits are (I believe) not at the cost of prisoner benefits; they are not mutually exclusive.

In an evaluation conducted of the TFD course, which involves students and inmates (Hurst, Nkala, and Young, 2002), many positive impacts were found to have resulted (Hurst, Nkala and Young, 2002). In my focus on Westville Female Prison, firstly, the project enabled the women to see drama as a communicative and consciousness-raising tool, and secondly it enabled them through dialogical action to mobilise/organise through the promotion of social cohesion. One Zulu speaking inmate, who was serving 25 years for murder and robbery commented:

> The first time it was very difficult for me [to act], I didn't even know if I can make it – if I can do it; but in the end I was playing in front of the other people like inmates and members…it was such a difficult thing on top of all our stresses, but we can really make it and we are proud of ourselves and because we are proud of ourselves we can make it! (Thembisile *)

Increased confidence and raised self-esteem came across the major outcomes experienced by the female inmate participants. This can be seen as a result of both the involvement in the creative process, which was collaborative, as well as the performance day. The participatory nature of the plays, which are devised around issues which the inmates are personally knowledgeable about such as spousal abuse, addiction, HIV/ AIDS and racism, enables inmates to feel validated by their ability to contribute expertly to the discussion with other inmates and particularly students who are perceptibly more knowledgeable than they are.

Raised self-esteem and confidence, most significantly was found to have encouraged positive risk-taking behaviour. Many women in prison retain a hardened persona as a survival strategy. Hughes (1998, p.49) similarly observes that maintaining a strong or 'tough' image in prison is very important to prevent bullying and scapegoating. Involvement in a project that not only requires and encourages generous, supportive behaviour, but also places the participant in an emotionally vulnerable position is both risky and brave. This was evident in the conflicting and often contradictory behaviour demonstrated by certain 'tough' women during the project. While they expressed sincere positive feedback after the event, and ultimately followed through, their behaviour during the process demonstrated a great deal of resistance – to each other, the project and me. The women used absenteeism, for example as a form of inactive resistance, which they would then apologise for. I once went in twice over a weekend at their request to help them with their play, which they then refused to do for me because a few people didn't arrive.

Aside the fact that mere participation in a drama project was risk-taking behaviour for many participants, the project did encourage even further behaviour and attitude change of this nature. One inmate commented:

> Before this play I wouldn't care what people thought of me. Now it worries me. I don't want people to have that opinion of me. I want to try and better myself in life. (Joelle*)

It is defensive/guarded behaviour propagated by an oppressive environment that reinforces low self-esteem that paralyses the possibility for social cohesion and the positive unifying effects that this can manifest. The subjects of the plays too (mentioned above) were also effective in the promotion of tolerance within a heterogeneous community.

> Before the drama programme I was too shy to speak to people of different nations [Xhosa's, coloureds, whites, Indians] ...but since I played the drama it is easy for me...I am not shy or scared of the people. (Thembisile*)

Through nurturing self-esteem, which encourages risk-taking behaviour and promoting tolerance through the form and content of the plays, the project was shown to have promoted social cohesion. Initially the effects seemed primarily to have affected quality of life; but their later organisational use of drama as the medium of communication for the Justice for Women Campaign, demonstrated the incarnation of Freirean pedagogy. Effectively, social cohesion enabled the women to mobilize and organize themselves using drama as a form of activism. Inmates expressed:

> We are more friendly with people: Especially this race thing we did...say for instance she had something against me being white, I would try and talk and get over that barrier. (Joelle*)
>
> Another thing that I learned from my sisters: we are unity as we are playing these drama - no matter she was fighting with me before or maybe she has got bitterness about me, as we are playing we are just sisters, we are the same family. (Tombi*)

Inside/Out Activism

It is Freire's (2000, p.175) conviction that 'to achieve...indispensable unity [among the oppressed] the revolutionary process must be, from the beginning cultural action'. Cultural action liberates and is therefore in essence dialogical, since dialogue is concerned with unity and the (re)naming/creating the world. Anti-dialogical communication is typically the mode of communication used by the oppressors since it is anti-unity and serves only to domesticate and divide the oppressed. To take it further, Freire (2000, pp.175, 176) asserts, 'The internal unity of the dominant elite which reinforces and organizes its power requires [my italics] that the people be divided'. The danger of unity amongst the oppressed is for the oppressors the danger of organisation, since 'organisation is not only directly linked to unity, but is a natural development of that unity'.

The Event Day, for the Justice for Women Campaign, which took place on 8 December 2001, was a demonstration of organisation as a result of unity made possible primarily by the social cohesion amongst the drama group (many of whom are serving sentences for murdering abusive men and most of whom have been victims of physical/sexual abuse) as well as the support of the social workers. Freire (2000, p.66) states that 'true reflection – leads to action'. The Event Day organised as conscientised action can thus be regarded as indicative of 'true' reflection and not 'mere activism' (ibid., p.65), 'action for action's sake' (ibid., p.88), which for Freire implies that it is devoid of serious reflection. For while I would choose to call it activism, I would not describe it as without reflection, since it was born out of and expressed through cultural action.

Aside from creating a general awareness of women abuse, the campaign centred specifically on 15 women who are all serving life sentences for murdering their abusive husbands. These women are requesting that they be released on time served or at least have their cases reviewed. Their argument is based on the grounds that their crimes were provoked by torturous abuse and the laws under which they were tried and convicted were not gender sensitive. Inmates, staff, representatives from the Justice for Women Campaign, the Justice Department, the Gender commission and members of the media were present.

As an activist in women's prisons, Faith (2000, pp.163, 164) has isolated 'seven organizing and unifying principles'. She states as the third principle: 'As a form of expression, music [and by extension all performance] is at the heart of social change'. She also states: 'Grassroots organizing are the only effective means of growing a social movement'. Both these aspects were intrinsic to the event. The method of articulating grievances through cultural activity is also regarded as appropriate since it is a natural cultural response for Zulu women in communicating for change within an oppressive/patriarchal society. 'Zulu society has always been largely patriarchal. Its women have been given minimal or marginal opportunity to air their views. Women have used visual and oral forms to express their feelings' (Magwaza, 2001, p.25). Thus the Freirean pedagogy, which informed our work was in harmony with the innate customary response of the majority of the women. This is how the event unfolded:

The day began with individual testimonies from two of the women convicted for murdering their abusive husbands, they were heart wrenching and ended in emotional collapse. One woman, clearly in the final stages of AIDS told of her contraction of the virus through her husbands adulterous behaviour. The other Phindile Nkosi, an active and enthusiastic member of the drama group, described torturous abuse to both her and their children. Other cultural activities such as singing by the prison choir and Zulu dance group performed, with the climax being the performance of the play by the drama group. The play was devised and workshopped by the inmates themselves. I was invited to facilitate later in the rehearsal to give them some staging advice.

The story told was a synthesis of stories - a narrative owned by everyone. It told of a woman whose husband is abusive to both her and her son. She goes to her family for advice – they tell her that they have paid *labola*, and that they can do nothing since she has been exchanged. The payment of *labola* or 'bride-price' is a traditional Nguni cultural practice, which is extensively practiced by urban and rural Ngunis today. It involves the payment of cattle (the amount to be agreed by the two families involved) as compensation (or thanks) to the bride's family by the groom in the case of marriage. It is controversial in that it is often perceived and experienced as being 'bought'.

She then goes to the priest, who tells her to kneel down and pray. Realising the futility of this gesture in the light of her life circumstances, she goes to the police to report the abuse. Her husband knows the policemen. He drinks with them regularly at the *shabeen* (bar). The policemen themselves beat their wives. One policeman sees her at the police station and gives Mr. Nene (her husband) a call. He comes down to the station and beats her in front of them. She then, in desperation hires another policeman to kill him for R1000-00. He does so and she is convicted for the murder with a maximum sentence since she has struck a deal with a fellow policeman. The tragic ending however lies not in the prejudice she endures at the hands of the criminal justice system that declares her a cold-blooded killer who murdered her husband for material gain, but the fact that her son, who is now effectively orphaned turns to crime. The play ends with his arrest, his cries for help, which no one hears. Shelters are not considered as an option for most black women. There are no shelters in the rural areas and are very few in the cities. Durban, a city of some 4 million people has only two. In addition, marriage is seen as a test of endurance and commitment, thus going to a shelter is considered going against family will (interview with inmates, 11 December, 2002).

The 15 women at the centre of this campaign have been seated around the action; they have enclosed it. As it ends they stand up, singing 'Emhlabeni sibuthwele ubunzima…' [In this world we are bearing hardships, our heavenly father, oh what have we done to deserve this…(translated by Ntokozo Ndlela)], a protest song typically sung at the funerals of those who died in political violence during apartheid. Here, it has been appropriated by the women where political oppression has been substituted for patriarchal oppression. One by one they recite a few lines of personal testimony using a 'spot-lighting' technique. One of the most memorable testimonies was from a middle-aged Indian woman who stated: 'The 15 years of abuse by my husband, was nothing compared to 20 years of having to live without my children'. This poignant statement encapsulates the concerns of many women inmates around the world; indeed these concerns of violence against women and inmates as mothers have been the primary motivating factors for activism in women's prisons the world over (Barry, 2000; Faith, 2000; Sudbury, 2000).

Activism in women's prisons in the West has been closely aligned with the feminist movement and began with the upsurge of women's issues which Second-Wave feminism brought to the foreground in the 1970s (Barry, 2000). The mantra 'the personal is political' brought with it awareness and legitimacy for concerns previously delegated to the private sphere: motherhood and interpersonal relationships. These issues touched women inmates even more sharply and continue to do so. Consequently groups with a concern for gender and race, since the majority of women (and men) in prison are black, have tended to rally around women inmates as indicative of what it is to be triply oppressed. The concern, which still resonates today, lies in the fact that women are most often the glue that keeps families and communities together. The incarceration of women means the breakdown of families and communities that in turn leads to more crime. World-renowned criminologist Pat Carlen actively campaigns for the abolition of women's incarceration entirely, outlining a strategy in her book, *Alternatives to Women's Imprisonment* (1990).

The 1970s in South Africa was a different story. It was a time of extreme repression where issues of resistance centred on political rebellion against the apartheid regime. Political men and women had, and needed, a common enemy: The Nationalist Government and the racism it enshrined. Consequently, with the focus on race, gender issues in South Africa have tended to be sidelined (Young, 1997). This propensity has unfortunately been carried over to the new dispensation. Despite our government's commitments to gender equality, which have been written into the constitution, gender issues continue to take a back seat within the public sphere. Over a period of 16 months, Media Tenor South Africa, Institute for Media Analysis, situated in Pretoria, and part of the International Media Monitoring Association analysed the importance of women-related issues in 178,160 news reports in South African daily, weekly and television media. They found that 'although females make up the majority of the South African population and are entering more and more powerful positions, issues relating to them are virtually ignored by the media' (http://*www.mediatenor.co.za* accessed 28 March, 2002). Further discussion will show, that when they do get the media's attention it is often not the attention they want or deserve.

Nevertheless, while media and other enforcement bodies (such as the police) are less committed to gender issues, the structural and conceptual changes that have occurred within the country, and by extension the prisons, have created the conditions, which make it increasingly possible for organised resistance to occur. This active resistance, which involves cultural expression, is important for galvanising social change by providing the structures or people through which concerns/injustices can be voiced in the interests of human rights. Rebecca, an American activist on the 'inside' describes the role of prison(er) activist:

> To be an activist in prison you need to talk to and for people who don't have a voice or the courage to talk in front of others. You have to find out what the problems are, pass the information on to others, yell real loud and

> not be afraid of that might happen to you (Chandler and Kingery, 2000, p.153).

It is the association of voice as agency that is most relevant here. The idea is that the voice carries with it some power to effect change. Agency is key to the process of the intervention and the practice in critical resistance/activism. Traditionally agency has been concerned with intentionality, action, will and the ability to exercise that will. However, in cultural terms, issues of agency involve 'the possibilities of action as interventions into the processes by which reality is continually being transformed and power enacted' (Grossberg, 1996, p.99). It is the ability to rearticulate and determine your own reality. This involves dialogue – participation. Yvonne Banning (1996, p.69) also asserts the dialogic nature of agency since it implies both acting on and being acted on. It involves 'action on the part of all participants – the speaker in speaking and the listener in listening'. Thus the extent to which the inmates are seen to have agency is concerned with the extent of the dialogue in which they were engaged and the extent to which they were actively listened to. To reiterate Gayatri Spivak's view in which she states (1990, pp.59-60):

> I will speak for myself as a Third World person – this is an important position for political mobilisation today. But the real demand is that, when I speak from that position that I should be listened to seriously.

During the 'barter' (Barba cited in Watson, 2000) with the students of the TFD course, the dialogue was mutually empowering. Prisoners became experts and felt a sense of self worth (Hurst, Nkala and Young, 2002). In response to a discussion on what inmates 'learnt' from the interaction with the students, one inmate emphatically retorted: 'The students also learn from us!'

The Event day for the Justice for Women Campaign in itself went well. Although an intensely emotional experience for all involved, inmates felt positive and strengthened by the practice of their own liberation and of literally fighting for freedom. The media were invited to give legitimacy to the event and in particular to enable their voices to be heard beyond the bars. Indeed, Faith (2000, p.166) writes, 'It is an important time for feminist activists to mobilise media and movement attention to women in prison'. The assumption was that the media is a powerful educative force, which is able to drum up the support needed to pressurise government authorities to bring about institutional change. However, to what extent can the media be trusted to 'truthfully' and without bias convey the message that it was intended to convey. And to what extent is the media even an appropriate mechanism to mediate, in this case, the gap between the oppressed and the oppressor in the practice of their mutual liberation? Taking the case of the *Sunday Tribune's* reportage of 9 December, I would say not at all.

The Media Merge

The headline on page five of the *Sunday Tribune* (December 9, 2001) reads in bold quotations: 'I would kill him again' (Vapi, 2001, p.5). A smaller article on page one that entices us to the bigger article has the headline: 'Jailed husband killers say "set us free"' (Vapi, 2001, p.1). As Eric Louw (1984) and John Keane (1991) point out, journalists are not all-knowing subjects but situated interpreters, mere products of their collective pasts, influenced by class position, ethnic background and of course gender. In this case the journalist was a black male.

The article begins with what appears to be a quote, but is in fact just an exercise in creative writing. 'We killed our husbands, we do not regret our actions but we do believe that we should go free' (Vapi, 2001, p.1). In the first small paragraph, he has effectively undermined the entire event – for the reading public – and labelled the inmates both psychopathic and delusional. He later goes on to say that 'Most did not regret their actions and that they had no other way of ending years of emotional and physical violence' (ibid); he does not explain why these women felt there was no other way. Without providing us with this information, which would point to our societies serious lack of infrastructural and financial support for its women, we are left thinking there must have been another way – why didn't she just leave?

Within the articles the quote 'I would kill him again' appears three times as do the words unrepentant/do not regret. For a skill in which space is an issue and every word counts, this is quite a lot of repetition. The first paragraph of the main article is equally sensational and biased.

> 'If he had to rise from the grave, I would kill him again.' These are the handwritten words on the orange t-shirt which fluttered on a makeshift clothesline at Westville Prison yesterday as part of an "open-day" anti-abuse campaign at the prison. The woman responsible [my italics] for the words says she should go free (Vapi, 2001, p.5).

The rest of the article is ambivalent but the damage was already done; the bold headline alongside a picture that can only be described as zoolike, alien and depressing is enough to make the average person think 'criminal' and leave it at that. The following section will attempt to theorise why in this instance certain media (for it would be false to assume that media are normatively homogenous) have chosen to subvert the intended message and not listen 'seriously' to the women, and by doing so confirm the lack of agency felt by the majority of women as prisoners.

Hegemony Hurts

'Cultural action either serves domination (consciously or unconsciously) or it serves the liberation of men and women' (Freire, 2000, p.179). The drama projects in the prison were action for the purpose of liberation; the reportage served the interests (consciously or unconsciously) of domination. When I asked Phindile Nkosi and the drama group how they felt about the newspaper article which they had all seen she replied 'I just cried'. When I asked why, she said that it was because firstly it had reminded her of the emotions of the day and secondly that they had 'turned it all around'. This statement met with fierce nodding and exclamation from the rest of the group. Be assured, hegemony does hurt.

The concept of hegemony, developed by Lenin to describe the need for intellectual and moral leadership, rather than force to sway the peasants to support the revolution (1917), was used by Antonio Gramsci to describe the way in which the 'ruling classes obtained the consent of the subordinate group to their own domination' (McLellan, 1979, p.185). The manner in which the ruling classes were/are able to look after their own interests without resistance from subordinate groups was/is primarily through cultural power – through 'the so-called organs of public opinion – newspapers and associations – which...in certain situations are artificially multiplied' (Gramsci, 1971, p.80).

This cultural power used for the purposes of domination ultimately serves only one master – the powerful. Looking at class/race/gender power dynamics as reflected in South African society today, those that constitute what it is to be powerful are specifically male and specifically middle-class of either black or white race. Black men tend to dominate in the government sector while white men still dominate the private sector. The manner in which cultural power is able to serve the interests of the oppressors is through social control gained through the well known adage 'Divide and Rule' as enforced through difference and fear (of crime and criminals). As discussed previously, 'the [powerful] minority cannot permit itself the luxury of tolerating unity of the people, which would undoubtedly signify serious threat to their own hegemony' (Freire, 2000, p.141). Consequently, media that serves the interests of big capital/ (white) patriarchy functions to reinforce difference (perhaps unconsciously) amongst the population to secure the power of the oppressors. Difference is established through the effective dehumanising of the oppressed – in this case prisoners, which feeds into what will now be discussed – the fear industry.

The Fear Industry

> If the humanisation of the oppressed signifies subversion, so also does their freedom; hence the necessity for constant control. And the more the oppressors control the oppressed, the more they change them into apparently inanimate 'things' (Freire, 2000, p.59).

This desire by the oppressors to dehumanise humans, which for Freire is the essence of sadism, demonstrates a fear within the oppressor to see 'the other' within 'the same'. It demonstrates what Freire (2000, p.46) terms a 'fear of freedom'. This fear exists both within the oppressed and within the oppressor. Within the women inmates it was quite literally demonstrated:

> Some of us have been here [in prison] a long time, so it made me think that when I go back home one day, people are going to back off from me because I come from Westville Prison – that's how I felt…this fear, it is in you. (Joelle*)

Through the positive interaction with the students, who for the inmates represented 'the outside'/freedom, the drama programme enabled the inmates, to some extent to overcome this fear through praxis. Within the oppressor, a fear of freedom is based on recognition of his role as the one who oppresses and the inevitable relinquishing of power, necessary for his liberation. The fear industry operates to reinforce those binaries in every effort to ensure that oppressive structures remain in place for the profit of the few. For:

> The fear of crime is the greatest fear of all, and no domestic segment of society is more demonised than the one consisting of criminals. The alleged offender is no longer part of 'us' but has suddenly become one of 'them' (the other upon whom evil can be justly visited) (Mead, 2000, p.11).

This binary of 'us' and 'them', which polarises, divides and effectively paralyses the population, is perpetuated by this media hysteria, which whips up fear in the population by creating a perception of criminals as 'psychopathic, deviant, sadistic madmen [and women] bent on ravishing a helpless prone citizenry' (Abu-Jamal, 2000, p.22).

In the light of the crime increase in South African society, most do not need much convincing; many need to take the moral high ground and pronounce what is right and wrong, who is good and evil in black and white terms, where a growing desire to 'Bring Back the Death Penalty' is being increasingly publicly expressed by South Africans of all class and ethnic backgrounds. Opportunistic politicians feed into this frenzy, hoping to benefit from what Abu-Jamal terms the Industry of fear: 'Nail em and Jail em!' shout Democratic Alliance (DA) banners of the 2000 election. Newspapers flash sensationalist headlines and consumers put their mouth where their money is – another crime story to swap at the dinner table.

This climate of insecurity which financially benefits those 'peddlers of real or fictional terror…the police, the justice system, industry and the weapons and security trade' (Duclos, 1998 cited in Parenti 2001, p.23) as well as the capitalist press, which sell newspapers and politicians who use it as a rallying point, actually serves as a means of social control (Parenti, 2000; Foucault, 1980). Crime and fear of crime as embodied in the myth of 'the criminal', as Parenti (2000) discusses, short-circuits the social cohesion necessary for political mobilisation since communities are afraid to knock on doors or go out after dark. If we ask, 'who benefits?' in this instance we come up with an uncomfortable yet familiar answer: those whose 'business' it is to serve communities. They include politicians, the police (since no crime means no police), the justice system and ultimately (and perhaps inadvertently) the capitalist media.

Out and About

The revolutionary and transformative potential of art and culture is articulately express by Angela Davis (1984, p.199):

> Art and culture are...special forms of consciousness that can potentially awaken an urge in those affected by it to creatively transform their oppressive environments. Art and culture can function as sensitisers and catalysts propelling people towards involvement in organised movements seeking to effect radical change. Art and culture are special because of their ability to influence feelings as well as knowledge.

Thus while cultural production acts as the principle means to ensure hegemony (Gramsci, 1971) and thus patriarchy, it can also function as the method to conscientise, mobilise and revitalise communities and individuals through the retelling of their own histories (Freire, 1972, 2000) with the agency that affords. Consequently, the fact that media and other systemic forms of cultural endeavour can be domestication does not, and must not, negate the positive achievements of 'the oppressed' in their struggle for liberation through the praxis of cultural action.

That we should be more suspicious of media which exists to serve another master, I heartily agree, for their hegemonic agenda can only harm those who threaten to expose their injustice. We need to talk directly to the people who matter; fortunately members of non-governmental organisations and government who ultimately have the power to effect change were present at the Event day.

Prison activist and inmate on death-row in the United States, Mumia Abu-Jamal (2000) proposes a two fold strategy to counteract the effects of the fear industry, in which I include the notion of a 'fear of freedom' (Freire, 2000, p.46): to deconstruct and expose the false presumptions upon which it is based and to embrace a grassroots approach that encourages consciousness-raising since 'Authentic thinking' writes Freire (ibid., p.77) takes place at the grassroots not in ivory towers. Abu-Jamal motivates with the energy of his words:

> Let us organise around that which is uplifting, and essentially human about us. We can then relegate the fear industry to the dusty museum basement of history. Ona Move. Down with this New Age slavery! (2000, p.23.)

Note

1. This material is based upon work supported by the National Research Foundation (NFR) under Grant number NRF5542. It has also been partially funded by the Community, Higher Education, Service Partnership (CHESP). Any opinion, findings and conclusions or recommendations expressed in this material are those of the author(s) and do not necessarily reflect the views of the National Research Foundation. The names of the inmate respondents are fictional.

References

Abu –Jamal, M. (2000), 'The Industry of Fear', *Social Justice: A Journal of Crime, Conflict and World Order*, vol. 27, no. 3, pp.22–25.

Acey, C. (2000), 'This is an Illogical Statement: Dangerous Trends in Anti-prison Activism', *Social Justice: A Journal of Crime, Conflict and World Order*, vol. 27, no. 3.

Agozino, B. (1997), *Black Women and the Criminal Justice System*, Ashgate, Aldershot.

Balfour, M. and Poole, L. (1998), 'Evaluating Theatre in Prisons and Probation', in Thompson, J. (ed.), *Prison Theatre: Perspectives and Practices*, JKP, London.

Barry, E.M (2000), 'Women Prisoners on the Cutting Edge: Development of the Activist Prisoners' Rights Movement', *Social Justice: A Journal of Crime, Conflict and World Order*, vol. 27, no. 3.

Boal, A. (1979), *Theatre of the Oppressed*, Pluto Press, London.

_____ (1992), *Games for Actors and Non-actors*, Routledge, London.

Carlen, P. (1990), *Alternatives to Women's Imprisonment*, Open University Press, Buckingham.

Chandler, C. and Kingery, C. (2000), 'Yell Real Loud: HIV Positive Women Prisoners Challenge Constructions of Justice', *Social Justice: A Journal of Crime, Conflict and World Order*, vol. 27, no. 3.

Davis, A. (1984), *Women, Culture and Politics*, The Women's Press, London.

During, S. (ed.) (1993), *The Cultural Studies Reader*, Routledge, London.

Faith, K. (2000), 'Reflections on Inside/Out Organizing', *Social Justice: A Journal of Crime, Conflict and World Order*, vol. 27, no. 3, pp.158-167.

Fanon, F. (1990/1965), *The Wretched of the Earth*, (4th Edition), Penguin, London.

Foucault, M. (1984), 'Space, Power and Knowledge', an interview with Paul Rainbow, in During, S. (ed.) (1993), *The cultural Studies Reader*, Routledge, London.

Freire, P. (1973), *Education for Critical Consciousness*, Continuum, New York.

______ (2000), *Pedagogy of the Oppressed*, (3rd Edition), Continuum, New York.

Gramsci, A. (1971), 'Selections from Prison Notebooks', in Nowell-Smith, G. and Hoaew, Q. (Trans and eds), Polity Press, London.

Grossberg, L. (1996), Identity and Cultural Studies: Is That All There Is? in Hall, S. and du Gay, P. (eds), *Questions of Cultural Identity*, Sage, London.

Habermas, J. (1994), 'The Emergence of the Public Sphere', in *The Polity Reader in Cultural Theory*, Polity Press, Cambridge.

Hall, S. (1996), *Critical Dialogues in Cultural Studies*, Routledge, London.

Heritage, P. (1998), 'Theatre, Prisons and Citizenship: A South American Way', in Thompson, J. (ed.), *Prison Theatre: Perspectives and Practices*, JFK, London.

______ (1998), 'Rebellion and Theatre in Brazilian Prisons: An Historical Footnote', in Thompson, J. (ed.), *Prison Theatre: Perspectives and Practices*, JFK, London.

Hooks, B. (1989), *Talking Back: Thinking Feminist Thinking Black*, Sheba Feminist, London.

______ (1993), *Yearning: Race, Gender and Cultural Politics*, Turnaround, London.

Hughes, J. (1998), 'Resistance and Expression: Working with Women Prisoners and Drama', in Thompson, J. (ed.), *Prison Theatre: Perspectives and Practices*, JFK, London.

Hurst, C., Nkala, B. and Young, M. (2002), *Theatre for a Developing Nation 2001: An evaluation*, Unpublished Report on the first level service-learning course run by the Drama and Performance Studies Programme at the University of Natal in partnership with Westville Prison. Keane, J. (1991), *Media and Democracy*, Polity Press, London.

Kerr, D. (1995), *African Popular Theatre*, David Phillip, Cape Town.

Loots, L. (2001), 'Re-situating Culture in the Body Politic', *Agenda: Empowering Women for Gender Equity*, no. 49, pp.9-14.

Louw, E. (1984), 'The Libertarian Theory of the Press: How Appropriate for the South African Context?', *Communicato*, vol. 10, no. 1, pp.31-36.

Macedo, D. (2000), 'Introduction', in Freire, P. (ed.), *Pedagogy of the Oppressed*, Continuum, New York.

Magwaza, T. (2001), 'Private Transgressions: The Visual Voice of Zulu Women', *Agenda: Empowering Women for Gender Equity*, no. 49, pp.25-33.

McLellan, D. (1979). 'Gramsci', *Marxism after Marx*, 2nd edn, Papermac, London.

Mead, E. (2000), 'Reflections on Crime and Class', *Social Justice: A Journal of Crime, Conflict and World Order*, vol. 27, no. 3, pp.11-15.

Munns, J. and Rajan, G. (eds) (1995), 'Antonio Gramsci (1891-1937)', *A Cultural Studies Reader: History, Theory, Practice*, Longman, London.

Parenti, C. (2000), 'Crime as Social Control', *Social Justice: A Journal of Crime, Conflict and World Order*, vol. 27, no. 3, pp.43-50.

Simon, B., Ngema, M. and Mtwa, P. (1983), *Woza Albert*, Methuen, London.

Spivak, G. (1990), *The Post-colonial Critic: Interviews, Strategies, Dialogues*, Routledge, London.

Sudbury, J. (2000), 'Transatlantic Visions: Resisting the Globalisation of Mass Incarceration', *Social Justice: A Journal of Crime, Conflict and World Order*, vol. 27, no. 3.

Thompson, J. (ed.) (1998), *Prison Theatre: Perspectives and Practices*, Jessica Kingsley Publishers, London.

Watson, I. (2000), 'Towards a Third Theatre', in Goodman, L and de Gay, J. (eds), *The Routledge Reader in Politics and Performance*, Routledge, London.

Worrall, A. (1990), *Offending Women: Female Lawbreakers and the Criminal Justice System*, Routledge, London.

Young, M. (1997), *Gender Dynamics and the Role of Participatory/Development Theatre in a Post-apartheid South Africa: The Example of DramAidE*, unpublished Master's Thesis, Graduate Programme in Cultural and Media Studies, University of Natal, Durban.

Internet Source

Media Tenor: http://www.mediatenor.co.za

9 Women and (African) Indigenous Justice Systems

OGBONNAYA OKO ELECHI

Introduction

This chapter examines the African indigenous justice systems from a restorative and transformative paradigm. In particular, inquiries into gender relations in African indigenous justice systems are undertaken. The author maintains that African indigenous justice systems employ both restorative and transformative principles in conflict resolution. Furthermore, that individual rights and interests are better protected and advanced within groups. Women, mindful of their social, economic and political disadvantage in the society, and conscious of their special interests, have put to good use their superior social organization and group identification capabilities to protect and promote their common interests.

In addition, women like men have access to constitutionally enshrined sanctionary powers, which they can invoke to counter the oppressive policies of the men. Amongst the Igbo people of Nigeria, women have analogous institutions where they mediate on disputes amongst themselves. Similar to men, women age-grades and village groupings are involved in the resolution of conflict. Women can also take cases directly to any of the indigenous institutions of conflict resolution just like men. It is widely believed that what affects the individual affects the community too. Women are therefore encouraged to bring up their marital problems to the public institutions of conflict resolution for adjudication. Being an interventionist culture, relatives, friends and neighbours do not hesitate in intervening in what many might otherwise consider the domestic problems of others.

While one can claim that all have equal access to the institutions of conflict resolution, it is important to point out that the indigenous institutions of conflict resolution are male dominated. However, all litigants and defendants are supported by friends, well wishers and family members. Again, participation in the African indigenous institutions of conflict resolution is voluntary. Litigants therefore, have the right to appeal against resolutions of indigenous courts to state courts. State courts have power and rights to review and overturn decisions of the indigenous courts.

African indigenous justice systems recognize that crime damages people, communities, and relationships. The needs of victims for validation, restitution, and support are a priority in Africa. Efforts are therefore made to restore the injury, property and relationships affected by the conflict. Furthermore, the community's peace, stability, harmony and trust, which are undermined by the conflict, are recognized and addressed. Victims, offenders, their families and friends, and community members as primary stake-holders in the conflict are involved in the definition of harm and search for resolution. Decisions are reached through a consensus and are devoid of any semblance of power.

Believing that individuals are inherently good, offenders are treated with respect and their need for reintegration into the community recognized. Ample opportunity and encouragement are provided offenders to appreciate the harm they caused victims and the community, and to work to make things right. Offenders' needs and competencies are taken into consideration and addressed. This African principle of justice is similar to Braithwaite's (1989) concept of reintegrative shaming. According to Braithwaite, 'reintegrative shaming' dispenses social disapproval and shaming of the wrong, while maintaining respect and understanding for the wrong-doer.

African indigenous justice systems see crime not just as a violation of people and relationships, but also as an opportunity for transformative healing for all – victim(s), offender(s), family members, friends, witnesses and members of the community. Conflict resolution creates opportunities for education, socialization and resocialization of not only the victims and the offenders, but of all community members. Conflict is appreciated as an opportunity for moral growth and transformation. The values, and socio-economic condition of the community are further re-examined in the process. It is generally believed that crime indicates a failure of responsibility. While the primary responsibility is that of the offender, the culpability of the family and the community is not overlooked. The mutual responsibility of community members' for each other in Africa is acknowledged. Akin to the peace-making perspectives, African people view crime and non-conformity as resulting mostly from the socio-economic marginalization of the individual, and work always to transform the social, economic and political environment. (For more on peace-making criminology, see Pepinsky and Quinney, 1991.)

It is further contended that restorative and transformative justice systems satisfy victims, communities, and offenders better than state-based retributive justice systems. Restorative and transformative justice systems recognize that crime damages people, communities and relationships. It therefore, seeks to empower victims, offenders, and the community members in non-adversarial community-based processes to attend to the needs created by the offence. The devolution of power to the community to address conflicts raises other concerns. Questions asked are whether restorative and transformative justice, being a community-based justice system will take into account the power imbalance and the disadvantaged position of women and other minority groups? This chapter addresses these concerns by examining the relationship between women and the African indigenous justice systems. African indigenous justice system is premised on a restorative and transformative model, which involves mediation, restitution and compensation principles. Materials for this chapter derive mostly from the author's research on the indigenous justice system of the Afikpo Igbo of Southeast Nigeria. However, much of the discussion has relevance for other African countries.

Principles of African Indigenous Justice Systems: A Brief Overview

There are two justice systems in operation in contemporary African societies. One is the state administered justice system modelled on the western judicial systems. Like the erstwhile colonial authorities' judicial system, its process is adversarial and focuses on punishment and rehabilitation of offenders. Received laws are said to be power and rule-based. On the other hand, African indigenous justice system remains relevant and dominant for the majority of conflicts in Africa. African indigenous justice system is process-oriented and has its goal as the restoration of relationships and social harmony disrupted by the conflict.

Received laws according to Parnell (1988) rule with power, while indigenous courts rule with principles. As such, everybody has equal access and participation in the justice system. No one can arrogate to him or herself the role of professionals thereby subjugating the voices of the laymen. It therefore, in an environment devoid of the semblance of power, provides opportunities for the primary stakeholders of conflict – victims, offenders, their relations and supporters and the community to be heard, and for the stakeholders' fears and concerns to be addressed. It is reiterated here that while everyone has equal access and participation in the institutions and processes of conflict resolution in Africa in principle and in practice, the contradictions of generational, gender and class inequality combine to disadvantage many.

The goal of African justice system is to heal what has been broken and to reunite relationships divided by the conflict. As Armstrong et al. (1993, p.14) rightly observed, 'African systems of justice focus on the processes of achieving peaceful resolutions of disputes rather than on adherence to rules as the basis of determining disputes'. Strenuous efforts are made to bring about a resolution which parties to the conflict believed just and fair. Primary stakeholders of the conflict – victims, offenders, their families and supporters and the community, must consider the processes of conflict resolution procedurally fair, and they must be satisfied with the outcome.

African indigenous justice systems measure the quality of justice through the well-being of victims, the community and the offenders too. It views crime as a violation of one person or persons by another, and not simply as law breaking. It further recognizes crime as an offence against human relationships. In other words, it recognizes that in any conflict there is sometimes a victim and that the community also suffers victimization in a conflict between community members.

African indigenous justice systems do not only seek to restore relationships broken due to conflict, but also seeks to understand and address the underlying causes of the conflict. Conflict becomes an opportunity to review and address socio-economic conditions prevailing in the community. The principle underlying this thinking is as Morris (1995, p.70) eloquently put it, 'you can't restore a community to wholeness that never was whole'. For justice to be meaningful, it has to address the underlying socio-economic problems in the community from which the conflict arose. Morris describes it best when she observes that 'transformative justice is a better approach for all parties involved in the triangle of crime: victims, offenders, and community. It prioritizes responding to the challenge of crime creatively in a way that transforms the problem of crime into opportunity' (ibid). Furthermore, restorative and transformative justice views a conflict situation as a learning opportunity for both the offender and all primary stakeholders. Every participant gets re-socialized into new ways of acting and being in community.

In traditional African societies, according to Gyekye (1996) and Motala (1989), the individual's right to food and shelter was respected and protected. Everyone had access to land, since land was owned both privately and communally. The mainstay of African economy was agriculture. Everyone was encouraged to work, and idleness carried a social stigma. African societies being gerontocratic, the elders are the custodians of the community wealth. The elders, as custodians of the community land administered the land to the best interest of the lineage or community.

Old age is deferred to in recognition of the contribution and wisdom of the elders. Besides, almost everyone will get old and enjoy the same status. However, it is important to note that the elders do not own or control the community land, but only hold it in trust for the lineage or community. An abuse of the position could result in replacement and or denial of other privileges. Land in Igbo communities for example is not a marketable commodity, and so the individual has the right to use the land for the production of food and development for residential purposes only.

African religion is human-centered (Mbiti, 1970). The human-centeredness of African religion is an indication that the human being is paramount in value and is an end in itself. Morally speaking, the human being is the foundation of values. Ifemesia (1978) describes it best when he characterizes Igbo societies as humane. A humane living according to him is a

> … a way of life emphatically centered upon human interests and values, a mode of living evidently characterized by empathy, and by consideration and compassion for human beings … Igbo humaneness is deeply ingrained in the traditional belief that the human being is supreme in the creation, is the greatest asset one can posses, is the noblest cause one can live and die for (cited in Iro, 1985, p.4).

That human beings are at the center of the universe does not suggest that other animals, plants and all of nature are expendable. As Kamalu (1990, p.14) points out, 'human-beings are very much part of the animal kingdom and of nature. It is recognized that human survival depends on the maintenance of an equilibrium or harmony in human-beings' relationship with other life-forms'.

African indigenous justice systems focus mainly on the victim rather than on the offender (Nsereko, 1991, p.22). The goal of the justice systems is to vindicate and protect the victim's rights. It is widely believed in Africa that victims, whose needs are un-addressed may likely become offenders. As such, strenuous efforts are made to create opportunities for victims to speak about their feelings and fears, and for the community to address the victims' concerns. Again, victims have suffered both material and emotional losses and need restitution. Further, victims need societal recognition of their pain and suffering. Victims of crime need the restoration of their power and dignity taken away by the experience of an offence. Most of all, victims need to understand the offender's motivation for committing crime against them.

Furthermore, the imposition of punishment on the offender was designed to bring about the healing of the victim rather than to punish the offender. In any conflict, rather than punish the offender for punishment sake, the offender was made to pay compensation to the victim. This practice, according to Nsereko (1992, p.22), was 'intended to restore the victim to the position he was in prior to the commitment of the offense. This was, of course, limited to the extent to which money or property could solve the problem'. Compensation goes beyond restitution according to Nsereko (1992). Compensation symbolizes apology and atonement by the offender to the victim. Above all, compensation ceremonies dissipate the animosity that victimization may engender between both the victim and the offender and their families. Furthermore, the African indigenous judicial processes also 'facilitated speedy and inexpensive justice to the victim' (Nsereko 1992, p.25). A major objective of African indigenous justice system is the re-establishment of the dignity of both victims and offenders and the re-integration of persons harmed and alienated.

Victim care is a priority because of the strong social solidarity and a prevailing spirit of good neighbourliness in the society. Morality is a corporate affair and it is recognized that crime affects not only the victim but the whole community. As such, victims and the community are central to the justice process. African judicial processes allow for the full participation of victims, offenders, their families and co-villagers. As primary stakeholders in the conflict they are involved in the definition of harm and search for resolution. In other words conflict resolution processes involve negotiation and dialogue. Decisions are arrived at through consensus of members present. The focus is in healing what was broken and to reunite the relationship that was divided as a result of the conflict. The full participation of victims, offenders, their families, supporters and the community in conflict resolution strengthens community bonds. The free exchange of information, participation and discussion by the stakeholders further enhances crime detection, prevention and resolution.

The needs of offenders are not neglected. Offenders are provided opportunities to be heard and to make amends. African indigenous justice systems value offenders' needs to end their alienation and to be re-integrated into the community. Giving rise to this practice is the African philosophical understanding that no individual is innately bad. A person is not inherently good or evil but may act in ways which are good, when they conform to the customs and regulations of his or her community. A person can exhibit evil behaviour when he or she acts in ways that go against the customs and regulations of his or her community. This explains why African justice systems are able to differentiate the actor from the act. Hence, African judicial systems are capable of condemning an act and retaining understanding and respect for the actor.

African indigenous justice systems acknowledge offenders are sometimes harmed by their own actions. Since Africans view themselves as a collective and therefore responsible for the well-being of their members, the needs of their members, including victims and offenders are addressed. The offender is confronted and challenged in a friendly and supportive environment. Offenders are held accountable for their actions. When sanctions are imposed, they are for compensatory aim intended to restore victims to their previous positions rather than for the punishment of the offender. Compensation goes beyond restitution; it represents some form of apology and atonement by the offender to the victim. However serious an offence is in Africa, it can be atoned for with a commensurate sacrifice or reparation.

African indigenous justice procedures are flexible, dynamic and apply a wide concept of relevance for many facts affect the settlement of conflicts. Rigid pursuit of individual rights by litigants is considered inappropriate and is discouraged. However, Gluckman (1969) observes that the judges of African indigenous courts, in deciding a case, take into consideration the nature of the relationships out of which the disputes emanate. Legal rights of litigants are sometimes therefore de-emphasized and discouraged, as the history of the relationships between litigants, are given primacy. The sphere of power of African indigenous courts is wide, as they exercise both administrative and legal functions. 'Civil suits' can consequently be converted into 'criminal hearing' if the interests of litigants and the community will be better served as a result.

African indigenous courts concept of relevance is rather extensive. Considerable weight is given to the relationship existing between litigants. Distinction is given between 'blood-kin' and 'fellow-villager' relationships for example. In disputes between husband and wife, which in comparison with that between blood-kins could be considered more ephemeral, the focus of the judges could be the 'relevant facts.' The range of relevance could even be reduced much further if the dispute is between strangers. Gluckman observes that strenuous efforts are generally made to reach a compromise 'acceptable to, and acceptable by all parties'.

African peoples according to Gluckman (1969) are notoriously litigious and could go to court for various reasons, even when they are aware that the case may not be decided in their favour. Gluckman notes:

> … the litigants in coming to court have appealed for a public hearing of their grievances, and these are examined against the norms of behavior expected of people. The judges therefore upbraid all the parties where they have departed from these norms. Judgments are sermons on filial, parental, and brotherly love (1969, p.157).

Litigants are also aware that the judges are capable of drawing a line between legal and moral rules. The judges are empowered to protect and enforce legal rules. While moral values are taken into consideration, the judges know they cannot enforce moral rules. However, the judges will frown at a litigant who insists on legal rights as against seeking 'justice'. People easily differentiate between legal and moral victories.

Uchendu (1965) further observes that amongst the Igbo, a fair and just judgment must take into account a wider range of facts and interests, including that of the community, without necessarily compromising the facts of the matter in dispute nor the interests of litigants. Uchendu states:

> Igbo legal procedures aim essentially at re-adjusting social relations. Social justice is more important than the letter of the law… The resolution of a case does not have to include a definitive victory for one of the parties involved. Judgment among the Igbo ideally involves a compromise and consensus. They insists that a good judgment 'cuts into the flesh as well as the bone' of the matter under dispute. This implies a 'hostile' compromise in which there is neither victor nor vanquished, a reconciliation to the benefit of – or a loss to both parties (1965, p.14).

Empowering communities to do justice raises other questions and challenges. Does the system equally protect and serve women and other groups who are marginalized in African societies? It is recognized here that when there is a power imbalance between members of the community, it may be difficult to engage in equitable conflict resolution, especially one that depends on full and free exchange of information, participation, discussion and consensus amongst participants. Some women's rights advocates posit that the rights of women and other minority groups are better protected by the state.

A major finding of this study is that individual rights and interests are better protected and advanced within groups. African women protect their rights and interests through women's organizations. In Afikpo for example, women, like men, are organized along age lines. They are also natural members of family groupings, patrilineal and matrilineal groupings. These organizations are expanded and strong forms of peer groups, which though hierarchical, have a high degree of social solidarity. These organizations in addition to providing economic and social support to members, are also strong rights protectors and advocates for its membership. Furthermore, participation in the African indigenous institutions of conflict resolution is voluntary. Litigants therefore, have the right to appeal against resolutions of indigenous courts to state courts. State courts have power and right to review and overturn decisions of the indigenous courts.

African Pre-Colonial Political Organization

To understand the African indigenous justice systems and processes, a brief review of African pre-colonial political organization is imperative. The social history of Africa falls into three periods: the pre-colonial, colonial, and post-colonial. The interest in African pre-colonial societies is because of the relevance of these institutions in African peoples' life today. African indigenous justice systems hold sway in the rural areas where the majority of the people reside.

Elias (1962) categorized African pre-colonial political organizations into two broad groups. African societies in the first group had a centralized political authority, 'administrative machinery' or 'judicial institution'. Societies in this group are generally heterogeneous according to Elias, but defer to one political superior, usually the 'Paramount Chief' or the 'King-in-Council.' Societies in this group are the Zulu, the Ngwato, the Bemba, the Bayankole etc. These Southern African societies comprise several ethnic groups, which explain the necessity for the use of force to hold them together. There are class distinctions based on wealth, privilege, and status and the 'incidence of organized force which is the principal sanction in a society based upon cultural and economic heterogeneity' (p.11). However, there are exceptions to this rule according to Elias, for the Zulus and Bemba kingdoms are culturally homogenous for example. The Ashantis' of Ghana also belong to this latter group.

The Ashantis of Ghana is a good example of a pre-colonial African society with a hierarchical political arrangement. Busia Jr. (1994) citing Busia (1951) observes that the social organization of the Ashanti was and remains based on kinship lineage networks. The political body was centered around the kinship system and the heads of the various lineages. The Ashantis operated a federal system of government that comprised about twenty-two chiefs (petty kings). The political authority rested on the king, together with the other paramount chiefs who constituted the 'Ashanteman' council. The head of the council remained the king whose headquarters was in Kumasi. The council, as the major authority, had power to maintain law and order. It also had the authority to declare war and also enter into treaties with other tribal groups. Each member of the council had a different role. Next to the King who had executive powers was the Prime Minister. Each of the other councilors managed a portfolio like finance, public relations and so on. Two other offices worthy of note were the head of all the women within the federal system known as the 'Queen-mother' and the head of the youth whose office had no political significance.

The King-in-council held court to try both civil and criminal cases. The cases brought before the king were of two kinds, namely the public and private. Homicide and treason, for example, are tried in the King's supreme court. Other cases like adultery, slander, and assaults, were handled as private cases within the lineage units.

The office of the King was an elective one. Eligibility, however, was limited to members of the royal family. The Prime Minister acts in the event that the incumbent dies, abdicates his office or is deposed from power. The Queen-mother, as the head of the royal family, is constitutionally empowered to nominate a candidate for the office of the King.

Busia (1951) and Busia Jr. (1994) note that the King did not rule for life, and that he remained in office for as long as he enjoys the good will of his people. Any of the King's subjects has constitutional rights to institute impeachment proceedings against the King. The case succeeds if the applicant is able to convince the majority of the councilors that the king has breached his oath of office. However, if the case fails, the applicant could pay with his life.

The Igbos of Nigeria

In the second category are the African societies with a decentralized political authority. These societies were erroneously believed to possess no laws or leaders and to be strongly individualistic. Societies in this group include the Logoli of Western Kenya, the Tallensi of Northern Ghana, the Nuer of Sudan and the Igbos of Southeast Nigeria. It is important to note that few Igbo societies have constitutional monarchy. Uchendu (1965) lists the Onitsha, Agbaja, and the Aro-Chukwu as few of the Igbo societies that were not completely acephalous. However, the villages in these communities remained autonomous and leadership was exercised through the Council of Elders. Further, the participatory democracy and egalitarian outlook of the people were not affected by the hierarchical socio-political arrangement. It is noted however, that at certain levels of political discourse, women and children were not allowed full participation.

The system had certain internal mechanism for the maintenance of law and order, and also for the enforcement of political decisions. The Igbo people of Nigeria are a good example. The Igbos had no political arrangement that could be called a federation, a confederacy or state. When there is a case or matter that affects the whole village groups, representatives of the villages meet in a general assembly. Jones (1965, p.5) notes that no village 'could be bound by a law or decision made at a meeting in the absence of its representatives' (cited in Uchendu, 1965, p.45).

All persons, including the villages, had equal rights and privileges. Decisions reached at these general meetings were through consensus, which was essential as sanctions against recalcitrant persons or groups were rarely enforced by force. All had a voice in these meetings, even though the elders, especially the ruling age grade, wielded a lot of influence. At the village level, however, what obtains can be considered a direct democracy, notes Uchendu (1965). All adults, including men and women are, represented. It is important to point out that the talks are dominated by men. Women talk only when they are directly involved, either as witnesses, plaintiffs or defendants. Women can also initiate the proceedings as a group or make a representation as a group. The set-up is aptly summed up by, Uchendu (1965, p.46):

> The picture of the Igbo political community which emerges from these settings is one that is territorially small enough to make direct democracy possible at the village level as well as representative assembly at the village-group level; and in which there are leaders rather than rulers, and political cohesion is achieved by rules rather than by laws [sic] and by consensus rather than by dictation.

In Igbo society, the middle-age grades make up the Council of Elders, and they are the major authority in the town and constitute the traditional government. The society is relatively egalitarian, as such, the chances of an individual's rights being violated are minimal. Again, most social and political activities are carried out either through the age grade, family groupings and the lineage, so that the individual's rights are better protected. The powers of the elders are well defined and limited with sufficient breaks such that the individual's rights are not encroached upon.

Depending on the task at hand, a capable individual could emerge to direct the course of events. Such an individual, as against collective leadership of the elders, only lasts for the duration of the event. For example, in Afikpo there have been instances where hippopotamuses were terrorizing villagers, sometimes leading to their evacuation. On one occasion, a brave man organized other men to attack and kill the beast. The community honored the individual with the title of the 'hippo killer'. Again, according to the rules of hunting, it is the individual that inflicts the first wound on the animal that is recognized as the owner of the kill, no matter who eventually kills the game. Yet, he is required to share with others in the hunt and those at home, the meat from the kill. As a matter of fact, the recognized killer of the game is entitled to only the head of the animal, and the rest of the animal is shared among hunting mates, relations and others according to culturally established hunting rules.

An individual leader can also emerge in times of war or other emergencies. Basden acknowledging the collective leadership of Igbo people posits:

> In times of emergency a dominating character automatically came to the front, and the people accepted him as leader until the trouble ceased. He then reverted to his former position in common with other citizens. Nor were any hereditary rights attached to the erstwhile leadership; the basic principle of no ruling families in Iboland remained inviolate. Where such prerogatives are beginning to appear, they are the fruit of modern innovations; they are really contraventions of native laws and customs (cited in Amadi, 1982, p.96).

Women and the African Indigenous Justice System

Social control in society is effected through formal and informal mechanisms. Formal social control methods are coercion-oriented, as in the functions of criminal justice officials. Men tend to be more controlled through formal mechanisms, since they dominate the public sphere. On the other hand, informal mechanisms of social control tend to be persuasion-oriented and relate to the controls exercised by the institutions of marriage, family, and peer groups. It is generally believed that women are more controlled through informal mechanisms since they prevail in the private sphere. Morris (1987, p.17) however, considers such characterizations an overstatement, noting 'men and women are both controlled by such mechanisms as the family, marriage, work and concepts of "masculinity" and "femininity."' Regardless, Morris (1987) agrees that social control mechanisms can operate differently on men and women.

To understand the status of African women under the community's traditional justice system, an examination of the institutions of marriage and family as well as the laws and customs of the people is very important. The marriage systems and the African extended family not only reflect both the social and economic conditions of societies but also have implications for the status and rights of the women. In addition, customary laws have been known to reproduce oppressive patriarchal values and practices. Recent experiences of Canadian Aboriginal women with customary laws, according to Nahanee, confirm 'customary sanctioning of sexual offenders in particular has been ineffective in curbing sexual violence against women, children. Besides, certain customary cultural values of kindness, reconciliation and family cohesiveness may in fact prevent Aboriginal women from officially reporting violence in the home' (Jackson, 1994, p.17). Informing this viewpoint is the belief that the modern state by its nature and agenda has a better view of the rights of women and other minority groups. For an examination of the institutions of marriage, family, divorce and African feminist theories, see Elechi (1999).

To understand how African women cope with the African indigenous justice system, a brief review of two women's organizations is imperative. As earlier observed, pre-colonial African societies can be categorized into two: centralized and decentralized political structure. The Igbos of Nigeria from where most of the empirical data for this study was gathered operated a decentralized political system. A few Igbo societies, as earlier noted, however, had a centralized, hierarchical political structure. The Onitsha Igbos is a good example.

Nzegwu (1995) describes pre-colonial Igbo political culture as 'dual sex'. Arguably, there is no generic or universal woman. Women under the African system operated a parallel social and political institution as that of the men. According to Nzegwu,

> under this dual-symmetrical structure, women had their own Governing Councils – *Ikporo-Onitsha, Nd'inyom* – to address their specific concerns and needs as women. The councils protected women's social and economic interests, and guided the community's development. This dual-symmetrical structure accorded immense political profile to women both in communities with constitutional monarchies (on the western side and some parts of the eastern banks of the River Niger – Onitsha, Ogbaru, and Oguta), and in the non-centralized democracies of the eastern hinterland (1995, pp.445-6).

Nzegwu (1995) observes that despite the fact that Igbo society was polarized along gender lines, that the relationship between men and women could hardly be described as antagonistic. It is generally believed in Igboland that a harmonious gender relationship was essential for the stability and progress of the community. Decision making in the community was generally arrived at through a consensus, and as such full consultation and participation of relevant actors was the norm. Women were fully involved and actively participated in some of the decision-making bodies of the community. Women's involvement in decision making in the community, according to Nzegwu (1995) is not because they are women but because of their unique insight into community affairs 'by virtue of their spiritual, market and trading duties, and their maternal roles' (p.446). For example, the *Obi* of Onitsha according to Nzegwu worked in partnership with the *Omu* (the female monarch) in governing the Onitsha people before the advent of colonial rule. This was also the case in the Ashanti Kingdom of Ghana earlier noted, where the Queen-mother's constitutional role was entrenched and protected.

Prior to 1890, when colonial authorities asserted their foothold in Nigeria, Onitsha women were led by a female monarch – the *Omu*. The *Omu* exercised her authority through the women's council – the *otu ogene*. Their role complemented that of the *Obi* of Onitsha – the male monarch. According to Nzegwu (1995), the *Obi* and the *Omu* institutions were responsible exclusively for the actions and activities of the Onitsha men and women respectively. However, their powers and functions complemented one another. Further, at the national level the two institutions worked together to formulate and execute policies of national interest.

When the British colonial authorities instituted the indirect rule system in Nigeria, the *Omu* and other womens' organization were greatly destabilized. While the colonial masters recognized and appointed men as representatives of 'natives' in governance, women were not accorded this recognition nor represented at any governmental level. Women's autonomy and public functions were as a result eroded. Subsequent colonial policies further derailed women's economic, social and political interests and independence. One notable example of this policy was that only men were enrolled in the newly introduced colonial schools at the time. Paid employment was therefore accorded men since they possessed the requisite skills. Nzegwu (1995, p.451) notes:

> Whereas in the past Igbo men had to share power with women, as they succeeded educationally, economically, and politically, they egoistically

> clung to power and could not be depended upon to distribute resources equitably. The co-optation of African men into the Western gender stereotypes did incalculable damage to modern Nigerian political culture. Freed from the restraining checks and balances that had curtailed sexism, male bias was massively built into policies, programmes, and structures of the system to safeguard it for men. The results were the denial of effective representation to an inordinately large number of women; the exclusion of women's corrective influence in governance; and the creation of a politically passive female citizenry and sexist, dictatorial men.

To meet their present social, economic and political needs, Onitsha women have transformed the *Omu* into a new organization known as the *Ikporo Onitsha*. The organization is headed by the oldest surviving woman known as *Onye-isi-ikporo Onitsha* (the head of Onitsha women). Nzegwu (1995) notes that while the power and prestige of the new organization does not equal that of the *Omu,* the women's organization still commands the respect and loyalty of both men and women in Onitsha today. Assisting the *Onye-isi-ikporo-Onitsha* in the management of the affairs of Onitsha women is a 35 member Governing Council. In addition, there is a general secretary and six to seven women leaders of opinion whose role are of advisory nature. Again, each of the nine founding villages of Onitsha has three representatives in the Council. This organization represents and promotes the interests of Onitsha women both within and beyond Onitsha town.

Amadiume (1987) further raises issues with the notion of the generic woman and the assumption that women's interests and roles were one and the same at all levels. Amadiume insists there was no rigid conception of gender in pre-colonial Igboland. This gender flexibility made it possible for women and men to share important social roles and status. Women and men therefore shared power in economic, social and political arena. Furthermore, the interests and roles of the woman in Igboland as daughter and member of the patrilineage differed considerably with that of the woman as a wife. According to Amadiume (1987, p.16),

> The mere fact of daughters' acting in collaboration with the patrilineage men in the interests of their patrilineage – whether as a police force against the wives or as ritual specialists dealing with confessions of infidelity or adultery by wives, and cleansing the patrilineage of pollutions and abominations – shows that one cannot talk of women's common interests being represented at all levels.

Afikpo is the Igbo town in which the author grew up and in which the fieldwork for this research was conducted. Unlike the Onitsha society, it has a decentralized government structure. Afikpo is a republican society in which age grades, lineage heads and social organizations are actively involved in the administration of the area. All power and authority in Afikpo is exercised through the age-grade system.

The age grade is perhaps the most significant indigenous social and political institution in Afikpo. Most social and political activities are organized through the age grade system. The age grade is a strong medium for conflict resolution and the enforcement of compliance to social norms. The age grade system is built on a cohort principle that organizes people born within approximately three-year intervals, initially at the village level. The village age-groupings identify and relate with their counterparts in other villages to exercise roles that affect the village-group as a whole.

The age grade system cuts across descent and class lines. Social class division and consciousness is low in Afikpo, and this is partly due to the age grade that groups together people of different socio-economic status. The only social distinction that the Afikpo people recognizes is that based on age. It is noted that gender and wealth is important but doubtful if wealth bestows political power, since leadership is exercised through the age groupings. The age-grade system has the following leadership hierarchy:

1. the junior elders made up of men in their fifties and early sixties known as the *Ekpuke Eto* age grades.
2. the middle and senior sub-grade consists of members in their mid-sixties and above and they are known as the *Ekpuke Essa* age grade.

These last two sets make up the Council of Elders and they are the major authority in the town and constitute the traditional government. However, Afikpo now has a traditional ruler in the office of the *Omaka-Ejali Ehugbo* created by the Federal Government of Nigeria in 1976. Beyond minimal involvement in conflict resolution in Afikpo, the Chief-in-Council's role is primarily symbolic. The Chief wields no traditional political role of any significance. The Chief represents Afikpo in both State and Federal traditional rulers meeting. The institution with the highest authority in Afikpo is the *Okpota* General Assembly. It functions as the Supreme Court of the land. It is the court of last appeal and deal with issues bordering on the security of the community and is an assembly of all adult males in Afikpo.

It is important to emphasize that female social and political activities are carried out separately from those of males. While females have a distinct organized age grade set, they are linked with their male counterparts. Women's age groupings are limited mostly to married females, widows and divorcees. Women age groupings however, meet with their male counterparts occasionally to discuss matters of common interest. Within the villages however, women have one overarching grouping of all the married women, divorcees and widows, variously called welfare or development associations. These organizations meet regularly – once a month to discuss issues of concern to all the women. In Afikpo town with 26 villages, there are twenty-six autonomous women organizations. The organizations are headed by the junior elders in their fifties. These organizations are pretty popular and enjoy a high level of legitimacy. One reason why the women's organizations are popular and perceived as legitimate is the interest free loans they provide their members and also the moral and social support members receive from the groupings in times of need. The women's village groupings, apart from protecting and promoting the interests of the women, also constitute into judicial panels to mediate on conflicts amongst their membership.

Discussion

Nzegwu (1995) describes gender relations in Africa as 'dual-sex'. This is because women operate separate social and political organizations through which they exercise power over their membership. These organizations are very effective in regulating women's behavior, and also providing, social, economic and moral support. In national affairs the organizations provide advocacy for their members. African women strongly believe that what affects one of them also affects the group as a whole. Efforts are therefore made to protect and promote their interests. Most of all, women's 'access to sanctionary powers and the judicial and constitutional backing to use its powers if need be...' acts as a major check on the power of the men (Nzegwu, 1995, p.447).

In Afikpo, the two political bodies with the highest power and authority in the town are the *Okporta* General Assembly and the Council of Elders. It is within these institutions that laws and policies for the administration of the town are made. Women do not participate in their meetings. However, it is believed that women are consulted before policies that would affect them are enacted. The process through which women are consulted is not clear. It is doubtful too that such consultations are made before decisions are reached considering that proposals for policies or laws are thoroughly debated until participants in the general assembly reach a consensus on the matter. What is clear however, is that men in making decisions are guided by their sensitivity particularly to the interest of the general well-being of the people as a whole, and the interests of women in arriving at any decision. As Nzegwu (1995) noted, men conscious of the consensus-seeking traditions of African society, must do everything to avoid antagonistic gender relations.

Sometimes men make policies that impinge on the rights of women. Attempts are first of all made by women to persuade the men to rescind the decision or have a rethink on the matter. Where such appeals fail, women who have a heightened sense of gender and class-consciousness will invoke their sanctionary powers. As Nzegwu (1995, p.447) observes,

> women's independence was fostered by cultural traditions that placed a premium on female assertiveness and collectivity, and did not define power as socially deviant. If men usually capitulated and were, or seemed politically 'helpless' before the collective strength of women, it is not because they were passive or timid. It was more that they were *accustomed* to women *being* in positions of power and influence, and had consequently developed respect for their administrative skill. The

> indigenous structures of governance publicly validated and reinforced women in ways that normalized their presence in the judicial, economic, and political spheres of life.

A case in point where women invoked their sanctionary powers to back up their demand was in the famous 1929 Women's War. According to Nzegwu (1995), Igbo women sensing that colonial policies had marginalized and reduced them to dependent status repeatedly took their protest to the offices of the colonial masters. Women demanded to be represented and consulted in the formulation of policies and general administration of the land, which they were accustomed to in the indigenous government. They also demanded to be exempted from paying tax since the colonial policies had undermined their economy, and the situation was exacerbated by the 1920s global economic recession. While this political protest started in one part of the Igboland, women putting to use their superior administrative and networking skills, had no difficulty in mobilizing other women in other parts of the land to their cause. The colonial authorities tried to placate the women by removing the Warrant Chiefs who the women accused of corruption. This failed to assuage the thirst of the women for justice, as some of the vexing issues such as their representation and consultation by government and their demand to be exempted from paying tax were not also addressed.

Recently in Afikpo, the indigenous government passed a decree restricting women travelling to certain towns for business, ostensibly for the security of the women. The women protested and refused to abide by this policy. The women rightly interpreted the policies as attempts by the men to control their movements and economic activities. Their militancy and political activism is not limited to indigenous governments. They have also successfully challenged the policies and appointments of the state government. In 1997 the Afikpo women organized to protest the retention of the principal of one of the secondary schools in the town that was oppressing and exploiting students. The state government in attempting to avert breakdown of law and order in the town responded by transferring the principal to another school in another town.

Afikpo women have successfully resisted certain cultural practices they find discriminatory and oppressive. A good example of this is their recent refusal to swear to the customary oath of chastity. Married women in Afikpo have on a regular basis been subjected to the swearing of oath of chastity to prove their faithfulness to their marital vows. Women have all the time lamented this cultural practice that look on women's sexual indiscretion as a problem but not that of men. A women's organization of one of the villages saw the opportunity to challenge this cultural practice when they noticed that the wives of the prominent politicians and some middle-class ladies who claim swearing an oath to a deity violated their Christian beliefs. The women argued and insisted that until every woman residing in the village was made to participate in the swearing of the oath of chastity, that none of their members would abide by the chastity oath swearing tradition. The men's elders' council could not get every woman in the community to swear to this oath of chastity. That ended this contentious patriarchal cultural practice. Soon after, every village in the town adopted the same argument and strategy to defy the chastity oath swearing tradition.

In the mid-1970s in Afikpo, the men in one of the villages met to discuss what might be responsible for the lack of birth in the village for about three years. Unaware to the men, the women had collectively decided to boycott their husbands' bed within this period to protest what they considered the waywardness of the men. The men after receiving agricultural loans from the government started staying out late and neglecting the family. The women met as a group to discuss this and tried individually but failed to call the men to order. The women's collective and unique approach no doubt got the attention of the men.

Women use mass divorce as the last resort to get men to rescind decisions found inimical to the well-being of the women. A well-known case where the women applied this method was when their member – a widow – was denied access to a farmland contrary to laid down practices. After all appeals to all the community's institutions of conflict resolution failed, the women protested by parading themselves naked through the village playground. Even this rarely applied customary means of protest failed to get the men to change their mind. The women therefore walked out en masse out of the village only taking with them their children that were still breast-feeding.

Women have also used satire to great effect for both psychological and social benefit to address their social standing. Cultural practices that discriminate against women are sung about to draw the community's attention to them. Authoritarian and irresponsible men are used in songs. Women have also used state agencies of social control to their advantage. The welfare offices in the town have been effective in enforcing alimony and child support payments. These are areas where the traditional institutions of social control have been found to be ineffective.

It is pertinent to observe that the average Afikpo woman is economically independent. Women do most of the peasant farming although men are custodians of the lineage farmlands. Men and women as individuals also own lands. Lineage lands are available to anyone interested in farming. The lineages own most of the land and make land available to lineage members, both men and women. However, men are more involved in the cultivation of yam, which is the cash crop. Most Afikpo men are subsistence farmers. The high status of yam crop in Igboland is of more symbolic value than its wealth-generating worth. Women can also cultivate yam but rarely do. When women are involved in yam cultivation it is not in large scale as that of men. Unlike other crops, yam cultivation is labor intensive and involves intricate processes. Other farm products where women farmers are dominant such as cassava, coco-yam, okro, vegetables, groundnuts and so forth are readily sold by women both at the local and distant markets. Certain crafts such as pot making, ropes, and cloth dyeing are areas where Afikpo women excel. They are also highly profitable ventures. Women also dominate the local market activities. Women make a lot of money through farming and trading, and exercise full control over their resources. One positive aspect of polygyny is that women tend to have high social and economic autonomy.

Ottenberg's (1959) and Amadiume's (1995) viewpoints contrast with the above position. Amadiume (1995, p.24) citing Ottenberg (1959) argues that 'not even in the face of colonialism and the subsequent growth of petty commodity trade, did this sexual imbalance change for Afikpo women, who remained immobile, unorganized, and under the firm control of their menfolk'. Amadiume also claims that since Afikpo women are not incorporated into the lineages of their husbands, the women's statuses in their husbands' households are usually ambiguous. Furthermore, that since most of the lands are controlled by the matrilineal lineage, women's usefulness to their husbands depended on the amount of land they can provide to their husbands. This position hardly describes the lot of Afikpo women today. There is also no indication that this describes the lot of Afikpo women in the 1950s when Ottenberg carried out the fieldwork. Afikpo women arguably dominate the subsistence economy. Women just like men have unfettered access to matrilineal lands.

Most farmlands in Afikpo are owned by the matrilineages. Women are the spiritual leaders of the matrilineages. They are the custodians of the matrilineage shrines. Women are likely to depend on their matrilineage for their farmlands rather than on their husbands. Husbands may benefit from their wives' lineage lands. One should have thought this arrangement would accord the woman more bargaining power in the marriage. The woman's dominant position in the control of farmlands, the most important factor of production in agrarian communities accords her certain degree of economic independence and autonomy from her husband. One is tempted to argue that the high divorce rate in Afikpo has a lot to do with this economic independence and autonomy enjoyed by Afikpo women. Until recently, over 75% of marriages in traditional Afikpo were likely to end in separation or divorce. It is not uncommon to find a woman in Afikpo who married over four husbands in her lifetime. The high divorce rate in Afikpo could also result from the fact that family members do not hesitate to intervene in the marriages of a family member if they have reason to believe either their daughter or son is having a bad deal in her or his marriage. As Amadiume (1995, p.82) rightly observes, in 'Igbo culture, it is her brothers that a woman expects to fight for her and protect her, *not her husband*' (emphasis in original). African families look after their own and this protection does not cease after the daughter is married away for example. It is important to note also that divorce does not attract stigma in Afikpo. Again, men tended to marry women much younger than them. Young women were expected to remarry after their husbands passed away.

In conclusion, it is important to note that in Afikpo, men dominate the major indigenous institutions of dispute resolution like in most patriarchal societies. Many cultural practices underscore the subservient position of women in society. During many cultural ceremonies, women's freedom of movement is sometimes affected. Women are penalized in the courts for violating these cultural practices. Women's sexual freedom and chastity especially in marriage remain open for public control. While there is no evidence to suggest that gender affects the outcome of cases at the indigenous courts, gender bias is implicated by the nature of the cases that come before the courts. Further, cases are determined according to the customs and traditions of the land. The argument here is that Afikpo women have a heightened sense of gender and class-consciousness. They have organized and successively resisted certain cultural practices they find oppressive.

On the other hand, the middle-class Afikpo woman's point of view on the relationship between women and the indigenous justice system differs somewhat from that of the rural woman. In the author's interview with a female university professor, she was of the opinion that status rather than gender was more likely to influence the course of justice. She was of the opinion that the court processes were politicized. She believed some of the indigenous court judges were greedy and corrupt. The educated woman according to her was greatly disadvantaged. The educated woman's behaviour was viewed with suspicion. People were quick to label her a liberated woman and attach motives to all her behaviours and utterances. She believed that the rural Afikpo women ware better organized, economically independent and had established customary lines of resistance against the oppression and control of the men.

Conclusion

This chapter examined the relationship between Women and the African indigenous justice systems. African indigenous justice systems employ restorative and transformative principles in conflict resolution. This study addressed the concerns often expressed regarding community based justice systems in a patriarchal society. Findings from this study indicate that individual and group rights are better protected and advanced within groups. Women conscious of their relative weaker economic and political position in the society, have employed their superior social organization, group identification and solidarity capabilities to protect and promote their common interests. Women are also encouraged to bring up their marital problems to the public institutions of conflict resolution for adjudication because of the belief in the community that what affects the individual also affects the community.

Most of all, women use their access to culturally and constitutionally enshrined sanctionary powers to counteract the oppressive policies and powers of men. Moreover, judgments of the indigenous courts can be appealed against to the state courts that have the ultimate power in the society.

Again, participation in the indigenous institutions of conflict resolution is voluntary. It is difficult to assume that the litigants' gender affected the outcome of a case in the African indigenous justice system. Litigants are supported by friends, well-wishers and family members. There is no reason to believe women lack confidence in the African indigenous justice system. All participants in the justice process are equal and actively participate in principle. However, men play dominant roles and tend to have stronger public speaking skills. All cases are publicly adjudicated.

References

Amadi, E. (1982), *Ethics in Nigerian Culture*, Heinemann Educational Books, (Nigeria) Ltd, Ibadan.

Amadiume, I. (1995), *African Matriarchal Foundations: The Case of Igbo Societies*, Karnak House, London.

Amadiume, I. (1987), *Male Daughters, Female Husbands: Gender and Sex in an African Society*, Zed Books Ltd, London.

Armstrong, A., Beyani, C., Himonga, C., Kabeberi-Macharia, J., Molokomme, A., Ncube, W., Nhlapo, T., Rwezaura, B. and Stewart, J. (1993), 'Uncovering Reality: Excavating Women's Rights in African Family Law', *Women and Law in Southern Africa*, Working Paper no. 7, WLSA Harare, Zimbabwe.

Braithwaite, J. (1989), *Crime, Shame and Reintegration*, Cambridge University Press, New York.

_______ (2002), *Restorative Justice and Responsive Regulation*, Oxford University Press, New York.

Busia, Jr. N.K.A. (1994), 'The Status of Human Rights in Pre-Colonial Africa: Implications for Contemporary Practices', in McCarthy-Arnolds et al. (eds) *Africa, Human Rights and the Global System*, Greenwood Press, Westport, Conn.

Cayley, D. (1998), *The Expanding Prison: The Crisis in Crime and Punishment and The Search for Alternatives*, The Pilgrim Press, Cleveland, Ohio.

Christie, N. (1981), *Limits to Pain*, Universiteteteforlaget, Oslo.

______ (1973), *Criminological Data as Mirror for Society*, Institute for Criminology and Criminal Law Stenciseries, no. 15, Oslo.

______ (1976), *Conflict as Property*, Institute for Criminology and Criminal Law Stenciseries, no. 23, Oslo.

Dike, C.P. (1986), 'Igbo Traditional Social Control and Sanctions', in *Igbo Jurisprudence: Law and Order in Traditional Igbo Society*, papers presented at the Ahiajoku Lecture (Onugaotu) Colloquium, Ministry of Information and Culture, Owerri, Nigeria.

Elechi, O.O. (1991), *Alternative Conflict Resolution in (Ehugbo) Afikpo*, Institute for Criminology and Criminal Law, Stenciseries, no. 67, Oslo.

______ (1996), 'Doing Justice Without the State: The Afikpo (Ehugbo) Nigeria Model of Conflict Resolution', *International Journal of Comparative and Applied Criminal Justice*, vol. 20, no. 2.

______ (1999), 'Victims Under Restorative Justice Systems: The Afikpo (Ehugbo) Nigeria Model', *International Review of Victimology*, vol. 6, pp.359-375.

Elias, R. (1993), *Victims Still: the Political Manipulation of Crime Victims*, Sage Publications Inc, Newbury Park, CA.

Elias, T.O. (1956), *The Nature of African Customary Law*, Manchester Press.

Fattah, A.E. (1995), 'Restorative and Retributive Justice Models – A Comparison', in Kuhne, H. (ed.), *Festschrift fur Professor Koichi Miyazawa*.

______ (1998), 'A Critical Assessment of Two Justice Paradigms: Contrasting the Restorative and Retributive Justice Models', in Fattah, E. and Peters, T. (eds), *Support for Crime Victims in a Comparative Perspective: A Collection of Essays dedicated to the memory of Prof. Frederic McClintock*, University Press, Leuven.

Gibbs, Jr., J.L. (1973), 'Two Forms of Dispute Settlement among the Kpelle of West Africa', in Black, D. and Mileski, M. (eds), *The Social Organization of Law*, Seminar Press, New York.

Gluckman, M. (1969), 'The Judicial Process Among the Barotse of Northern Rhodesia' (originally published 1955) in Aubert, V. (ed.), *Sociology of Law*.

Gyekye, K. (1996), *African Cultural Values: An Introduction*, Sankofa Publishing Co., Accra, Ghana.

Harris, M.K. (1989), 'Alternative Visions in the Context of Contemporary Realities', in *Justice*: *The Restorative Vision: New Perspectives on Crime and Justice*, Occasional Papers of the MCC Canada Victim Offender Ministries Program And MCC US Office of Criminal Justice, February, Issue no. 7.

Iro, M. (1985), 'Igbo Ethics and Discipline', in *The Igbo Socio-Political System*, papers presented at the 1985 Ahiajoku Lecture Colloquium, Ministry of Information, Culture, Youth and Sports, Owerri, Nigeria.

Iwuagwu, A.O. (1980), 'The Ogu Corpus and the Igbo Concept of the Moral Law', paper presented at the 1980 Ahiajoku Lectures Colloquium, Ministry of Information and Culture, Owerri, Nigeria.

Jackson, M. (1994), 'Aboriginal Women and Self-government', Crim. 840 Casebook Compiled by Prof. Joan Brockman, Simon Fraser University.

Kamalu, C. (1990), *Foundations of African Thought: A Worldview Grounded in the African Heritage of Religion, Philosophy, Science and Art*, Karnak House, London.

Morris, R. (1995), *Penal Abolition: The Practical Choice*, Canadian Scholars' Press, Toronto.

Morris, R. (1999), *7 Steps From Misery Justice to Social Transformation*, Rittenhouse, A New Vision, Toronto.

Njaka, E.N. (1974), *Igbo Political Culture*, North Western University Press, Evanston.

Nsereko, D.D.N. (1991), 'Extenuating Circumstances in Capital Offenses in Botswana', *Criminal Law Forum*, vol. 2, no. 2.

Nsereko, N. (1992), 'Victims of Crime and Their Rights'. in Mushanga, T.M. (ed.), *Criminology in Africa*, United Nations Interregional Crime and Justice Research Institute (UNICRI), Rome.

Nsugbe, P.O. (1974), *Ohafia: A Matrilineal Ibo People*, Oxford University Press, Clarendon.

Nzegwu, N. (1995), 'Recovering Igbo Women's Traditions for Development: The Case of Ikporo Onitsha', in Nussbaum, M. and Glover, J. (eds), *Women, Culture and Development*, Oxford University Press.

Ogundipe-Leslie, M. (1993), African Women, Culture and Another Development, in James, S.N., Abena, P. and Busia, A. (eds), *Theorizing Black Feminisms: the Visionary Pragmatism of Black Women*, Routledge, New York.

Okere, T. (1986), 'Law-Making in Traditional Igbo Society', in *Igbo Jurisprudence: Law And Order in Traditional Igbo Society*, papers presented at the 1986 Ahiajoku Lectures Colloquium, Ministry of Information and Culture, Owerri, Nigeria.

Onwuachi, C.P. (1977), 'African Identity and Ideology', *Festac "77*, African Journal Ltd., London.

Ottenberg, P.V. (1959), 'The Changing Economic Position of Women among the Afikpo Ibo', in Bascon, W.R. and Herskovits, M.J. (eds), *Continuity and Change in African Cultures*, The University of Chicago Press, Chicago.

______ (1965), 'Inheritance and Succession in Afikpo', in Duncan, J. and Dekkett, M. (eds), *Studies in the Laws Of Succession in Nigeria*, Oxford University Press, London.

______ (1968), *Double Descent in African Society – the Afikpo Village Group*, University of Washington Press, Seattle.

Ottenberg, S. (1971), *Leadership and Authority in an African Society: The Afikpo Village-Group*, University of Washington Press, Seattle.

Otuu, M.O. (1977), *Afikpo (Ehugbo) Age-Grade Organization (A Study in Continuity And Change)*, unpublished B.Sc. Thesis, June 1977, Nsukka, University of Nigeria.

Parnell, C.P. (1988), *Escalating Disputes: Social Participation and Change in the Oaxacan Highlands*, The University of Arizona Press, Tucson.

Pepinsky, H.E. and Quinney, R. (eds) (1991), *Criminology as Peace-making*. Indiana Press, Bloomington.

Rattray, R.S. (1929), *Ashanti Law and Constitution*, Oxford University Press, Clarendon.

Ross, R. (1996), *Returning to the Teachings: Exploring Aboriginal Justice*, Penguin Books, Toronto.

Uchendu, V.C. (1965), *The Igbo of Southeast Nigeria*, Holt, Rinehart and Winston, New York.

Umozurike, U.O. (1981), 'Adjudication Among the Igbo', in *Perspectives on Igbo Culture*, papers presented at the 1981 Ahiajoku Lectures Colloquium, Ministry of Information and Culture, Owerri, Nigeria.

Van Ness, D. (1989), 'Pursuing a Restorative Vision of Justice', in *Justice: The Restorative Vision*, Occasional Papers of the MCC Canada Victim Offender Ministries Program and the MCC U.S. Office of Criminal Justice, February, Issue no. 7.

Van Ness, D. and Strong, H.K. (1997), *Restoring Justice* (2nd Edition), Anderson Publishing Co, Cincinnati, Ohio.

Wilson, A.R. (1986), 'Customary Marriage and Divorce in Igbo Society', in *Igbo Jurisprudence: Law and Order in Traditional Igbo Society*, papers presented at the 1986 Ahiajoku Lectures Colloquium, Ministry of Information and Culture, Owerri, Nigeria.

Wiredu, K. (1997), 'Democracy and Consensus in African Traditional Politics: A Plea For a Non-Party Polity', in Eze, E.C. (ed.), *Postcolonial African Philosophy: A Critical Reader*, Blackwell Publishers, Cambridge, Massachusetts.

Zehr, H. (1989), 'Stumbling Toward a Restorative Idea', in *Justice: the Restorative Vision: New Perspectives on Crime and Justice*, Occasional Papers of the MCC Canada Victim Offender Ministries Program and the MCC US Office of Criminal Justice, February, Issue no. 7.

______ (1990), *Changing Lenses: A New Focus for Crime and Justice*, Harald Press, Waterloo, Ontario.

Acknowledgements

My very special thanks and appreciation go to Professors Biko Agozino and Anita Kalunta-Crumpton for this great opportunity and for their editorial comments and advice.

10 Crossing the Wrong Boundaries: The Dilemma of Women's Drug Trade Participation in Jamaica

MARLYN J. JONES

Introduction

This chapter explores women's drug trade participation dilemma in Jamaica. Through an examination of statistics from the Correctional Services of Jamaica, the Jamaica Constabulary Forces and Jamaican media reports of drug offences committed by Jamaican women either in their own country or abroad. It addresses the following questions: (1) In what ways does drug trade affect Jamaican women? (2) Are women in Jamaica incarcerated for the same category of offences as those women in North America or Europe? (3) What can be done to correct the situation? The chapter concludes with the recommendation that in order to develop policies to address increased female participation in drug crimes within the Caribbean region, ethnographic studies should be conducted with (1) Jamaican females incarcerated in Jamaica and in foreign jurisdictions and (2) female foreign nationals incarcerated in Jamaica.

The chapter fills, in part, a gap in the literature in respect of drug offences of Jamaican females. Drawing on feminization of poverty and underdevelopment theses, the chapter highlights some consequences of prohibitionist drug policies. It suggests that the source country focus of US drug policies contribute to the underdevelopment of the Caribbean region. Although underdevelopment of 'Third World', and specifically Caribbean nations, has had adverse economic consequences, women are disproportionately affected. Consequently, many women have adopted poverty alleviating strategies, with increasing rates of drug related arrests showing that not all strategies are legal. A brief description of the US drug policy ensues to give context to the discussion.

US Drug Policy

The National Drug Control Strategy (NDCS), produced by the Office of the National Drug Control Policy (ONDCP) represents the official drug policy of the United States government. This strategy includes elements of demand reduction, supply reduction, user accountability and zero tolerance. The United States drug control has undergone a number of distinctive phases in which a wide variety of policies, strategies and tactics have been used to control the illegal drug problem. Despite the range of responses, two primary focuses are supply and demand reduction. The dominant drug policy response remains prohibitionist in nature with supply reduction emphasizing elimination of drugs at the source.

As part of the drug-free 21st century mandate, the NDCS has established a number of supply reduction targets for drug producing and transit countries. An underlying assumption of these targets is that social, political and economic conditions will not prevent countries from attaining the imposed goals. Additionally, the United States has arsenal such as the certification process to ensure cooperation in achieving its imposed reduction targets. The certification process assesses whether countries have taken adequate steps on their own to meet the goals and objectives of the 1988 United Nations drug convention. Non-complying countries may be decertified. De-certification involves the withdrawal of all but humanitarian and anti-narcotic aid and the withholding of US vote from international funding agencies such as the International Monetary Fund (ONDCP, 2002). Although de-certification has economic consequences, supply reduction targets are implemented without regard for the social, political and economic environment in which drug producing or transit nations operate.

Anti-drug legislation allows the United States to regulate both domestic and international jurisdictions. Simultaneously, the National Drug Control Strategy, annually reiterates that the US federal government will resist all attempts to legalize marijuana, hemp and hemp products (ONDCP, 2002). Consequently, concerns about the consequences of practices such as US drug certification restrict Caribbean nations from implementing policies that respond to the particularities of their local society. For example, US drug supply reduction initiatives also incorporate the supposition that the United Nations will not change the schedule for drugs, thus maintaining marijuana as a Schedule 1 drug. A Schedule 1 designation means that marijuana has no legally accepted medical use.

The NDCS identifies most Caribbean nations as major source and/or drug transit areas. However, the 2001 International Narcotics Control Strategy Report (INCSR) released in March 2002 categorizes Jamaica as the leading transit point for cocaine entering the United States from South America. Although Jamaica is both a producer of marijuana and a transit point for cocaine, statistics from the Jamaica Constabulary Force indicate that there has been a decline in the amount of marijuana (ganja) produced with a concomitant increase in cocaine transiting the island.

Recognizing the need to address cocaine trafficking through its borders, in 2000 Jamaica established a commission to study the decriminalisation of (ganja) marijuana. The Commission found that the majority of Jamaicans favoured the legalization of marijuana. Rastafarians are among the most verbal stakeholders long seeking legalization of marijuana in Jamaica. Horace Campbell's *Rasta and Resistance* and myriad other publications discuss efforts of the Rastafarians to have marijuana legalized within Jamaica. Consequently, Rastafarians were also active participants in making submission to the Ganja Commission. However, The Ganja Commission represents governmental acknowledgement of legalization as an alternative drug policy with the potential for addressing some of the island's crime problems.

While acknowledging legal and international challenges, The *Report of the National Commission on Ganja* (Chevannes, 2001, p.41) recommended decriminalisation of ganja for personal use. More importantly it notes:

> [P]unitive sanctions administered by the justice system to users of small quantities [of marijuana] is not only unjust but is a major source of disrespect and contempt for the legal system as a whole. Moreover, the punishment meted out to such offenders has not had and is not likely to have the desired effect of a deterrent. Administering the present law as they apply to possession and use of small quantities of ganja not only puts an unbearable strain on the relationship of the police with the communities, in particular male youth, but also ties up the justice system and the work of the police, who could use their time to much greater advantage in the relentless pursuit of crack/cocaine trafficking (Chevannes, 2001, p.56).

The commission's report was tabled in the Jamaican parliament. However, soon after its release, US embassy staff in Jamaica reiterated that the United States would consider Jamaica's adherence to drug protocol in its annual drug certification review (Williams, 2001).

The importance of being able to respond to local particularities is underscored by national drug statistics from Jamaica (see Tables 10.1a, 10.1b and 10.2) indicating that marijuana-related offences comprised the majority of drug related arrests. Therefore, marijuana decriminalisation would help to reduce court cost, eliminate the reported backlog of cases, and reduce Jamaica's correctional population and its criminal justice expenditures. The ability to reduce and/or reallocate criminal justice expenditures would allow the island to direct the resources where they are most needed. For example, approximately 60% of Jamaica's budget is currently being used for debt servicing, leaving the remaining 40% to cover all other category of expenses. During the 2000/1 fiscal year 62.7% of the total budget was earmarked for debt service charges. Payment of principal accounted for 36.3% (The Expenditure Budget, 2001). Consequently, social services, health and education are grossly under funded. Nonetheless, concerns about the consequences of de-certification result in resources being disproportionately allocated to curtail drugs destined for the United States.

Jones (2002, p.120) identifies women's increased involvement to be one of the consequences of the displacement effects of drug policies on Jamaica. Although increased participation emanates, in part, from displacement effects of the drug trade, women's economic position has become a significant contributor to their drug trade participation. Other contributors include Jamaica's current status as the leading Caribbean drug transit nation and the gendered nature of the drug trade.

Consequences of Drug Policy for Women

The drug war's contribution to an increase in the female prison population is reflected in the number of women incarcerated on drug related charges (Human Rights Watch 2000; Szalavitz, 1999; Mauer et al., 1999). The feminist literature uses the term feminization of the drug trade to describe this phenomenon. As used, the term suggests that the war on drugs has disproportionately affected women (Szalavitz, 1999). Women still constitute a minority of all offenders and prisoners worldwide. However, the past decade has seen an unprecedented increase in the female prison population in Britain, Canada and the United States. The population is disproportionately the poor and women of colour incarcerated for drug offences (Greenfeld and Snell, 1999; Pollock, 2002, p.53; Sudbury, 2001; Heaven, 2001; Carlen, 1999).

Foreign nationals convicted on drug related offences now represent a growing sub-population within women's prisons worldwide (Sudbury, 2000; Heaven, 2001; Richards et al., 1995). In 1996, approximately one-third of the population at Dublin Female Correctional Facility in California were foreign nationals (Buck and Whitehorn, 1996). Bureau of Justice Statistics data on non-citizens also show that the 'criminal alien' population in the US is steadily rising. It is important to emphasize that within the United States, the criminalisation of women is racially and geographically disproportionate. Minority women (black and Hispanic) represent a disproportionate share of the women sentenced to prison for a drug offence. Human Rights Watch (2000, np) reports that while incarceration rates for both black and white women have increased by approximately two-thirds since 1990, in 1997 black women were more than eight times as likely as white women to be in prison. For example, in 1990 the ratio of female prisoners for all women in the United States was 31 per 100,000 with 19 and 117 for whites and blacks respectively. This increased to 57 per 100,000 populations with a ratio for whites of 34 and 212 per 100,000 populations for blacks (Greenfeld and Snell, 1999, p.10).

Correctional Services of Canada recognized the increase of females in Canadian federal facilities and established a Working Group on Foreign National Offenders. However, the Canadian working group reported that a central issue raised by foreign national women concerned having to rely on immigration lawyers for information. More significantly, many had problems retaining lawyers for their case since legal aid does not provide one for them. In September 1994, the

Working Group identified only 23 female foreign nationals at Kingston's Prison for Women (P4W) (*http://www.csc-scc.gc.ca/text/prgrm/fsw/fsw17/toce.shtml*) but by 2001 these numbers had increased significantly. In Canada, sentences less than two years are served in provincial facilities. Ontario and Quebec, two provinces with large immigrant populations, reported an increase in the number of incarcerated immigrants from the Caribbean. Consequently, information based on Canadian federal statistics exclude a large percentage of the incarcerated population and may be a conservative estimate of Jamaicans in Canadian institutions.

Sudbury (2000, p.134) notes that while the British prison industrial complex is small in comparison to that of the US, the dramatic increase in the British prison industrial complex disproportionately affected people of color and specifically, African-Caribbean women. For example, in 1998, 24% of Britain's prison population were women while men comprised only 18%. Furthermore, while British born African-Caribbean persons comprised 2% of the free population, they comprised 12% of women prisoners and 10% of men prisoners. Foreign nationals including women were 14% of Britain's female prisoners and 7% of male prisoners (Sudbury 2000, p.134). Pollock (2002, p.207 cited in Carlen, 1999, p.124) notes that in 1997 only 4% of Britain's prison population were women, however, 16% were foreign nationals. Richards et al. (1995) note that foreign nationals in British prisons often experience a more harsh prison environment than their native counterpart.

A review of the literature indicates that women in prison in the United States, Britain and Canada are disproportionately low income, with low levels of educational attainment, high rates of substance abuse and mental illness (Mauer et al., 1999, p.1; Heaven, 2001). Many women under correctional supervision are mothers of minor children (Greenfeld and Snell, 1999, p.1) and have experienced prior sexual and or physical abuse (Greenfeld and Snell, 1999, p.1; Mauer et al., 1999, p.1; Weston-Henriques and Gilbert, 2000). This leads one to question whether the profile is similar in other jurisdictions? Much is known about women incarcerated in North American and British jurisdictions, however, little information exists on women incarcerated in the Caribbean region.

The Jamaican Situation

The statistics on women offenders from the Jamaica Constabulary Force and the Correctional Services of Jamaica are not as extensive as statistical information found in the United States, Canada and Britain. Nonetheless, the Jamaican criminal justice statistics and media reports indicate that while the majority of arrests continue to be of males, the number of women arrested in Jamaica for drug offences continues to increase. Simultaneously, Jamaican women are highly represented in correctional population in other jurisdictions and Jamaica's female prison also has a large foreign national population (Burrell, 2001).

Jurisdictions such as Britain have experienced an increase in apprehension of Jamaican drug couriers, many of whom are women. Jamaica's news media daily run headlines such as *13 more drug mules charged in London, 22 J'cans Charged.*

Drug Mules held in London, British dental nurse fined, British prison home to many Jamaican women, Drug mules spark visa debate in UK, J'cans crowd UK prisons, More Drug Mules Caught in Britain, UK may deport drug mules, Cocaine kills 10 'mules – over 150 nabbed this year, Female Drug Smugglers. Jamaican news report from January 18, 2001 indicates that there were 1,296 Jamaicans in UK jails. The number of Jamaican women in British prisons increased from 100 to over 400 in three years (Roxborough, 2001). In January 2002, 795 of 4,023 women in jail in Britain were incarcerated for drug offences with 311 of these offenders being Jamaicans.

Statistics from the Narcotics Division, Jamaica Constabulary Force (2002) indicates that of individuals arrested for violation of Jamaica's Dangerous Drug Act between January 1999 and June 30, 2002, the majority were local males and the majority of arrests were for marijuana-related offences. Females accounted for 9% or 2,234 persons (see Tables 10.1a, 10.1b and 10.2). Of all persons (both males and females) arrested at airports in Jamaica between 1999 and June 30, 2002, the top three nationalities for non-Jamaicans apprehended were Americans, British and Canadians. Together, these countries represented 5% (1,314) of the total arrests (Table 10.2). Interestingly, of the 1,615 cases where the destination was stated, 28% were destined for the US, 65% for the UK and 6% for Canada. The number of persons apprehended who were destined for the US has seen a steady decline, down from 156 cases in 1999 to 27 on June 30, 2002. The reverse is true for the UK where there has been an increase from a total of 107 arrests in 1999 to a total of 405 in 2001. By June 30, 2002, there were 326 persons apprehended destined for the UK.

Table 10.1a Total Drug Arrests, Jamaica 1999 – November 30, 2002

	1999	2000	2001	November 30, 2002	Total
Total Arrests	6714	8857	6443	4536	26550
Local Males	5898	7951	5567	3881	23294
Foreign Males	201	225	226	180	832
Local Females	483	488	454	394	1819
Foreign Females	132	193	196	81	602

Table 10.1b Drug Statistics, Gender and Substances, Jamaica 1992-1999

Total Arrests	1999	1998	1997	1996	1995	1994	1993	1992
Local Female Cocaine	100	81	69	106	99	83	705	50
Local Female Ganja	385	387	246	230	321	195	1450	131
Foreign Female Cocaine	67	48	54	15	52	15	112	27
Foreign Female Ganja	65	61	47	88	148	94	303	149
Local Male Cocaine	473	479	202	251	249	148	1310	133
Local Male Ganja	5425	6146	2629	2415	3679	939	2352	452
Foreign Male Cocaine	71	41	37	24	52	40	130	36
Foreign Male Ganja	130	201	183	552	151			
Yearly Totals	6716	7444	3467	3681	4751	1514	6362	978
Per cent females (rounded)	9	8	12	12	13	26	40	37

Source: Compiled from data provided by Narcotic Division, Jamaica Constabulary Force, 230 Spanish Town, Kingston, Jamaica, W.I.

Table 10.2 Drug Couriers Apprehended, Jamaica, 1999 – June 30, 2002

Nationality of All Drug Offenders Apprehended	1999	2000	2001	To June 30, 2002	Total
Jamaicans	6,381	8,439	6,021	2,461	23,302
Americans	134	127	114	53	428
British	94	166	227	72	559
Canadians	33	49	36	3	121
Others	72	76	43	15	206
Airport Arrests					
Norman Manley	148	243	286	214	891
Donald Sangsters	176	222	329	169	896
Destination					
U.S.A.	156	140	137	27	460
United Kingdom	107	217	405	326	1,055
Canada	25	35	38	2	100
Ingestion	2	5	47	202	256
Death (from overdose)	N/A	N/A	10	3	13

Source: Compiled from data provided by Narcotic Division, Jamaica Constabulary Force, 230 Spanish Town Road, Kingston, Jamaica, W.I.

Increased apprehensions and arrests have consequences for the correctional population. In 1992, there were 126 females housed at Fort Augusta Adult Correctional Centre, Jamaica's only facility for adult females (Wolfe, 1993). As demonstrated in table 10.3, except for 1997 when there was a slight decline, Jamaica's female prison population is steadily increasing. Correctional Services of Jamaica statistics indicate that at the end of November 1999, of the 3,548 people incarcerated, 201 or 5.7% were females (see Table 10.3).

Table 10.3 Females, Fort Augusta Adult Correctional Centre, Jamaica, 1992- 1999

Year	Totals
1992	126
1993	176
1994	166
1995	185
1996	192
1997	168
1998	197
1999	201 (November)

Source: Compiled from information obtained from Correctional Services of Jamaica, Kingston, Jamaica.

Drug law violations and violent offences are the two leading categories of women's offending in Jamaica, however violations of the Dangerous Drug Act account for a significant number of women in Jamaica's prison (see Tables 10.4 and 10.5).

Table 10.4 Admission by Offences, Fort Augusta Prison for Women, 1998

	Age						
Offence Category	17-20	21-25	26-30	31-35	36-40	Over 40	Total
Murder/ Manslaughter	0	1	2	1	1	1	6
Wounding	1	5	4	5	1	0	16
Drugs	64	25	27	16	6	3	141
Other	11	7	0	1	0	0	19
Total	76	38	33	23	8	4	182

Source: Compiled from information obtained from Correctional Services of Jamaica, King Street, Kingston, Jamaica.

Table 10.5 Dangerous Drug Act Violators as a Percentage of Total Female Inmates, Jamaica 1997, 1998

Age	1997			1998		
	Drug offences	Total Inmates	% Drug Offenders	Drug Offences	Total Inmates	% Drug Offenders
17-20	26	48	54	64	76	84
21-25	17	47	36	25	38	66
26-30	36	61	59	27	33	82
31-35	10	29	34	16	23	69
36-40	6	6	100	6	8	75
Over 40	2	4	50	3	4	75
Total	97	195	49	141	182	77

Source: Compiled from data provided by Correctional Services of Jamaica.

In 1998 drug offences represented 77% of total offences for which women were incarcerated in Jamaica, increasing from 49% in 1997. Hence, consistent with statistics from other jurisdictions, drug offence convictions account also for the majority of females in Jamaica's correctional facilities. Whereas the majority of male offenders within Jamaica's correctional facilities are below the age of 30, the ages of women convicted for offences are more dispersed, nonetheless the majority of female offenders are below age 40 (see tables 10.4 and 10.5).

Jamaica's National Task Force on Crime (Wolfe Report) reported that of 126 women housed at Fort Augusta in 1992, 36% were foreigners convicted of Dangerous Drugs Act violations (Wolfe, 1993). Jamaica's female correctional population by nationality shows that while the majority of women were Jamaican, until 1999, the majority of individuals from other jurisdictions were Americans. In 1993, 58% (70 of the 120) inmates of American Nationality in Jamaica's correctional facilities were women. While there has been an increase in the number of women incarcerated since, those classified as American have declined significantly from 70 in 1993 to 22 in 1998 (Table 10.6).

As noted previously, the drug trade displays much displacement activities. Displacement includes changes in substance, geographical location, mode of transportation and more recently conduit. An example of geographical displacement is evident in route changes since 1999. For example, there has been an increase in persons destined for the United Kingdom whereas previously they were predominantly destined for the US.

Table 10.6 Inmates by Nationality, Fort Augusta, 1993, 1995, 1998

Nationality	Year		
	1993	1995	1998
Jamaican	84	104	139
American	70	55	22
British	5	4	16
Canadian	8	7	12
Other	9	15	8
Total	176	185	197

Source: Compiled from data provided by Correctional Services of Jamaica.

To evade detection, couriers have developed many methods of transporting drugs, many of which are life-threatening. While the methods of transporting drugs are quite varied, two frequently used methods are 'swallowing' packets of cocaine wrapped in condoms. The other method is 'insertion' where individuals carry the drug in orifices such as vagina and rectum. A less frequently used practice, 'strapping' refers to the method of carrying the drugs strapped on body parts.

Between 1999 and 2001, approximately 2500 individuals were apprehended at Jamaican ports for drug trafficking. Jamaica Constabulary Force National Drug Statistics on apprehensions indicate no death from overdose in 1999 and of the individuals interdicted with drugs, only 2 had ingested (swallowed). However, there was a steady increase in incidences of ingestion with 202 cases in June 30, 2002, an increase from five cases in 2000 and 47 in 2001. For the first six months of 2002, there were 3 recorded deaths due to ingestion of cocaine and of 150 couriers apprehended smuggling cocaine from Jamaica in 2001, 10 died. News reports suggest that during 2001, British Customs officers rushed several people to hospital from the airport after cocaine packets broke and began to leak inside them (Davenport, 2001). Technology adopted by Jamaica's Customs and Immigration at mid-year, 2002 initially resulted in the interdiction of more drugs and the apprehension of more drug couriers (Buckley, 2002).

Although many Jamaican women in British jails in 1998 were found to be from inner city areas and were enticed into being a courier because of their economic situation, economics is not the only factor. Current arrest statistics indicates that participants come from all socio-economic backgrounds. This includes women with children, families, and college students as well as others who may not typically raise suspicion in authorities when travelling abroad. While some people are recruited and assume the attendant risks, many others such as children are coerced. Olga Heaven, Director of Hibiscus, a UK charity that campaigns for the welfare of the inmates while they are in British prisons, is quoted as saying:

> The typical 'mule' is in fact a poor, unsophisticated, naive, poorly educated woman in her mid-30s, a lone parent who is the sole provider for four or five children, sometimes also an aged or sick parent. She

> tends to be unemployed, partly employed, or self-employed as a small-time higgler, dressmaker, or hairdresser. Most come from inner-city communities... some complained of being threatened or forced to carry drugs by dealers or friends, while others claimed they were set up, or ignorant of what they were carrying. There is occasionally quite graphic police evidence to back up the claims of these victims. In one recent case, a woman claimed to have been raped and buggered by two men who inserted packages of drugs in her anus. She was not believed until the doctor who examined her testified that she suffered severe trauma, and that the insertion involved a great deal of force. Unfortunately there was not much sympathy in the courts and she was given an 11-year sentence (*Jamaica Gleaner*, March 2002).

Poverty is also cited as the major factor accounting for women apprehended in Britain (Heaven, 2001). Similarly, a 1994 report in *Toronto Life* indicates that of the 436 persons held at Toronto's Pearson International Airport for drugs smuggling in 1993, the typical profile was female, young, single, with children, and poor. A 1997 *MacLean's* Magazine article entitled *The Perils of Paradise* reports that of Canadians arrested each year in Jamaica for attempting to smuggle drugs, the typical profile is 'young, financially strapped females'.

Another devastating effect of the drug trade is that within developing countries the reallocation of resources into anti-drug activities is felt disproportionately by women. All these have repercussions for women's economic situation, which, in turn, contributes to women's offences, with war on drugs policies significantly contributing to increased incarceration of women. International efforts such as the 1995 Beijing Conference have sought to globally improve women's conditions. Simultaneously, women have adopted poverty alleviating or 'wealth creating' mechanisms. Unfortunately, some of these adaptations have increased their criminal justice involvement. Consequently, drug courier profile indicates another example of displacement.

Developing countries are disproportionately ranked among the poor on the United Nations Human Development Index. Jamaica Ranks 86 on the 2002 United Nations World Development Index. In addition *World Bank Global Development Finance*, a yearly report on developing countries' external finance, released on March 13, 2002, indicates that while 'developing countries now suffering from a global economic downturn are likely to experience a rebound in growth this year, [the] growth rates in many poor countries still will be too low for rapid poverty reduction' (World Bank, 2002). Jamaica was one of the worst economic performers in Latin America and the Caribbean during the 1990s (King and Handa, 2000; Anderson 2001; Moser and Holland, 1997). However, Jamaica's economic crisis had a far greater impact on women (Barrow, 1993; Anderson, 2001; Heaven 2001). Citing King and Handa (2000) Anderson (2001) notes that while the percentage of Jamaicans classified as poor fell from 30.5% in 1989 to 16.9% in

1991, there were age, gender and regional differences. Individuals living in rural areas, especially households with seven or more persons were more likely to be living below the poverty line. By extension, children constituted 49% of the poor in 1998 (Anderson, 2001, p.6).

Women are disproportionately affected by the Jamaican economic climate. For example, Jamaica's post secondary educational institutions graduate greater percentages of women. Of the 2,358 students graduating from the University of the West Indies, Mona, in November 2000, only 554 or 23.5% were males. In 1999, Jamaica had an unemployment rate of 15.8%. However, closer scrutiny reveals that the rate for males was 10.3% while that for women was 22.3% (United Nations Statistics Division, 1999). Information from the Statistical Institute of Jamaica, 1999 also indicates that females comprised two-thirds of persons outside the labour force. Information from the 1999 Economic and Social Survey of Jamaica (ESSJ), which registers annual changes in Jamaica's social and economic sectors, shows that females were also more likely to be unemployed for longer periods. Of individuals out of work for more than a year, the rate for men was only 18.7% however the corresponding rate for women was 30.5%.

The 2002 United Nations Development Index summaries on gender inequality in education and economics and governmental spending for Jamaica indicates that while women's economic activity rate was 67% and female economic activity rate (as % of male rate, 2000) was 85%; only 15% of Jamaican women are employed in industry with 85% in the service sector. The governmental spending priority for 1998 shows a 2.6% increase over 1990 in budgetary expenditures (as a % of GNP) for education. And, despite an increase, in 1998 health expenditure was only 3%. It is important to note however that Jamaica's spending priority is conducted in conditions not of its own choosing. That is, in addition to drug imposed mandates, structural adjustment programs also impose stringent criteria that have had devastating economic consequences. Lundy (1999), discussing the social and environmental consequences of structural adjustment policies noted that the conditions were particularly harsh for Jamaica.

Structural adjustment programs imposed on developing nations as part of the globalizing project have had and continue to disproportionately affect developing nations in regions such as the Caribbean. Exacerbated by The United States anti-drug activities and an expansion of the prison industrial complex, this lead one to question whether the imposition of initiatives on drug producing and transit nations is part of what Rodney (1972) describes as the process of underdevelopment. Walter Rodney in *How Europe Underdeveloped Africa* posits that Europe deliberately underdeveloped Africa, with the Transatlantic slave trade being its greatest manifestation. An element of underdevelopment is that the metropolis develops at the expense of the satellites. Anderson (2001), discussing poverty in Jamaica identifies elements characteristic of the underdevelopment of the satellite by the metropolis. She notes:

> Jamaica promulgates policy statements that poverty will be eradicated, while on the other hand, the international lending agencies press for social

> security reform and improved targeting of social assistance to the poor. And in this continuing dance around the crisis of poverty, the distinction between cause and consequence has become increasingly blurred, with the result that poverty-reduction policies have little chance of reducing the extreme risks and hardships which Jamaicans face on a regular basis.

Consequently, while traditional conception has been that globalization has been positive for every sector of society, as pointed out by Thomas (2001, p.201) and Thomas and Canterbury (2001) the beneficiaries have been selective. Essentially, globalization or 'allowing the economy, politics, culture and ideology in one country to penetrate another, forced a large number of states into the periphery' (Thomas 2001, p.215). The result is an emergence of a new era of global apartheid characterized by polarization along racial lines. Global apartheid, explains Thomas (2001, p.216) 'is a structure of the world system that combines political economy with racial antagonism. It is a system in which a minority of whites occupies the pole of affluence, while a majority composed of other races occupies the pole of poverty'. Hence, global apartheid is a system of extreme inequality in political, social, economic, cultural, racial, military and legal terms (Thomas 2001, p.216 cited in Kohler, 1987). Drawing on the work of Barnet and Cavanagh (1994), Thomas notes that this new world order is stratified economically and racially into a pyramid comprising of seven grouping of nation-states. The final two tiers are composed of the poor nations of Asia, Africa, the Caribbean and Latin America 'whose prospects for development are dim, making them vulnerable to exploitative investments and economic dependence' (Thomas, 2001, p.217). Globalization did not universally reduce poverty, improve the standard of living, or political and social freedom. Instead globalization appears to have 'deepen[ed] the process of the transfer of wealth from poor to the rich countries' (Thomas and Canterbury, 2001, p.221). Consequently rich nations are getting richer and the poor are becoming more impoverished. Thus within a post cold war era, the Caribbean region has been economically marginalized.

Economic downturn in many Third World countries disproportionately affects women on whom the responsibility for childrearing falls. The intersection of race, class, and gender conflate with geography to prevent poor black women in developing countries from optimizing their possibilities for advancement and thereby minimize their capacity to earn reasonable and steady incomes (Apena, 2001 cited in Barrow, 1993). Critique of the essentialist notion of women's oppression led Black feminists such as Patricia Hill Collins to define and redefine the marginal position of Black women as one characterized by double jeopardy, multiple jeopardy and multiple consciousness. Using the intersectionality concept as an analytical tool allows feminists to make meaning of the multiple sites in which individuals are located. However, for Collins (1998) rather than examining gender, race, class, and nation as separate systems of oppression, intersectionality explores how these systems mutually construct one another. Therefore, an intersectional analysis suggests that certain ideas and practices surface repeatedly across multiple systems of oppression and serve as focal points or privilege social locations for these intersecting systems. Thus intersectionality implies that not only is there multiplicity of voices but that identities also intersect. Stuart Hall (1996) describes the recognition of these multiple positions that individuals occupy as being the process of articulating identities.

A recognition of the marginalization of women in developing regions of the world helps in understanding the interconnections among systems of oppression. Thus, placing Jamaica's economy within an under-development framework makes evident some of the processes that constrain Jamaican women in their pursuit of optimum growth and hence, make consideration of participation in the illegal drug trade a viable alternative. Such disadvantages have led women to pursue economic opportunities within diverse arenas including across activities and geographical boundaries.

Underdevelopment and Female Drug Dilemma

Jamaica's economic context and women's victimization can be seen as part of the underdevelopment of the Caribbean region. Underdevelopment of the Caribbean emerges from several sources. First, disproportionate attention to drug related concerns reduces systematic attention to other areas such as research and development. Second, many Caribbean governments are unable to implement policies that respond to their local particularities. Third, the imposition of structural adjustment programs associated with the global network of new actors that emerged with the process of globalization constrain nation states in decision making regarding economic development. Consequently, re-allocation of resources results in under funding of social services and provision of other infra- and super-structural development. For example, prison building or a disproportionately large criminal justice budget reduces the funding for health, housing and education. Since women are the primary employees and recipients of social services, reallocation of resources contributes to their economic marginalisation and leads them to adopt poverty alleviating mechanisms.

As more women see drug couriering as a viable economic alternative, their marginalisation makes them more vulnerable to being recruited as drug trade participants. However, participation in the drug trade is gendered with women participating primarily as facilitators, occupying roles such as couriers (drug). While there is a paucity of research on drug dealers, there is even less discussing female participants in the drug trade. Denton and O'Malley (1999) note that the majority of research on drug dealers focuses on men. Examining a group of successful women drug dealers in Melbourne, Australia, most of whom were also illicit drug users, Denton and O'Malley (2001) found that property offences were tightly integrated with the women's drug businesses to provide a lucrative source of income, gifts, payments and rewards as well as excitement and other valued, intangible satisfactions including status and self-esteem. In an earlier observational study of successful women drug dealers in Melbourne, Denton and O'Malley

(1999) found that skills and orientations associated with familial relations played a key part in the most sensitive aspects of women's drug business. However, ruthlessness and violence were comparatively peripheral even though the women demonstrated that they were capable of utilizing violent means (Denton and O'Malley, 1999). Although women have the capacity for violence, they are more likely to be victims of violence (Sommers and Baskin, 1997). For example, Jamaican law enforcement intelligence personnel suggest that increased participation in, and/or the role of women as dominant players in, Jamaica's drug trade may be a contributing factor to an increase in female homicide victims in Jamaica.

In June 2002, Ion Scan drug trace detection machines were installed at Jamaica's two international airports. There was an immediate increase in the number of individuals apprehended trying to smuggle drugs though Jamaica's ports. Jamaican Customs reported a 66% reduction (85 drug couriers as opposed to 254) in the number of couriers dealt with compared to the same time period the previous year. This led the Jamaican government to report an overall reduction in the number of couriers attempting to smuggle cocaine from Jamaica to the United Kingdom.

The drug control arena exhibits a high degree of displacement. This flexibility in trafficking and distribution routes contributes not only to geographical displacement but also to mode of transportation. Displacement effects have already become evident. News report on October 26, 2002 notes that UK drug smugglers are now targeting wheelchair pensioners. In November, 19 Britons were also apprehended at Montego Bay's Donald Sangster's International Airports attempting to smuggle over 1700 pounds of ganja (*Jamaican Observer*, 2002). Consequently, technology implementation and subsequent increase in apprehensions generally result in shifts in the method of operation, changes in geographical areas of operation, substances, and the mode and conduits used to transport drugs.

In addition, there is a high level of violence associated with the drug trade. Therefore, as detection technology increases the likelihood of apprehension, recruitment efforts will become more coercive. Thus, women who courier drugs to and from Jamaica may become vulnerable to particular forms of violence during the recruitment process. Thus, within the Jamaican context women's vulnerability to, and their propensity for, violence need to be examined.

Finding a Solution for the Drug Dilemma

The drug war has little to do with public health. Instead, anti-drug activities and an expansion of initiatives such as the eradication of marijuana and the spraying of coca in drug producing areas lead to an expansion of the prison industrial complex. Furthermore, the imposition of supply reduction targets create undue hardships on societies that are required to expend resources in order to comply with US imposed mandates, thus diverting scarce resources from domestic economies that are already underdeveloped. Areas in need of urgent attention to reduce participation of, and consequences for female drug couriers, especially those crossing foreign boundaries, are media, government policy-making and drug participants sensitisation. With respect to media sensitisation, Heaven (2001) notes that the media has adopted a hostile attitude towards couriers, ignoring the kingpins who are mainly men in ships, trains and planes. Media depiction of drug trade participants as 'mules' and other derogatory labels contributes to the stigmatisation of females who participate in the drug trade as couriers. Media sensitisation would help to change the depiction and subsequent treatment of drug couriers.

Government and other stakeholders such as criminal processing employees also need to be receptive to the implementation of alternatives to prison. For example, along with the implementation of Ion Scan drug trace detection machines, Jamaica embarked upon a media campaign directed at drug trade participants emphasizing likely apprehension. While women themselves need to be educated about the perils that await them for drug trade participation, as epitomized by the axiom, a drowning man will clutch at straw, education is not sufficient to eradicate women's drug trade participation. Investing in women is the most direct way to lift families out of poverty. Hence skills building and social support are required to transform the lives of the poor and powerless.

Policy makers also need the flexibility to implement best practices from other jurisdictions or policies that best respond to their local particularities. An example is Jamaica being able to decriminalize marijuana to free up resources. However, for women to realize an improvement in their life conditions, the regions in which they live must also be elevated economically. This, however, is less likely when these nations are constrained in policy implementation but instead are required to allocate a disproportionate portion of their budget to drugs rather than general domestic problems. In addition to such constraints, structural adjustment programs divert resources from social programs and lead to the underdevelopment of said countries.

The literature on women and crime has proliferated in response to an increase in the rate of female incarceration. Despite increased representation of Caribbean nationals in drug-related activities, this area receives scant attention in drug policy literature. Consequently, very little criminological information is available on native women or foreign nationals incarcerated in Caribbean jurisdictions such as Jamaica. Instead, accounts tend to be primarily journalistic.

Although feminists critiqued *malestream* criminology for being androcentric and ethnocentric, contemporary feminist analyses also ignore women in non-European or non-North American countries. For example, a 2002 publication, discussing women incarcerated in jails and prison around the world discussed in addition to the US, Great Britain, Canada and other countries. The 'other countries' category could encapsulate the rest of the world, however, it simply discussed Australia and New Zealand. It is interesting therefore that the author concluded by noting that 'it is clear that women across the world share the same issues as women incarcerated in prisons and jails in the United States' (Pollock, 2002, p.213).

Criminology, like other western disciplines, often make the assumption that what pertains in one locale can be applied universally. Similarly, essentialist notions of women leads to gross generalizations that may, in their entirety, be applicable either to white women or women in particular geographical regions. The racial exclusion is reflected in the title of the publication, *All the Women are White, All the Blacks are Men, But Some of Us Are Brave* (Hull et al., 1982), and also observed by bell hooks (1981) who notes that racialised groups remain marginalized and excluded because often when race is mentioned, the reference is to men with 'women' referring specifically to white women. Women of colour are often ignored. Thus combined with poverty, racism creates a dual ghetto for racialised and ethnic women (hooks, 1981). Africans on the continent and in the Diaspora have highlighted differences in the life conditions of women of colour. Since there are variations in women's lived experiences, it is necessary to undertake specific studies to elucidate the geographic and specific differences of women's life (Peake, 1998, p.2). It is imperative then that women in all locations and positions are allowed to speak of their experiences, and in their own voices. These conversations can then provide text to illuminate the problematic of specific women's experiences.

Hence the absence of the Caribbean region from the drug policy literature highlights several reasons why ethnographic studies should be conducted on women incarcerated in and from the Caribbean. The importance of said research is elucidated by Cain (1990b) who notes that what happens to girls and women in courts and prisons connect to what happens in the playground, in the family and at work. Thus, researching women helps to illuminate ways in which relations of rulings including 'legal apparatus such as law, courts and prisons, embody and express a taken for granted ideology of family life in a form which profoundly limits women's opportunities' (Cain,1990b, p.6).

Ethnographic studies can illuminate women's needs, vulnerabilities and pattern of offending. Ethnography is central to feminist standpoint epistemology and methodology, which as a way of knowing 'create the space for an absent subject, and an absent experience that is to be filled with the presence and spoken experience of women speaking of and in the actualities of their everyday world' (Smith, 1987, p.107). Standpoint epistemology facilitates conversations with women in their respective sites. Consistent with feminist standpoint epistemology and methodology, it becomes important that the life experiences and concerns of Caribbean women are researched and incorporated into the knowledge that is produced concerning women's criminal justice participation. Another reason for researching women of diverse identities and settings is that attention needs to be paid to women's life stories in order to interrogate the constitution of gender but more so because women's life stories make evident the processes whereby they become participants in the practices that are often used against them. Life stories can, in instances, point out ways in which women wittingly or unwittingly participate in their own subordination. To illuminate the specifics of Jamaican women's law breaking, I recommend therefore that an ethnographic study be undertaken with Jamaican women in prisons in foreign jurisdictions as well as

Jamaicans and foreign nationals in Jamaican prisons. This information is a crucial precursor to policies aimed at reducing women's participation in the drug trade.

Despite the human and monetary resources allocated to the drug problem, there has been no decline in the amount of drugs crossing the US borders, nor in the problems associated with drug abuse and addiction. But, the myopia associated with US prohibitionistic drug policy has hampered the development of effective solutions to the drug problem by circumventing serious consideration of the systematic social inequalities of which drug abuse and trafficking are merely symptoms. Consequently, the US drug war has failed to address the root causes of the drug problem. Instead, the supply side focus of the US drug war has been fought on foreign shores where economic opportunities are limited. Nonetheless, while US drug control policies have consistently been critiqued for being a failure, irrational and ineffective, they have been remarkably rational and successful as agents of social control and stratification.

Additionally, analysis has shown that increased enforcement simply displace not replace the source of drugs and the shift is often to an area of less resistance often characterized by vulnerable socioeconomic and political conditions. US drug law enforcement therefore exacerbate and force drugs into regions where there is less counter-narcotic interference resulting in an increase in drug consumption and level of violence.

To conclude, this discussion provides some preliminary information on female offenders in Jamaica. It situates the participation of Jamaican women in the drug trade within the general economic framework that disproportionately affects women. The linkages between drug dealing/trafficking and economic underdevelopment among both Caribbean producer countries and Caribbean immigrants, lead one to ask whether drug trade is a form of adaptation. The discussion suggests that the presence of poor women in drug trafficking must be understood as a by-product of Third World underdevelopment. And, by highlighting the need for improved economic relations and redistribution of wealth to improve economic conditions in developing countries, the discussion problematizes the underdevelopment of specific regions.

Additionally, anti-drug policies need to be reformed. Instead, the US continues to reinforce its zero-tolerance prohibitionist policies both domestically and internationally. Simultaneously, it imposes conditions on other nations that can ill afford to expend the level of resources required to sustain US imposed targets. Consequently, the United States intent on eliminating drugs at the source displaces the responsibility for the drug war on areas of least resistance. Consequently, women who comprise a significant portion of the unemployed in these regions are disproportionately affected.

Jamaican crime statistics indicate an increase in women's criminalisation for drug related offences. However, poverty is only one of the many factors predisposing drug trade participation. Nonetheless, taking geographical and economic conditions into account show that instead of focusing disproportionately on more narrowly constituted issues such as drugs, there needs to be a broader focus on ameliorating general social, economic, cultural and psychological disparities within the world. These factors will elevate women's economic position and reduce the likelihood of their participation in criminal activities. Therefore, it is imperative that alternative drug policies seek to ameliorate the conditions that make participation in the drug trade an attractive alternative for women. While long-term strategies are being developed short-term alternatives to prisons should be explored.

References

Anderson, P. (2001), 'Poverty in Jamaica: Social Target or Social Crisis?', *Souls: A Critical Journal of Black Politics, Culture and Society*, vol. 3, no. 3, Summer 2001.

Apena, A. (2001), 'Africana Women's Liberation and the Twenty-First Century: A Historical Focus on the Caribbean Region and Nigeria', *International Journal of African Studies*, vol. 3, no. 1, pp.47-62.

Barnet, R. and Cavanagh, J. (eds) (1994), *Global Dreams: Imperil Corporations and the New World Order*, Simon and Schuster, New York.

Barrow, C. (1993), 'Small Farm Food Production', in Momsen, J. (ed.), *Women and Change in the Caribbean*, Indiana University Press, Bloomington.

Buck, M. and Whitehorn, L. (1996), 'Legal Issues for Women in Federal Prisons', The Prison Law Project of the National Lawyers Guild, reprinted from *The Legal Journal, Newletter of the Prison Law Project,* vol. 4 (1), Issue 10, http://www.prisonactivist.org.

Buckley, B. (2002), 'Fewer Drug Swallowers: Ion Scans dent Narcotics trade', *Jamaica Observer.Com*, http://www.jamaicaobserver.com/news/html/2002 0811T210000-0500_30320_OBS_FEWER_DRUG_SWALLOWERS.asp [2002-08-13].

Burrell, I. (2001), 'Prisoners Overseas: Record Number of Drug Offenders in Jail Abroad', *The Independent* (London-Lexis Nexis), March 5 2001.

Cain, M. (1990a), 'Realist Philosophy and Standpoint Epistemologies or Feminist Criminology as a Successor Science', in Gelsthorpe, L. and Morris, A. (eds), *Feminist Perspective in Criminology*, Open University Press, Milton Keynes.

______ (1990b), 'Towards Transgression: New Directions in Feminist Criminology', *International Journal of The Sociology of Law*, vol. 18, pp.1-18

Campbell, H. (1987), *Rasta and Resistance: From Marcus Garvey to Walter Rodney*, Africa World Press.

Carlen, P. (1999), 'Women's Imprisonment in England', in Cook, S. and Davies, S. (eds), *Harsh Punishment: International Experiences of Women's Imprisonment,* Northeastern University Press, Boston.

Chevannes, B. (2001), *The Report of the National Commission on Ganja*, Government Printing Office, Kingston, Jamaica.

Collins, P.H. (1998), 'It's All In the Family: Intersections of Gender, Race, and Nation', *Hypatia: A Journal of Feminist Philosophy*, vol. 13, no. 3, p.62.

Correctional Services of Canada (2002), 'Foreign Nationals: Need Identification Meeting', retrieved from the World Wide Web, http://www.csc-scc.gc.ca/Text/prgrm/fsw/fsw17/toce.shtml [2002-04-16].

Correctional Services of Jamaica (1998), *Annual Report Kingston*, Government Printing Office, Jamaica.

Damner, M.J.E. (2002), 'Three Strikes and its Women Who are Out', in Muraskin, R. (ed.), *It's a Crime: Women and Justice*, Prentice Hall, New Jersey.

Davenport, J. (2001), 'Horror as "cocaine mule' Dies on BA Holiday Flight', *The Evening Standard* (London-Lexis-Nexis), October 17 2001.

Denton, B. and O'Malley, P. (1999), 'Gender, Trust and Business: Women Drug Dealers in the Illicit Economy', *The British Journal of Criminology*, vol. 39, no. 4, pp.513-30.

______ (2001), 'Property Crime and Women Drug Dealers in Australia', *Journal of Drug Issues*, vol. 31, no. 2, pp.465-86.

Greenfeld, L.A. and Snell, T.L (1999), *Bureau of Justice Statistics Special Report on Women Offenders*, NCJ 175688, http://www.ojp.usdoj.gov/bjs/pub/pdf/Wo.pdf [2002-03-14].

Hall, S. (1996), 'Introduction: Who Needs 'Identity'?', in Hall, S. and DuGay, P. (eds), *Questions of Cultural Identity*, Sage, London.

Harlow, C. (1998), *Bureau of Justice Statistics Special Report on Profile of Jail Inmates 1996*, April, NCJ 164620, http://www.ojp.usdoj.gov/bjs/pub/pdf/Pjim00.pdf [2002-03-22].

Heaven, O. (2001), *Working with Women Prisoners from Jamaica, Colombia and West Africa in the United Kingdon: Recognizing the Needs of Foreign Nationals*, European Institute for Crime Prevention and Control, vol. 36, pp.79-83.

Hooks, B. (1981), *Ain't I a Woman? Black Woman and Feminism*, South End Press, Boston, M.A.

Hull, G.T., Scott, P.B. and Smith, B. (eds) (1982), *All the Women Are White, All the Blacks are Men, But Some of Us are Brave*, The Feminist Press, The City University of New York, New York.

Human Rights Watch (2000), 'Punishment and Prejudice: Racial Disparities in the War on Drug', http://www.hrw.org/reports/2000/usa/.

_____ (2001), *World Report: United States Human Rights Development*, http://www.hrw.org/wr2k1/usa/.

Jamaica Constabulary Forces (2000), *National Drug Statistics, 1990 – March 30, 2000*, Narcotics Division, 230 Spanish Town Road, Kingston, Jamaica.

______ (2002), *National Drug Statistics, 1999-June 30, 2002*, Narcotics Division, 230 Spanish Town Road, Kingston, Jamaica.

Jamaica Gleaner (2002), 'I Was Misled, Says Prisoner', http://www.jamaica-gleaner.com/pages/drugmules/story2.html [2002-03-30].

Jones, M.J. (2002), 'Policy Paradox: Implications of U.S. Drug Control Policy for Jamaica', *ANNALS, AAPSS* 582, July 2002.

King, D. and Handa, S. (2000), 'Balance of Payment Liberalization, Poverty and Distribution in Jamaica', retrieved from http://www.undp.org/rblac/liberalization/docs/jamaica.pdf, 21 September 2002.

Lundy, P. (1999), *Debt and Adjustment; Social and Environmental Consequences in Jamaica*, Ashgate, Aldershot.

Mauer, M., Potler, C. and Wolf, R. (1999), 'Gender and Justice: Women, Drugs and Sentencing Policy' *The Sentencing Project*, November, http://www.ihra.org.uk/paris/proceedings/rosenbau.htm [July 23 2000].

Moser, C. and Holland, J. (1997), *Urban Poverty and Violence in Jamaica World Bank Latin American and Caribbean Studies*, The World Bank, Washington, D.C.

Office of the National Drug Control Policy (2002), *National Drug Control Strategy*, Executive Office of the President, Washington, DC, http:// whitehouse drugpolicy.gov/publications/policy/03ndcs/index.html [2002-09-04].

Planning Institute of Jamaica (1999), *Economic and Social Survey of Jamaica*. Government Printing Office, Kingston, Jamaica.

Pollock, J.M. (2002), *Women, Prison and Crime*, (2nd edn), Wadsworth Publishing, United States.

Richards, M., McWilliams, B., Batten, N., Cameron, C. and Cutler, J. (1995), 'Foreign Nationals in English Prisons: Some Policy Issues', *Howard Journal of Criminal Justice*, vol. 34, no. 3, pp.195-208.

Rodney, W. (1972), *How Europe Underdeveloped Africa*, Howard University Press, Washington. D.C.

Roxborough, P. (2001), 'J'cans Crowd UK Prisons – British Team Coming to Probe Reasons Local Women Smuggle Drugs', *Jamaica Gleaner Online*, http://www.jamaica-gleaner.com/gleaner/20010514/lead/lead2.html [2002-04-16].

______ (2001), 'British Prisons: Home to Many Jamaican Women', *Jamaica Observer.Com*, Monday, September 10 2001, http://www.jamaicaobserver.com/magazines/allwoman/html/20010910t090000-0500_13925_obs_british_prisons_home_to_many_jamaican_women.asp.

Smith, D. (1987), *The Everyday World as Problematic: Feminist Sociology*, North Eastern University Press, Boston.

______ (1990), *Text, Facts and Femininity: Exploring the Relations of Ruling*. Routledge, London.

______ (1992), Sociology from Women's Experience: A Reaffirmation, *Sociological Theory*, vol. 10, no. 1, pp.88-98.

Sommers, I. and Baskin, D.R. (1997), 'Situational or Generalized Violence in Drug Dealing Networks', *Journal of Drug Issue*, vol. 27, pp.833-49.

Sudbury, J. (2000), 'Transatlantic Vision: Resisting Globalisation of Mass Incarceration', *Social Justice*, vol. 27, no. 3, pp.133-49, http://wilsontxt.Hwwilson.com/pdffull/06597/3ZH11/IF8.pdf.

Szalavitz, M. (1999) 'War on Drugs, War on Women', reprinted from *Choices, On the Issue Magazine* 1999, vol. 8, no. 1, p.42, http://www.lindesmith.org/library /szalavitz2.html [2002-03-28].

Thomas, D. (2001), 'Between Globalization and Global Apartheid: African Development in the New Millennium', *The International Journal of African Studies*, vol. 3, no. 1, pp.201-220.

Thomas, D. and Canterbury, D.C. (2001), 'Resistance and Removal of Struggles Against Globalization', *The International Journal of African Studies*, vol. 3, no. 1, pp.221-225.

Turriff, C. (2001), 'Going after Swallowers – Drug Mules Risk Life and Freedom for $300,000 Reward', *Jamaicaobserver.com*, Sunday, December 30 2001 http://www.jamaicaobserver.com/news/html/20011229t230000-0500_18976_obs_going_after_swallowers.asp.

US Department of Justice Office of Justice Programs Bureau of Justice Statistics (1994), *Women in Prison*, NCJ-145321, http://www'ojp.usdoj.gov/bjs/pub /ascii/wopris.txt [2002-05-04].

______ (1996), *Noncitizens in the Federal Criminal Justice System, 1984-94, July 1996*, retrieved from http://www.ojp.usdoj.gov/bjs/pub/ascii/nifcjs.txt [2002-09-24].

______ (1999), *Women Offenders*, NCJ-175688, http://www.ojp.usdoj.gov/bjs/pub/pdf/wo.pdf.

US Department of Justice (1999), *Source Book of Criminal Justice Statistics*, Office of Justice Programs Bureau of Justice Statistics.

US Department of State (2000), *International Narcotic Control Strategy Report*, retrieved from http://www.state.gov/g/inl/rls/nrcrpt/1999/ 2002-05-30.

______ (2002), *International Narcotic Control Strategy Report*, retrieved from http://www.state.gov/g/inl/rls/nrcrpt/2001/ 2002-05-30.

United Nations Development Fund (1999), 'Jamaica', *Country Report*, http://www.undp.org/rblac/gender/jamaica.htm [2002-03-14].

______ (2002), 'Jamaica', *Country Report*, http://hdr.undp.org/reports/global/2002/en/indicator/indicator.cfm?File=cty_f_JAM.html retrieved from the World Wide Web 2002-12-26.

United Nations Statistics Division (1999), *Indicators on Unemployment and Indicators on Income and Economic Activity*, http://www.un.org.

Weston H.Z. and Gilbert, E. (2000), 'Sexual Abuse and Assault of Women in Prison', in Muraskin, R. (ed.), *It's A Crime: Women and Justice*, (2nd edn) Prentice Hall, New Jersey.

Williams, D. (2001), 'U.S. Backlash against Ganja – Embassy Official Warns of De-certification for Jamaica', *Jamaica Gleaner Online*, August 17, 2001, http://www.jamaica-gleaner.com/gleaner/20010817/lead/lead1.html.

Williams, P. (2001), 'British Dental Nurse Fined, Jailed for Ganja', *Jamaica Observer.Com*, Thursday, September 27 2001 http://www.Jamaicaobserver.com/news/html/20010926t190000-0500_14752_obs_british_dental_nurse_fined__jailed_for_ganja.asp.

Wolfe, L. (1993), *Report of the National Task Force on Crime*, Government Printing Office, Kingston, Jamaica.

World Bank (2002), 'Reducing Poverty in Changing Times', *Development News*, World Bank's Daily Web Zine. http://www.worldbank.org/development news/stories/html/031402a.htm [2002-03-14].

Other Internet Sources

Jamaica Observer.com, Friday, December 14 2001, '13 more drug mules charged in London. U.K. Targets Jamaican Drug Mules', http://www.jamaica observer.com/news/html/20011213t210000-0500_18356_obs_more_drug _mules_charged_in_london.asp

Jamaica Observer.com, Thursday, December 6 2001, '22 J'cans Charged. Drug Mules Held in London, Three Others Released', http://www.jamaica observer.com/news/html/20011205t200000-0500_17924_obs_j_cans_char ged.asp

Jamaica Observer.com, Tuesday, December 24 2002, 'Another Long Wait for Briton on Ganja Rap' http://www.jamaicaobserver.com/news/html/ 20021223T210000-0500_37076_OBS_ANOTHER_LONG_WAIT_FOR_ BRITON_ON_GANJA_RAP.asp

Jamaica Gleaner, Monday December 17, 2001, 'Cocaine kills 10 "mules" – Over 150 Nabbed this Year', URL: http://www.jamaica-gleaner.com/gleaner/ 20011217/ [2002-04-16]

Jamaica Gleaner, Tuesday December 18 2001, 'Drug Couriers Arrested and Charged', URL: http://www.jamaica-gleaner.com/gleaner/20011218/[2002 -04-16]

Jamaica Gleaner Online, 'Drug Mules a Strain on Health Services', http://www.jamaica-leaner.com/gleaner/20020708/news/news4.html[2002 -07-08]

Jamaica Observer.com, Monday, January 14 2002, 'Drug Mules Spark Visa Debate in UK', http://www.jamaicaobserver.com/news/html/20020113t200000-0500_19692_obs_drug_mules_spark_visa_debate_in_uk.asp [2002-04-16]

Jamaica Gleaner Online, Wednesday, May 16 2001, 'Female Drug Smugglers' URL:http://www.jamaica-gleaner.com/gleaner/20010516/cleisure/cleisure 1. html [2002-04-16]

Jamaica Gleaner, May 27 1999, 'Hibiscus Jamaica: A Helping Hand for the Destitute', URL:http://www.jamaica-gleaner.com/gleaner/19990527/news/ index.html [2002-04-16]

Jamaica Gleaner, Saturday, December 15, 2001, 'More Drug Mules Caught in Britain', http://www.jamaica-gleaner.com/gleaner/20011215/lead/lead4. html [2002-04-16]

Jamaica Gleaner, 'Smugglers Risking Their Lives, Say UK Cops', http:// www.jamaica-gleaner.com/pages/drugmules/story1.html [2002-03-30]

Jamaica Cleaner, 'The Expenditure Budget', available at http://www.jamaica-gleaner.com/gleaner/20010403/cleisure/cleisure1.html, retrieved on 20/10/2002.

Jamaica Gleaner, Thursday, December 6, 2001, 'UK May Deport Drug "mules"', URL: http://www.jamaica-gleaner.com/gleaner/20011206/ lead/ [2002-04-16]

Jamaica Gleaner Online, March 26 2000, 'Unemployment Rises in 1999', http://dev.go-jamaiica.com/gleaner/20000326/business/b3.html [March 26, 2000]

Jamaica Gleaner Online July 30, 2000, 'Women Hit Hardest By Job Loss', http://www.jamaica-gleaner.com/gleaner/20000730/arts/arts5.html [July, 30, 2000]

11 Gunboat Criminology and the Colonization of Africa

EMMANUEL C. ONYEOZILI

Introduction

'Gunboat Criminology' has been used to characterize the truncated relationship between the pre-colonial European interlopers and indigenous Africans. This early relationship represents a devastating epoch in the history of Africa when the European colonial powers used intimidation, threat and brute force to impose their economic and personal, selfish will on African people. It was an era immediately preceding colonization and extending to the post-colonial era. The relationship was one that the Ibadan School of History and the Ikime (1977) school of thought would characterize as 'gunboat diplomacy'. Ikime alluded to the events as a period when 'it was no longer "what is right" but "might is right"' (p.6). To Ohadike (1991), European predators were, at the time, driven by a policy characterized 'by diplomacy if possible, or by conquest, if necessary' (p.1). It was an absolute dispensation based on a concept of political expediency and illusion, which Anene (1966) termed 'find a chief or make one'.

To the current author, Gunboat Criminology goes beyond European arm-twisting politics with multifold purpose – conquest, occupation and exploitation designed to satisfy the economic needs of colonists and colonialism, and the imposition of alien wishes upon Africa. It radiates the trappings of deceit, perfidy, and guile of the Europeans who mortgaged their conscience and used traders, churches and missionaries as decoys to betray Africans' trust and hospitality. It also encompasses the colonial era, where colonial-style policing, military force, prisons, taxation, and civil service fronts were all introduced to provide a silhouette of a criminal justice system and an administrative apparatus, all in the quest for 'good government and free trade' for African cannibals. On the other hand, indigenous African kings utilized their limited resources to fight fiercely to protect their kingdoms and retain their autonomy. They fought to protect their culture, traditions, spirituality, religious beliefs and their God-given rights. The European military may have won the battle in the short run but in the end lost the peace by galvanizing African consciousness and independence movements. Gunboat criminology therefore encompasses a plethora of complex dynamics involving colonization, African consciousness, de-colonization, neocolonialism and problems of nation-building. It also includes the whole concept of Afrenaissance (Mazrui, 2003).

For a long period, Eurocentric writers have window-dressed the abolition of slave trade to justify the sad events that marked a 'dark age' in the history of mankind on the African continent. One major purpose of this work is to provide criminological and historical explanations of events from interdisciplinary and Afrocentric perspectives. It is the hope of this author that this work will help intellectuals to form a balanced and independent opinion.

Historical Background

The conquest and eventual colonization of Africa by certain European 'bounty hunters' marked a sad period in the history of Africa. For a thorough navigation and understanding of this tortuous terrain of history, this chapter will begin by exploring the much-avoided history of the European slave trade. The intent is to establish linkages between the imperial ego, exploitation and economic needs of colonialism. The sequence of events will then be fused to explain the reason why and the manner in which the colonial powers forced the subjugation of Africa. Hopefully, this trend will shed some light on many unanswered questions regarding African affairs.

Early European Contact with Native Africans

Although some Europeans had earlier visited some parts of the continent that was later known as Africa, it was not until the 15th century that there were any well-authenticated visits by Europeans to the West African coast. Financed by the great Prince Henry 'the Navigator', the Portuguese first reached the coast of Senegal, then Gambia (Beazley, 1894; Sanceau, 1947). In coming to Africa, the Portuguese were inspired by a mixture of economic, military and religious motives (Burns, 1972; Omer-Cooper, 1986). Economically the Portuguese wanted to discover a separate route of their own to the gold trade of West Africa, one that would not require them to pass through the territory of the Maghreb Muslims. They further hoped this would yield for them, a sea route to India for the rich trade in Indian spices (Burns, 1972; Omer-Cooper, 1986). Militarily, the Portuguese wanted to find the legendary Christian king, Prester John; they hoped he would help them attack the Muslims. Religiously and to a lesser extent, militarily, they sought to convert Africans to Christianity and to develop alliances with African kings. These alliances, they thought, would give them a trade advantage and strengthen their hand against the Muslims (Burns, 1972; Omer-Cooper, 1986).

Although the [Portuguese] African 'marathon' started with the capture of Ceuta in 1415, it was not until after a series of voyages between 1441 and 1445 that they reached the Guinea coast. They had to wait until 1482 to reach the Gold Coast (modern Ghana), where they established a fort, São Jorge da Mina (now called Elmina Castle) (Beazley, 1894; Omer-Cooper, 1986). In 1472, the first contact with Nigeria was recorded; in 1485 John Affonso d'Aveiro visited the Oba of Benin City and this marked the first European visit to a Nigerian king (Burns, 1972; Egharevba, 1960). In line with Prince Henry's policy, a cordial relationship was established between the King of Benin and the King of Portugal. Portuguese missionaries were sent to 'sow the seeds' of Christianity, and King John II (1481-95) of Portugal opened a friendly correspondence with the King of Benin. Churches and monasteries were established to boost the new faith in Benin, and even the king of Benin, who reigned in 1553 was purported to have learned to speak Portuguese, which he had learned as a little child (Burns, 1972; Egharevba, 1960).

It is important to note that the relationship between the Portuguese and the Benin Empire was characterized by equality and mutual respect. Royal gifts were exchanged between the kings (Egharevba, 1960). It is equally significant to note that at first the Portuguese who visited West Africa were mainly interested in the gold trade although they also wanted slaves to sell in Portugal, where there was a great shortage of labor. In Benin the relationship was simply associated with the trade in goods, spreading the new religion, and friendship.

The Portuguese in Kongo (Congo) and Angola

By 1471, Portuguese explorers had reached Costa da Mina (Gold Coast or modern Ghana), and by 1483 'discovered' the Congo River. In 1491, King John II of Portugal sent a band of artisans and missionaries to the court of Manikongo Mzinga Mkuwu of Kongo to convert the kingdom into Christianity and to exchange western technology. The Portuguese pressed into the hinterland to the port of Luanda, and in 1556 encouraged the local authority of Angola to assert their independence from Kongo.

In 1571, the Portuguese king presented Angola as a proprietary colony to one of his followers (July, 1992). Thus, with a combination of skill and conquest, Portuguese's presence and domination of the coastal regions of East Africa was established. In time, a colonial administration had been imposed on Kongo and Angola.

The Dutch Activities and Influence in Africa

July (1992) contends that the arrival of the Dutch in Africa was part of a grand geopolitical design to checkmate the colonial ambitions of rivals, Portugal and Spain. The Dutch escapades started with the founding of the Dutch East Indian Company in 1602. By 1617, Dutch fighting ships prowling the coasts of West Africa had raided São Tome and São Jorge da Mina. They occupied the island of Goree in 1617, and in 1633 captured Arguin. Towards the end of the first quarter of the 17th century, the Dutch control of West African trade has been completed. Emboldened by their imaginative merchandising ability, and superior seamanship, more ships were equipped to circumnavigate the rest of Africa with an eye on monopoly of Indian trade. In 1652, a fleet of three small Dutch ships arrived in Table Bay, or in what is today, South Africa. At first, the Dutch commander Jan van Riebeeck kept to his home government's instructions to avoid trouble with the region's indigenous Khoikhoi inhabitants. Eventually, however they established a small truck farm and bartered cattle with the Khoikhoi.

In 1657, nine of the Dutch East India Company employees were given the status of free Burghers and allocated small individual farms to help increase production. The following year they imported slaves from Madagascar to augment the labor supply, and with time the free Burghers converted their temporary settlement to a permanent colony. Between 1679 and 1707, and under the administrations of Simon van der Stel and his son Willem, an active immigration policy was encouraged to populate the region with Dutch and German settlers. Van der Stel founded the village of Stellenbosch from where the Boers spread to other parts of the cape region. Company employees were also encouraged to bring their wives along therefore discouraging mixed marriages between the settlers and native Khoikhois.

In 1795, some frontier farmers (trekboer) proclaimed republics, independent of Cape Town, over the districts of Graff-Reinet and Swellendam. Unfortunately for the new republics, during that same year, in arrangement with the Dutch government as a checkmate against seizure by the French, an English squadron temporarily occupied the Cape region. That occupation became permanent in 1806. With the foundation having already been put in place by the Dutch, the British inherited an Apartheid policy. Again, trade and profit has proven to be driving forces behind what later became the worst colonial policy in history – Apartheid. With the ceding of their holdings in Cape region, and the containment of French expansion in that part of the continent, the Dutch influence (though not their legacy) in Africa dwindled.

The French Colonial Policy in Africa

France's initial interest in Africa was mercantile activity and in the form of national trading monopolies. The pioneer French business interests in Africa were the Royal African Company chartered by Charles II in 1660, and the French West Indies Company, established by Colbert in 1664. In league with the commercial interest representatives of the Swedes, Danes, and Brandenburgers, the French, in 1659, occupied Saint-Louis Island at the mouth of River Senegal. From here they challenged the Dutch West African activities and captured the slave depot of Goree from the Dutch in 1677 (July, 1992).

Crowder (1976) argued that on the French coastal colonies of Dahomey, Cote d'Ivoire (Ivory Coast) and Guinea, traders showed the way to military occupation. Like the British colonizers, the French were of the conviction that conquest was a moral right, and that the invaders were actually bringing 'light' to the 'heart of darkness'. The fact of the matter remains that trade and profit was at the apex of all European activities in Africa, and all future French incursions on the African continent would be grounded on this guiding principle. In effect, the French occupation of West Africa was achieved by military conquest rather than diplomacy and treaty (Crowder,, 1976). Driven by desire for promotion rather than by the realistic economic potential of the territories, the French commander Archinard epitomized the arrowhead of French forced penetration and colonization of several West African kingdoms. Beginning in 1878, the French engaged in sustained attacks on both Ahmadou Sekou's Tokolor Empire and Samory Toure's empire. By 1893, Ahmadou's brother, Aguibou colluded with the French to defeat him. Ahmadou fled to Sokoto Caliphate where he died in 1898.

During 'the seven years war', Samory remained defiantly fierce in his resistance by playing the British in Sierra Leone against the French. However, he was later tricked while suing for peace with the French. He was captured and deported to Ogowe, an island off the coast of Gabon where he died in 1900. At Somory's death in 1900, the French had annexed the two territories into the new and expanding French West African colonies of Mali, Upper Volta, Niger, Senegal, Guinea and Dahomey. In 1902, Morocco and Mauritania were added to the list as North African colonies while the pacification of Cote d'Ivoire (Ivory Coast) was completed in 1917.

In 1900, in another part of Africa, the French Army in Algeria had marched southward and aided the defeat of Sudanese Rabih at the battle of Kuseri (in the Kanem Bornu region). With this victory, the French gained control of the Equatorial African region. In 1905, they organized four territories of Gabon, Middle Congo, Ubangi-Chari and Chad. These states later became a federation of French Equatorial Africa in 1910. July (1992) states that a head tax and forced labor were also introduced to insure the exploitation of rubber and ivory of the region while at the same time indigenous land was appropriated to French developers.

The Belgians

The Belgian influence in Africa was limited to the region of the Belgian Congo. The Belgian adventure was born out of ambitious desires of King Leopold of Belgium who embarked upon a Congolese exploration as a private venture. With a combination of tact and skilled machinations, Leopold's legal claim over the Congo territory was ratified at the 1885 European Berlin Conference on the scramble for and partition of Africa.

Beginning in 1887, Leopold granted extensive landholding concessions on Congo, over which he held a 'legal monopoly' as a personal property. In 1908, Belgium annexed the Congo Independent State. While Belgium formerly assumed the administration of Congo state, Leopold retained monopoly of the concessions he sold to independent developers, from which he still collected royalties estimated at 71,000 francs a year. The indigenous Africans suffered collateral loss in the form of lands lost to government grabbing and confiscations, and loss of their independence.

The British Presence in West Africa

The first visit by Europeans to the region that is today called Nigeria was in 1485. Nearly seven decades later in 1553, the first English ships reached the Benin River (Burns, 1972; Ryder, 1969). This fleet of three ships was commanded by Captain Windham and was piloted by an experienced Portuguese seaman, Penteado. This landing marked the beginning of a relationship that would culminate in the colonization of Nigeria by the British (Burns, 1972; Egharevba, 1960; Ryder, 1969). Anchored at the Ughoton port on the Benin River, the English merchants crossed over into the city of Benin, where they were brought before the *Oba* (i.e. King). First, stated Ryder (1969), 'Penteado and the English merchants knelt before the *Oba* who told them to rise' (p.77). He then asked why they had come to his country. It is important to observe that kneeling as a form of salutation before the *Oba* indicated the reverence in which the Portuguese and the English merchants held the *Oba* as the monarch of the empire of Great Benin. *Oba* Orhogbua (c. 1550-1578), who spoke fluent Portuguese, then negotiated trade terms with the British merchants. Penteado acted as interpreter (Egharevba, 1960). They agreed that Benin pepper would be exchanged for unspecified British goods.

The next visit to Benin by the British was in 1588 under the captainship of James Welsh. After a two-month stay the merchants traded their goods for a cargo of pepper, elephant tusks, curiously woven cloth made of cotton wool, and barrels of palm oil (Burns, 1972; Ryder, 1969). In spite of the death toll that afflicted the crew, the desire for profit brought Welsh back in 1591 (Burns, 1972; Egharevba, 1960; Ryder, 1969). For their pains, the merchants exchanged their goods for 589 sacks of pepper, 150 elephant tusks, 32 barrels of palm oil, and cloth curiously woven and made of cotton wool made from the bark of palm trees (Burns, 1972; Ryder, 1969).

Three points of great significance must be conveyed in our treatment of early British contact with Nigeria (Benin Kingdom). First, British merchants treated the *Oba* with marked reverence as a king of an empire in his own right. Second, the trade relationship between the *Oba* and the early Portuguese, and later with the British merchants, was conducted on equal terms and with mutual respect. Finally, the *Oba* of Benin dictated the exchange rate at which this trade was carried on and the British were satisfied as exemplified in their eagerness to return in spite of the high death tolls on British personnel. At no point during the early-contact period of this relationship were Africans treated as second-class citizens.

The European Slave Trade (Social Violence), 1500-1850s

The history of colonization would not be complete without a discussion of the role the slave trade played in the history of Africa of the period. In discussing the first European contact with West Africa, it was mentioned that the Portuguese did capture some natives whom they took home as slaves. Initially, Prince Henry the Navigator had hoped to Christianize and educate these captives and send them back to Africa to act as missionaries and as a buffer to stem the fast pace of the growth of Islam in the region (Beazley, 1894). With the passage of time this policy was abandoned and their labor was diverted to meet the agricultural and domestic needs of Portugal (Omer-Cooper, 1986).

It has been pointed out that slave trade became a massive affair only after the development of sugar plantations in São Tomé and later in Brazil and the West Indies (Omer-Cooper, 1986). Accordingly, this development, 'created an almost unlimited demand for labor' (p.30). The Portuguese, the Dutch, the Danes, the French and the British then transported millions of Africans across the Atlantic. The balance of trade thereafter would be tilted forever in favor of the Europeans.

Three major reasons are advanced in connection with the precipitation of the slave trade. The first was Henry the Navigator's idea of converting Africans to Christianity as part of his offensive against Islam. Second was the realization that these initial slaves were useful as farmhands in the under populated areas of Portugal. Finally, the discovery of America and the establishment of Spanish colonies in the Americas and in the West Indies led to the realization that Africans were better workers than the native Indians who worked in the Spanish mines and plantations in the West Indies (Burns, 1972). By 1650, African slaves had become West Africa's major export commodity (Burns, 1972; Omer-Cooper, 1986).

In the beginning, the Portuguese enjoyed a monopoly on the slave trade, the Papal Bull dividing the world having prevented Spain and other nations from going to Africa for slaves. The Reformation however weakened the Papal Bull and allowed the entry of other Europeans (other than Portugal) into the lucrative trade in African slaves. The 16th century, therefore, marked the beginning of an epoch that culminated in the greatest crime in all human history, trans-Atlantic slavery. The involvement of the British in the slave trade did not begin until 1562 after the Reformation had weakened the Papal Bull. During that year, the infamous John Hawkins (the first Englishman to engage in this traffic) took 300 slaves from Sierra Leone to Haiti. The profit garnered from this first attempt was so immense that the following year, Hawkins easily obtained financing (from Queen Elizabeth I) for another trip to Africa. He was given command of a squadron of seven ships (the flagship vessel was named Jesus) to sail to Africa and then carry slaves to the West Indies (Burns, 1972).

The British entry into the slave trading business opened the floodgate of competition among the British and other European merchants. It also marked the beginning of three centuries of agony for the unfortunate Africans, to the eternal shame of Europe, especially Britain. Beginning in 1618 (Burns, 1972), and armed with King James' charters, various English companies flooded West Africa. Beginning from the mouth of River Gambia, various forts were built, the first of which was named 'Fort James' in honor of the 'king of slave dealers' (King James I of England). With ever-increasing acceleration, and in her mad scramble to monopolize trade in slaves from Africa to the Spanish colonies in the West Indies, the British had by the close of the 17th century virtually edged out all the other competing European powers. Omer-Cooper (1986) noted that the British did not start the slave trade. In fact, there had always been a slave trade with the Arabs in parts of Africa, and European slaves had long been bought and sold in North Africa. However, he observed that 'the trade across the Atlantic was to eclipse in scale anything of the kind that had happened before' (p.29).

The factors that sustained and heightened the immoral traffic in human beings across the Atlantic were the great impetus given to the trade by the King of England, and the hypocrisy of the Protestant churches. Royal charters aside, a synod of Protestant churches held in France in the year 1637 issued a declaration stating that 'slavery was not condemned "in the Word of God" and was of the right of nations' (Spears, 1907, p.40). The Archbishop of Canterbury was a member of this synod and raised no objections.

In 1772 Justice Mansfield reached a landmark decision in favor of Granville Sharp who had gone to court to protect the freedom of James Somersett, a runaway slave. In his ruling Mansfield declared that 'as soon as any slave sets his foot on English ground he becomes free' (Burns, 1972, p.76). In spite of this ruling in 1776, a proposed resolution that 'the slave trade is contrary to the laws of God and the rights of men' failed in the British Parliament (Burns, 1972; Durant and Durant, 1975). England was now the leader in slave traffic across the Atlantic Ocean. Durant and Durant (1975) observed that in 1790 alone, British vessels transported 38,000 slaves to America, French ships 20,000, Portuguese 10,000, Dutch 4,000, Danish 2,000, and 'each nation contributed according to its ability in what was probably the most criminal action in history' (p.368). From Liverpool and Bristol, the British ships carried liquor, firearms, cotton goods and diverse trinkets to the slave coasts of Africa.

On the continent of Africa, the slave trade led to a loss of about five generations of able-bodied men and the subsequent depopulation of the continent. Omer-Cooper (1986) noted that the 'colossal business in human beings had terrible and widespread effects on the development of African societies, making *internecine* (italics supplied) wars more profitable' (p.30). Constant outbreaks of tribal wars arose to satisfy the insatiable appetite of African kings in their royal hunt for war prisoners. Even years after its abolition, the slave trade left the continent a legacy of another century of wars and rumors of war, and the enmity and animosity it generated persisted between different African societies (Rodney, 1972). Crowder (1968) argued that it is ridiculous and beyond comprehension that despite the wars between these nations, the merchants still found a common ground to agree on the slave trade. Most of the slaves were shipped to Haiti, the West Indies, the U.S.A., Guyana, Jamaica, and of course, to England and other British colonies. It is on record (Rodney, 1972) that the African trade led to the rise of seaport towns, notably Bristol, Liverpool, Nantes, Bordeaux and Seville. Again, direct and indirect connection with these ports led to the rise of various European manufacturing centers.

In England, Lancashire was the first major center of the Industrial Revolution and the economic advance of Lancashire was closely tied to the growth of the port of Liverpool through trade in human beings (Durant and Durant, 1975; Rodney, 1972). In a well-documented account, Williams (1944) noted that in Bristol around the year 1730, it was estimated that 'on a fortunate voyage the profit of a cargo of about 270 slaves reached £7,000 or £8,000, exclusive of the returns from ivory' (p.36). In Liverpool, the minimum profit margin was said to be as high as 100% to 300%. By the 1780s, the slave trade alone was generating a clear profit of £300,000 a year for each merchant (Rodney, 1972; Williams, 1944). This is good evidence of a direct linkage.

The slave trade that flourished for over three centuries was in no small part a result of the patronage given it by the British monarch (Queen Elizabeth I), the British Parliament and the Church of England. Elizabeth 1 is on record as the Financier-in-Chief of John Hawkins, the first Englishman to carry slaves from Africa. For his meritorious service in perpetrating social violence in the name of the Queen, he was knighted by Queen Elizabeth I who called the slave trade 'a detestable act which would call down the vengeance of Heaven upon the undertakers'. The Queen knighted Hawkins anyway (Burns, 1972, p.69; Williams, 1944, p.39). Even the Quakers who later became critical opponents of the slave trade, traded, owned and kept slaves up until 1756. The principal amongst these Quaker families were the Barclays and the Barings who together owned a slave ship, *The Willing Quaker* (Williams, 1944, p.43).

Evidence abounds (Williams, 1944) to show that the increase in the slave trade was synonymous with the rise of the big English cities like Liverpool. The wealth associated with the trade was so relevant to the British economy and politics that its abolition was not under consideration in the 18th century. Williams (1944) contended that 'the age which had seen the mortality among indentured servants saw no reason for squeamishness about the mortality among slaves' (p.34). Since the exploitation of slaves on plantations did not differ fundamentally from the exploitation of the feudal peasant in European cities, the proponents of free trade in slaves put pressure on their parliamentary representatives to ensure that no restrictions, whatsoever, be considered in Parliament concerning the slave trade.

The famous Cardinal Manning of the 19th century was the son of a rich West Indian merchant dealing in slave-grown produce. Further, until the British government paid him over £12,700 compensation for their freedom in 1833, the Bishop of Exeter fought feverishly to retain his own 655 slaves (Williams, 1944). The church dared not condemn the trade.

This essay does not focus on the slave trade. The author has, however, delved into the subject as a foundational step toward helping the reader to understand the British involvement in the planning and promotion of this horrendous trade. It is on the strength of this involvement that one can understand the reluctance and dilemma of Africans and their initial failure to understand the European, albeit British 'Chameleon theory' regarding the slave trade — a theory of financing the slave trade today, and sending Christian missionaries to preach against its horrors the next day.

The Industrial Revolution

The term *Industrial Revolution* connotes an epoch that culminated in 'a major discontinuity in the process of industrialization during which the British economy was launched irreversibly into "self-sustained growth" within a couple of decades (1783–1802)' (Deane, 1996, pp.14-15), to use economics parlance. Some authorities, including Deane (1996), argue that the cataclysm that precipitated the economic shift in 18th century England was a forest fire that had been in the making for many decades. The event should therefore be seen as a shift in economic history and not as a revolution. However, others like Beales (1958) may beg to differ. According to Beales:

> It may be true that each particular aspect of that change, when examined under the statistician's microscope, shows a change not of kind but of degree. But the sum of these changes was overwhelming, and the process of adding sum to sum, like the process of compound interest, amounted to a revolution (1958, p.29).

Viewed from this dimension, the Industrial Revolution replaced one social system or one civilization by another. A civilization 'based on the plough and the pasture perished – in its place stood a new order, resting, perhaps dangerously, on coal, iron and imported textile materials' (p.30).

That the Industrial Revolution is seen as a historically unique breakthrough in an evolutionary process of technological change, or as a discrete event occurring in a brief and sharply demarcated time span is not the issue. What is important is that its effect was so profound that if we were to divide the sum of changes into 70, the per annum change would be far-reaching enough to dwarf all previous changes in British history since the Dark Ages. In other words, the changes occasioned by the Industrial Revolution would eclipse all other changes in history put together (Beales, 1958; Deane, 1996). The Industrial Revolution has been construed as the application of science to industry and society. The tangible outcome was the quicker conversion of raw materials into manufactured goods. This, in turn, implied a greater need for raw materials to meet the machinery needs of the newfound industries. The three highly productive and progressively improved machines were the Hargreaves's spinning-jenny, Arkwright's water-frame and Crompton's mule. In combination with one another, they transformed both the quantity and quality of yarn that could be delivered by an individual spinner (Deane, 1996; Omer-Cooper, 1968).

The reason for mentioning the Industrial Revolution and its attendant effects is threefold. First, because it was grounded on the production surplus of slave labor; the Industrial Revolution was strongly affected by the slave trade, both directly and indirectly. Second, this author wishes to establish the obvious linkages among the European slave trade, the Industrial Revolution, and the colonization of Africa. Finally, it will highlight the academic tragedy and rectify the hypocrisy of most European authors and historians who persistently refuse to give recognition to the contribution of Africa to the wheels of the Industrial Revolution and the subsequent technological advancement of the West. This is to restate the point that the wealth and advancement of Europe were anchored on the backs and in the sweat and blood of the African slaves. Any less credit would be uncivilized in the 21st century.

African Perspective and Collision

Up until 1781, the British had taken a leading role in the trafficking of slaves (Burns, 1972). However, they suddenly began to preach the gospel of the evils associated with the inhumane traffic in human beings. To contemporary Africans (Dike, 1956), 'the European movement for abolition was extremely puzzling, especially as Englishmen who were foremost in the trade became overnight the most zealous in opposing it' (p.13). Not only had the slave trade been the mainstay of their economies but also slave-trading kingdoms such as Lagos, Dahomey, Bonny and many others owed their origins and greatness to the rise of the slave trade. That the trade had become part and parcel of the people's way of life can be derived from the statement of the King of Bonny in 1807:

> We [the King and Council] think that this trade must go on. That also is the verdict of our oracle and the priests. They say that your country, however great, can never stop a trade ordained by God himself (Dike, 1956, p.13).

The King of Bonny was dead wrong on this. As Dike (1956) noted, the economic change taking place in Europe at the time had unified the various discordant elements (European governments) toward a set goal (the looting of Africa) and provided a common ground for unity or alliance among some strange bedfellows. Still not realizing the changing tide in the affairs and economics of trade, King Opubu in 1824 said:

> I declare emphatically that I can never compromise my sovereign powers. On this issue I am adamant. Consider my kingdom, this land which I hold in trust for the Bonny country and the spirits of my ancestors. What would be my excuse if my father or grandfather were to rise from their graves and demand to know the reason for the presence of English warships in the territories they had entrusted to my charge? (Dike, 1956, p.17.)

That a clash and great upheaval would occur was only a matter of time, a fact which, up till then, only the British had fathomed.

In what later became Nigeria, the substitute trade the British introduced to replace the slave trade was palm oil trade. Although the rulers and peoples of the delta states of Nigeria were naturally unwilling to give up the trade in slaves at the dictates of the British, they did, in fact, begin to organize for the palm oil trade soon after the institution of the British anti-slave-trade naval squadron in West Africa (Ikime, 1977). Ikime (1977) further stated that by 1840, all of these states, except Brass, were already fully involved in the palm oil trade. For all practical purposes, this marked the beginning of the second phase of the European thrust into the African continent that would result in the Africa's loss of its sovereignty. The trade in palm oil was totally different in organization from that of the slavers. Being a successful palm oil trader required a large capital outlay, a large labor force for manning the trade canoes and the goodwill of suppliers as well as a large fleet of canoes for the cargo. In a bid to ease the transition from slaves to produce trade, a trust system was developed between the European merchants and the coastal middlemen on the one hand, and between the coastal middlemen and the hinterland suppliers/manufacturers on the other. The trust system implied the advancing of manufactured goods from the Europeans to the African middlemen who in return would deliver the agreed upon quantity of palm oil (Ikime, 1977).

This new system of trade naturally created conflicts between the European and African coastal traders often resulting in the closure of markets, especially on the eastern delta coasts. The main areas of conflict ranged from loss of count on the quantity of oil owed on trust to disagreement on the price of oil to be exchanged. Trade monopolies or attempts at monopoly by certain European groups sometimes resulted in conflicts when the African coastal merchants refused to toe the line, but instead selling to other trading customers thereby generating competition. It was the desire to break the coastal monopoly of the African middlemen that at first forced some Europeans to entertain the thought of going inland. As expected, the coastal chiefs did everything in their power to ensure that the Europeans would be frustrated in every attempt at inland direct trade. Bound by tradition not to leave their capitals, the coastal chiefs used their domestic slave elements to penetrate the hinterlands to secure not only the trade in palm oil but also trading alliances and the goodwill of the hinterland communities (Ikime, 1977).

Beginning in 1836 in Nigeria, British involvement in the affairs of Delta society deepened. For example, in the 1836 agreement imposed by the British, 'Bonny authorities were forbidden to imprison, detain, or in any other way maltreat British subjects' (Ikime, 1977, p.20). Two subsequent treaties, both designed to advance British political and commercial interests, were agreed upon in 1841 and 1848 even though the British did not intend to honor any portion of the treaties that dealt with their own behavior. From then onward, British traders and agents began to flout African laws at will while hiding behind the power of the gunboats to protect their malfeasance.

Appointment of John Beecroft as Consul for the Bights of Benin and Biafra

On June 30 1849, John Beecroft, a British trader, was appointed consul for the eastern and western delta region by Palmerston, the British Foreign Secretary. This appointment was in response to the memoranda sent by the British traders in the Itsekiri Kingdom, whose factories and firms were looted by the aggrieved Itsekiri traders, albeit for noncompliance with trading principles (Anene, 1966; Ikime, 1977). The personality of Beecroft was that of a man whose political activities were guided by narrow general principles. According to Dike (1956), Nigerian kings who:

> favoured slave abolition, embraced Christianity, encouraged legitimate commerce, and supported missionary enterprise were good kings. Those who stood for the old abstentionist policy and resisted encroachment, whether they dealt in slaves or not, were to him enemies of "progress" and were singled out for attack...cloaked by his diplomatic manoeuvres, his efforts to discredit... African rulers who dared to defend their "savage independence" (p.130).

With this mind-set, there was no second-guessing as to how he would handle power in his encounters with the kings who were determined to uphold their sovereignty. Rightly dubbed 'a firm believer in the use of force or the show of force for the furtherance of British interests' (Ikime, 1977, p.22), he did not hesitate to swing into brigandry. Henceforth, between 1841 and 1848, lawlessness, intimidation and genocide became the hallmark of British-Nigerian relations.

In 1851, Beecroft seized on the clash between the British traders and the Itsekiri to bombard Bobi (an Itsekiri town) and imposed a heavy fine on their leader. In his report he wrote, 'These scoundrels must be well chastised with powder and shot' (Ikime, 1977, p.23). Further, he lured the Itsekiri elders on board his man-of-war (gunboat) and imposed a treaty of commerce on them similar to the Bonny Treaty of 1836. The treaty provided for the protection of the lives and property of British traders, forbade the molestation of British subjects under any pretext whatsoever, and laid down the amount Itsekiri traders were to be fined if they stopped the trade of any British subject who had paid his *comey* (duty). The imposed treaty, however, did not make any provision enabling Itsekiri to punish British offenders. Again, only brute force and the presence of the gunboat could force the Itsekiri to sign such a one-sided treaty (Ikime, 1977).

In 1852 Beecroft committed similar excesses in Calabar. He not only employed gunboats to protect the British supercargoes but went further to preside over the election and installation of King Archibong on the throne of Calabar (Anene, 1966; Dike, 1956). By this single act, he not only became the Consul but also arrogated to himself the title of kingmaker, an act regrettably copied by his successors in the politics of Opobo, Ebrohimi, Lagos and Benin. Following Beecroft's example, it also became the trademark of the British representatives to fabricate and trump up charges and thus create a *casus belli* to justify an attack on innocent citizens (Afigbo et al., 1986; Anene, 1966; Cookey, 1974; Ikime, 1968, 1977).

It will therefore be proper to conclude that the method of penetration adopted by the British was dubious, deceitful and carefully thought out. It also serves to support the claim that of all the intentions and motives behind the British abolition of slave trade, the economic motive was the most dominant. In the words of Morel (1968):

> What are we in West Africa for? What do we hope to do there? What object took us there? What main purpose keeps us there? The answer is not for a moment in doubt. Commerce took us to West Africa; commerce keeps and will keep us in West Africa. It is the *fons et origo* of our presence in West Africa. The day it ceases to be so, West Africa ceases to be of use to the Empire... but commerce will remain the backbone, as it ever has been, of European intercourse with West Africa (p.21).

The British Conquest of Nigeria (Gunboat Diplomacy): General Overview

Ikime (1977) stated that 'the bulk of what is now Nigeria became British territory in the period between 1885 and 1914' (p.3). In the year 1885, the Niger Coast Protectorate was declared. The author would, however, side with Ohadike (1991) to contend that the British government conquered and colonized Nigeria after a series of military operations that began with the annexation of Lagos in 1852.

In the preceding section, the author had attempted to establish a linkage between the Industrial Revolution and the European slave trade. In the same manner in which African labor powered British technological ascendancy so did the Industrial Revolution precipitate the desire for raw materials to feed the industries. The British who had traded in Africa were of course quite aware of the availability of the desired raw materials (vegetable oil, rubber, indigo, cotton, ivory, timber, etc.) in Africa. In the past, these materials were formally purchased by exchanging British manufactured goods for them (Burns 1972; Omer-Cooper, 1986).

Naturally, therefore, Britain looked to Africa for the procurement of the desired raw materials. To do this more effectively, and in order to encourage alternative modes of production, European kidnapping of Africans for slave trading had to be halted. It was therefore no accident that the 18th century, which encompassed the peak of industrialization in Europe, also witnessed Justice Mansfield's decision in favor of Granville Sharp.

Perspectives

Based on this development and contrary to established opinions, the author argues that Justice Mansfield's decision of 1772, the Imperial Acts of 1807 and 1833, the abolition of the slave trade and slavery, and the Christian missionary activities dating from 1792 (Buxton, 1968; Durant and Durant, 1975; Omer-Cooper, 1986;

Spears, 1907; Williams, 1944) were no accidents of history. That is, the chain of events was a calculated grand design engineered and nurtured by the British to exploit Africa and extend her imperial designs. Mountains of evidence abound to substantiate this argument (Buxton, 1968; Durant and Durant, 1975; Morel, 1968; Omer-Cooper, 1986; Spears, 1907; Williams, 1944).

It has already been mentioned that John Hawkins took his first 300 captives from Sierra Leone to Haiti in 1562. The following year he was rewarded with the command of a squadron of seven ships, led by the flagship named 'Jesus', to go to Africa and kidnap more captives. Hawkins's only credentials for knighthood were of course the royal dividends from the slave trade. It was no accident that Hawkins chose as his coat of arms the representation of an African in chains (Rodney, 1972). The Queen of England was the underwriter of the expedition and the profit was destined for the royal treasury (Burns, 1972; Rodney, 1972). In 1637, a synod of Protestant churches decided that slavery was not condemned 'in the word of God' and was thus the right of nations (Burns, 1972, p.69). The 'field commander' of the Church of England, the Archbishop of Canterbury was part of this body; and the 'commander-in-chief' of the Church of England, the monarch of England did not condemn the resolution. This resolution also explains why Queen Elizabeth had not been against naming her slave ship '*Jesus*'; the slave ship was, figuratively, her 'son of God'.

While much has been written about Justice Mansfield 1772 judgment (on Granville Sharp's case) by all European writers who are constantly seeking triumphs of humanitarianism, very little, if any has been written about Justice Mansfield being the same judge who ruled on the *Zong* case in 1783. The *Zong* case dealt with a British captain who had thrown 132 slaves overboard and later brought action against the insurance company seeking compensation (Durant and Durant, 1975; Williams, 1944). In this 1783 case, Justice Mansfield ruled that 'the case of slaves was the same as if horses had been thrown overboard', and awarded the ship owners £30 in damages for each of the 132 slaves they murdered (Williams, 1944, p.46). This ruling is the crux of the author's argument that the 1772 ruling was mere window-dressing designed to legitimize abolition and to advance the British economic and political agenda. The ruling also lent moral and legal legitimacy to the formation of missionary societies from 1792 onward to evangelize and 'save the souls of Africans from idolatry, cannibalism, and eternal damnation'.

The logic of this line of argument is supported by other developments, namely, in spite of the 1772 ruling, and yet because of it, a resolution to the effect that 'the slave trade is contrary to the laws of God and the rights of men' failed to pass in Parliament in 1776 (Burns, 1972, p.76; Crowder, 1978b, p.98; Durant and Durant, 1975). Twelve other such resolutions presented by William Wilberforce in 1789 were lost by large majorities. Where then lay the morality of the British 'courts of justice' or that of the Parliament dominated by royal robots? The author wishes therefore to say thanks but no thanks to both Mansfield and Granville Sharp for 'saving' the freedom of poor James Somerset.

Furthermore, the author argues that the hypocrisy of the British is also clearly exposed by their treatment of freed slaves. Sheltering under the guise that 'the freed slaves could not fend for themselves effectively, with the result that they resorted to begging and thus became a nuisance in English society', the British government hatched yet another of its plots (Afigbo et al., 1986, pp.56-57). In 1786 the Committee for Relieving the Black Poor was hurriedly formed. By February 1787, the British government funded the repatriation of 'freed slaves' to Sierra Leone, albeit to 'eradicate the nuisance from English society'. No English history book is yet proud to report that by March 1788, only 130 of the 411 initial deportees who were dumped without adequate shelter and food supplies survived. The St. George's Bay Company was also chartered to run the affairs of the new Sierra Leone settlement as another slave colony (Afigbo et al., 1986). Between 1788 and 1802, the British were rounding up the 'liberated slaves' everywhere they could be found – England, Nova Scotia and Jamaica – and transporting them to Sierra Leone.

Further contradictions in the British policy that strengthen the author's argument concern the method of acquisition of the land to which the 'liberated slaves' were deported. The basic question here is, was the permission of the paramount Temne king (Miambana) of the territory obtained before establishing this new outpost? The obvious answer is an emphatic No! By this act of omission or commission, the lives of the new settlers were further endangered by drawing the wrath of the king (Afigbo et al., 1986). In addition, this was a violation of international law regarding the sovereignty of the Temne people. The bigger question, then, is, since most of these men and women knew where they came from, why did the British fail to return these slaves to their homelands?

At this point, it is safe to argue that economically speaking, the unfortunate captives were grafted into Sierra Leone so as to be rendered permanently dependent, and thus more readily compliant with future exploitation. By this time the British had set their eyes on Africa as the prime source of much-desired industrial raw materials, and the raw materials product of Sierra Leone would therefore be subjected to British-dictated prices. Furthermore, only the desired raw material-related crops were initially introduced to those marooned folks. The conquest and colonization of Sierra Leone was accomplished through this unorthodox method.

For the record, it is important to note that the argument that Britain's primary motive for abolishing the slave trade was purely economic, does not in any way disparage the well-meaning humanitarian efforts of people like Granville Sharp, Thomas Clarkson, William Wilberforce, and later Olaudah Equiano (Gustavus Vasa). The author's argument is intended only to categorically reject, as hypocritical, the religious connotation attached to the British motive. Argument to this effect need not be repeated. The main idea of the author is that such humanitarians were so scarce and so underfunded logistically that it was nearly impossible for them to make any significant impact on the monarchy, Parliament or British public opinion. Their efforts were therefore only a voice in the wilderness. In fact, it was the turn of events (the Industrial Revolution) and the attendant consequences that lent the hand of providence, in this case, the dire need for African raw materials (cotton, rubber, vegetable oils, indigo, ivory, timber and so forth) (Afigbo et al., 1986). It forced Parliament (which was traditionally influenced by plantation merchants) to vote not only for the abolition of slavery but also for the naval force to back up the resolutions.

Politically and strategically, the Mansfield decision encouraged the rise of abolitionist movements that were sponsored by various religious organizations. The political legitimacy conferred by the decision fulfilled the religious and moral desires of the church which hitherto had remained aloof on the unspeakable sacrilege of the church's involvement in the slave trade. The bishops could now condemn slavery; they organized missions to 'evangelize' and propagate the Christian faith, and ultimately encourage Africans to adopt a 'legitimate trade'. It must be emphasized here that this is the same Protestant church whose bishops, along with the King of England, had in 1637 declared that slavery was not condemned 'in the word of God' and was therefore the right of nations. It is also the same Protestant church whose bishops and cardinals retained their slaves until they received £12,700 compensation in 1833 (Williams, 1944).

Still on the political front, the Mansfield decision provided Britain with the springboard from which she persuaded other nations of Europe to ban slave trade for their nationals after the Imperial Acts of 1807, which after 1833 had effectively banned slavery and slave trade in all British territories and possessions. France banned slave trade in 1815, Spain in 1817, Portugal in 1819, and Brazil in 1830 (Afigbo et al., 1986; Burns, 1972). The United States of America had earlier abolished it in 1808, Sweden in 1813, and the Netherlands in 1814 (Crowder, 1978).

Again the sincerity of the British in abolition remained suspiciously circumspect considering that this was:

> a nation that carried on public executions of children for petty theft right up till the middle of the century (19th) and instituted a system of child factory labor whose conditions, in many cases, were far worse than those for the slave on the sugar plantation (Crowder, 1978b, p.99).

As early as 1729, the question of the rights of slaves on British soil had been considered by the Solicitor General (Talbot) and Attorney General (Yorke) [of Britain]. In their judgment, 'baptism did not bestow freedom or make any alteration in the temporal condition of the slave. [In addition] a slave did not become free by being brought to England [from the West Indies], and remained the property of his master' who could legally compel his return to the plantations (Bready, 1939, p.104; Crowder, 1978b, p.98; Klingberg, 1926, p.37; Williams, 1944, p.45).

It must also be noted that in his *Commentaries on the Law of England* in 1765, William Blackstone wrote to clarify the opinion handed down in 1729. He stated that '...with respect to any right the master may have lawfully acquired to the perpetual service of John or Thomas, this will remain exactly in the same state of subjection for life' in England and elsewhere (Bready, 1939, pp.104-05; Williams, 1944, p.45). Prior to the 1772 Mansfield decision, Blackstone had explicitly told Granville Sharp (in the latter's fight for the liberty of the maltreated slave, Jonathan Strong) that the 'legal rights of the slave owner' over his human property existed 'in England' (Bready, 1939, p.105). A notice published in the *Liverpool Advertiser* in September 1766 helps to confirm (contrary to current popular belief) that slaves were openly sold and bought in England. The notice read:

> To be sold at the Exchange Coffee House, in Water Street, this day, the 12th instant, September, at 1 o'clock precisely, eleven negroes imported by the *Angols* (Bready, 1939, p.105).

These concomitant and subsidiary evils of slavery, together with the accursed institution [of slavery] itself, combine to lend credibility to the argument that most British abolitionist maneuvers were grounded in economic motives. The credulous arguments by mainly European authors forced Dike (1956) to take a stand. He argued that although non-economic forces may have played a role in abolitionist endeavors and European penetration into West Africa, yet '... in a curious way [European] writers have tended to harp unduly on these external manifestations of a movement that was at root economic' (p.14).

Other developments elsewhere that had cowed and diminished British pride and imperial integrity included the loss of America as a colony. Britain therefore had to hide under the cloak of the Mansfield decision to look elsewhere to boost her self-esteem without losing face. Africa particularly fitted into the grand sche, because it promised to become a rich source for the much-needed industrial raw materials for European factories. Ohadike (1991) contended that until gold and diamonds were discovered in large quantities in South Africa in the 1880s and 1890s, the British regarded southern Nigeria as the most valuable part of Africa in the 19th century. It was the major source of palm oil and palm kernels and held out promise for trade in other raw materials for British manufactured goods. The British therefore could not resist the temptation of acquiring such 'a valuable territory by diplomacy, if possible, or by conquest if necessary' (Ohadike, 1991, p.1).

Having passed a law against the slave trade, Britain proceeded to bully, persuade and bribe other European nations to do the same (Ikime, 1977). While it is true that surplus capital generated by the slave trade launched Britain into the Industrial Revolution, by the middle of the 18th century the same could not be said of other European countries. They were therefore reluctant in both the abolition and their enforcement of the abolition provisions. In fact, many of the nations were not prepared to cooperate with Britain (Afigbo et al., 1986). Afigbo et al. asserted that this policy of non-cooperation was 'partly because they suspected that the British zeal was not entirely the result of humanitarian intentions, but was also connected with a desire to promote her economic interests' (p.53).

The West African (Preventive) Squadron

In order to add some bite to its barking, the British government sent out several detachments of the navy to patrol the coastal waters of West Africa with the dual purpose of seizing slave ships and later intimidating African kings into submission. The two instruments of diplomacy (abolition treaties) and naval force (the Preventive Squadron) were supposed to complement each other. The squadron's work was not easy given the limited right Britain had over international waters. She therefore persuaded other European slave-trading countries to negotiate reciprocal search treaties and to recognize the Courts of Mixed Commission established in Sierra Leone for trying captured slavers (Afigbo et al., 1986).

The failure of these treaties – Abolition Treaties, Reciprocal Search Treaties, the Mixed Commission, and Equipment Treaties – to exterminate the slave trade led British thinking in another direction. This new direction was to stop the slave supply at its source, Africa. This she did using the gunboats.

Dike (1956) found it necessary to emphasize that the contemporary movements connected with the changes wrought by the Industrial Revolution were a European, not a West African, phenomenon. This was particularly true of events on the ideological plane. He thus remarked:

> The nineteenth-century West African middleman was not only ignorant of the ideological battle raging in Europe on the question of abolition, but his ideas of life, of society, and of man belonged to a world poles apart from that in which the Benthamites argued and the Clapham sect preached (p.12).

Be that as it may, and irrespective of the opinion of Africans, British policymakers resolved to uproot slavery at its source, and in its place, introduce 'legitimate and free trade'.

The Fall of Lagos

European authors (Burns, 1972; Geary, 1965) and their cohorts have always painted, labeled, and stigmatized Lagos with the much-maligned name of 'slave coast'. These European historians have therefore understood (by choice) and explained the British conquest of Lagos between 1851 and 1861 in terms of the British anti-slavery policy (Asiegbu, 1984). In effect, King Kosoko of Lagos was a recalcitrant slave dealer and therefore could not be spared by the anti-slavery British.

The author will, however, take sides with Asiegbu (1984), Ikime (1977) and Ajayi (1961), and argue that the slave trade was only a speck in the catalogue of events that led to the assault on Lagos in 1851. This argument is all the more defensible when it is placed in perspective with the fact that Brazil and Portugal whose merchants and governments were still buying slaves up until 1860s, were not attacked. It is against this background that one can logically and without contradiction assert that British commercial and colonial interests ranked highest among the factors that led to the British attack on Lagos in 1851. In his brilliantly documented book, Ikime (1977) convincingly established that Lagos was subjugated because 'Britain wanted a share, perhaps the lion's share, of the trade of Lagos from which she had been excluded for nearly 40 years' (p.93).

On balance, the chronology of events that culminated in the British conquest could be traced to the ascendancy rivalry for the throne of Lagos, which became vacant in 1841 following the sudden death of *Oba* Oluwole. The people of Lagos sided with and made Akitoye the king, and the defeated Kosoko and his supporters were forced into exile (Ikime, 1977). In a spirit of reconciliation, and to reestablish trade and peace after the crises, Akitoye allowed Kosoko to return to Lagos in 1845. This singular act was to be the greatest source of his undoing, for in the same year Kosoko plotted and overthrew Akitoye from the throne of Lagos (Asiegbu, 1984; Ikime, 1977).

The overthrow and expulsion of Akitoye to Badagry, a neighboring kingdom, and the consequent skirmishes that followed between the supporters of the two created a loophole for Akitoye's plea to the British to help restore him to the throne. Not only did the Christians on the coast of Badagry persuade him to ask for British support, they also made him write to Queen Victoria, pledging to help abolish the slave trade in Lagos. *Oba* Shoron of Abeokuta, who needed British arms to protect his kingdom from Dahomey invaders, also was persuaded to write to the queen in support of Akitoye's claims to the disputed throne. It was on the strength of these presentiments that the Foreign Office urged Beecroft to visit Kosoko and sign a treaty for the abolition of the slave trade in Lagos (Burns, 1972; Ikime, 1977). With four British warships in presence in November 1851, Consul Beecroft visited Kosoko and urged him to sign the treaty, which he of course was smart enough to refuse. Using a delaying tactic, Kosoko claimed he had to consult with his chiefs and the King of Benin before he could sign anything on behalf of his kingdom.

Entreated further to sign the accord, Kosoko plainly intimated to Beecroft that 'the friendship of England was not wanted' (Burns, 1972, p.122; Geary, 1965, p.26). Angered and rebuffed, Beecroft returned to the warships and ordered Commander Forbes to attack Lagos. The attack was repulsed by Kosoko who was armed and ready. Two British officers were killed and 16 wounded (Burns, 1972; Geary, 1965; Ikime, 1977). Ikime (1977) stated that the one thing the Europeans hated most was defeat by an African force. The defeat of Beecroft at Lagos was therefore a major disgrace for the British navy. It is against the background of this initial defeat that one can assess the British resolve for a total bombardment of Lagos, at least to redeem the British pride that had been trampled under King Kosoko's feet. The surprise attack started on December 25, 1851, and after three days of fighting Kosoko was defeated; Akitoye was restored to the throne of Lagos on New Year's Day, 1852. British pride was redeemed.

Akitoye was forced to sign an anti-slave treaty with accompanying clauses that reduced him to a mere puppet of the British. Less than 10 years later, on August 6, 1861, Lagos was annexed and declared a British possession. The following year, Lagos was established as a colony, and this effectively stripped the *Oba* of all judicial and administrative powers over his kingdom (Burns, 1972).

To summarize, the manner of British occupation of Lagos was unprecedented in the history of civilized society. Viewing it from a legal perspective, this author would describe the British action as international terrorism and a violation of international law. First, the *Oba* of Lagos, Kosoko, did not enter into any treaty of cooperation with the British to justify the intervention. Second, there was no formal declaration of war before Lagos came under British attack. Third, custom demanded that the *Oba* of Benin install an *Oba* of Lagos and not Britain.

The Lagos incident is only one in a series that is evaluated by the author in the course of this chapter. Looking at the claim by European authors that the central goal of British intervention was humanitarian, begs the question, and the validity of the argument is found wanting. In a manner characteristic of British imperial policy, and in order to obtain Foreign Office approval for the attack, many damaging and unsubstantiated lies were fabricated against Kosoko. The assertion that the attack itself was premeditated and had no real bearing on Kosoko's refusal to sign the treaty is borne out by instructions from the Foreign Office, which *inter alia* ordered Beecroft to conclude a treaty with Kosoko. Beecroft was further instructed, should such a treaty be refused, to remind him [Kosoko]:

> that Lagos is near to the sea, and that on the sea are the ships and the cannon of England; and also to bear in mind that he does not hold his authority without a competitor, and that the chiefs of the African tribes do not always retain their authority to the end of their lives (Burns, 1972, p.122).

Geary (1965) explained that the 1852 treaty signed by Akitoye:

> abolished slavery and human sacrifices, and provided for freedom of trade for British subjects... It further provided for protection and freedom from molestation of missionaries...and no subject of the king and chiefs of Lagos was to be molested from embracing Christianity (p.27).

The terms of this treaty did not leave anyone in doubt that commerce rather than humanitarianism was the driving force behind British intervention in the affairs of West Africa.

The systematic use of intimidation and falsification of facts to secure subjugation of kings will of course reverberate in all future discussion concerning British relations with Africa in the pre-colonial and colonial periods. While this miscreant practice and official lawlessness may not manifest any immediate visible effect on social control in the areas encountered, the long-term effects on the problem of social control will impact on Nigerian criminology and postcolonial administration.

With Lagos colonized and a protectorate government established, Britain put out its feelers to evaluate events in the rest of Yorubaland. Missionaries spread from Lagos and Abeokuta to the hinterland, and by 1894 they became the principal factor in the events that led to the subjugation of the rest of Yorubaland. The Lagos Protectorate was later extended to cover the rest of Yorubaland. The kidnapping of king Jaja, the illegal bombardment of Prince Nana Olomu and the fall of Igboland completed the routing, and eventually the total subjugation and colonization of Nigeria.

The British occupation of Kenya, Tanganyika and Uganda took the same systematic pattern of introduction of trade, religious pacification and finally military decapitation of opposition. The systemic poverty, official corruption, military *coup d'etats* and failed economies in Africa are reverberations of the failure of colonialism as a viable policy.

References

Afigbo, A.E., Ayandele, A.E., Gavin, R.J., Omer-Cooper, J.D. and Palmer, R. (1986), *The Making of Modern Africa*, vol. 1, Longman, Inc, New York.

Ajayi, J.F.A. (1961), *The British of Lagos, 1851–1861: A Critical Review*, Nigeria Magazine 169.

Anene, J.C. (1966), *Southern Nigeria in Transition, 1885-1906: Theory and Practice in a Colonial Protectorate*, Cambridge University Press, Cambridge.

Asiegbu, J.U.J. (1984), *Nigeria and its British Invaders 1851-1920: A Thematic Documentary History*, NOK Publishers International, New York.

Beales, H.L. (1958), *The Industrial Revolution, 1750-1850*, Kelley & Miliman Inc, New York.

Beazley, C.R. (1894), *Prince Henry the Navigator*, O.P. Putnam's Sons, New York.

Bready, J.W. (1939), *England: Before and After Wesley*, Hodder and Stoughton Limited, London.

Burns, A. (1972), *History of Nigeria*, Unwin Brothers Ltd, Old Woking.

Buxton, T.F. (1968). *The African Slave Trade and its Remedies*, Dawsons of Pall Mall, London.

Cookey, S.J.S. (1974), *King Jaja of the Niger Delta: His Life and Times*, 1821-1891, NOK, New York.

Crowder, M. (1968), *West Africa Under Colonial Rule*, Northwestern University Press, Evanston, Illinois.

______ (1976), *West Africa Under Colonial Rule*, Hutchinson & Co. (Publishers) Ltd, London.

______ (ed.) (1978), *West African Resistance: The Military Response to Colonial Occupation*, new ed, Hutchinson, London.

______ (1978b), *The Story of Nigeria*, 4th edn, Revised, Faber, London.

Deane, P. (1996), 'The British Industrial Revolution', in Teich, M. and Porters, R (eds), *Industrial Revolution in National Context*, Cambridge University Press, Cambridge.

Dike, K.O. (1956), *Trade and Politics in the Niger Delta, 1830-1885: An Introduction to the Economic and Political History of Nigeria*, Clarendon Press, Oxford.

Durant, W. and Durant, A. (1975), *The Age of Napoleon*, Simon and Schuster, New York.

Egharevba, J.U. (1960), *A Short History of Benin*, Ibadan University Press, Ibadan.

Geary, W.N.M. (1965), *Nigeria Under British Rule*, Frank Cass, London.

Ikime, O. (1968), *Merchant Prince of the Niger Delta: The Rise and Fall of Nana Olomu, Last Governor of the Benin River*, Heinemann Educational, London.

______ (1977), *The Fall of Nigeria: The British Conquest*, Heinemann, London.

July, R.W. (1992), *A History of the African People*, Prospect Heights Waveland Press Inc, Illinois.

Klingberg, F.J. (1926), *The Anti-Slavery Movement in England*, Yale University Press, New Haven.

Mazrui, Ali A. (2003), 'Afrenaissance: Struggles of Hope in Post-Colonial Africa', in Onwudiwe, E. and Minabere, I (eds), *Afro-Optimism: Perspectives on Africa's Advances*, Praeger, Westport, Connecticut.

Morel, E.D. (1968), *Affairs of West Africa*, Cass, London.

Ohadike, D.C. (1991), *The Ekumeku Movement: Western Igbo Resistance to the British Conquest of Nigeria, 1883-1914*, Ohio University Press, Athens.

Omer-Cooper, J.D. (1986), 'Introduction', in Afigbo, A.E., Ayandele, E.A., Gavin, R.J., Omer-Cooper, J.D. and Palmer, R. (1986), The Making of Modern Africa, vol. 1, Longman Inc, New York.

Rodney, W. (1972), *How Europe Underdeveloped Africa*, Tanzania Publishing House, Dar es Salaam.

Ryder, A.F.C. (1969), *Benin and the Europeans, 1485-1897*, Humanities Press, New York.

Sanceau, E. (1947), *Henry the Navigator*, W.W. Norton & Company Inc, New York.

Spears, J.R. (1907), *The American Slave Trade: An Account of its Origin, Growth and Suppression*, Scribner, New York.

Williams, E.E. (1944), *Capitalism and Slavery*, Andre Deutsch, London.

12 Reparative Justice: A Pan-African Criminology Primer

BIKO AGOZINO

Introduction

> Europe is literally the creation of the Third World. The wealth which smothers her is that of the underdeveloped peoples. The ports of Holland, the docks of Bordeaux and Liverpool were specialized in the Negro slave trade, and owe their renown to millions of deported slaves. So when we hear the head of a European state declare with his hand on his chest that he must come to the aid of the poor underdeveloped peoples, we do not tremble with gratitude. Quite the contrary; we say to ourselves: "It's a just reparation which will be paid to us." Nor will we acquiesce in the help for underdeveloped countries being a program of "sisters of charity." This help should be the ratification of a double realization: the realization by the colonized peoples that it is *their due*, and the realization by the capitalist powers that in fact *they must pay* (Fanon, 1963, pp.102-103).

In this chapter, I will demonstrate the lessons that criminology could learn by paying attention to the struggle for reparations by people of African descent in connection with crimes of slavery. The chapter is intended as a criminology primer because it could help to introduce African scholars to a discipline of criminology in a transgressive way that is capable of transforming the imperialistic discipline and making it more sensitive to the needs of the victimized. Reparative justice differs from punitive justice by seeking how to address the wrongs done to the victimized instead of being obsessed with how to punish the offenders. The chapter will begin by introducing a video documentary text that I completed recently on the subject. Even though many readers have not seen the video, it is being used here as the equivalent of ethnographic material which researchers report and which readers understand without actually having seen the video of the fieldwork. The questions raised for criminologists in the video will be reiterated in the introduction and the textual material used in the video will be reproduced for a closer analysis in the chapter. Following the introduction will be a section on comparative arguments in favour of reparations. This will be followed by arguments against reparations. Then finally, a concluding section of the chapter will highlight the lessons for criminology and identify a theoretical framework suitable for the development of reparative justice.

Reparative Justice is the title of a criminological discourse on the African Holocaust otherwise known as the Trans Atlantic Slavery that I completed as a videotext recently (Agozino, 2002). The 33-minute video was given a broadcast premier by the African Independent Television, Lagos, Nigeria, in June 2002. I have used the video to facilitate some criminology classes and a doctoral candidate in England found it useful for his dissertation research. This chapter will be framed around the video by elaborating on some of the iconography. For example, the above epigraph from Fanon was also quoted in the video. As in the video, I see this chapter as challenging the reader to imagine innovative theoretical strategies for coming to terms with what the United Nations Organization has since recognized as Crimes Against Humanity – the African Holocaust.

The documentary questions the failure of criminological imagination when it comes to tackling one of the most enormous crimes that ever took place in an organized manner for centuries and that involved the genocidal destruction of over 100 million lives. When criminologists glance at the history of this terrorism, they tend to focus on the cruel and unusual 'punishment' of the enslaved but criminologists mostly indulge in what Cohen (1993) calls the culture of silence on human rights crimes. (see also Schwendinger, H and J., 1970).

This chapter, like the documentary, attempts to develop a critical application of the insights that criminology could gain from the struggles for reparations. The documentary opened by asking the viewer to imagine that it was Europeans and not Africans who were enslaved and subjected to enslavement for 400 years and then colonized for another 100 years before being held under imperialist repressions ever since in a system of domination that Nkrumah recognized as neo-colonialism (Nkrumah, 1968). Why am I asking you to imagine this? I am asking you because most criminologists are people of European descent and or scholars trained in the Eurocentric tradition. Perhaps criminologists are too slow to develop interest in this subject because it did not happen to Europeans and by challenging you to simply imagine it, do not feel threatened, it is only your imagination for a minute.

Do you think that the governments of the USA and the UK would threaten to walk out from a United Nations Conference Against Racism just because the issue of reparations was tabled for discussion if people of European descent were the people victimized by such enormous historical wrongs? Do you think that Eurocentric criminologists would have continued for centuries to worry about pick-pockets and desperados while conveniently ignoring the most violent and most sustained form of organized crime ever known? Imagine that you were hired by the descendants of the survivors of the Holocaust as a consultant criminologist to advise them on the struggle for reparations; which criminological theory would you base your recommendations on? Would you follow the demonological perspective that assumed that the devil is responsible for leading otherwise moral people astray when the perpetrators of the African Holocaust were known for their religious ethics?

Or would you base your recommendations on the classical perspective with the assumption that people use their free will to break the social contract and should be made to pay the price but the slave holders were supported in their depravity by the philistine philosophy of classicism? Would you consider the relevance of the pathological perspective that assumed that the slave-holders were genetically superior to their victims and gave the impression that there was nothing wrong with their rational-psychotic debasement of human beings? Would you turn instead to the social disorganization perspective with emphasis on how immigrants in a crimogenic environment are responsible for most crimes whereas the perpetrators of the slave holocaust were more likely to occupy the commuter zones that the Chicago School saw as relatively crime-free?

How about the theory of anomie with a view that it is those who lack access to the legitimate means of achieving cultural goals who are more likely to innovate illegitimate means of achieving those goals whereas the means adopted by the organized criminals of the trans Atlantic European slavery had more than adequate access to the legitimate means of genocidal practices? Perhaps you will be more attracted to the learning perspective with emphasis on how the slave-holders learnt their crimes against humanity except that they were not regarded as crimes at that time and instead, it was the victims who were 'punished' or victimized for attempting to revolt or flee from the inhuman conditions of slavery. Maybe the labeling perspective would provide a framework for your recommendations by focusing on how certain acts come to be labeled criminal while other acts remain perfectly legal because deviance is anything that is defined as such by those who have the power to label others as deviant.

Perhaps, you will like to move beyond the liberalism of labeling and attempt to develop a critical perspective from Marxist, feminist, anarchist or radical multicultural perspectives in order to come to terms with the enormous historical wrongs that have been visited on people of African descent for centuries (Pfohl, 1994). Whichever perspective you adopt, you will be certain to discover many opportunities to advance criminological theory and so the silence of criminologists on the reparations debate is actually not in the interest of the development of criminology.

Anita Kalunta-Crumpton has reviewed the poverty of western criminological orientalism in Chapter 1 of this book and so there is no need for a rehash in this concluding chapter. The question is not what criminology can contribute to the struggle for reparations because the struggle will be fought and won with or without criminologists. The question is what the struggle could contribute to criminology. This kind of discussion should be the core of any introduction to criminology course aimed at students of African descent and other students interested in understanding the political and economic relationships between law and society (as part of what Onwudiwe and Lynch, 2000, called black criminology). Lack of such interest by criminologists is part of the reasons why their discipline is rarely found as an autonomous department in Africa with the obvious exception of South Africa (Agozino, 2003).

Arguments for Reparations

Professor Chinweizu (1994), author of *The West and the Rest of Us*, argues that people of African descent are late-comers to the demand for reparations and concluded that if the demands of people of other descent have been addressed with more seriousness than the demand by people of African descent, the only explanation would be the deep-seated racism that was nurtured during the African Holocaust and that is still being sustained by white supremacist countries that benefited from that holocaust. Chinweizu listed the following nine cases of the demand for reparations and a careful study of them could provide some strategic lessons for people of African descent in their own struggle for reparations. The advantage of starting the campaign for reparation relatively late is that people of African descent can learn from the mistakes and successes of earlier campaigns for reparations. The analysis of Chinweizu was summarized in the documentary as follows:

1. In 1921, the US paid $25m to Colombia for excising Panama from Colombia.
2. The Mapuche of Southern Chile are seeking the return of 30 million acres stolen by Europeans since 1540.
3. The Inuit (Eskimo) of Canada were offered 850,000 sq. miles of their ancestral land in 1992.
4. In the US, claims by the Sioux to the Black Lands of South Dakota are in court and the US government is planning to give 400,000 acres of grazing land to the Navaho and some more to the Hopi in the South-West of the USA.
5. In 1988, the US government admitted wrongdoing in the internment of 120,000 Japanese-Americans under executive order 9066 of 1942, during WW II and awarded each internee $20,000.00.
6. Japan paid reparations to the Asian countries that it occupied in WW II and North Korea is seeking $5b in damages for 35 years of Japanese colonialism.
7. European allies after WW I demanded reparations from Germany, fixed at 132 billion gold marks in 1921. Further reparations were demanded at the end of WW II from Germany to the tune of $320b.
8. Germany also paid reparations to the Jews for the Nazi Holocaust including an initial sum of $2b, plus $952m in personal indemnities; $35.70 per month for each concentration camp inmate; $820m for the resettlement of displaced Jews in Israel; and other unspecified amounts.
9. With such precedents, it would be sheer racism to deny reparations to people of African descent for the 500 year-long holocaust.

To the cases listed by Chinweizu, we could add the more recent cases of Aboriginal Australians (who are of African descent) who are waging an uphill struggle to regain some of their ancestral lands and for reparations to the survivors of the stolen generations of children taken from their parents and given to white families. Also more recently, the Heroro of Namibia are campaigning for reparations from Germany for the imperialist genocide that nearly wiped out the Heroro nation. Similarly, black South Africans have been demanding reparations from the government for the crimes of Apartheid against humanity. The struggle for land in Zimbabwe, South Africa, Namibia and Kenya could also be seen as part of the struggle for reparations and all these cases should be studied closely for the lessons they could provide to both criminology and the struggle of Africans for reparations. Also relevant here is the demand by the Organisation of African Unity that the United Nations and countries that neglected to do something to halt the predictable Rwanda genocide in 1994 and or who facilitated it should pay reparations to the survivors (Torpey, 2001).

It has also been suggested by Amadiume (2000) that Biafra could be used as a model of reconciliation in Africa perhaps because at the end of that civil war in Nigeria, the military government of Yakubu Gowon declared no victor no vanquished. Mazrui (2003) also cited this case as one of the examples of the readiness of Africans to forgive even when they have defeated their foe. This view of Mazrui raises the question, what was there to forgive the Biafrans who were the ones that took the brunt of a genocidal war in which an estimated three million, mostly Biafrans, were killed and whose entire life-savings were confiscated in return for a flat payment of twenty pounds at the end of the war? Perhaps Amadiume was hinting at this when she invoked the memory of Biafra in her introduction to the edited volume, perhaps, like Soyinka (2000) in the volume, she was hinting that Africans also owe reparations to one another that need to be addressed truthfully as part of the healing process.

It is easy for a genocidal army to turn round to the survivors and say, we extend to you the mythical African readiness to forgive but what does African forgiveness mean from the point of view of the victimised? The answer lies in the fact that recently, the Igbo of Nigeria appeared before the Oputa Commission that was set up to review past cases of human rights violations in the country and tabled a claim for US$9 billion as reparations for the crimes of the civil war that Mazrui assumed were forgiven. Mazrui's stance on the civil war is understandable since he was vociferous in his partisan condemnation of patriots like Christopher Okigbo who died fighting to end the genocidal war in Nigeria. The assumption that Africans are ever ready to forgive is a dangerous assumption that could invite more atrocities from bullies who would be encouraged by the expectation that Africans will be ready to forgive even the gravest of violations. Since no reparations have been paid to the victims of the genocidal was in Nigeria, it is not clear in what sense Amadiume used Biafra as a model of reconciliation for the rest of Africa unless it is in the sense that the Igbo rebounded from the tragedy with unprecedented vigour despite atrocious attempts to keep them marginalized as Ikpeze (2000) argued in his contribution to Amadiume's editorial. The task of African scholars interested in criminology is to passionately and objectively study the crimes against humanity that have been disproportionately visited on Africans with unprecedented lack of reparations by Europeans in collusion with a few Africans.

Although Chinweizu observed that people of African descent are late-comers to the demand for reparations, he was probably referring to Africans in Africa who, according to Ali Mazrui (2003), are exceptional in their readiness to forgive wrongdoing instead of seeking to profit from past wrongs as other groups of people have successfully done. African Americans have had a longer history of demanding for reparations than the other groups that have successfully been paid reparations as listed by Chinweizu above. For example:

> Bishop Henry Turner of the African Methodist-Episcopal Church and the International Emigration Society in Atlanta, Georgia was probably the first African-American to demand reparations from the federal government. Bishop Turner was attempting to raise money to send blacks back to Africa. He estimated that America, in 1896, owed approximately four million African-Americans $50 billion in back wages. For re-settlement purposes however, he only sought $500 million from Washington. It is believed he received not a penny (Damu, 2000).

The call of Bishop Turner was preceded by the call of several white clergy in support of reparations for African Americans. The call was taken up in the 1920s by Marcus Garvey in the form of the campaign for people of African descent to be returned to Africa as part of the reparations for the crimes that they suffered in the New World. Support for black nationalism as part of reparations also came from Harry Haywood, a California dock worker who was also active in the Communist Party of the US, and who called for a black nation to be created in the southern states of America as part of the reparations for the wrongs of slavery. Around this time, W.E.B. Du Bois and others were campaigning through the Pan African Congress Movement to raise awareness about the unique wrongs suffered by people of African descent (Du Bois, 1998). Following the formation of the United Nations, Du Bois and others were given a powerful platform in 1951 to present charges of genocide against the US government for crimes against people of African descent and call for remedies. The Black Panther Party took up the call from the mid-1960s by including the demand for '40 acres and two mules' in their ten point program. The Nation of Islam has also been supportive of the call for reparations since the 1960s (Damu, 2000). The first Reparations Bill (H.R. 29) was presented to the US Congress by Theddeus Stevens of Pennsylvania in 1867, calling for the seizure of the public land in the ten Confederate states and the distribution of such land to the formerly enslaved African Americans. The reason why no reparations have been paid to people of African descent is not because of any mythical willingness to forgive or even because of silence on the matter. The reason is because white supremacy continues to thrive on the soil fertilized with the blood, sweat and tears of African ancestors since slavery as Chinweize inferred.

One thing clear from the above cases is that cases in which the victimized relied on legal action in courts as a strategy in the struggle for reparations have realized less success than cases in which direct action, legislative action, or simply lobbying of the executive were adopted as main strategies. The huge victory won by black farmers in the US for reparations from the government for systematic discrimination over the years is an indication that victory can be won in courts but such victories usually benefit lawyers more than they benefit victimized individuals when it comes to sharing the damages awarded by the courts. While the claim of the Sioux to the Black Lands of South Dakota are still in court and while Aboriginal Australians won limited access to their land through the Mabo decision, such court victories tend to bring only symbolic benefits to the victimized. On the other hand, those cases in which diplomatic pressure, lobbying, legislation or militant direct action were the strategies, more substantial reparations had been secured. For example, attempts to use legal means to redistribute land in Zimbabwe were frustrated until the landless started seizing land, forcing the government to either support them or fight them but the government chose to support them. This suggests to people of African descent that while litigation remains an option, its potential impacts must not be exaggerated. Rather, we must realize that the form of legal reasoning is under the domination of individual rights and so arguments based on group rights would be difficult to sell in court (Block, 2002). Despite the relative failure of the law to win victories for the victimized in the struggle for reparations, it has been strongly argued that there are firm legal grounds that support the struggle for reparations:

1. The enslavement of Africans was a crime against humanity.
2. International Law recognizes the right of victims of crimes against humanity to claim reparations.
3. There is no legal barrier to prevent those who still suffer the consequences of crimes against humanity from claiming reparations.
4. The claim is on behalf of all Africans at home and in the Diaspora.
5. The claim would be brought against the governments (and the corporations) that benefited from the crime of slavery.
6. Experts can be relied upon to fix the amount of reparations due.
7. If the claim is not settled by mutual agreement, it will go to an international tribunal recognized by all parties (Gifford, 1993).

This opinion was cited in the documentary, *Reparative Justice*, but because it flashed by in a few seconds, readers can follow the web link in the references here to read it in detail. Note that Lord Anthony Gifford, Queens Counsel, did not advocate the use of litigation as a privileged strategy in the struggle for reparations. The emphasis is on making a claim and not on filing a lawsuit. Instead of privileging litigation, it is being suggested that mediation and arbitration should be the first option under the assumption that since the crime is internationally recognized, both parties would reach an agreement on reparations. Failing a mutual agreement, it is suggested that an international tribunal that is recognized by all parties should be able to settle the dispute. The reason why the mediation approach is favoured by lawyers and activists alike is not simply because the language of law is individualistic while the platform of the reparations movement is collectivist. A more important reason is that if the legal personalities that benefited from the African Holocaust refuse to pay any reparations, the weakness of African countries that were divided by the colonial powers means that no one could compel an unwilling country to pay reparations to people of African descent even if there is a court judgment to that effect. For instance, Nicaragua won cases in the International Court of Justice against the US over the illegal mining of her seaports in the 1980s but US simply ignored the ruling and carried on with business as usual. Given the circumstances, mass action by concerned citizens could lead to mediation and arbitration, which could work better than the threat of litigation. Despite the appeal of mediated and arbitrated solutions to the reparations debate, Randall Robinson cautions that people of African descent should not see themselves as beggars (also quoted in my documentary, *Reparative Justice*):

> Blacks should come broadly to know that we do not approach this looming national debate as supplicants. The appeal here is not for affirmative action but, rather, for just compensation as an entitlement for the many years of heinous U.S. government-embraced wrongs and the stolen labor of our forebears. We make only the claims that other successful group complainants have made in the world. Put simply, we too are owed. Let us as a national society have the courage to approach the future by facing up at long last to the past (Robinson, 2000, p.246).

In recognition of the legitimacy of the demands by people of African descent, John Conyers of the Congressional Black Caucus and a member of the House of Representatives from Michigan introduced the 1989 Bill (H.R. 3745) seeking the establishment of a commission 'to examine the institution of slavery' and 'to make recommendations to the Congress of appropriate remedies'. The bill was buried in Congress for many years but it was never voted out. The bill was reintroduced in 1993 as H.R. 40 to commemorate the promise of 40 acres and a mule that was not delivered to African Americans.

Arguments Against Reparations

'Ten Reasons Why Reparations for Slavery is a Bad Idea and Racist Too' was written by David Horowitz as a commercial for which he bought spaces on the pages of newspapers across 50 campuses in America. The advertisements were paid for by the Center for the Study of Popular Culture at an average of $700.00 per paper. Some of the campus newspapers (Brown, Duke, Arizona, UC Berkeley,

UC Davis, Chicago, and Wisconsin) sold the space for his article while most rejected the offer. Some mainstream newspapers have since published the opinion too. The arguments of Mr Horowitz, a white male who confessed that he was a former sympathizer with the Black Panther Party but is now a right-wing ideologue, can be summarized as follows:

1. There is no single group clearly responsible for the crime of slavery.
2. There is no single group that benefited exclusively from slavery.
3. Only a tiny minority of white Americans ever owned slaves, and others gave their lives to free them.
4. Most Americans have no connection (direct or indirect) to slavery.
5. The historical precedents used to justify the reparations claim do not apply, and the claim itself is based on race not injury.
6. The reparations argument is based on the unfounded claim that all African American descendants of slaves suffer from the economic consequences of slavery and discrimination.
7. The reparations claim is an attempt to turn African Americans into victims and it sends a damaging message to the African American community.
8. Reparations to African Americans have already been paid.
9. What about the debts that Blacks owe to America?
10. The reparations claim is a separatist idea that sets African Americans against the nation that gave them freedom.

Each of these 'reasons' was examined and rejected by Allen and Chrisman (2002). They state that the relativist argument of Horowitz implies that no society is ever responsible for large-scale social wrongs and so only when an individual can be proven guilty can we admit that there is a remedy. Just because it could be argued that everyone was responsible for slavery, it does not lead to the conclusion that no one is responsible for it. The argument that African Americans benefited from slavery by inheriting a better condition of living compared to Africans at home begs the question whether Africa would have been the same had 100 million of its citizens not been destroyed or shipped away. To compare the annual income of African Americans favourably against the GDP of many African countries is to ignore the fact that African Americans are not a nation state and raises the possibility that they could be living in yet better social conditions were their ancestors not enslaved.

Concerning the excuse that white men died to free African Americans from slavery, there is ample evidence that many white troops in the Union Army were reluctant conscripts who often rioted against African Americans following racist propaganda that freed African Americans would take over the jobs of white men while they were away fighting the Confederates. By comparison, the former enslaved Africans did not wait to be conscripted, they enlisted en masse and fought bravely to preserve the Union. In fact, their bravery was acknowledged by one of the Union officers, General William Sherman, who issued Field Order 15 in January 1865 to empower Union commanders to grant 40 acres and a mule to the head of every African American family whether male or widowed and to every adult male among the formerly enslaved (Wells-Barnet, 2002). The Order was quickly rescinded by President Andrew Johnson in the same year. Instead, during the era of Jim Crow, thousands of African Americans were lynched across America following often false accusations of raping white women and/or their lands were seized to force them into working as sharecroppers under conditions similar to slavery. More recently, many former Confederate states started flying the Confederate battle flags in defiance of the limited protection that African Americans won through the Civil Rights Act of 1964. Given that white women are the primary beneficiaries of the civil rights act and given that African Americans shed their blood in all the wars that America has fought, it is ridiculous for anyone to argue that African Americans owe their freedom to whites while maintaining that nothing is owed to African Americans. As Ekwe-Ekwe (1993) convincingly stated, it is ridiculous for anyone to suggest that Africans owe anything to Europeans. The reason for Ekwe-Ekwe's opinion was elaborated in his article for US Africa Online as follows:

> In the past 20 years, Africa has consistently been a net-exporter of capital to the West, a trend that has been accentuated by the debilitating consequences of Africa's servicing of its so-called "debt" to the West. In 1981, Africa recorded a net capital export of US$5.3 billion to the West. In 1985, this transfer jumped to US$21.5 billion and three years later it was US$36 billion or US$100 million per day. In 2000, Africa's net capital transfer to the coffers of the West stood at US$150 billion (Ekwe-Ekwe, 2003, *http://www.usafricaonline.com/ekweekwe.nepad.html*).

Although Ekwe-Ekwe added a note on the hypocritical western admonition of African leaders to respect human rights and end corruption, the above trend could be said to be a version of the advance-fee fraud or 419 crimes that Osisiogu and Onwudiwe analyzed in Chapters 5 and 6 of this book. The imperialist Four-One-Niners give the impression that they are the ones giving aid to Africa when they are mortgaging the future of generations of Africans to the modern debt slavery. To claim that African Americans do not deserve reparations because most living Americans have no direct link to slavery is to ignore the fact that most living Americans had no direct connection with the internment of Japanese Americans during World War II and yet they were paid reparations by the US government. The same observation applies to the payment of reparations to Jews by the German government and corporations. As Michael Moore (2001) stated in *Stupid White Men*, the era of slavery is not ancient history but a recent one in which someone can still remember a great grandfather or great grandmother who was enslaved. Many westerners oppose the demand for reparations on the ground that they are almost certain that the reparations would be embezzled by a few greedy leaders. However, if you owe someone, you do not refuse to pay up simply because you suspect that he or she would waste the fund you are obliged to pay back. It is the responsibility of African democrats to make sure that when reparations are paid, that a few despots would not be able to seize it and share it with their imperialist fellow Four-One-Niners in whose money markets they invest the loot.

The legacy of slavery in America is evident in the fact that in 1998 the median family income in America was $49,023 while that of African Americans was $29,404. The poverty line was estimated at $17,029 for a family and 23.6% of African American families lived below this poverty line. Only 25% of white American families had zero assets compared to 51% of Hispanic American families and 61% of African American families. This is ignored when comparison is made between African Americans and black Jamaicans who came to America of their own free will since 1836 when the British government paid reparations to the slave holders to the tune of $100,000,000 to free 90% of the Island's population from slavery but without paying anything to the enslaved. To demand that the descendants of the enslaved should be paid reparations is not the same as trying to turn them into victims. As Cornel West (1993) argued, it is possible to recognize that people have been victimized without jumping to the conclusion that they remain victims instead of being the survivors that Bob Marley and the Wailers sang about. The legacy of slavery and colonialism in the administration of criminal justice in Britain has been analyzed by Agozino (1997), Hall et al. (1978), Kalunta-Crumpton (1999) and many others who point out that although black people make up less than 2% of the population of England, they make up more than 12% of the prisoners due to the continuation of colonialist policing and trials of black populations in Britain. The proportion of black women among all women prisoners is double the proportion of all black prisoners to all prisoners in England (24%). Other chapters in this book indirectly reflect the legacies of the unequal relationships between people of African descent and Europeans since the days of slavery. See especially the conditions of women of African descent in the chapters on Brazil (7), Jamaica (10), Ghana (2), and South Africa (8). In the US, a similar picture is painted by Manning Marable who observed that:

> The racial oppression that defines U.S. society as a whole is most dramatically apparent within the criminal justice system and the prisons. Today, about one-half of all inmates in prisons and jails...are African-American. In 1992, of every 100,000 black American males, 2,678 were prisoners. Black men from age 30 to 34 were imprisoned at a rate of 6,299 per 100,000; for younger black men aged 24 to 29, the rate was 7,210 per 100,000 (Marable, 1997, p.44).

Walter Block (2002) reviewed the arguments in favour of reparations by Randall Robinson in contrast with the advertisement of Horowitz against reparations and came to the conclusion that:

> Owning a slave is a crime under libertarian law. The Nuremburg Trials have established the validity of ex post facto law. Those people who owned slaves in the pre civil war U.S. were guilty of the crime of kidnapping, even though such practices were legal at the time. A part of

> the value of their plantations was based on the forced labor of blacks. Were justice done in 1865, these people would have been incarcerated, and that part of the value of their holdings attributable to slave labor would have been turned over to the ex-slaves. Instead, these slave masters kept their freedom, and bequeathed their property to their own children. Their (great) grandchildren now possess farms which under a regime of justice, would have never been given to them. Instead, they would have been in the hands of the (great) grandchildren of slaves. To turn those specific lands to those blacks in the present day who can prove their ancestors were forced to work on these plantations is thus to uphold private property rights, not to denigrate them.

Block's support for the reparations struggle is too limited to be of much use. First of all, he is convinced that the punitive individualism of classical criminology or what he called libertarian law would be adequate for addressing the demands for reparations. On the contrary, the demand for reparations is best understood in terms of the restorative justice philosophy that Ogbonnaya Elechi (Chapter 9 in this book) found more effective for the resolution of disputes in traditional African societies. The emphasis of the reparations movement is not on the punishment of individual offenders but on justice for the victimized. Moreover, Block appears to be blocking the demand for reparations by suggesting that only those families who owned slave farms should pay back with only land to only those families whose ancestors worked on such specific land. Such a 'libertarian' framework will rule out any reparations from the corporations that insured the slave ship and insured the slave farms as well as the government that benefited from cheap slave labour for public works and tax revenue from slave wealth. Such a strategy would further antagonize white taxpayers against the idea of reparations even though many of them have their privileged positions today because of the unjust government-sponsored restrictions of opportunity for African Americans. What Block was proposing could be part of the reparations package but cannot be the whole or adequate reparations for crimes as huge as the African Holocaust. Such a formula would completely deny reparations to African nations that were impoverished as a direct consequence of the Holocaust.

Such a divisive tactic is already working to weaken the reparations movement by encouraging African Americans to fight for reparations exclusively for themselves rather than in solidarity with their African brothers and sisters. For example Charles J. Ogletree Jr. (2002) listed the members of the recently formed Reparations Coordinating Committee and it is noticeable that none of the committee members is an African-African. While calling for all Americans to support the issue of reparations because it is not simply a 'Black issue', he did not extend the call across the black Atlantic to people like Chinweizu, Ali Mazrui and the late Moshood Abiola and Bernie Grant who were very active in the struggle for reparations for the people of African descent as a whole. As a member of the Eminent Persons' Group set up by the Organisation of African Unity 'to explore the modalities and strategies of an African campaign of restitution similar to the compensation paid by Germany to Israel and the survivors of the Nazi Holocaust', Ali Mazrui (1993) addressed this issue of divisiveness and urged unity among people of African descent especially in the struggle for reparations for the trans-Atlantic Slavery. To him, the reparations can be calculated on the basis of the harm done to Africa and the benefits accrued to Europe and should include the transfer of capital and skills, support for democratization and power-sharing in international organizations like the World Bank and IMF. Such capitalist reparations package differs markedly from the Third Way that Fanon (1963) advocated but which Mazrui rejected in preference for an English poet who wrote about the death of a mad dog and the survival of the good man who was inoculated with morality against the rabid bite. Without wondering if Europeans are the good men and dying Africans the mad dogs in this analogy, it is timely to point out that Fanon was not an advocate of violence; he was only explaining as a psychiatrist how nuerotic victims of imperialist violence understood violence as cleansing. Instead Fanon saw nationalist violence as full of pitfalls into which the liberation struggle would fall especially when the external enemy is defeated and the violence turns inwards to consume internal enemies instead of uniting the people.

The question of unity raises the reservation by apologists of the European slave trade by asserting that Europeans were not the only ones involved in the slave trade. Before the Europeans came to Africa to kidnap and sell human beings, Arabs had been trading on African captives and when the Europeans arrived, they found that Africans were not only enslaving one another but were willing to sell each other into slavery. As far as the apologists were concerned, the European slavery was a legitimate trade involving the laws of demand and supply. In the video documentary (Agozino, 2002), this issue was raised by comparing it to the argument by some men that the rape victim precipitated the rape or that the rapist should not pay reparations to the victimized if the victimized had an orgasm during the rape. The work of Walter Rodney (1972) was cited in the video to underscore the fact that it was only the ruling elite in the fledging kingdoms that engaged in the slave trade under terms that were dictated by the Europeans. Those kings like those of Dahomey and Opobo who tried to resist the slave trade were dealt with through what Emmanuel Onyeozili calls gunboat criminology in Chapter 11 above (see also Agozino, 2003). On the question of African complicity in the slave trade, it is important to note that Bauman (1987) indicated that some Jews were co-opted or coerced to assist in the Nazi Holocaust but that the responsibility for the Holocaust remained with the Nazis and not with the Jewish collaborators or facilitators. Similarly, we should not blame victimized Africans who survived the African Holocaust just because a few Africans were co-opted into the crimes. In every system of oppression, be it those of black people by white people, those of poor people by rich people or those of women by men, there are always members of the oppressed group who exercise the little choice they have or lack of choice to end up being the instruments for the oppression of people like them. This historical fact does not mitigate the crimes of the oppressors in any way.

The above argument about the European slave trade does not answer the questions raised by the Arab slave trade. Should Arab countries pay reparations to Africans for the Trans Saharan Slave trade? Many people of African descent are demanding that this should be the case especially because many Arab countries are wealthy enough to start paying back to Africa for the historic injustice, and those who are too poor to pay should come forward with sincere apologies. Even if they do not pay as much as the Europeans because they too have been exploited by imperialism and because their enslavement of Africans was not to the same extent or intensity as European slavery, they should offer moral leadership to the Europeans by paying something. Under Islamic law or *Sharia*, offenses against people (as opposed to unforgivable offenses against Allah) can be settled through the law of *Quesas* that allows for reparations and forgiveness to be offered instead of seeking punishment of the offender under the European idea of the rule of law. The urgency of an acknowledgement by the wealthy Arab states of the debt they owe to Africa is highlighted by the fact that in parts of Arabised Africa, black Africans are still held for generations as indentured labourers by Arabs in conditions similar to, but not identical with, chattel slavery.

It was on this point that the documentary by Henry Louis Gates, *Wonders of the African World*, was subjected to severe criticism especially when he kept reminding Africans he met that his ancestors were sold into slavery (presumably by the ancestors of the Africans) but he never reminded any of the Europeans that his ancestors were enslaved by theirs. However, it should be pointed out that Gates did not 'make' that documentary in the sense that production is understood in the television industry. It is the Director who really owns a production and who shares the credits with a lot of people behind and in front of the camera. Gates was in front of the camera and obviously did some research behind the camera too but in the scheme of the British Broadcasting Corporation that produced it, he was a small fish who could not control the content or the spin given to the final edited version, his Harvard Professorship not withstanding. As I pointed out in my contribution to the debate, Gates should have been asking the Africans how it felt for one survivor to meet another (Agozino, 2000). Instead of dividing Africans into slaves and slave traders, we should recognize that the majority of Africans are survivors of the slave raids and did fight bravely and desperately against the odds of genocidal technology to save their own lives the way that the ancestors who were captured and dehumanized by the Europeans struggled to become the black survivors of Bob Marley. For example, there are corrupt politicians who loot the public coffers today but it will be wrong to accuse the entire populace of being complicit in the corruption brought about by absolute power when they cry out against it and struggle against it in different ways. The fact that the documentary by Gates generated passionate debates in the US whereas it was first shown in the UK without anyone lifting a stiff upper lip is an indication of how much better organized people of African descent are in America where they have successfully struggled for Black Studies programs that are nonexistent in the UK.

Conclusion

Michael Moore (2001), a white man, wrote that he is scared of white men because of the historical wrongs that they have done not just to himself but to others as well. He was wondering why white men are not profiled as criminals by criminal justice officials given the overwhelming evidence that they are dangerous. Instead, it is the relatively powerless, especially African Americans who are profiled as criminals when they were the victims of the longest running organized crime in history. He concluded by adding his voice to the demand for reparations.

The above discussion of arguments for and against the demand for reparations has implications for criminological theory that should be addressed. Criminology is overwhelmingly fixated on how to punish the crimes of the poor more effectively. What the demand for reparations teaches criminologists is that punishment is not always the most effective response to crime. Sometimes, restorative justice works much better than punitive justice. Some criminologists are aware of this lesson and are campaigning for the application of restorative justice principles as alternatives to punishment (see Chapter 9).

However, even the criminologists who are adherents of the philosophy of restorative justice rarely extend their interest to the demand for reparations by people of African descent. Black South Africans have already demonstrated how forgiving Africans can be by winning the struggle for majority rule without witch-hunting the architects of apartheid. Instead of seeking punishment for the crimes against humanity, they organized a Truth and Reconciliation Commission. Some critics point out that such a public search for truth and reconciliation is not enough and that reparations will have to be paid by the New South Africa to the vicitmized in order to do justice to the wrongs they suffered. Zimbabwe and Kenya demonstrated similar kindness towards their former oppressors even without a truth and reconciliation commission but lack of reparations meant that the desire for justice remained among the people and manifested in the struggle for land by the landless. Wole Soyinka provides a clue to the reluctance of Europeans to express remorse and pay reparations for the wrongs they inflicted on others in the essays that he was forced to present in the department of Anthropology when the department of English at Cambridge University refused to host the lectures. According to him some scholars mistakenly see the similarities between Yoruba cosmology and Greek cosmology as 'conclusive evidence' that the Yoruba borrowed their religion from the Greeks without recognizing the sharp contrasts:

> But the morality of reparation appears totally alien to the ethical concepts of the ancient Greeks. Punishments, when they occur among the Olympians, invariably take place only when the offence happens to encroach on the mortal preserves of another deity and that deity is stronger or successfully appeals to Father Zeus, the greatest reprobate of all. And of course, it was generally accepted that the rape, mutilation, or death of a mortal minion of the offending deity could go some way towards settling

> the score to the satisfaction of all... The penalties which societies exact from their deities in reparation for real or symbolic injuries are an index of the extent to which the principles of natural restitution for social disharmony may be said to govern the moral structure of that society and influence its social laws... Divine memory is not permitted (by Africans) to rest and prayers are uttered as reminders of natural responsibilities. Of course, it must be admitted that the actualities of the continent today reveal no such awareness to the observer (Soyinka, 1976, pp.13-15).

Here Soyinka reminds us that the African ethical value of holding even the gods accountable when they misbehave is at risk of being eroded by the floods of militaristic Europeanized political regimes which misapply the Yoruba saying that the king is god to mean that the king is above the law. However, despite this moral erosion, he was actually supporting the argument of Ifi Amadiume that colonialism failed to destroy all aspects of positive African culture and values (Amadiume, 2000). Although Soyinka did not add this to his comparison of world views, it is interesting to note that the only place in the Bible where God was told by a human being to 'repent' was when an African, Moses the Egyptian, told God to repent of his anger and awesome threat to wipe out the Jews after they worshipped a Golden Calf in the wilderness. Soyinka did not explain why the Europeans are quick to demand reparations from one another and to pay them to some groups while steadfastly refusing even to apologize to Africans perhaps because the reality of the African Holocaust was not the subject of his Cambridge lectures on mythology, literature and the African world. Reparations for slavery was specifically addressed by Soyinka (2000) when he cautioned that the politics of reparations could be divisive given that some Arab Africans may also be asked to pay reparations for the Trans Sahara Slavery while some African Muslims would try to argue against that and seek only to build solidarity around the Trans Atlantic Slavery or around colonialism.

The African model of accountability, forgiveness and reparative justice could benefit the criminal justice system by doing away with the death penalty, the war on drugs and the prison industrial complex. The people of African descent are not seeking to execute those who caused the Holocaust that resulted in an estimated 100 million deaths during the middle passage alone. Nor are Africans demanding that the countries that benefited from slavery should be imprisoned, whatever imprisonment would mean for a country as powerful as America. The slave holders may have been high on the opium of profits to carry out such inhuman crimes but people of African descent are not calling for a war on drugs like tobacco and alcohol that continue to kill our people while making huge profits for Massa.

Instead, all the people of African descent ask for is that the historic wrongs be studied in order to find remedies for the continuing legacies of the crimes. W.E.B. Du Bois (1998) provided the theoretical foundation for reparative justice in his monumental book, *Black Reconstruction in America*. The book documents the atrocious crimes committed against African descendants in America and how the Africans survived the Holocaust against huge odds by campaigning for the reconstruction of the whole country in the interest of all and not only in the interest of African Americans. One example stands out in the achievements of people of African descent in America – the foundation of public education for all. During slavery, it was against the law of the Black Codes for Africans to learn to read and write but many learnt the skills by any means necessary. Then after the civil war, African Americans started demanding for publicly funded education to be made available. Just as many white men oppose the demand for reparations today, they rose up in arms against reconstruction and claimed that it would only bring disaster to America. Even the cracker who assassinated Abraham Lincoln gave as his reason that Lincoln was leading African Americans to ruin by making the emancipation proclamation. Du Bois was one of the first to defend reconstruction as bringing benefits to all Americans while prominent scholars like the future president, Woodrow Wilson, dismissed reconstruction as a total disaster. For example, the struggle for African Americans to have the voting right was opposed by poor whites who later realized that rich whites were the ones benefiting from the disenfranchisement of poor blacks. As Du Bois put this:

> It was not until after the period which this book treats that white labor in the South began to realize that they had lost a great opportunity, that when they united to disenfranchise the black laborer they had cut the voting power of the laboring class in two. White labor in the Populist movement of the eighties tried to realign the economic warfare of the South and bring workers of all colors into united opposition to the employer. But they found that the power that they had put in the hands of the employers in 1876 so dominated political life that free and honest expression of public will at the ballot-box was impossible in the South, even for white men. They realized that it was not simply the Negro who had been disenfranchised in 1876, it was the white laborer as well. The South had since become one of the greatest centers of exploitation of labor in the world, and labor suffered not only in the South but throughout the country and the world over (Du Bois, 1998, p.353).

Needless to add that the struggle for black suffrage paved the way for white women's Suffragette Movement with the vital support of black men like Frederick Douglas. Incidentally, Du Bois was prophetic in the above passage because Al Gore as Vice President was among the policy makers who disenfranchised millions of African American voters on the pretext that they were convicted felons. It turned out that the presidential election was 'stolen' from Gore who won 500,000 more votes than George W. Bush partly because thousands of black voters were disqualified from voting in Florida. Asante (2001) analyzed the 'stealing of black votes' in the Florida Electoral College Presidential Election of 2000 and found that it represented 'archetypical crimes' that activists like Fannie Lou Hamer had campaigned against in the 1960s when bogus constitutional tests were used to prevent African Americans from registering to vote.

According to Du Bois, white labour unions were not very supportive of the black struggle for reconstruction because they feared that racial equality would mean lesser jobs or lower pay for white men but some of them saw that the subjection of black people to second-class citizenship would mean that the plight of poor white workers would remain desperate. Thus many white teachers volunteered to go down south and help to start the colleges that are known as historically black today. Despite the fact that poor white men were mobilized with racist propaganda to attack black public schools more viciously than they attacked black owned farms, according to Du Bois, white men and white women are today the prime beneficiaries of the publicly funded higher education that African Americans campaigned for as part of reconstruction.

Similarly, the African philosophy of reparative justice is not designed to benefit only the victimized but also to benefit the offenders by promoting a more healthy society for all (Fanon, 1963). As the Civil Rights Movement and the Anti-Apartheid Movements have shown, when people of African descent are paid adequate reparations, the resources would help to strengthen the global community to the benefit of all. The options are not only financial, however. As I pointed out to the Deputy Lord Mayor of Liverpool City Council in the video documentary, *Reparative Justice*, the reparations could take the forms of a dream come true. In the DREAM:

- D stands for democratization of civil societies where people of African descent live to make sure that they participate adequately in governance through, for instance, the cancellation of the foreign debts that hold Africans and Caribbeans in the modern slavery and the ending of the disenfranchisement of African Americans under the pretext that they are former felons;
- R stands for reparations that must be paid at a fixed annual percentage of the GDP of European and American countries into a fund to be administered by people of African descent as opposed to aid that is dependent on the willingness of the donor countries;
- E stands for more educational opportunities through special scholarships set aside for people of African descent in Europe and North America and also funded in Africa in addition to affirmative action that benefits other minorities and white women even more than African Americans;
- A stands for apology which President Bill Clinton initiated during his trip to Africa but which remains inadequate because many European politicians still refuse to apologize and the Deputy Lord Mayor interviewed for *Reparative Justice* did not apologize on behalf of past slave-trading mayors despite a City apology (Christian, 2002);
- M stands for more mobility or the expectation that people of African descent should be given the right to travel to Europe and north America without a visa requirement given that there are many people in the world

> who have such privileges when they have not earned it the way Africans have (Agozino, 2002).

The Deputy Lord Mayor requested that I should send him the above proposals in writing and I did so after reformulating the proposals in easy to follow itemization similar to the one above but I never got an acknowledgement. To remind us of the visionary words of Frantz Fanon that we started with, let us conclude this with a quotation from the great Osagyefo Kwame Nkrumah (1968):

> Africa is having to pay a huge price once more for the historical accident that this vast continent brought fabulous profits to western capitalism, first out of the trade in its people and then out of imperialist exploitation. This enrichment of one side of the world out of the exploitation of the other has left the African economy without the means to industrialise (quoted in Robinson, 2000, p.179).

The final lesson from Nkrumah and Du Bois here is that it is possible for the case for reparations to be hijacked by imperialism the way that decolonisation was hijacked and turned into neo-colonialism. For this reason, it should be made clear that the campaign for reparations is not simply targeted at European and/or Arab citizens by Africans as if everything will be fine when a few comprador bourgeois elements are given 'transfer of capital' to set up exploitative phantom capitalist subsidiaries in Africa whereas it is clear that Africa is the entity forced to make a net 'transfer' of capital and skills to Europe and North America (Ekwe-Ekwe, 2003, 1993). The case of Israel is a good warning to those who campaign for reparations on the basis of the Nuremberg principle since the reparations funds could be hijacked by the ruling class for the development of satellite states under the domination of imperialism and for the continued exploitation and oppression of Africans and the masses elsewhere. It is for reasons such as this that Nkrumah and Du Bois, among others, tirelessly campaigned for a united Africa in which development will be the collective task of the people rather than the current situation that favours imperialism in which undemocratic puppet regimes and unaccountable multinational corporations are supported so long as they facilitate the exploitation of Africa by imperialism.

Bibliography

Agozino, B. (1997), *Black Women and the Criminal Justice System: Towards the Decolonisation of Victimisation*, Aldershot, Ashgate.

______ (2000), 'Wonders of the African Crisis', *West Africa Review* vol. 1, no. 2. and also in *The Black Scholar: Journal of Black Studies and Research,* vol. 30, no. 1.

______ (2002), *Reparative Justice*, Lagos and Indiana, Iva Valley Media and Omala Media, 33 minutes, Audio Visual, Colour.

______ (2003), *Counter Colonial Criminology: A Critique of Imperialist Reason*, Pluto Press, London.

Allen (Jr.), E. and Chrisman, R. (2001), 'Ten Reasons: A Response to David Horowitz, *Black Scholar*, vol. 31, Issue 2, pp.49-56.

Amadiume, I. (2000), 'Introduction', in Amadiume, I and An-Na'im, A. (eds), *The Politics of Memory: Truth, Healing & Social Justice*, Zed, London.

______ (2000), *Daughters of the Goddess Daughters of Imperialism*, Zed, London.

Asante, M.K. (2001), 'Criminal Archetypes in the 2000 Presidential Election: How Black Votes were Stolen', *Black Scholar*, vol. 31, Issue 2.

Bauman, Z. (1989), *Modernity and the Holocaust*, Polity Press, Cambridge.

Bennett, L. (1961), *Before the Mayflower: A History of Black America*, Penguin, New York.

Block, W. (2002), 'On Reparations to Blacks for Slavery', *Human Rights Review*, vol. 3, no. 4, pp.53-73.

Chinweizu, no second name, (1993), 'Reparations and a New Global Order: A Comparative Analysis', paper presented at the First Pan African Congress on Reparations, Abuja, Nigeria, April 27-29, http://www.arm.arc.co.uk/NewGlobalOrder.html.

Christian, M. (2002), 'An African-Centered Perspective on White Supremacy', *Journal of Black Studies*, vol. 33, no. 2, pp.179-198.

Cohen, S. (1993), 'Human Rights and Crimes of the State: The Culture of Denial', *Australian & New Zealand Journal of Criminology*, vol. 26.

Damu, J. (2000), Creating Shared Visions: H.R. 40 and the Reparations Movement, http://www.campusaction.net/news/fight_racism/reparations_article.htm.

Du Bois, W.E.B. (1998), *Black Reconstruction In America 1860-1880*, Free Press, New York.

Ekwe-Ekwe, H. (1993), *Africa 2001: The State, Human Rights and the People*, The International Institute for Black Research, Reading, England.

Fanon, F. (1963), *The Wretched of the Earth*, Penguin, Middlesex.

Gifford, Lord Anthony, Q.C. (1993), 'The Legal Basis of the Claim for Reparations', paper presented at the First Pan African Congress on Reparations, Abuja, Nigeria, April 27-29: http://www.arm.arc.co.uk/legalBasis.html.

Hall, S., Critcher, C., Jefferson, T., Clarke, J. and Roberts, B. (1978), *Policing The Crisis: Mugging, the State, and Law and Order*, Macmillan, London.

Ikpeze, N. (2000), 'Post-Biafran Marginalization of the Igbo in Nigeria', in Amadiume, I. and An-Naim, A. (eds), The Politics of Memory, Zed, London.

Kalunta-Crumpton, A. (1999), *Race and Drugs Trials: The Social Construction of Guilt and Innocence*, Ashgate, Aldershot.

Mazrui, A. (1993), 'Who Should Pay For Slavery?', *World Press Review*, vol. 40, no. 8.

______ (2003), 'War, Refugees, and Environment in Africa', Keynote speech at the 2nd Edinboro University African Studies Conference, April 3-5.

Moore, M. (2001) *Stupid White Men and Other Sorry Excuses for the State of the Nation*, Regan Books, New York.

Nkrumah, K. (1968), *Neo-Colonialism: The Last Stage of Imperialism*, Heinemann, London.

Ogletree, C.J. (2002), 'Reparations, A Fundamental Issue of Social Justice', *The Black Collegian*, First Semester Super Issue.

Onwudiwe, I.D. and Lynch, M. (2000) 'Reopening the Debate: A Re-Examination of the Need for a Black Criminology', *Social Pathology*, vol. 6, no. 3, pp.182-198.

Pfohl, S. (1994), *Images of Deviance and Social Control: A Sociological History*, McGraw-Hill, New York.

Robinson, R. (2000), *The Debt: What America Owes to Blacks*, Penguin, New York.

Rodney, W. (1972), *How Europe Underdeveloped Africa*, Bogle-L'Ouverture, London.

Schwendinger, H. and J. (1970), 'Defenders of Order or Guardians of Human Rights?', *Issues in Criminology*, vol. 5.

Soyinka, W. (1976), *Myth, Literature and the African World*, Cambridge University Press, Cambridge, 1976, pp.13-15.

______ (2000), 'Memory, Truth and Healing', in Amadiume 1and An-Na'im, A. (eds), *The Politics of Memory, Truth, Healing & Social Justice*, Zed, London.

Torpey, J. (2001), 'Making Whole What Has Been Smashed: Reflections on Reparations', *The Journal of Modern History*, vol. 73, pp.333-358.

Wells-Barnet, I.B. (1892, 2002), 'Southern Horrors: Lynch Law in All its Phases', in Gabbidon, S.L., Green, H.T. and Young, V. (eds), *African American Classics in Criminology and Criminal Justice*, Sage, New York.

West, C. (1993), *Race Matters*, Beacon Press, Boston.

Index

Note: page numbers in bold refer to tables.